THE YOM KIPPUR WAR

Other books by The Insight Team of the London *Sunday Times* published in the United States:

THE YOM KIPPUR WAR

by The Insight Team of the London *Sunday Times*

DOUBLEDAY & COMPANY, INC., GARDEN CITY, NEW YORK, 1974

PICTURE ACKNOWLEDGMENTS

Most of the photographs in this book are by *Sunday Times* photographers Kelvin Brodie, Frank Herrmann, Bryan Wharton, and Sally Soames.

Additional photographs were provided by:
Romano Cagnoni: 12, 13, 23, 39
Leonard Freed: 24
Michel Astel, Bamahane: 64, 65, 66, 67, 68, 69
Micha Bar-Am, Magnum: 19, 30, 31
Associated Press: 3, 14, 21
Camera Press: 4, 8, 9, 15, 29
Rex Features and Sipapress, Paris: 16, 20, 40, 42, 58
UPI: 5, 6, 18

ISBN: 0-385-06738-0
Library of Congress Catalog Card Number 74–2719
Copyright © 1974 by Times Newspapers Limited, London
All rights reserved
Printed in the United States
First Edition in the United States of America

ACKNOWLEDGMENTS

This book derives from the extensive coverage of the fourth Arab-Israeli war in the London *Sunday Times* during October 1973. Research into the causes and conduct of the war continued, however, for some time after the cease-fire. We have also taken advantage of the lag between publication of the British and the present American edition to incorporate considerable material not earlier available and to correct several errors of fact or interpretation in the previous work. The text has thus been extensively rewritten and greatly expanded. The efforts of other inquirers and the pressures of politics in several countries, not least the United States, make it inevitable that new facts and assessments on aspects of the war will continue to emerge for some years. But sufficient facts can already be pieced together, it seems to us, to make it possible to outline with some precision the main events of a remarkable conflict. That is what this book tries to do.

A note on sources. We have rejected footnotes in the text as being too cumbersome—one working draft to which we did append sources ran up to twenty footnotes to a page. For the most part, our sources are obvious from the context or may be deduced from the nature of the material. Where we have obtained information from private sources beyond the reach of a normal inquirer, we have indicated this, unless to do so would point to the identity of someone who specifically requested anonymity. We should add that although we write before publication of the report of the Israeli judicial inquiry into aspects of the war, we have had access to some of its preliminary findings. As for material already in the public domain: A great deal was published, at the time and subsequently, about almost every aspect of the Yom Kippur War. A disheartening amount was incorrect. We have thought it outside our brief to examine the role and effectiveness of the press in the conflict, though it is worthy of considerable study. (A first stab can be found in the January 1974 issue of the Columbia *Journalism Review*.) Where our own researches have led us to facts or conclusions different from those published at the time—as they frequently did—we have, by and large, thought it worthwhile neither to point out contemporary errors nor to relate the process of inquiry through which we decided in favor of one version against another.

Insight reporters in the Middle East were Peter Kellner in Cairo and Philip Jacobson and Peter Pringle in Tel Aviv. The Insight editor, John Barry, and two former Insight editors, Bruce Page and Lewis Chester, combined to write and edit the book. Research in London was by Parin Janmohamed and Marjorie Wallace. The project was coordinated by Ron Hall.

We depended heavily on the skill and experience of Eric Marsden, the resident *Sunday Times* correspondent in Israel, and many other *Sunday Times* reporters and correspondents made valuable contributions, including: Stephen Aris (New York), John Bonar (Amman), Henry Brandon (Washington), William Dullforce (Cairo), Paul Eddy (Tel Aviv), David Holden (London), Martin Meredith (Cairo and Beirut), Brian Moynahan (Beirut and Damascus), Tony Rocca (Cairo), William Shawcross (Washington), and Ed Stevens (Moscow).

The graphics and maps are by Peter Sullivan, Duncan Mil, and John Grimwade, under the art direction of Edwin Taylor. The photographs are mostly by Kelvin Brodie, Bryan Wharton, Frank Herrmann, Sally Soames, and Romano Cagnoni, who worked often under dangerous conditions near the front lines.

Special arrangements were made with leading news organizations for particular aspects of the coverage: the BBC monitoring service, Caversham (which provided texts of Middle East radio broadcasts); *Al Ahram*, Cairo (whose then editor, the distinguished journalist Mohammed Heikal, conducted revealing interviews with General Ismail and Henry Kissinger, and whose writings 1969–73 provide essential clues to the real course of Egyptian-Soviet relations); *Ma'ariv*, *Tel Aviv* (which first published a vivid tape recording of the opening of the war, edited in Hebrew by Aaron Dolav); *Ha'aretz*, Tel Aviv (whose authoritative military correspondent Zeev Schiff provided us with valuable commentaries while the war was in progress); the staff of *An Nahar*, Beirut; *Arab Report and Record*; and the New York *Times* News Service. We used much documentary material compiled by the Department of Defense, Washington.

Technical advice was provided by Edward Luttwak, whose authoritative study of the Israeli Army will be published by Harper & Row, Publishers, later this year; and by Edgar O'Ballance, author of *The Sinai Campaign, 1956*, *The Third Arab-Israeli War*, and other works of contemporary military history. (His *The Electronic War in the Middle East, 1968–1970*, is to be published by Faber and Faber, London, later this year.) Geoffrey Pardoe, managing director of General Technology Systems Ltd., advised on missiles. And Richard Ogorkiewicz of Imperial College, London, author of *Design and Development of Fighting Vehicles*, advised on tank warfare. The responsibility for accuracy, however, remains entirely our own.

It also goes without saying that in reconstructing some aspects of the war, we have drawn upon the observations of other reporters. Particular debts we gratefully acknowledge are to the news agencies Reuters, AFP, and AP: to the Jerusalem *Post*, which published graphic accounts from the survivors of several battles; to *Al Akhbar*, Cairo, which published an important interview with General Shazli by its editor, Moussa Sabri; to Ronald Payne and Christopher Dobson of the London *Sunday Telegraph*; to Israeli journalists Yashayahu Ben-Porat, Yehonatan Geffen, Uri Dan, Eytan Haber, Chazi Carmel, Eli Landau, and Eli Tabor, whose joint work *Hamechdal* (Special Edition, Tel Aviv) revealed controversial new evidence on Israeli political actions throughout the war; to *Aviation Week & Space Technology*, for its coverage of the air war; to Rowland Evans and Robert Novak, particularly for their work *Nixon in the White House*; to Joseph Kraft, for his work in the New York *Times* and *The New Yorker*; to Eric Rouleau of *Le Monde*; and to the newsmagazines *Time* and *Newsweek*, which were, like most of the media, caught on the hop by the outbreak of war, but rallied to provide well-informed coverage of its aftermath. We thank Time-Life, Inc., for permission to reproduce an extract of David Niven's article on Henry Kissinger in *Life* magazine.

We wish also to thank Elizabeth Collard, Rupert Pengelly of *International Defense Review*, and Leon Charney, all of whom gave useful help. We regret that we cannot thank by name the many diplomats, government officials and military men who gave us their time, in several capitals, but because of their jobs wished to remain anonymous. We can thank the long-suffering staff of Doubleday, particularly Betty Prashker and Diane Matthews, who bore with the rewriting required by a seemingly endless flow of new information.

Finally, and with great sorrow, we recall our *Sunday Times* colleague, Nicholas Tomalin, who was killed while covering the war on the Golan front. He was one of Britain's most distinguished journalists, and superb war reporting was only one of his many talents. Before his car was hit by a Syrian missile on October 17, he had filed reports that guided us with remarkable clarity through the confused events of the first days of fighting. This book is dedicated to him.

London and New York, February 1974

CONTENTS

THE YOM KIPPUR WAR

A Bunker by the Suez Canal

Avi Yaffe had just emerged from the shower and was hanging his clothes to dry on the coils of barbed wire when the first shells began to fly. A flight of MiGs screamed overhead, and canisters on either side of the canal exploded into clouds of belching dark green smoke. Through the smokescreen, it was just possible to make out commando boats maneuvering into the water. Avi sprinted back to his post. It was 12:05 P.M. on Saturday, October 6, 1973. The fourth Arab-Israeli war had begun. Avi was signalman in an Israeli bunker beside the Suez Canal. Coming over the water toward him was one of the main thrusts of the Egyptian Army.

Avi—short for Abraham—had kissed goodbye to his wife Dassy just two weeks earlier, leaving her in charge of the recording studio he runs in Jerusalem. As with all able-bodied Israelis of military age, he had to spend thirty-three days each year on duty as an Army reservist. This time his unit had been posted to the Bar-Lev Line, the string of Israeli forts along the canal.

In construction, some forts were more complex than others. Avi's was little more than a piled-up sand hill perhaps thirty feet above the surrounding dunes. On the summit, facing the canal, were two or three sandbagged firing positions and a watchtower; another couple of firing positions guarded the fort's rear. Buried in the center of the hill was the command bunker, a corrugated-iron shelter underground. The fort was so small that it was only a few yards' sprint from the firing posts down the trench to the bunker. Around the whole, coils of barbed wire, broken by a single gate, gave dubious perimeter protection. It suddenly seemed very little to stop the Egyptian Army.

For five days before the attack, Avi's unit—their fort was in the central sector, almost opposite Ismailia—had been aware of unusual activity on the Egyptian bank. On October 1, a convoy of missile trucks had been seen entering Ismailia. The roar of armored columns could sometimes be heard behind the high sand ramparts on the Egyptian bank. Groups of Egyptian officers conferred by the canal, and a resplendent lieutenant general was once seen making a long examination of the scene through the telescopes of a lookout post. Later in the week, a party of Egyptian sappers had arrived to drive stakes in the ground near the water's edge, while bulldozers leveled the approaches.

But none of this had created much surprise: elsewhere along the bank the Egyptians had been careful to keep up appearances of normality. Unarmed soldiers sat, as usual, on the bank, dangling their feet in the cooling water. Tractors continued their monotonous work of piling up defensive sand dikes. And the regular gardener turned up each day to water the gardens of the long-abandoned villas near Ismailia.

It was around noon on Saturday, October 6, that Avi's unit became aware of more ominous signs of trouble. The soldiers in the forward observation positions reported that their opposite numbers on the Egyptian bank had pulled back. And the tractors had stopped working. A suspicious silence had fallen over the Egyptian lines. About noon, too, a message from headquarters came via Avi's communications center: Arrange to evacuate two smaller forts to the south. The message was passed to Avi's commander, known to his men as "Meyerke" (a diminutive of his name, Meir), a reservist from a kibbutz near Jerusalem. The evacuated men rolled up in an armored personnel carrier, bringing the complement of Avi's fort to thirty-two. Minutes later, the first Egyptian shelling began. The time was 12:05 P.M.

Avi, with a sense of detachment not uncommon among people in extreme danger, now became not only a participant in the drama that followed, but a remarkable observer of it. He had as usual brought along a heap of electronic equipment from his recording studio, including test gear for better servicing of his army radio sets and a high-quality tape recorder plus spools of tape. He had been using the tape machine mainly for playing music to entertain his fellow soldiers during their tedious tour of duty. As the Egyptian assault began, Avi automatically switched his machine to "record" and reeled out a microphone. For sixty nerve-wracking hours, while Avi and his fellows were trapped in their bunker, the tape recorder picked up snatches of conversation and radio messages, with an occasional commentary that Avi spoke into the microphone. The resultant tapes, which Avi preserved through a near-miraculous rescue, vividly convey the courage and confusion of men in battle.

First there is a long series of reports from the men in the forward firing positions, the sandbagged dugouts a few yards ahead of the command bunker on the forward, canal side of the fort:

"Egyptians are putting in boats directly below us . . . they're crossing now . . . full of crowds of infantry . . . landing with antitank missiles . . . a few odd tanks rushing at Egyptians . . . artillery fire . . . shells falling close, closer, fire getting nearer. Armored troop carriers crossing . . . lots of them jumping on the bank and running forward with missiles . . . six helicopters—Egyptian commandos—flying over. [The Israeli soldiers were so stunned by the attack that they didn't even fire at the helicopters; but later, as the helicopters returned empty, the Israeli soldiers opened up on them with machine-gun fire.]

"T-54 tank is opposite . . . it's shooting at us. More boats crossing, wave after wave . . . they're fanning out in our area . . . they're putting up a commando flag . . . Egyptians are laying a bridge . . . automatic trailer is lowering floats . . . huge convoys, lots of armor . . . tanks, halftracks, trucks with missiles, lines of Jeeps and batteries of artillery."

The forward spotters are complaining—why isn't the Israeli Air Force in action? Planes could make mincemeat of such a traffic jam. A battery of mortars from a wood across the canal ranges in. The yard of the fort is soon pockmarked with craters. The Israelis reply with all their weapons, shooting at the massed crossing and the artillery batteries. Shells fall on the fort, filling it with yellow, choking smoke. The men are afraid: They consult the fort's doctor (in civilian life a hospital intern from Kfar Saba). He reassures them it is not poison gas, just a smokescreen. Now, with Egyptians all around them, the men prepare their small arms for hand-to-hand combat.

But the assault on the fort does not come. The shelling is ranging deeper and deeper into Sinai, and at 5:30 P.M. there is a complete pause. The men begin to realize they have been by-passed by the attacking troops. They are now totally cut off.

Underground in the command bunker, Avi and Meyerke listen by radio as the meager Israeli armored forces in the area try to check the Egyptian onslaught. One mile behind the fort, on a road that runs parallel to the canal, is an Israeli tank unit and, somewhere in the area, a mobile artillery unit. The artillery commander wants to join forces with the tanks for a joint attack on the Egyptian bridgehead across the canal, but before that can happen the enemy attacks. The Egyptians are armed with deadly Sagger antitank missiles, and the artillery commander sends out an urgent warning to the tanks: "Take care not to get hit. Take cover! I want you to save all your strength for a counterattack."

The artillery opens fire on the Egyptian tanks, but it, too, is attacked with missiles. From his firing position at the eastern, Sinai, side of the fort, Meyerke's deputy, Yehoshua—known as Shuki—can see the battle raging and reports that the tanks will not now be able to come to the aid of the fort. "They're pretty messed up," he says. The tank commander radios the fort to ask Meyerke if he would like a platoon of armored infantry.

MEYERKE: Armored infantry? Sure!

However, after a pause the tank commander changes his mind.

TANK COMMANDER: Sorry. Armored infantry can't do anything there. There's an unbelievable fog [smokescreen]. Can't see a thing. I'm withdrawing them back a bit so they can change their positions.

Meyerke joins Shuki in the firing position from where they can see tanks on the road a mile away.

MEYERKE: Are those Egyptian tanks over there?
SHUKI: Yes, but they are not firing on us at the moment. (He makes a spitting sound—tfu, tfu—for luck.)
MEYERKE: Shuki, get hold of a piece of wood real quick and make touchwood.

By radio the fort learns that the Egyptians have dropped paratroops from transport planes ten miles inside Sinai. Behind the fort, by moonlight, the battle rages on, and at last Israeli planes fly over and drop bombs.

MEYERKE (to Shuki): Why didn't they do that at five, or at four?

As Saturday night becomes Sunday morning the fort again comes under attack. Shells explode, and one of the lookouts, known as "Marciano," is injured in the neck by a ricochet. "Not serious. He can make it to command bunker himself." But on the radio comes news that in the fort to the north the commanding officer is seriously wounded and two men killed. They keep calling for help.

Headquarters at Tasa has troubles too. A MiG bombing raid has killed several soldiers and the girl secretary of the commander. Even so, a rescue operation is launched to relieve the northern fort, but Egyptian commandos, flown in by helicopter, ambush the relief column and force it to retreat.

The artillery commander comes through on Avi's radio to ask if the artillery is hitting well.

SHUKI: Negative. Tell him to range two hundred southward.
HEADQUARTERS (on the radio): What's new with you?
SHUKI (in a voice of unflappable calm): Nothing special here, Headquarters. There's fire around us. We've seen one more boat cross the canal. Aside from that, there are people around us.
HEADQUARTERS (puzzled): You asked for artillery?
SHUKI: Yes, we asked.
DOCTOR: Bloody hell! Don't allow Shuki to send situation reports. For him everything is always fine, even now.
AVI (shouting into the radio): We've lots of Egyptians around us.
MEYERKE (taking charge): Hello, Headquarters. I don't know what's happening with you. The guns are firing far from target. They're hitting a dead area. I can't see but it's far from target. It's nowhere near the right direction.

Headquarters and artillery attempt to range in the guns more effectively. Meyerke still can't see the hits. Calls for help continue to arrive from the northern fort.

AVI (offering a water flask to the doctor): Here, take water. Have three sips to make up for what you've lost sweating. I'm after you. Holy Allah! All this war. Who invented it?

DOCTOR: Craziness! Fighting! Getting killed!

AVI: And what do we get out of all this business? Instead of getting leave we'll have to stay till the end of the reserve tour.

MEDICAL ORDERLY: After the war they'll let you go home.

AVI: After this business is over, our fort will be in the rear. That's clear. We'll sit in the rear because the boys will be in Cairo, right? Then we won't be in the first line, we'll be in the rear.

MEDIC: You're laughing now, but in a few days our army will really be across the line.

AVI: I've never had this sort of thing before. The situation has always been that the enemy is a kilometer from me, two hundred meters from me, no distance at all. But enemy from all sides? By the way, we'll soon be able to dial home. What day is it now? Sunday? [There is a roster that allows front-line troops to telephone home between certain hours.] We can call home from three to four in the morning. I'm dying to call home. I'd just want one call home. They don't know what's happening here.

MEDIC: They're more worried than we are.

AVI: I'm not worried so much for myself as for my family.

A few hundred yards away from the fort a lone Israeli tank is hit by shellfire. The tank commander calls up the fort.

TANK COMMANDER: I'm hit. I'm going down to check the damage. We've had a report that there are Egyptian paratroops in this area. Look a little to the left of their tanks. There are paratroopers there now.

AVI: Well, Egyptian paratroopers. That's something.

MEDIC: Where are our paratroopers?

(The tank in radio contact with the fort is unable to move and is surrounded by Egyptians. Three of the crew surrender and are, apparently, shot. The fourth man hides in the tank pretending to be dead. After nightfall on Sunday he crawls to the fort, bringing its complement to thirty-three men.)

Meanwhile, a second attempt to relieve the northern fort is being made by an Israeli unit of halftrack armored cars.

HALFTRACK UNIT (on radio): There are three enemy tanks at the gate to the [northern] fort. We've hit them. All three are burning now.

COMMANDER OF MOBILE ARTILLERY: Watch out! They're firing missiles at you. Change your positions and be on the lookout at all times.

The halftrack unit is eventually forced to withdraw to refuel and take on more ammunition. The northern fort keeps calling for help. The condition of the injured commander is deteriorating. But Headquarters can still only provide artillery support for the forts. And they are still having problems.

HEADQUARTERS: Hello. Say, how is it with our artillery fire? Does it need correcting?

MEYERKE: I don't see any hits. Maybe they aren't shooting at all.

HEADQUARTERS: What do you say? Are you ranging them?

MEYERKE: Ranging? That's not our thing at all. I don't see any hits. He should hit farther west. No?

AVI: Shuki, who's shooting?

SHUKI: Egyptians.

AVI: On whom?

SHUKI: On us, I think. They just stopped.

MEYERKE: Give me Shuki. Shuki, do you hear armor in the Egyptian concentration?

SHUKI: So Marciano says. [Dull noises can be heard—the roar of many Egyptian armored vehicle motors. The whole front wakes up.]

AVI (into mike): The time is twenty to five, early Sunday morning. In the morning, there'll certainly be a serious battle. There's tension in the air. [Avi hangs photographs of his three children and his wife over the communications equipment. The doctor rakes through his wallet for pictures of his daughter.]

AVI: You know she looks like you.

DOCTOR: They say she's more like my wife.

AVI: What do you photograph on?

DOCTOR: On Kodak.

AVI: Nice colors.

Over the radio the men in the fort can hear two Israeli tank units that have reached the road a mile away but are now in trouble. The commander radios headquarters.

TANK COMMANDER: Egyptian infantry is all around us. Send reinforcements and help extricate us.

At that moment bombs explode on and around the fort. One of them scores a direct hit on the command bunker. The corrugated iron roof gives way, and earth and stones rain down on the men inside, filling the air with choking dust. At first the men do not realize they have accidentally been bombed by their own aircraft.

AVI: Now it's starting.
DOCTOR: Wake everyone in the bunker.
MARCIANO (by telephone from a firing position): I can see our planes flying over.

Headquarters has sent Phantom fighter-bombers to support the tank units and the fort. Belatedly the tank commander radios the fort a warning.

TANK COMMANDER: Take care of yourselves. We're putting planes over this area.
MEYERKE: Moment, moment. North of us there is a target. Between us and the Egyptian crossing, seven hundred to a thousand meters, there is Egyptian infantry well dug in.
TANK COMMANDER: I see giant yellow mushrooms over your positions. Is there any danger?
AVI (repeating to Meyerke): Two giant yellow mushrooms over our position. Is there any danger?
MEYERKE: No, it's a smokescreen.
TANK COMMANDER: Can you see the bridge across the canal?
MEYERKE: No. There's still some fog [yellow smoke].
TANK COMMANDER: Try and look out for it. And take care of yourselves.
FORWARD POST: Hey, the Egyptians are shooting heavy antiaircraft fire into the sky at the planes that were bombing us.

SOLDIER: Proves they're *our* planes, right?

MARCIANO (from his outpost): Our planes are blasting rockets on the Egyptians.

AVI: Excellent. You're a darling, Marciano. What time is it?

DOCTOR: Ten to seven in the morning.

AVI: I thought it was already twelve. [The Egyptians are apparently aware that the fort is spotting and reporting and bring down another heavy smokescreen on it.]

MEYERKE: Avi, tell the artillery we don't see any hits on the Egyptian infantry.

ARTILLERY COMMANDER: They said on the telephone that you will have to wait. It's being taken care of.

MEYERKE (impatiently): I want to know why I don't get fire on the Egyptian infantry. I want to see one hit, already.

AVI (ironically): Now you'll see a hit. A bull's-eye on us!

They wait in vain for artillery fire, but suddenly two more Israeli Phantoms swoop in to bomb Egyptian concentrations near the fort on the banks of the canal. Part of the bombload goes into the canal itself, and a huge quantity of water is sprayed on the fort. The men in the canalside firing positions run soaked into the bunker shouting with glee.

SOLDIER: What a shower. Wow-eem! You should see what planes can do. You see four bombs fall like that and four Egyptian trucks go up in flames. Two of them went up together with one hit. There's a boat down here below—may have got here from the blast.

That is one of the rare exuberant moments in sixty-eight terrifying hours. By now, the fort had become of vital tactical importance to the Israelis: It was the last remaining spotting unit for artillery and bombing strikes in the sector of the central Egyptian crossing. Meyerke's unit could not expect to be relieved in a hurry: They were clearly too valuable to the new sector commander, Major General Ariel ("Arik") Sharon, who just at this time had arrived to try to sort things out.

The fighting had begun very differently for Arik Sharon, the man who in many Israeli eyes was to become the hero of the war. Just three months before, at the age of forty-five, he had retired from regular service to become a politician.

In retirement, however, Sharon had remained in command of a reserve division. But not until 9:30 A.M. on Saturday morning, barely four hours before the war began, had the telephone order come to Sharon at his ranch near Beersheba to mobilize this division—though he had been briefed earlier on the signs of crisis. The order to head for the canal front came as soon as the Egyptian attack started; but then there were serious problems of transport. Not until noon on Sunday did the main body of Sharon's overstrength division of three armored brigades, an artillery group, and other specialized units, begin to take up position along the central sector of the front opposite Ismailia.

"The situation was very grave," Sharon said. "It was impossible to understand exactly what was going on." Just before his division became operational he picked up the field telephone to get some firsthand information.

Toward noon on Sunday the telephone in Avi's communications bunker rings. The commanding officer is on the line.

MEYERKE: I have a force here, not just mine but all sorts of hangers-on and people who got stuck here. No injured, Al-Hamdu-Lellah [praise Allah], except a few small ricochets, but not serious.
SHARON: Are you getting knocked up?
MEYERKE: We, not directly at this moment. But they're getting organized around us. Two platoons of infantry behind us. We can see armored troop carriers going in, perhaps also tanks.
SHARON: Tell me, is there much traffic on the canal road?
MEYERKE: Well, earlier on they were moving on it, a few hours ago, a number of armored personnel carriers that got as far as us. We began to hit them so they turned around and left soldiers, a few groups. I still can't understand the logic of their scattering soldiers along the road. And they return north, northwest, to the area where all their tanks are—the tank battalion that got it from the Air Force earlier.
SHARON: Were there some good hits?
MEYERKE: There were some good hits. We saw some scenes you'll probably remember from the good old days of the Six-Day War.
SHARON: Where are you from?

MEYERKE (naming his kibbutz): Nativ Halamed-Heh.

SHARON: And your men are Jerusalemites?

MEYERKE: Jerusalemites.

SHARON: Their tanks went up in flames, or what?

MEYERKE (tone of satisfaction): Yes.

SHARON: When the Egyptians are not attacking you, are they doing anything else?

MEYERKE: Not so far as I can see, no. What is happening in my direction is directly on the banks of the canal. Armored personnel carriers and tanks have approached there in my direction to a range of seven hundred and eight hundred. They have dug-in infantry. When they raise their heads we shoot. And also with the 81mm [mortar].

SHARON: Do you have ammunition?

MEYERKE: Yes. We try not to just shoot away. I've started going stingy with the 81 [mortar].

SHARON: Did you have artillery support?

MEYERKE: I had, then they stopped it.

SHARON: They stopped the artillery support?

MEYERKE: Now I have it from the south.

SHARON: Tell me, opposite you, north, close to the crossing area, are there any enemy forces between you and them?

MEYERKE: I went down about five minutes ago and there weren't any of them. One moment, I'll see if No. 2 is listening in. Shuki, Shuki, speak.

SHARON: Peace to you. Tell me . . .

SHUKI (in one of the firing positions): Peace and blessing.

SHARON: . . . how many tanks do you see there?

SHUKI: Some forty, forty-five.

SHARON: On what formation? Concentrated?

SHUKI: Some are concentrated, others are standing in rows.

SHARON: Were there any tanks burned?

SHUKI: Not burned, but it seems they were damaged without burning.

SHARON: The men ran away?

SHUKI: The men all came down from them. They're around now. They have like dikes. They're on top of the dikes and in the area on the dikes. [Sharon cross-questions him on distances, but the description remains confused.]

MEYERKE: Arik, understand, they're holding a sort of flat area, do you hear? A flat area a few hundred meters long and a few hundred meters wide, and they've taken up directions facing the area from which, it seems, our armor is blocking them. . . . It seems that together with everything they have behind them, with trucks and everything, they're taking up an area of almost a kilometer long.

SHARON: Tell me, your impression in general is that—all these Egyptians, are they tired or are they swinging?

MEYERKE: I tell you. When you look at them after the Air Force came down on them, you remember what it was like six years ago.

SHARON: Were you a soldier then, or what?

MEYERKE: Of course I was a soldier. Look, I'm already fourth time—no, third time—a soldier in wartime. You're talking to an old man of nearly forty-one.

SHARON: Look fellows, we've only just got here. Now I'm planning to make every effort to extricate you. A little bit later we'll contact you, tell you what to do. . . .

[Sharon inquires about transport at the fort, says he will get the artillery to give further instructions on spotting, and repeats his promise to extricate them, then hangs up.]

Shortly before Sharon's call ends, the most serious shelling to date begins on the fort. By now, 24 hours after the war had begun, 150 tanks—almost a tenth of the Israeli total—have been lost in Sinai alone. A key commander is only just starting to pick up the threads. And Israel, the triumphant victor of the Six-Day War, is gravely threatened. How could this happen?

We will return later to Avi, Meyerke, and Shuki, and the controversial war of "Arik" Sharon. But first we must look at the Arab side, the diplomatic decisions that led up to war, and the puzzling failure of the Israelis to read the signs of danger.

ONE

NO PEACE, NO WAR:
A FAILURE OF DIPLOMACY

1. The Unclosable Gap

The conflict between Israel and the Arab states, and the failure of the superpowers and the United Nations to bring peace between them, go back decades. Historically, the conflict has involved the competing claims of two peoples—the Jews and the Palestinian Arabs—to the same strip of fertile land between the river Jordan and the Mediterranean Sea. On three occasions, in 1948–49, 1956, and 1967, Israel fought to make the Jewish state secure. Each time it won a decisive military victory; but each time it was unable to translate its victory into peace with its Arab neighbors. The Middle East stayed at the brink of war.

For Israel, when, for the fourth time, open warfare began on October 6, 1973, the central issue was once again the security, the existence, of the Jewish state. But for Egypt and Syria, who launched their attack after months of meticulous planning, this war was different from the previous three. This time their stated war plans contained no intention of destroying Israel; nor were the claims of the Palestinians among their main considerations. Israel's principal offense by now—so far as Egypt and Syria were concerned—was not its existence, but its continued occupation of the lands it had seized from them in 1967.

Yet that demand—in contrast to previous Arab threats to the heartland of Israel itself—was not unreasonable. And there were many in Israel who pointed this out. Why, then, had peace proved so elusive?

The history of the six years between the wars falls into four phases: Three were attempts at peace; the last was a preparation for war. First, the United Nations tried to achieve a settlement by virtually public diplomacy. Then President Nixon tried, initially by more covert means. When both failed, the Soviet Union unwillingly stepped in. The United States' efforts had, at least in part, collapsed through Soviet unhelpfulness. Now, as Egypt's President Sadat abandoned diplomacy, the Soviets belatedly tried to restrain him. But, in the final phase, Sadat broke free of them and—convinced that his sole chance of forcing peace terms upon Israel was to manipulate the impact of a renewed conflict—he launched again into preparations for war.

From the start, the six-year struggle for peace had been uphill. The June 1967 fighting stopped in response to cease-fire demands by the United Nations Security Council—demands only possible when the Soviet Union relaxed its veto power to save the Arabs from even more crushing defeat. It was inevitable, therefore, that the first attempt to translate this cease-fire into a permanent peace should also be made at the United Nations. But the aftermath of humiliating defeat is not the best time for reflective negotiation.

Early in August 1967, Arab leaders met in Cairo, where they rejected any form of negotiations with Israel. In return, Abba Eban, Israel's Foreign Minister, said that the map of the Middle East had been "irrevocably destroyed," though he held out the hope that Israel would withdraw from most of the occupied lands following peace negotiations. A fortnight later, an Arab summit conference in Khartoum called for "political efforts at the international and diplomatic level to eliminate the effects of the aggression"—but within the impossibly unyielding framework of what became known as the "Three Noes": no peace with Israel, no recognition of Israel, no negotiations with it, and insistence on the rights of the Palestinian people in their own country. It was, in effect, a call for somebody else to bail out the Arab cause.

The cornerstone of international attempts to bridge this gap was Security Council Resolution 242, adopted unanimously—and therefore with both American and Soviet support—on November 22, 1967. It called for "a just and lasting peace" in the Middle East based on two principles:

> 1. Withdrawal of Israeli forces from territories occupied in the recent conflict.
> 2. Termination of all claims or states of belligerency and respect for and acknowledgment of the sovereignty, territorial integrity, and political independence of every state in the

area and their right to live in peace within secure and recognized boundaries free from threats or acts of force.

The resolution also affirmed the necessity

1. For guaranteeing freedom of navigation through international waterways in the area.
2. For achieving a just settlement of the refugee problem.
3. For guaranteeing the territorial inviolability and political independence of every state in the area, through measures including the establishment of demilitarized zones.

To "promote agreement" in the Middle East, U Thant, the UN Secretary General, was asked "to designate a special representative" as mediator.

In all respects except the most important one, Resolution 242 was a triumph for behind-the-scenes UN diplomacy, and for its main sponsor, Britain's UN representative, Lord Caradon. It carefully balanced Israel's desire for security with the Arab states' demand for recovery of the occupied territories. It was acceptable to the two superpowers. And it spelled out a procedure for moving toward peace negotiations. But it failed to prevent another war.

The problem was that Resolution 242's demand for Israeli withdrawal "from territories occupied in the recent conflict" contained an important ambiguity: Did it mean *all*, or merely *some*, of the occupied territories? The Soviet Union and the Arab states argued for the "all the territories" interpretation; the United States, Britain, and Israel replied that it left open the possibility of readjusting Israel's borders. In reality, the confusion was necessary: Had the resolution been more explicit, one or other superpower would certainly have vetoed it—or at best abstained.

"A constructive ambiguity," Israel's Abba Eban called it—a description adopted somewhat smugly by its British authors. But it is arguable that, on the contrary, Resolution 242 was ultimately destructive. It papered over differences instead of forcing their frank appraisal; it was diplomacy when the need was for *realpolitik*. Israel could claim that the imperative of "secure borders" necessitated certain, always unspecified, annexations; the Arabs could reject even the most sensible adjustments. Both could claim in

242's ambiguity the support of "world opinion." Neither felt any pressure to negotiate—as speedily became clear.

On November 23, 1967, U Thant named Dr. Gunnar Jarring as his special representative. Jarring was a Swedish diplomat with a finely tuned ear for delicate negotiations. He came from a neutral country with no history of partisan behavior in the Middle East. As ambassador to Moscow—and previously to Washington— he had developed a sophisticated understanding of both Soviet and American diplomacy.

But although Jarring succeeded in retaining the support of both those governments, he made only limited progress in closing the gap between Israel and the Arab states. For a start, Syria still refused to contemplate any kind of *modus vivendi* with Israel. On December 12, the Syrian Government—at that time about the most erratic and bellicose regime in the Middle East—announced that it would not work with the Jarring mission, because it was "useless to meet Dr. Jarring as long as his mission is limited to the framework of the resolution adopted by the Security Council and completely rejected by Syria." The leaders of Israel, Jordan, Lebanon, and Egypt did, however, agree to meet Jarring. But it quickly became clear to him that peace talks—let alone their conclusion—were way off.

The Israeli Government told Jarring that the steps to peace had to take place in the following order:

1. Direct negotiations between Israel and the Arab states, leading to:
2. Peace treaty, followed by:
3. Israeli withdrawal to the borders agreed in negotiations.

Egypt and Jordan insisted on a different sequence:

1. Israeli withdrawal to the pre-1967 lines, before:
2. Indirect negotiations through the United Nations, leading to:
3. Peace agreement.

Israel's insistence on direct negotiations was based on the argument that the two sides could hardly live in peace in the

future if they were not prepared to speak to each other now. But
the Arabs equated Israeli insistence on direct talks with a demand
for *de facto* recognition of Israel before talks began. In defeat,
however, the Arabs saw recognition of Israel as one of their few
bargaining cards. More important, Egyptian and Jordanian leaders
were afraid that their defeat had been so humiliating that they
would be unable to reach a fair settlement without a middleman
to hold the ring.

Yet there were soon signs that Egypt, at least, was beginning to
depart from the intransigence of the Khartoum declaration. In
February 1968, Yugoslavia's President Tito reported after a visit
to Cairo that President Nasser would accept UN demands for
demilitarized zones, the ending of the state of war, and the
freedom of Israeli shipping to use the Suez Canal.

By the end of that month, Jarring was sufficiently hopeful that
peace talks might begin, to return to the Middle East carrying
two draft letters he intended to send to U Thant, if the combatants agreed. One referred to talks with Israel and Egypt, the
other to talks with Israel and Jordan. Their otherwise identical
contents conveyed the willingness of each county "to devise
arrangements, under my auspices, for the implementation" of
Resolution 242; and their acceptance of Jarring's invitation to
meet with him separately—in Nicosia "for conferences within the
framework" of the resolution.

Jarring's stratagem failed. Israel eventually accepted the draft
letters but insisted on Nicosia as a prelude to direct talks. Egypt
and Jordan dropped their demand for Israeli withdrawal prior to
negotiations, but wanted "a more precise declaration by Israel of
its willingness to implement Resolution 242." They also wanted
the talks to take place at the UN's New York headquarters.

Jarring persuaded the Arabs to drop the demand for clarification. But Israel could not be persuaded into a change of venue.
Eventually, Jarring simply decided to hold the meetings in New
York—but without formal invitations. By now it was clear, anyway, that the discussion would be desultory at best. And so it
proved. When Foreign Minister Eban unveiled Israel's avowed
plan for peace at the UN General Assembly on October 8, 1968—a
plan that laid down no timings, nowhere defined Israel's idea of
secure borders, and gave no hint of Israel's solution to the

Palestinian problem—the Jarring mission finally went into hibernation.

No mediator stood a chance unless the two sides could be forced into serious talks. That was now clear. A settlement in the Middle East, in other words, depended upon the wishes of the superpowers—and the degree to which they imposed their wills upon the client states they were so busily supplying with weaponry. As the Jarring mission faded, it was America's turn to try—the first task of President-elect Richard Nixon.

As a Middle East peacemaker, Richard Nixon had one remarkable advantage. In the 1968 election, Democratic candidates depended, as usual, upon Jews for more than half their campaign contributions of more than ten thousand dollars. Nixon, by contrast, got little Jewish cash and only 15 to 18 per cent of the Jewish vote. In his victory over Hubert Humphrey in November 1968, therefore, Nixon did not owe American Jewry a thing. It gave him unprecedented freedom of maneuver.

But Nixon also bore one singular disadvantage. The Soviets trusted him even less than they trusted most American politicians. And on the Middle East, if on nothing else, Nixon had earned that distrust. It is worth recounting in detail a complex little powerplay in the closing weeks of the 1968 campaign. It provided the background against which President-elect Nixon began work on the Middle East. It suggests that the Soviets were sufficiently fearful of a Nixon victory to intervene—delicately but actively— to aid Humphrey. Finally, it encapsulates the persistently destructive influence of domestic politics upon America's Middle East policy throughout the decade of the sixties.

Nixon the candidate precipitated the sequence. Inevitably, he too was wooing the Jewish vote—though with a desperation that suggested flagging conviction. On one foray, he met twelve Jewish leaders in his New York apartment and informed them that he was aware of the pro-Arab bias in the State Department. "I intend to have many Jews in my Administration," he proffered, "not just because they are Jews but because they are smart."

That was standard, if clumsy, electioneering. But on September 9, Nixon caused trouble. He told a Washington convention of B'nai B'rith—one of America's more flintily Zionist organizations—that Israel should possess "a technological military margin to more than offset her hostile neighbors' numerical superiority." Israel should be helped "to maintain peace in the Middle East." One Arab diplomat later presumed, acidly, that Nixon intended to appoint Israel sheriff. B'nai B'rith were delighted, of course. It was a seductive appeal to the hard-line Jewish vote. The danger was that Nixon apparently advocated scrapping America's policy, under Kennedy and Johnson, of sending to Israel only those arms necessary to preserve parity with Arab equipment from the Soviet Union. Nixon's policy was an invitation to a spiraling arms race.

Lamely, President Johnson had to use his scheduled appearance before B'nai B'rith the next day to appeal obliquely to the Soviet Union to curtail its shipments to the Arabs: "We continue to hope that our restraint will be matched by others." But everyone in his audience knew that for nine months Johnson had been sitting on an Israeli request for McDonnell-Douglas Phantom F-4s —supersonic fighter-bombers and, by some margin, the most sophisticated weapon yet envisaged by either side in the conflict. Even when Johnson's Defense Secretary, Clark Clifford, declared himself "not conscious of any serious imbalance in the level of forces between Israel and the Arab states," the attraction of Nixon's bold appeal remained.

The Soviet Union intervened. In mid-September, the Soviets leaked the news that they had allegedly offered Egypt and Syria more tanks, aircraft, and pilot instructors. Privately, the Soviet Union also approached America with another peace plan. It was, of course, idiotic to propose serious diplomacy in the midst of an American election, and the Soviet Union must have known it. And the alleged supplies had already been taken into account when Clifford gave his verdict.

But the Soviet Union had supplied Johnson with the excuse he needed. On October 9, Johnson announced that he had authorized negotiations to begin on the Phantom deal. These, Johnson solemnly said, would be "to provide Israel with an adequate deterrent force, capable of . . . offsetting the sophisticated weapons received by the Arab states." The timing of his announcement—midway through the UN debate on the Middle East— wrecked whatever fragile hopes still clung to the Jarring mission. But it hauled back the Jewish vote for Humphrey. It was still not enough.

Nixon the President-elect was, however, vastly more realistic than Nixon the candidate. Nixon's real views on the Middle East had been revealed in a campaign speech on September 29. "There could," he said, "be nuclear war in the Middle East unless America and Russia sit down and talk." (He had said this before, but only as a postscript to more vote-catching remarks.) And this coincided with his general aim to move, as he grandly put it, "from an era of confrontation into an era of negotiation." Once elected, therefore—and with more domestic freedom than any President since the 1956 Aswan-Suez debacle had fragmented Western influence in the Middle East—Nixon proposed, as his first foreign policy target outside Vietnam, a deal with the Soviet Union to settle the conflict. It was not his fault that he failed.

The priority that Nixon gave to a Middle East peace stemmed from more than an awareness of the risks of a superpower confrontation—though that was the starkest aspect to sell to the American public. In the long term, Nixon was also convinced, a settlement was the essential precursor to any policy of undercutting Soviet influence in the region. And finally, even before Nixon had been inaugurated, events demonstrated that time was not on the side of peace.

Until 1968, the Palestinian guerrilla movements were irritants rather than major protagonists. But with the dwindling of hopes for a settlement, the guerrillas gathered momentum—though their activists have never comprised more than a tiny minority of Palestinians. And in 1968 first Syria and then other Arab states began once more to give them proper military training. The early postwar guerrilla raids were in Israel itself, the targets being restaurants, bus stations, and markets. But Israeli security forces all but crushed those groups operating inside the country, and border patrols decimated bands slipping over the frontiers. Meanwhile, Israeli strikes on guerrilla bases in Jordan and Syria escalated. The guerrillas were forced to operate farther afield, outside the immediate arena. The resulting international headlines made them harder to ignore. Israel did not try.

On Boxing Day 1968, two Palestinians from Lebanese camps killed one Israeli and wounded another in an attack upon an El Al Boeing at Athens Airport. Already irate over the deaths of twelve people and the wounding of fifty more in an explosion in a

Jerusalem market in November, Israel decided upon massive retaliation. On December 28, Israeli commandos assaulted Beirut
Airport. In a forty-five-minute raid, thirteen aircraft—eight from
the Middle East Airlines—were destroyed. (The Security Council,
unanimously condemning Israel's "premeditated military action,"
made no mention of the Palestinian attacks.) The swiftness of
Israel's response, however, could not conceal the Palestinians'
growing capacity to hinder any peace settlement. The longer a
peace settlement was delayed, the harder it would be to implement.

It was against this darkening background that, a few days before New Year 1969, Nixon's newly nominated Secretary of State,
William Rogers, began to plan America's Middle East policy
afresh. Roger's knowledge of the area was slim: When he first met
the State Department's Middle East desk officers, he is said to
have scanned the map behind them and remarked: "Why, that's
all the Middle East? You fellows do have a large area on your
hands." His indispensable aide was thus one of America's more
able career diplomats, Joseph Sisco—the Assistant Secretary for
Near Eastern Affairs, whom he had inherited from Rusk. At their
first meeting in late December 1968, Rogers spelled out to Sisco
Nixon's new ground rules.

The first was that, as Nixon had implied, the United States
would deal directly with the Soviet Union. Indeed, as Nixon saw
it, America had no choice. Already, Nixon had absorbed the
doctrine of his new national security advisor, Henry Kissinger: If
America was unwilling to carry through the logic of nuclear
confrontation to defend anything outside America, the only alternative to defeat was nuclear condominium. To put that across
inside America, of course, would require tact; and it was uncertain
how far the Soviet Union would cooperate. Nixon's second guideline was equally controversial. The peace settlement Nixon sought
envisaged Israel's withdrawal virtually to the pre-1967 borders—
keeping only the most minor territorial gains for reasons of security.

The latter had, in fact, been the precise policy of the Johnson
administration—though, in deference to the Jewish lobby, the
Democrats had deemed it prudent to blur this. Besides, whatever
formal policy might have been, strong factions in both the

Pentagon and the State Department questioned the wisdom of any Middle East strategy other than a reliance upon the only regime in the region both pro-Western and stable, Israel. So, in practice, Israel had gotten its own way. Behind general injunctions, the Johnson administration had been content to let Jarring ask the hard questions.

Nixon wanted to change all that—but in secret. Sisco, charged by Rogers with drafting papers on the implementation of the new policy, had to work in the evenings, after everyone had gone home. Still, Nixon did signal the change. Barely a month after his election, he sent William Scranton, sometime Republican governor of Pennsylvania, on a tour of the Middle East. To all he met, Scranton reiterated that America proposed a more "even-handed" policy in the area. "It is important," he told the Israelis, "for the United States to take into consideration the feelings of all peoples in the Middle East and not necessarily espouse one nation over some other." He even hinted that Nixon might make Israel wait three years for the Phantoms Johnson had promised. And while the White House press secretary, Ronald Ziegler, said: "His remarks are Scranton remarks, not Nixon remarks," few could have doubted that Scranton was flying presidential kites.

It was, indeed, a policy of even-handedness—or, as it was put in Washington, "objectivity"—which was endorsed at Nixon's first and most crucial policy meeting on the Middle East. At an all-day meeting of the National Security Council on February 1, Sisco's policy papers were discussed. According to the well-informed account of those indefatigable reporters, Evans and Novak, President Nixon, Kissinger, Rogers, Defense Secretary Melvin Laird, and CIA chief Richard Helms all agreed with the policy proposed.

In outline, it was simple. The United States would seek to reach agreement with the Soviet Union on the broad sweep of a settlement, including borders. The channel of communication would mainly be the Soviet ambassador in Washington, Anatoly Dobrynin. Amplifying Nixon's brief, Sisco's papers even outlined what the United States might accept by way of a settlement. Israel would withdraw from all of Sinai and the Gaza Strip, and from most of the Golan Heights and the West Bank of the Jordan. The intractable problems of Jerusalem and the Palestinian refugees would be worked out later, under tacit superpower guarantees of mutual compromise. In return, Egypt would have to sign a peace agreement and permit Israeli passage through the Suez Canal and the Straits of Tiran, the Sinai gateway to Israel's oil port of Eilat. If necessary, a peace-keeping force—perhaps including superpower troops—would be inserted once more into the area.

To sell this deal internationally, Sisco proposed that any American-Soviet agreement should be endorsed by the "Big Four": the superpowers plus Britain and France. (Besides fancying that they still had a role to play in their old sphere of influence, Britain and France were the other permanent Western members of the Security Council.) As a final stage, the package would be handed to a revitalized Jarring to sell in detail to the participants.

The Big Four rapidly proved as cosmetic as the more cynical State Department officials had prophesied. From April 1969, meetings were held among their UN representatives—formally, to thrash out Resolution 242. The meetings were to drag on, convening spasmodically, until September 1971. No common interpretation ever emerged.

But the talks that mattered were those, simultaneously, between the United States and the Soviet Union alone. And those did, as we shall see, come remarkably close to success. The stumbling block was that neither superpower—despite being the armorer of its respective client states—had, in the last resort, the will to force an unpopular deal upon them.

2. The World's Smallest Superpower

Mrs. Golda Meir became Prime Minister of Israel less than two months after Nixon took office. Her misfortune was to confront an activist President with a paralyzed government. She had little choice. Israel ballots by proportional representation—the votes going to party slates rather than to individual candidates. The aim is democratic, the result stagnation. Historically, the Labor party has consistently returned to power, but equally consistently without an over-all majority. Fringe parties have wound up holding the balance, with disproportionate influence inside successive Israeli Cabinets.

The paraplegic nature of the government Mrs. Meir had to run is indicated by the composition of her Cabinet after the 1969 elections. One group—her most senior ministers—was from the Labor party, itself an uneasy alliance of three factions. Another group represented the United Workers party (Mapam). A third hailed from the National Religious party. A final element was from Gahal. The two broadly Socialist parties were, more or less, prepared to withdraw from the occupied lands—though few even of these ministers could agree on the details. The National Religious party, on the other hand, asserted Israel's historic right to the "Promised Land"—the boundaries of which they defined to include the West Bank of the Jordan. And Gahal wanted Israeli sovereignty over almost all the 1967 gains. It was scarcely surprising that, in response first to the Jarring and then to the American initiatives, the Israeli Government would produce no details of what "secure borders" it wanted. The Cabinet would have fallen apart—in the end, it did just that—the moment its ministers began any such exercise.

As much by necessity as by calculation, the Israelis' policy on a peace settlement was thus to wait for the Arabs to approach them.

When the early Khartoum conference signaled Arab intransigence, that merely relieved Israel of any need to consider what it really wanted. The demand for "secure borders," like the Arab demand for "justice" for the Palestinians, disguised a bankruptcy of policy.

There were other reasons why Israel saw no need to settle. The 1967 War—and the "no peace, no war" tensions after that—tapped a torrent of cash from the Jews of the Diaspora. In the five years 1962–66, world Jewry gave Israel about $400 million; in the five postwar years, they gave $1.2 billion. On top of those donations, investment in Israel doubled over the same period. By the end of 1972, nine in ten Israeli households had a refrigerator, and two in three had television; both percentages had doubled in three years. And to man Israel's booming industries, who better than the Arabs from the occupied territories?

Politically, the outlook was equally bullish. "Israel is now a military superpower," "Arik" Sharon proclaimed. "Every national force in Europe is weaker than we are. We can conquer in one week the area from Khartoum to Baghdad and Algeria." It was the extreme expression of a common confidence. With the superpowers locked in nuclear stalemate, it was argued, Israel alone had the ability to take the initiative in the Middle East. Ergo, Israel was the effective arbiter of the region.

Nor did the Israeli military establishment appear to doubt that America would always support them. As the importance of that dwindling commodity, crude oil, became steadily clearer through the late 1960s, the Israelis persuaded themselves that this enhanced *their* importance rather than the Arabs'. One commentator, a fervent supporter of Israeli Defense Minister Moshe Dayan, wrote: "Israel became the only possible sanction that the Americans, the Europeans and the Japanese could call upon in their confrontation with the Arab and international oil barons. . . ." He was taken seriously. In Washington, Israel argued that it was the lone democratic bastion holding back the Soviet advance in the Middle East; even, that Israel's presence alone prevented the overrunning of the oil-rich Gulf states by the "revolutionaries" of Egypt and Syria. The argument gained wide credence.

It was scarcely surprising that Nixon wanted to keep his first steps to a new American policy secret. Nor was it surprising that

Mrs. Meir regarded his aims with implacable suspicion. An element of paranoia is understandable in Israeli politics—as Henry Kissinger once remarked: "Even a paranoid can have real enemies." And, in an interview with the London *Sunday Times* in June 1969, Mrs. Meir rejected the apparent American intentions: "I cannot imagine that Israel would again consent to any deal under which we would have to depend for our security on others. We are more intelligent than that. One does not have to be very sophisticated to come to the conclusion, after the bitter experience of twenty years, that the only people we can depend on for our security are ourselves."

By this time, it was not only the Palestinians who threatened the peace. The Suez front had opened up once more. It had never been wholly quiet, but the artillery duels across the canal rose to a new intensity through the spring of 1969. Egypt had begun the sequence with a concentrated barrage early in September 1968—perhaps to concentrate the international mind on the eve of the proposed (and abortive) Jarring talks. Egypt, said Nasser, was abandoning "passive resistance" in favor of aggressive "preventive defense." To protect its soldiers against this barrage— and to provide a defense against a possible canal crossing—Israel began early in 1969 the construction of a line of strongpoints along the east bank of the canal. After their architect, the Israeli Chief of Staff of the time, these quickly became known as the Bar-Lev Line. Determined to prevent its construction, Egypt stepped up its barrage at the beginning of March 1969. Israel responded. By the end of April, U Thant described the canal zone as being in "a virtual state of active war."

Egypt raised the stakes. On May 1, President Nasser boasted that a series of commando raids across the canal had destroyed 60 per cent of the newly built Bar-Lev Line. The Suez Canal, he told UN officials, could no longer be considered a cease-fire line. The United States and the Soviet Union, still trying to map the rough outline of a settlement, were seemingly appalled. Through U Thant, they appealed for calm. Nasser's response was to authorize air strikes on Israeli positions in Sinai.

Nasser knew the risks he was running. But by the end of 1968 the Egyptian Army was severely disenchanted with the gulf between Nasser's rhetoric and the military activity he actually sanctioned. It was partly to still this dissent that Nasser had proclaimed the switch to "preventive defense." He had another reason, though. By early 1969, the superpowers were beginning to debate Nixon's ideas for a settlement in the Middle East. Nasser genuinely—and almost certainly correctly—felt that unless Egypt stirred militarily, the chances of the United States forcing Israel to swallow peace terms that Nasser would find acceptable were remote. The Soviet Union agreed.

For public consumption, the Soviets joined the United States in appealing for calm across the canal. But, according to sources in Cairo who were close to Nasser at that time, the secret advice the Soviets gave the Egyptian leader was to try his luck. Early in 1969, the Soviets apparently encouraged Nasser to see whether he could drive the Israelis back from the canal by a combination of artillery barrages and commando raids. According to these sources, it was in response to this advice that Nasser launched in April his commando assaults to blow up the embryonic Bar-Lev Line.

From the Soviet point of view, the advice made sense. It *was* unlikely that Israel would of its own accord throw away the bargaining counters that its hold on Sinai and the canal represented. Unless Nasser broke the deadlock, the chances of political progress thus *were* as low as he feared. Yet not even Nasser could balance forever on the pyramid of his own rhetoric—the mutterings inside the Army showed that. It was worth a military adventure.

Calculating the inevitable Israeli response, the Soviets presumably reassured themselves with the fact that through the winter of 1968–69 the Soviet Union had already supplied Egypt with an air defense system: a network of some of the most advanced Soviet antiaircraft missiles, the SAM-2, manned by Soviet troops drawn mainly from the air defense corps stationed around Moscow. With that protection, the Soviets might have been excused for thinking, nothing much could go wrong for Nasser. The trouble— for both Egypt and the Soviets—was that Egypt's gamble did go disastrously wrong.

By July, it was clear that Israel would have to reply. That month, thirty Israelis were killed and seventy-six wounded on the Suez front. Finally, on July 20, Israel launched the first of a series of devastating air raids on Egyptian air bases, missile complexes, and military installations west of the canal. Now it was

Israel's turn to raise the stakes. The so-called War of Attrition had begun in earnest.

Israel's strategy was twofold: first, to destroy the Soviet-supplied missiles, the SAM-2s, which protected Egyptian military and strategic industrial targets; then, having stripped away the air cover, to damage Nasser's industrial capacity to wage war. Through the latter half of 1969, the Israeli Air Force grimly set about the first stage of this task. By September, its pilots had discovered how to circumvent the missile defenses. By the end of the year, the radar controlling most of Egypt's twenty-four main SAM-2 complexes had been wiped out. (And, Egyptian sources say, more than 40 Soviet soldiers had been killed or wounded.)

But Israel could retaliate by land too. On September 9, its forces launched what became known as the Ten-Hour War. A force of torpedo boats and landing craft went ashore in Egypt at El Khafayev on the Gulf of Suez, about 25 miles south of the town of Suez. There, the Israelis disembarked 6 tanks and three armored personnel carriers—all Soviet-made, spoils of the Six-Day War. Manned by 150 Israeli paratroopers, all Arabic speakers and wearing Egyptian uniforms, the armor set off southward along the coast road. While Israeli air raids over the canal distracted attention, this force—in 10 hours—destroyed 3 major radar stations and killed about 150 Egyptian soldiers. Late in the afternoon, they re-embarked aboard the landing craft, shipping back with them a rare prize, 2 of the Soviet Union's latest tanks, the T-62, which had only weeks before been supplied to Egypt for the first time. (What happened to these T-62s is uncertain. One knowledgeable British Army source claims that at least one went to Britain for comparison trials in the deserted north of Scotland; but Ministry of Defence officials deny this.)

The raid had a purpose. Egypt had been storing its newer Soviet gear in the desert along the gulf, apparently assuring the Soviet Union of its security there. The raid was to demonstrate to the Soviet Union the imprudence of trusting its latest equipment—much of which the West was itching to examine—to the Egyptian defenses. Its untoward effect, however, was to demonstrate to the United States that Israel was in little need of help. Yet Mrs. Meir still appealed to Nixon, on a visit to Washington later in September, for another twenty-five Phantoms and one hundred Skyhawks on top of those authorized by Johnson. Nixon sat on the request.

As 1969 ended, Israel pulled off another spectacular coup. Its commandos removed—again from a coastal installation on the Gulf of Suez—one of the latest Soviet mobile antiaircraft radar sets, the P-12. This was an even greater blow than the loss of the T-62s, since the Soviet air defense system is the most intensive in the world and the P-12 was then one of its most advanced elements. Its removal was a bad setback to Egypt: That particular installation had been sited to cover one of the Israeli pilots' favorite approach routes, the long curve up from the southeast. (The P-12 was found, on examination by Israeli experts, to have a range of two hundred miles.) And its espionage value to the West was enormous. It was an expensive success, though. Under the impact of the steadily escalating Israeli air assault, the Soviet Union abandoned its talks with the United States to find a peaceful settlement.

The talks had begun in high hopes. Rogers had picked up in January 1969 the Soviet proposals made during the election campaign. They were a reasonable starting point: Israeli withdrawal to the pre-1967 borders; a UN presence to demilitarize the occupied territories; a four-power guarantee of Israel's security, with Jerusalem and the Palestinians to be sorted out later. Israel, of course, was appalled—"a plan to dismantle Israel by stages," Eban called it. Rogers simply did not agree, though he wanted Soviet clarification of how strictly they interpreted the withdrawal clause. And in response, Rogers gave to Dobrynin in March 1969 a thirteen-point American plan, meeting most of the Soviet demands.

The problem was that when Soviet Foreign Minister Andrei Gromyko went to Cairo in June, he was quite unable to sell any such deal to President Nasser. It was a stormy session. The United States too talked of demilitarizing the occupied territories, for instance; and Rogers thought he could persuade Israel to take back 10 per cent of the Palestinian refugees. But the United States was vague on whether Israel should abandon all of Golan or the Jordan West Bank, though all too clear on Jerusalem: That should remain unified. How difficult Gromyko's session was may be judged from the fact that Nasser simply reiterated two demands: total Israeli withdrawal before any talks, and separate negotiations with the Palestinians themselves.

Nasser was still buoyed up by the early successes of his fresh military adventure—which, after all, the Soviet Union had approved. Why, now, should he tamely follow the Soviets' new line, merely because their emphasis had shifted once more toward a peaceful settlement? And however irritated Gromyko might be with Nasser, the Soviet Union could not abandon him. He was their beachhead in the Middle East. So back went a discouraging Soviet reply to Washington. Rogers tried to see the bright side. At least the Soviet Union was thinking in terms of a "package deal," none of the terms of which would be implemented until all elements were agreed—which meant no prior Israeli withdrawal. And the Soviet Union was encouragingly vague on the Golan and Jordan borders, and on the Palestinian question.

So Sisco went to Moscow in July. And in September Gromyko came to the United States to see Rogers. When, on October 28, Rogers handed Dobrynin the United States' final outline settlement, he really thought he could get agreement. As Sisco's original policy papers had envisaged, the United States was trading territory for peace—while providing Israel with added security by means of four-power, effectively superpower, guarantees. There were even hints that King Hussein of Jordan would be pressured into allowing a separate Palestinian state to be set up on the Jordan West Bank.

It was too late. Having triggered a shooting war across the canal, Nasser was by the end of the year totally unable to cope with the increasingly severe and audacious Israeli counterstrikes. Unless the Soviet Union moved to bolster Egypt's air defenses, Nasser might fall. Certainly, Soviet prestige in the Arab world would suffer. So, on December 23, the Soviet Union rejected Rogers' document—reneging even on points previously agreed. The Middle East was back to bullets again. (But did the Soviet Union contemplate a more surgical alternative: the elimination of Nasser? In September, Nasser discovered that his Vice-President, Ali Sabry, had been sounding out Moscow on the possibility of a *coup d'état*. And in the first days of December—just before the Soviets finally delivered their rejection of the U.S. peace plan—

there is good evidence that Nasser was suddenly afraid that he was going to be assassinated by "foreign agents.")

Nassar survived. But it was Israel that held the immediate military initiative. In the early days of January 1970, Israel obtained from the United States the most advanced electronic gear it had yet acquired to defeat the SAM-2s. (Nixon's decision to release the equipment came in the wake of the Soviet Union's rejection of Rogers' efforts.) This ECM—Electronic Counter Measures—equipment was to be slung in pods beneath the wings of the Phantoms that Israel was now getting as the first fruits of the Johnson deal. For the first time, the Israeli pilots now had warning when the surviving SAM-2 radar locked onto them. With this to protect them, the pilots embarked upon the second phase of Israel's assault on Egypt. From January 7, 1970—when three of the main military airfields around Cairo were bombed—the Israeli raids on strategic military and industrial targets penetrated ever deeper into Egypt. Within three months, most of Egypt's early-warning radar had been wiped out, as had three quarters of its general radar cover. Egypt was virtually open skies. Israel even raided targets in the outermost suburbs of Cairo.

Inevitably, the civilian casualties mounted. When its aircraft killed seventy workers in a scrap metal factory and injured another hundred, Israel acknowledged a "technical error." But when its bombs destroyed a school in the Nile Delta, killing forty-six children and injuring twenty, Israel was adamant that it had struck a military target. This was, at best, no more implausible than the Palestinians' purported reason for firing a bazooka at a bright yellow Israeli school bus, a familiar daily sight as it trundled along the Lebanese border. The dead consisted of eight children, three teachers, and the driver, the wounded another twenty children. The guerrillas claimed that the bus had carried "Zionist experts."

The onset on January 7 of this new phase of Israeli counterattacks appalled Nasser. And when, on January 22, the Israelis made yet another audacious assault—an amphibious attack on the Egyptian-held island of Shadwan, which physically controls the entrance to the Gulf of Suez—the Egyptian President was thrown into a state verging on panic. On January 23, after a thirty-two-hour occupation, the Israelis withdrew from Shadwan (yet again lifting off by helicopter the interesting Soviet equipment they had found). But by then Nasser had flown secretly to Moscow. He was accompanied only by his Foreign Minister, Mohammed Riyad, and his War Minister, Lieutenant General Mohammed Fawzi. And Nasser's purpose was simple. He went to beg for more Soviet military aid.

This secret four-day meeting in the snowbound Soviet capital was to prove a turning point in the Soviet involvement in Egypt's cause. Yet it was only with the greatest possible reluctance that the Soviet leaders even considered Nasser's pleadings.

Politically, the Soviet Union was disillusioned by the seemingly irremediable inability of the Arabs to form a united front against Israel. (The latest failure had been a wholly fruitless meeting of Arab leaders at Rabat in December 1969—a meeting later derided by one shrewd Egyptian as "talks over a cup of coffee.") To one Arab minister visiting Moscow about that time, Soviet Premier Alexei Kosygin did not hide his exasperation. "You confuse us, Arab friends," he said. "We beg you for your own sake and for the sake of your friends to agree on one thing: Agree on the maximum or the minimum. It does not matter which. But agree. For heaven's sake, agree on something."

Already, the Soviet Union was tempted by the potential economic benefits of the détente that Nixon was dangling. If Vietnam could be wound down, only the Middle East would stand in the way. Now, despite massive Soviet aid, the Egyptians had got themselves into another mess.

Sufficient information has since leaked out about that crucial January 1970 meeting in Moscow to enable its outlines to be pieced together. Nasser wanted, first, more advanced antiaircraft defenses and, second, continued Soviet support for the idea of an Egyptian foray in strength across the canal. Neither prospect now appealed to Moscow.

Since the 1967 debacle, the Soviet leaders had been cautious which weapons they supplied to Egypt. They differentiated—insofar as this was possible—between defensive weapons, which they supplied in quantity, and offensive weapons, with which they were much more grudging. And, after the Israeli raids, the Soviets were even less anxious to risk their most advanced armaments on Egyptian soil.

Nasser explained to Soviet party leader Leonid Brezhnev—the main Soviet negotiator—that the SAM-2s had been neutralized. The Israelis had learned (or been told by the United States) that the missiles could not cope with low-level aircraft. Nasser said he now needed the SAM-3 to combat Israeli low-level tactics. And to match the Phantoms which Israel was now flying as the first fruits of the Johnson pre-election agreement, Egypt needed a more advanced fighter than the MiG-21s which the Soviets had supplied so far.

The Soviet Union had paused before supplying even the SAM-2s. Could they now risk the capture of a SAM-3? As Mohammed Heikal, then editor of the semi-official Cairo daily *Al Ahram*, wrote some time afterward: "This was a hard decision for the Soviet leaders to make because these weapons had never before been deployed outside the country. . . . The [Egyptian] request for new weapons was followed by a request that Soviet experts should help in the operation of the new weapons until Egyptian soldiers had acquired the necessary skills.

"This was an ever more difficult decision to make. Apart from the military point of view, the decision would signify in international terms that the Soviet Union would not allow a defeat to befall the Arab nation, under any circumstances."

There is good reason to think that Heikal—by some margin the best informed journalist in the Arab world—was reproducing faithfully the arguments of the Soviet leadership. British diplomatic sources even claim that the first Soviet proposal was that Nasser should send Egyptian technicians to the Soviet Union for a year's training on the missiles. Only when Nasser turned that down—fearing, presumably, what else they might be trained in—did the Soviets apparently face the choice of a greatly expanded military presence in Egypt.

But what else, in the end, could the Soviets do but accede to Nasser's demands—or abandon their game of power politics in the Middle East? So Nasser got a promise of SAM-3s. He got a promise of more advanced aircraft. He got continued Soviet support for a plan to "secure the reopening of the Suez Canal" by "helping the Egyptians to establish a bridgehead on the east bank of the waterway"—again, the phrasing of British diplomats shortly afterward. In a remark Nasser himself later let fall, he said that the

Soviets had even promised the first shipments of this new equipment within thirty days.

Thus, to stave off an Egyptian defeat in a war that Egypt had started, and to prop up the best Arab leader they had, the Soviets were sucked deeper into direct involvement in the Middle East. To the worried men of the Kremlin, it must all have looked unpleasantly like a rerun of the United States' experience in Vietnam.

Perhaps that was why the Soviet Union virtually appealed to the United States to help it out of the quagmire before it was too late. On January 31—less than a week after Nasser had left Moscow—a note from Kosygin was handed to Kissinger. (That it was to the White House rather than to the Secretary of State may be taken to indicate the seriousness with which the Soviet Premier hoped it would be viewed.) "We wish to inform you clearly," he said, "that the U.S.S.R. will put at the disposition of the Arab countries everything necessary for the expulsion of this insolent aggression so long as Israel persists in its adventures. . . . We believe it is our duty to draw to your attention the extremely grave consequences which could result. . . ." But the United States, too, had difficulty in standing up to its Middle East client state.

Paradoxically, however, the immediate effect of the new Soviet aid seemed to be a lessening of the tension. For the Soviets kept their promise to Nasser. In the first days of February 1970, an airlift of antiaircraft guns, radar units, and the first handful of SAM-3 missile installations began to arrive in Egypt, to be followed by shiploads of more equipment to the port of Alexandria— plus the first of thousands of technicians and troops. In the last week of February, the first Soviet pilots and ground crews arrived. By mid-March, there were 3,000 Soviet personnel in Egypt; by the end of March, the total was 4,500; by July, it had spiraled to almost 10,000. And from April, the construction of SAM-3 batteries continued apace.

Just in case Israel thought of catching these installations undefended, the Soviet pilots began in mid-April to fly operational missions over Egyptian territory. Israel subsequently claimed that twenty-four Soviet squadrons were based in Egypt, but Washington estimates were considerably more conservative. The Soviets were flying MiG-21Js, instead of the MiG-23s Nasser had requested. But the MiG-23 had only just entered squadron service in the Soviet Union. And the advanced fire-control system on the MiG-21Js made them formidable opponents of the Phantoms. (Meanwhile, squads of promising Egyptian pilots were flown to remote air bases in the Soviet southern state of Kazakhstan to train on these MiGs—the climate in Kazakhstan approximates to that around the northern Nile.)

The Soviet pilots' task in Egypt remained strictly defensive. Indeed, the Soviet Government had forbidden them to fly nearer than thirty miles west of the canal. Their job, as the Israeli pilots swiftly discovered, was to deter deep penetration raids on targets deep into Egypt. The tactic worked. The last thing that Israel wanted was to risk shooting down a Soviet pilot. (On one attempted Israeli raid, its Phantoms curving in over the Gulf way south of the canal, no fewer than forty Soviet pilots scrambled to meet them. The Israelis turned tail.) From mid-April, the Israelis had to abandon deep strikes into Egypt. Nasser had, at least temporarily, been saved.

If Israeli air strikes were thus politically confined to the area just west of the canal, the Soviets had the military answer to that too. They set about constructing a missile defense line between the canal and Cairo. The "box," as Israel came to call it, began about twenty-five miles back from the canal, was then about sixteen miles deep, and in all stretched north and south of the Cairo-to-Ismailia road for about fifty miles. If this "box" were ever completed—to interlock into a network of jointly controlled and coordinated missile batteries—Egypt would effectively be barred to Israeli air strikes. The destruction of this "box" became Israel's first priority.

To begin with, its pilots had some success. The Soviets had trouble working up their SAM-3 batteries: The batteries had never been in active service before and radar calibration apparently posed problems. And since one type of SAM-3 radar required a sixty-five-foot tower—giving rise to rumors in Cairo that minarets were being pressed into service—they made easy targets for Israeli strikes. The mainstay of Egypt's air defenses was still the SAM-2, to which Israel—by courtesy of the United States—now had total countermeasures.

It was to prove Israel's misfortune, however, that the cease-fire in this savage technological war came when it did. For it deprived Israel of the chance to learn just how formidable Soviet missiles could be when they were fully operational. It was a lesson in store.

The cease-fire came at Nixon's instigation. In a sense, it was his last throw. The Soviet Union's rejection of a year's patient progress toward a settlement, just when it seemed close to success, had shocked him. It had also strengthened the argument of Israel and its supporters in Washington that negotiations could never succeed. The only sane American policy, it was said, was to so arm Israel that the Soviet Union would be cowed from the Middle East for fear of sparking World War III. Nixon had bowed to this pressure to the extent of supplying the ECM gear necessary to neutralize the SAM-2s. But to preserve any hope of achieving his long-term aim—resconstructing America's relations with the Arabs—Nixon had to keep moving along the road to peace. A cease-fire would be a start.

The Soviet presence itself constituted a persuasive reason for action. However unwillingly the Soviet Union had become involved in Egypt, its contingent there was now massive. By June, the Soviets had actually taken over five major Egyptian air bases—three near Cairo and two in the north—and had the use of more than twenty others, besides having sealed off a sizable area of Alexandria docks as a naval and supply base.

Nor were the Soviets backward in making full use of these facilities. The U. S. Sixth Fleet in the Mediterranean was now regularly shadowed by Soviet "Badger" bombers—based in Egypt, wearing Egyptian markings, but piloted by their regular Soviet crews. (Not that such espionage was wholly one-sided. According to a source in the Washington intelligence community, the CIA managed fairly swiftly to penetrate one of the main Soviet bases in Egypt. The means of penetration was apparently Egypt's state-owned wine company, the *Société de l'Alexandre pour les Boissons Distilles et Vignobles de Gianaclis*—the name, of course, a splendid legacy of pre-revolutionary days. The story has a certain geographical plausibility, because the wine company's Alexandria premises did abut onto one of the main Soviet bases, Jiyanklis. According to the Washington source, the operation was blown in some fashion by the Egyptian security services. "It wasn't that

valuable," the source commented. "But the girl running the operation was just about the last American agent in Egypt. I guess
they just wanted to tidy things up." No arrests are traceable in
Egypt. Presumably, those involved were all foreign nationals and
were quietly expelled.)

Secretary of State Rogers launched the new U.S. peace initiative
on June 19, 1970. As a first stage, he asked Israel and Egypt to
agree to a three-month cease-fire. The canal could then be dredged
and cleared of ships stuck there since 1967. (One ship had been
carrying apples, by now well past their prime.) Israel was to
commit itself to withdrawal from occupied lands. The dormant
Jarring mission and Resolution 242 were then to be revived.

It is hard to say which side distrusted the offer more. President
Nasser arrived in Moscow on June 29 for another protracted
and difficult bout with the Soviets—whose acceptance of the
plan, though with reservations, Rogers had obtained in advance.
Twice Nasser delayed his return to Cairo until, when he left on
July 17, he had accepted the plan unconditionally. As if to emphasize the fragility of the plan's chances, Palestinians stormed
through the streets of Cairo denouncing him as a coward. Nasser
closed down their radio stations.

Israel was as unhappy as Nasser had been. Mrs. Meir was
by now seriously convinced that Nixon was conspiring with
Moscow to sell out Israel if necessary. She denounced the
Rogers plan as "a trick which would enable Egypt to prepare
for a renewal of the war in a more intense form." But Israel,
ultimately, could not say no—as U. S. Assistant Secretary Sisco
had somewhat bluntly reminded her on a visit to Israel earlier
in the year. There were tense, confused meetings of the Israeli
Cabinet. Some, like Eban, thought the plan was hopeless but
that Israel could not appear intransigent. Others, like Mrs. Meir
and Dayan, agreed about its hopelessness but were more concerned to re-establish their damaged "special relationship" with
the United States. Others, from the Gahal party, wanted a public
rejection of the whole idea. Mrs. Meir had no choice. On July 31,
1970, Israel accepted the plan—and the right-wing Gahal party
quit the coalition and went into opposition in protest.

The short-term imperative of a cease-fire is one thing; the long
haul of a political settlement is another. Having engineered the

40 NO PEACE, NO WAR

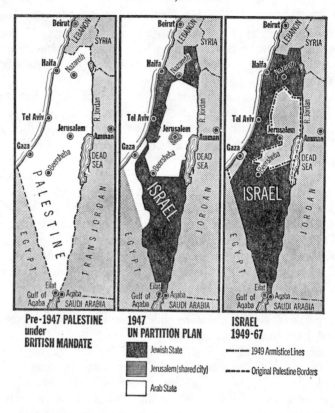

Pre-1947 PALESTINE under BRITISH MANDATE

1947 UN PARTITION PLAN

Jewish State

Jerusalem (shared city)

Arab State

ISRAEL 1949-67

—··— 1949 Armistice Lines

—— Original Palestine Borders

Map 1 The changing shape of Israel

Until 1948, Palestine—a land of two million people, in which two out of three were Arabs, and one in three was Jewish—was controlled by Britain under mandate from first the League of Nations and then the United Nations. In November 1947, the UN decided to partition the country into a Jewish state (57 per cent of the land) and an Arab state (42 per cent). Jerusalem was to be shared, and administered by the UN. The Jews accepted this advantageous plan, but the Arabs did not. When the British left in May 1948, Israel was born. Immediately, Arab forces attempted to crush the new Jewish state—and the Israelis attempted to extend their control over more of Palestine. The Israelis were more successful: In May 1949 Israel signed an armistice with its Arab neighbors, gaining more land than the UN had intended. Jerusalem was divided between Israel and Jordan. The proposed Arab state was never formed. Up to a million Palestinians fled from Israel and became refugees. The borders remained intact until 1967, despite the 1956 War, when Israel, in collusion with Britain and France, invaded Sinai.

Map 2
In the Six-Day War of June 1967, Israeli forces occupied the whole of what had been Palestine, together with the Sinai desert in Egypt and the Golan Heights in Syria. Israel subsequently offered to withdraw from most of the occupied territories, but not Sharm-el-Sheikh, the Golan Heights, or Jerusalem. In the absence of negotiations, Israeli forces continued to control the occupied areas.

easy part, the superpowers handed back to Jarring the task of once more cranking up his peace mission. The omens were inauspicious. Nasser had already delayed accepting Rogers' cease-fire for six weeks, while he rushed on with the completion of the missile "box". Now he promptly took advantage of the cease-fire not merely to complete construction of the "box," but to move new missiles forward almost to the west bank of the canal.

The scale of the breach indicates Soviet connivance. The best estimates suggest that on August 7, the "box" consisted of sixteen operational missile complexes. Within a week, six new sites had been constructed nearer the canal. Within a month, forty-five new sites had been built, of which around thirty were already operational. And all were sited progressively closer to the canal. The range of the missiles deployed was such that Israeli aircraft flying over the *east* bank—defending the Bar-Lev Line against amphibious assault, for instance—were now at risk. It was a decisive military gain for Egypt.

Yet Nixon had anticipated that this might happen. He had ordered that the cease-fire be monitored by reconnaissance over-flights. There was a hitch. The first U-2 spy plane did not take off from the British air base at Akrotiri in Cyprus until August 9, two days after the cease-fire had come into supposed effect. (In a foretaste of a problem that was to loom in the Yom Kippur War, the governments of Greece, Spain, and Italy asked the United States not to launch Middle East spy flights from bases on their soil. Belatedly, the United States had to beg use of Akrotiri.) By August 9, however, the construction of the new sites was already so advanced that it was clear to Washington that there was no practical way—short of scrapping the cease-fire and allowing war to break out again—of persuading the Soviet Union to halt this.

It was never publicly revealed what an advantage this breach of the cease-fire conferred upon its Soviet and Egyptian architects. The truth was, in the closing stages of the technological war across the canal, improvements in electronics had already begun to tilt the balance away from Israel.

From June 1967 until August 1970, the comparative air losses were approximately 110 Egyptian aircraft downed for 16 Israeli. But in the closing phase of that period—the 6 weeks before the cease-fire—the Israeli losses were running about level with the

Egyptian at around half a dozen each. The cease-fire came before that lesson had really sunk home in Israel. But Nasser's blatant breach of the cease-fire to consolidate and advance this newly effective missile screen could not be ignored.

On September 8, 1970, barely ten days after the revived Jarring talks had opened, Israel pulled out of them "so long as the cease-fire standstill agreement was not observed in its entirety." Mrs. Meir deserves some credit for so mild a response. She was grappling with extreme dissension with her own Cabinet. One faction even wanted a preemptive strike against the missile "box." And it is an indication of the equally extreme pressure the United States exerted that, in November 1970, Israel was persuaded to return to the Jarring talks. Mrs. Meir said later that Israel had to do so "because otherwise our arms supplies would have been threatened." Even so, Israel's renewed presence at the talks was scarcely productive: under instructions to stone-wall, its representative could only repeat that Israel's negotiating position was "under discussion in the Israeli Cabinet."

Yet now the situation had changed—surely for the better. On September 28, 1970, President Nasser died. He had a heart attack while trying to patch up a cease-fire in the short but savage war that King Hussein of Jordan had launched upon the Palestinian guerrillas in Jordan. (Hussein's Bedouin regulars slaughtered the guerrillas; the "Black September" movement commemorates the killings.)

Nasser's successor was his long-time collaborator, Anwar el Sadat. And without Nasser's hold on the Egyptian people, without his ability to demand from them unending sacrifice in a seemingly hopeless cause, Sadat would surely explore conciliation. He did. It was just catastrophically bad luck that, at this crucial moment, two separate peace initiatives should now have collided.

It was Sadat's intervention that was unexpected. On February 4, 1971, he announced that he would extend the cease-fire; that he would accept partial Israeli withdrawal in Sinai as a first stage; and that in return he would reopen the canal. Inevitably, there were snags to the offer. The cease-fire was renewed for only thirty days, for instance. And Israeli right of passage through the canal was linked to a settlement of the Palestinian question. But as the first peace offer of the new Egyptian President, it was—however incomplete—a historic departure. Comparison with the "Three Noes" of Khartoum, which had defined the initial Arab position, showed that.

Israel denounced the plan as merely an attempt to deprive its forces of what their Sinai commander called "the most important line of defense," the Bar-Lev fortifications. Still, the United States might once again have been able to pressure Israel into at least the appearance of accommodation. But Sadat's offer crossed, fatally, with Jarring's last weary effort.

On February 8, 1971—just four days after Sadat's offer—Jarring wrote to him and to Mrs. Meir. From Egypt he requested a commitment to enter into a peace agreement with Israel, to include:

1. Termination of all claims or states of belligerency.
2. Respect for and acknowledgment of Israel's sovereignty, territorial integrity, and political independence.
3. Respect for and acknowledgment of Israel's right to live in peace within secure and recognized boundaries.
4. Responsibility to do all in its power to ensure that acts of belligerency or hostility do not originate from or are not committed from within Egypt against the population, citizens, or property of Israel.
5. Noninterference in Israel's domestic affairs.

From Israel, Jarring sought a commitment to withdraw its forces from Sinai to the pre-1967 lines. This was to depend on "satisfactory arrangements" for demilitarized zones; freedom of access by Israeli ships to the Gulf of Aqaba past Sharm el Sheikh; and freedom of navigation through the Suez Canal.

Sadat replied in a week, making the commitment Jarring wanted. Egypt also undertook, as part of a peace settlement, to ensure freedom of Israeli navigation through the Suez Canal; freedom of access to the Gulf of Aqaba, with a United Nations peace-keeping force at Sharm el Sheikh; and a demilitarized zone "astride the borders in equal distance." Provided Israel agreed, Egypt would also accept a UN force on the borders, in which the superpowers could participate.

Eleven days later, Israel's reply arrived. It was long and detailed, and accepted many of Jarring's proposals. But on the central commitment that Jarring sought, the reply was highly discouraging; it agreed to withdrawal "to the secure, recognized and agreed boundaries to be established in the peace agreement. . . . Israel will not withdraw to the pre-June 5, 1967 lines." The letter made no reference to the idea of a demilitarized zone.

This flat refusal to withdraw to pre-1967 lines was a late addition to Israel's draft reply, inserted to meet strong feelings in the Israeli legislature, the Knesset. It was unnecessary, since Sadat had indicated privately that he would consider boundary adjustments— minor in Sinai, possibly more radical on Golan and the Jordan West Bank. And Rogers, who had been shown the draft Israeli reply, had urged Mrs. Meir to take out that clause. But Mrs. Meir was by now irreversibly suspicious of Rogers. She even thought that the coincidence of timing revealed the Jarring letter as part of a Rogers-Sadat plot. Israel, she declared, "could not trust what Mr. Rogers offers us"—scarcely soothing the insult by adding, "even if he does so with the best of intentions."

On March 5, U Thant blamed Israel for the diplomatic deadlock, appealing to Mrs. Meir to commit herself to withdrawal at least to the pre-1967 Sinai borders. Israel did not reply. Two days later, on March 7, Sadat refused to extend his cease-fire any longer. A *de facto* cease-fire did continue. But it was the effective end of diplomatic efforts to reach a peace settlement. The initiative now passed to President Sadat. And he saw no choice but war.

3. Sadat Decides on War

Anwar el Sadat is by nature a somewhat repressed man, prone to swoops between euphoria and depression—also a reflective man, not given to the outbursts of the expansive Nasser. He has thus always been harder to fathom than his predecessor. But, after the Yom Kippur War, President Sadat did unburden himself with considerable frankness in a long conversation with one Western friend. And he filled in other details in an emotional speech to students at Alexandria University seven months after the war. Sadat's explanations of the reasons that drove him to war provide a remarkable glimpse behind the scenes of international diplomacy in those last three years before October 6, 1973.

"From the day I took office on President Nasser's death, I knew I would have to fight," he said. "Nasser had known we would have to fight. It was my inheritance. But captivity by the British teaches you patience." (From 1942 to 1945, the young Sadat, hotheaded and anti-British for nationalistic reasons, was kept under house arrest in Cairo, after the British had uncovered a ludicrously bungled German plot in which he was involved.)

Practicing patience, Sadat was willing to give diplomacy a chance. "I did have slight hopes of Secretary of State Rogers in 1970 and 1971. And he came shopping here. But all he did was to extract more and more concessions from us and not a single one from the Israelis." (There was an element of truth in this.) And Sadat began to realize why: "Rogers thought we would never fight. The Israelis thought they could not be surprised. The West thought we were poor soldiers without good generals."

Complacency was indeed a factor in Israel's inflexibility. Its military acknowledged the decisiveness of their first strike in 1967, yet refused to recognize that much of the Egyptian Army's subsequent mess would, to some degree, have overtaken any fighting group so swiftly deprived of its air cover. But Israeli inflexibility stemmed, too, from legitimate doubts that the Arabs, whatever they told the world, really wanted peace. Israel's essays into Arabic to prove this need not be taken too seriously. Israel claimed that it demanded full peace—which it said was *sulh* in Arabic— while Egypt would at best offer only *salaam*, which Israel said was merely live-and-let-live, falling short of the friendly relations of *sulh*. Philologically, this was nonsense: The two words are used virtually interchangeably in the Koran. But there was a political truth in the point. Yet could Israel really expect the memories of a generation to be wiped away merely by a signature on a treaty?

Almost every olive branch offered by the Egyptians, however, contained a reference to "the restoration of the legitimate rights of the Palestinian people." And they were the group with the most bitter memories of all. Twice in a quarter century, hundreds of thousands of Palestinians had been uprooted following Israeli military victories in 1948 and 1967. By 1973, there were more than two million Palestinians, most living away from what they considered their home; six hundred thousand were still living in refugee camps. As the years passed and groups turned in despair to guerrilla warfare or acts of terrorism—most notably the killing of Israeli athletes at the Munich Olympics in September 1972—Israel could point to the Arab leaders' public tolerance of these exploits.

This was a half truth. Leaders like Sadat were privately unhappy and did on occasion utter carefully worded public condemnations. And while each reference to the rights of the Palestinians might have been a source of anxiety to Israel, for Egypt it was a necessary acknowledgment that any settlement that could not be sold to the Palestinians would be fragile indeed.

But through 1971 the chances of any settlement receded. And while Sadat steadily lost his slight faith in diplomacy, it also became apparent that the pressures of "no peace, no war" were wrecking what little unity the Arabs possessed. In August 1971, Syria had severed relations with Jordan; six months later, Sadat followed suit after a speech by King Hussein in which he offered to replace his own Hashemite Kingdom of Jordan with a United Arab Kingdom with two equal regions. The Jordanian region would still have its capital in Amman, which would also be the federal capital; the Palestinians would have their own region on the West Bank of the Jordan, and a capital in the old city of Jerusalem.

Hussein's plan was, not surprisingly, rejected by both Israel and the Palestinians. For Israel, the plan meant giving up too much occupied territory (in particular, the old city of Jerusalem); for the Palestinians it meant gaining too little. But the Egyptians and Syrians were the most disturbed of all: The fact that Hussein had launched the plan at all meant that he was envisaging a separate peace treaty with Israel, even outside the framework of Resolution 242—or so they thought. Politically, Sadat had no choice but to sever relations.

It was internal dissent, however, that finally brought Sadat to view in specific terms the necessity for war. In response to this internal pressure, Sadat had to promise that 1971 would be "the year of decision." The dissent—and the reasons why he made that vow—provide a case-study in Soviet-Egyptian relations.

The fundamental fact is that the Soviet Union tried to undermine Sadat even before he was established, and when that failed the Soviets supported an attempted *coup d'état* that Sadat thwarted only at the last minute. Many of the details of what became known as the Ali Sabry Affair are still hidden—and most of the principals are now serving life sentences beyond the reach of inquiring newspapermen. But it seems that the crisis had its roots even before Nasser's death.

Ali Sabry was an air force officer who had risen to become Prime Minister of Egypt in 1964 and Vice-President a year later. He was dismissed in September 1969—as we have already related—after Nasser learned that he had been sounding out the Soviet attitude to a possible revolt against Nasser. When, three month later, Nasser was worried by the possibility of assassination at the hands of "foreign agents," it was thus a prudent precaution to declare a new heir apparent. In December 1969, Nasser appointed as new Vice-President one of his oldest military colleagues, Anwar el Sadat.

Sadat had been a member of Nasser's original Free Officers group which, through the late 1940s, had planned the overthrow of King Farouk. Since then he had held a variety of ministerial and political posts, in all of which he had shown himself a competent administrator. When Nasser then died in September 1970, however, Vice-President Sadat had had less than a year in which to establish himself as heir presumptive. And Ali Sabry—forgiven by Nasser and appointed to command Egypt's air defenses—was still a strong contender.

Nasser died at 6:15 P.M. on September 28, 1970. Soviet Premier Kosygin flew into Cairo next day. The Soviets' interest in Nasser's successor was understandable. They had a gigantic military and political investment in Egypt. Now their most powerful collaborator—himself no easy ally—had died politically intestate. It was inevitable that the Soviets should try to influence the succession. They failed. Six days after Nasser's death, the executive committee of the Arab Socialist Union—Egypt's sole political party—nominated Sadat as the new President. The rest—the "approval" of the National Assembly and the popular referendum—was a formality.

Sadat was not a choice to Soviet liking. He was a nationalist, and willing to collaborate with the Soviets—or with the Nazis, as he had during World War II—if that would serve Egypt's purpose. But he was a devout Muslim and that, fundamentally, meant that he was anti-Communist. Ali Sabry, on the other hand, was a Marxist-Leninist. And while he was as devout and pragmatic a nationalist as Sadat—as Minister for Presidential Affairs in 1957–62, for instance, Ali Sabry had been one of the main advocates of improved Egyptian relations with the West—the Soviets regarded him as the better long-term bet. And it was undeniable that since 1967 Ali Sabry had been one of the most committed supporters of an increased Soviet influence in Egypt.

The differences between Sadat and Sabry ranged over the whole spectrum of Egyptian and Arab options for the future. Very roughly, Sabry was a "hawk," while Sadat was at least prepared to attempt the role of "dove." Sabry maintained that diplomacy held no hope: Egypt's only solution was war, as soon as possible. And he was optimistic about Egypt's chances of holding a bridgehead across the canal. Moreover, since the only country able to help Egypt in this task was the Soviet Union, Sabry held, Egypt should avoid entanglement with the anti-Communist members of the Arab world, such as Libya.

Sadat, by contrast, was willing to give diplomacy a chance—if necessary by making considerable gestures to this end. He was less than optimistic about Egypt's present chances of a victory over the Israelis. And he held that, while Egypt's relations with the Soviet Union were indeed important, the rebuilding of Arab unity was as crucial.

It was a clash of opposites. And Sadat, newly installed as President, had to balance these factions. There is good evidence that while Sadat embarked upon his unexpected February 4 peace offer, he simultaneously appeased the "hawks" in his own government by preparing for war. Israeli military sources are convinced that Egypt was preparing to launch an attack of some magnitude across the canal in the last days of March 1971 and again in December. And Sadat himself has confirmed the December date. So 1971 nearly was, after all, "the year of decision."

Through the first three months of 1971—as the power struggle between the new President and his rival gathered momentum—Sadat gave ground. By January 25, the Egyptians had completed preparations for an amphibious crossing of the canal at various places. On February 3, they moved heavy reinforcements of missiles and artillery into the canal zone.

Then came Sadat's peace initiative: his February 4 peace proposals and, parallel with these, his acceptance of the cease-fire for another thirty days, until March 7. But the month drifted away. No progress was made. The United States was clearly not going to provide the decisive pressure upon Israel.

On March 3 to 7, Egypt evacuated civilians from the west bank of the canal; Cairo was subjected to a partial blackout. By March 11, the Israelis were in turn moving heavy reinforcements into Sinai. And the United Nations observers along the canal were sufficiently worried to resume regular bulletins on the military situation. On March 13, the Cairo daily *Al Ahram* was reporting that peace was unlikely to last for more than another two weeks. (The Soviet contingent in Egypt seems to have agreed. In early March, Soviet personnel were moved even farther back from the front line.)

The final phase of preparation for war began on March 16, when Sadat called the first of a series of six meetings with his military advisors—to review "combat potential," *Al Ahram* reported, and to prepare "a comprehensive plan for the next battle." On March 25, Sadat gave special war powers to Egypt's provincial governors.

Everything seemed set for a major Egyptian assault across the canal in a couple of days.

The crisis oozed away. Next day, March 26, Sadat proclaimed that his decision to fight was irrevocable—but added, rather more significantly: "Timing is our own concern. And we are preparing ourselves with *patience* [our italics] and determination for that day." In other words, the war was off. Why? Largely, it seems, for the simplest reason. After reviewing the state of Egypt's forces with his advisors, Sadat decided that they were in no state to confront the thoroughly alerted Israeli Army. Besides, Egypt would be fighting alone. How much help the United States would give to Israel was uncertain. And, however strongly the Soviets were covertly backing Ali Sabry, they were doing nothing to help Sadat's immediate entry into war.

To the Ali Sabry faction, however, Sadat's last-minute retreat from battle was evidently the final straw. At the next gathering of Egypt's top political forum, the Arab Socialist Union central committee meeting on April 25, it became clear that Sabry and four supporters—including Minister of War Mohammed Fawzi— now openly challenged the basic fact of Sadat's rule. On May 2, Sadat dismissed Sabry and placed him under house arrest.

The details of the coup which Sabry's henchmen, notably War Minister Fawzi, then tried to mount remain obscure. It was, in any event, thoroughly bungled. (In a bizarre interlude, Fawzi and two colleagues even consulted a medium on their best move. The medium claimed to be in contact with a long-dead sheik. Unfortunately, he was rather more closely in touch with the Egyptian security police. The séance chamber was bugged.) Fawzi got as far as loading up some of his tanks with ammunition, but that was all. Later that summer, the trials of ninety-one alleged plotters began in Cairo. Sadat commuted the inevitable death sentences to life imprisonment. The threat from Ali Sabry was over.

But Sadat's juggling act had to continue—only now on a grander scale. Throughout the Ali Sabry Affair, Sadat had tried to minimize the damage to Egypt's relations with the Soviet Union—still, realistically, the only potential supplier of the arms Sadat had now decided he needed. Simultaneously, Sadat was trying to cajole the United States into diplomatic action. Neither superpower was too impressed.

After the visit to Cairo in May 1971 of U. S. Secretary of State
Rogers, Sadat waited for the United States to pursue the new
Egyptian peace offer. Meanwhile, on May 25, Soviet President
Podgorny followed Rogers into Cairo. Two days later, Sadat signed
a fifteen-year friendship treaty with the Soviets. "I did it to reassure them after the Ali Sabry business," Sadat told his visitor
after the war.

The United States was scarcely reassured, of course. Sadat's
account of the next phase was fairly frank: "We waited. May and
June passed. On July 6, I received notification from the U. S.
Secretary of State that the United States would intervene to
achieve a peaceful solution in accordance with the initiative I
had submitted. They asked some questions, including a question
about the Egyptian-Soviet treaty . . . and I answered them. My
answer has always been that all our decisions express our free
will. . . ." (Nasser would have given a more pungent reply.
Similarly asked once whether he was not afraid that arms sales
would give the Soviets undue influence, he roared with laughter.
"But because I am their debtor, I am the stronger of the two
parties," he said. "Their concern is to be reimbursed. Mine is
to pursue relations with them on a basis of equality.")

"July passed without anything happening," Sadat went on.
"August and September passed. On October 11, 1971, I went to
the Soviet Union. I had a long session with the three Soviet leaders
[Party leader Leonid Brezhnev, Premier Kosygin, and President
Podgorny]. . . . We removed the clouds that existed in our
relations. We agreed in October on specific arms deals. And
the arms were to arrive before the end of 1971."

"The Soviet leaders asked about the 'year of decision,' why I
held to this and why I insisted that the situation be reactivated
militarily. Because there was no other way, I told them. I explained
the matter to them very clearly and frankly and in a friendly
manner. As I have said, we agreed on arms deals; and the arms
were to arrive before the end of 1971."

Sadat's account of that meeting appears to have been a trifle
tactful. The joint communiqué afterward certainly talked of measures "further to strengthen Egypt's military might." But at the
main banquet in Sadat's honor, President Podgorny pointedly
referred to the Soviet willingness to strengthen "the defense

capability of Egypt and other Arab countries." And although Sadat at that lunch, said that "force and only force" was "the only method of putting pressure on Israel," Podgorny in reply emphasized the Soviet wish for a peaceful solution.

Still, Sadat had gotten the arms he wanted. Or he thought he had. "We were supposed to be able to make a decision on the war on December 8 [1971]. . . . October passed and so did November, and then December came. But there was absolutely no information about the arrival of any shipments or anything. On December 8, the fighting between India and Pakistan began. As we all know, the Soviet Union had commitments toward India. We entered December, and then more than half of December had gone by. Nothing had arrived. But the understanding was that these shipments would arrive in October, November, and December so that before the end of 1971 we could make a decision and begin operations.

"I notified the Soviet Union. About the middle of December, I told them that there were only fifteen days left before the end of the year, and we did not yet even have the dates of the arrivals of shipments or vessels. We had no information about them and they had not appeared. But I had fixed the year of 1971 as the 'year of decision.'"

Finally, Sadat recalled: "I decided that the time had come for a total clarification of our relations with the Soviet Union." In mid-December—facing the humiliation of the collapse of his vaunted "year of decision"—Sadat told the Soviet ambassador in Cairo, Vladimir Vinogradov, that he wanted to go to Moscow at once. "I asked if I could visit them in order to avert this situation [the collapse of the battle plan] and so that we could solve it together."

The Soviets were not disposed to be helpful. After some days' delay, Vinogradov returned with the Soviet reply. "They fixed a date for my visit—not in January 1972 but in February 1972," Sadat said. "I almost rejected the offer. . . . As I understood it, their purpose in delaying the date was to let me calm down, cool off a little. This was because I had fixed 1971 as the year of decision, and they did not approve of it. Actually, they did not approve of any action other than political or diplomatic action."

Sadat had to accept the humiliation. As 1972 thus indecisively

dawned, Cairo was plunged into two days of student rioting—
the first in the capital since 1968. On January 25, Sadat tried to
reassure a gathering of students, professional men, and union
leaders—itself proof that the discontent was widespread. A decision to go to war against Israel had already been taken, he said:
"It is not mere words; it is a fact." As Sadat said afterward: "I
understood the discontent. After six years, our men on the canal
and our students wanted action." But actions must depend upon
Soviet arms. On February 2, 1972, Sadat arrived in Moscow to
sort out his problems with the Soviets.

The Soviet Union was in a poor bargaining position. Its
influence in the Middle East largely depended upon a presence in
Egypt. Besides, the cyclical nature of American politics now in-
truded. Fresh American presidential elections were coming in
1972. From mid-1971 Nixon once more set about wooing the
Jewish vote. There was nothing halfhearted about the courtship.
In 1971, the United States sold Israel six hundred million dollars'
worth of arms—more than seven times the military assistance the
Johnson administration had supplied. (The campaign paid off.
The Israeli ambassador in Washington, Yizhak Rabin—he had
been Chief of Staff in the Six-Day War—openly rooted for Nixon.
"We have to display gratitude to those who acted in support of
Israel . . ." he said. The Democrats protested to Jerusalem.)

Against that background, it was remarkable that the Soviets
were as tough as they were. For Sadat arrived in Moscow bearing
a shopping list of offensive weapons. He came away disappointed.
Communist party leader Brezhnev and Prime Minister Kosygin
would not supply them. Sadat was disgusted: "It was clear that the
stalemate—no peace, no war—suited the superpowers. There was
some agreement between them about the level of arms supplies."
The Soviet Union did try to appease Sadat with fresh supplies of
defensive weapons. But the communiqué after his visit pointedly
reiterated the Soviets' aim of a peaceful settlement within the
ambit of Resolution 242.

Apart from any reasons of global strategy, Brezhnev was
frankly skeptical of the Arabs' ability to use even the weapons
they had. He was still shocked by the 1967 debacle. "If each of
your tanks had fired just one shot, the pattern of that war would
have changed radically," he told the Arabs. "But your guns were

untouched." To Sadat, however, this Soviet bluntness was further evidence that the balance of Soviet policy was tilting toward détente. And, quite contrary to Soviet intentions, this merely hardened Sadat's conviction that a war *soon* was his only hope. Détente, after all, would merely erode further his ability to capitalize upon superpower rivalry to lever a settlement. And his next visit to Moscow confirmed his fears.

"This time the Russians had asked that I visit them," Sadat recalled. "They insisted on it because Nixon was going to visit them in May." So on April 27–29, 1972—after a strong speech criticizing the Soviet Union for not supplying the weapons he wanted—Sadat returned to see Brezhnev. "I went to Moscow," Sadat said, "and I told Mr. Brezhnev that we would have to fight one day. There was no alternative. He said he did not want a superpower confrontation."

The discussion followed lines by now well worn—as Sadat explained afterward. "The core of the discussion between us was —and I always said it—that the issue would not be activated or solved without military action. The Soviet Union's view was against military action. The discussions used to finish up with the view that, even in order to reach a peaceful solution, Israel had to be made to feel that we were in a position to talk about this peaceful solution from a position of strength, not weakness. That was the conclusion we used to end up with. And the Soviets then used to promise to supply us with arms, etc., etc."

And this time Sadat at least persuaded Brezhnev of his seriousness of purpose. The Soviet communiqué after the visit declared at last that the Arabs "have every reason to make use of other means [than diplomacy] for the return of the Arab lands seized by Israel"—a careful limiting of objective. But still the Soviet Union would not give Sadat the arms he wanted. He recalled: "The Russians prevaricated throughout the summer and autumn of 1972. They said they were awaiting the American presidential election in November. Don't forget that when I was in Russia in April, they didn't know whether Nixon would come back, though he did go to Moscow after that—following his trip to China."

By midsummer, Sadat knew he had to bring matters to a head: "The Russians felt they had a presence on our soil, even if they kept discreetly out of sight." It was a considerable presence: four thousand to five thousand advisors with the Egyptian forces; ten thousand to fifteen thousand other personnel, some manning the fifty SAM-2 and SAM-3 missile sites; two hundred pilots with ground crew for the MiG-21J and Sukhoi-11 fighters; and heavy Soviet contingents at four Egyptian ports and by now virtually in control of seven airfields. Effectively, the Soviet Union could veto any of Sadat's military plans. This caused enough trouble for Sadat with his own officers. Many were pro-western; others were simply fed up with what they saw as Soviet arrogance toward them.

Yet still the Soviets would not commit themselves. "We agreed at the April meeting," Sadat said, "that after the summit meeting between President Nixon and Secretary Brezhnev in May, the process of consolidating Egypt's capability would begin quickly. Because we agreed that there would be nothing new in the U.S. position in 1972, since it was an election year in the United States. We also agreed that after the election—that is, immediately after November—we had to be prepared. The Soviets agreed to this."

After the Nixon-Brezhnev meeting on May 29, 1972, Sadat waited for news from Moscow. "I waited for a notification [of what had been agreed]. And after 14 days [that is, on June 13] I received notification—including an analysis by the Soviet Union similar to what we had predicted at the April meeting. That is, that there was nothing new in the U.S. position because the U.S. position viewed Egypt and the Arabs as a motionless corpse and the U.S. only respect force. So if Egypt and the Arabs were a motionless corpse, why should the Americans act or change their position? The Soviet analysis was thus the same as our predictions before the April visit. . . . I replied and said: 'All right, now that your analysis is the same as the one we [the Egyptians] agreed upon, the questions—as agreed with you—are the following."

Around June 15, Sadat sent his seven-point questionnaire to Brezhnev, seeking to elicit just how far the Soviets really were prepared to provide him with arms and diplomatic backing to re-open hostilities against Israel. The covering note warned that Egypt's relations with the Soviet Union depended upon the answers. Brezhnev did not reply; Sadat sent a reminder. Finally, around July 8, Ambassador Vinogradov delivered Brezhnev's answer. It was, according to Sadat, a three-page letter: the first page rehearsing the importance of Soviet-Egyptian relations, and the other two pages an attack upon Mohammed Heikal of *Al Ahram*, whom Brezhnev blamed for the worsening in relations. None of Sadat's seven points was answered.

"It included absolutely no mention of what we had agreed in April," Sadat said afterward. "There was absolutely no mention of anything about the battle except in the last three lines of the answer. Before that, there was a statement about the Moscow summit meeting between the two giants. The statement included the phrase 'military relaxation.' Military relaxation, while Israel had complete superiority and we were short of several things. We were asked to embark upon military relaxation." Sadat was so angry that, in Ambassador Vinogradov's stunned presence, he there and then ordered the departure of all Soviet military advisors from Egypt within ten days.

At the Soviets' dazed request, Sadat's Prime Minister, Dr. Aziz Sidqi, went to Moscow on July 13 to spell out precisely why Sadat was taking this step. But Sidqi was under strict instructions. If Brezhnev proclaimed his willingness to help, he was to be asked to furnish proof in the shape of MiG-23 fighter-bombers, which the Soviet Union had been denying to Sadat for more than a year. The talks were a failure. The Soviets would not supply more arms. And although Egypt was willing to gloss over the rift with a joint declaration "in order to cover anything that the West might exploit," the Soviets refused that too. On July 15 Sidqi flew home, and on July 17 the Soviet exodus began.

Sadat put the most diplomatic face on things and, of course, revealed no details of what had happened. Instead, speaking on July 19 to the central committee of Egypt's Arab Socialist Union —the sole and governing party—Sadat put the message politely: "The Soviet Union is a big country which has its own international role and its own strategy. As for us, our territory is partly under occupation and, therefore, our target at both the Egyptian and the Arab levels is to remove the consequences of the aggression." But he then hinted at the problem Sidqi had tried, in vain, to resolve. Egypt had never sought to create a confrontation between the Soviet Union and the United States, and Egypt had never expected Soviet soldiers to fight Arab wars, he said.

But whatever weapons Egypt obtained from abroad, their use was a matter for decision by the Egyptian people "without obtaining permission from any quarter whatever its importance."

Privately, Sadat at the time said merely: "I felt we all needed an electric shock." His real purpose he explained after the war: "I expelled them to give myself completely freedom of maneuver." But the alacrity of the Soviets' departure—and their lack of protest—scarcely indicates unwillingness on their part. Perhaps Vietnam was indeed on their minds?

Sadat's action strengthened his position remarkably: All whispers of Army disaffection were immediately stifled. At the same time, it raised the Army's hopes that Sadat would do something equally decisive about Israel. In the short run, however, there was no alternative but to attempt once more to break the deadlock diplomatically. At a private meeting of the Peoples' Assembly on August 17, he stated: "What we need now is to move with the Soviet Union, the United States, Western Europe, nonaligned and Arab nations in preparation for a new initiative."

Sadat, reasonably, thought that the United States would seize the opening created by his expulsion of the Soviets. He was not so naïve as to expect a "reward." He merely assumed that the United States would now pressure Israel to accept withdrawal, if only so that Washington could then step into Moscow's shoes in Egypt. A diplomatic initiative, as Sadat saw it, made sense.

But Sadat could not afford another year of failure. He would probably fall; the Egyptian economy could not indefinitely bear the staggering military burden; it was even doubtful whether Egypt's social structure could long survive the strains of "no peace, no war." While exploring peace, Sadat simultaneously began to prepare for calculated, successful, war. In October 1972, he appointed as War Minister and Commander-in-Chief one of his oldest Army colleagues and supporters, General Ahmed Ismail. (One of Egypt's most dashing and aggressive combat officers, Lieutenant General Saad el Shazli, was already Chief of Staff. The conflicting careers and personalities of these two generals were to affect the coming war at a crucial moment.)

But, inexorably, even the contemplation of war drove Sadat to a fresh acknowledgment of the need for weapons—which meant the Soviet Union. Once more, Sadat set about patching up relations with Moscow. Syrian President Hafez Asad had already acted as intermediary in the first stage of this rapprochement, and then, in mid-October, Egypt's Prime Minister Sidqi went to Moscow for two days. "It was clearly apparent that relations had begun to move again," Sadat said afterward. "However, that was on the surface only. In fact and in essence, relations did not move at all."

Ironically, the Soviets' continuing caution was the final catalyst of war, as Sadat subsequently explained: "After the November election, Mr. Nixon was returned. And I had a letter from Mr. Brezhnev saying that they wished to support the policy of détente and they advised me to accept the situation. They said they could not increase their normal arms supplies." On November 14, 1972, Sadat spoke to closed meetings of the Socialist Union central committee. "We had a meeting of our higher council," Sadat said, "and we rejected this. We started planning the October 6 offensive from that moment." For the final eleven months before war, the story thus has two simultaneous and parallel strands: Sadat's last, not very hopeful, diplomatic initiative; and General Ismail's slow, methodical, and brilliant planning for war.

The preparations for war began well. In February 1973, Sadat sent two final emissaries to Moscow. The first visit was by his national security advisor, Hafez Ismail—to stretch a likeness somewhat, Cairo's Henry Kissinger. At the end of the month, Sadat's new War Minister General Ismail—no relation to his namesake—went in turn. The Soviets capitulated. They agreed to provide the offensive weapons that Sadat demanded—but very unhappily.

"The two of them concluded a deal in Moscow," Sadat explained later. "After February 1973 our relations began to be, or to become, normal. Some of the arms concluded in the deal began reaching us after General Ismail's return in February. . . . We were happy that our relations should return to normal. But the Soviet Union persisted in the view that a military battle must be ruled out, and that the question must await a peaceful solution."

Yet, at the same time, the Soviets were even "allowed" by Sadat to teach the Egyptians how to use these new weapons. "Some [Soviets] did return with the task of teaching us how to use the new missiles," Sadat said. "We carried out this training well behind Suez." (Most of it was actually done at a base just south of Mersa Matruh, on the Mediterranean edge of the Western Desert.)

Sadat had won. To preserve its bridgehead in the Middle East, the Soviet Union had reluctantly bowed to its client state. It is unlikely that it occurred to the Soviet leadership that the most apposite description of their situation was that proverb of Chairman Mao Tse-tung to the effect that the tricky part in riding a tiger comes when you try to dismount. Unable to accomplish that feat, the Soviet Union thus became an accomplice as, irrevocably, the focus of Sadat's policy turned toward the cautious and ingenious planning of his Minister of War.

According to a highly detailed account he gave much later to *Al Ahram*, General Ahmed Ismail swiftly decided that merely to repeat the 1969–70 War of Attrition would be disastrous. "Any attempt on our part to do so would be met with a more violent reaction on Israel's part . . . greater than the political and military importance of any action we took," he said. He concluded: "Our strike, therefore, should be the strongest we could deal." But what sort of strike? Here, Ismail agreed with the long-held views of his Chief of Staff: The way to beat the Israelis was not to mimic their swift-strike *Blitzkrieg* tactics, but to chop them up in what Shazli called a "meat grinder" war.

The new year brought a further military option. On January 21, 1973, after several weeks of negotiation, Ismail was made Commander-in-Chief of the armies of the so-called Federation of Arab Republics. Since two members of this federation, Egypt and Syria, had somewhat ambivalent relations with the third, Libya, the post was seemingly honorific. But Ismail was more hopeful. "My second idea," he told *Al Ahram*, "was now that our strike should be dealt jointly from two fronts." Ismail's defense headquarters are a small compound of modest offices surrounded by a ten-foot wall on July 23 Street, in the Cairo suburb of Abbasiya. In the last days of January, the forty-strong Egyptian planning staff housed in these offices began to prepare for the new war. The irony no doubt occurred to them that the compound was only a few hundred yards from the new Nasser mosque, the tomb of the last man to take on Israel.

Sadat's final and parallel diplomatic initiative now reached its peak, in February 1973. The job was entrusted to Hafez Ismail, Sadat's national security advisor. Ismail set off on a tour that included Moscow, London, Washington, the United Nations, and Bonn. In addition, Egypt's Foreign Minister, Mohammed Zayyat, went to New Delhi and Peking. The only stops that mattered were Ismail's in Moscow and Washington—Moscow to patch up Egyptian relations; Washington for a final effort to persuade the United States to lean on Israel. The Moscow trip was, as related, a success. The Washington visit was not.

On February 23, Ismail met the re-elected President Nixon in the Oval Room of the White House. And Nixon was not discouraging. He spoke of the United States' wish to get negotiations going; later in the day, Rogers echoed his response. Their remarks were somewhat pointed: On January 18, Egypt had rejected Rogers' advance warning of a new U.S. initiative, to be based once again upon "negotiations of a Suez Canal agreement." Cairo had dismissed this as allowing Israel "to perpetuate her occupation of Sinai." Still, Ismail described his talks as "warm, objective and fruitful." Rogers next day spoke of a "new warmth" in relations with Egypt.

But Nixon, second term, was not as free from the influence of the Jewish lobby as he had been in 1968. This time, the best estimate was that he had gotten at least 35 and perhaps even 40 per cent of the Jewish vote. Careful handling could consolidate that into a permanent Republican bloc—another element in the new conservative coalition it was Nixon's dream to forge. On February 25, Assistant Secretary of State Sisco emphasized in an interview that the United States had no intention of using its position as Israel's armorer to put pressure on Mrs. Meir.

A few days later, on March 1, Mrs. Meir arrived at the White House. Afterward, she outlined Israel's policy. "If President Sadat is prepared to meet with us on any level, even indirectly, I could not welcome it more," she said. The helpfulness of this was offset somewhat by her caveat that the Golan Heights and Sharm el Sheikh were "nonnegotiable." While Sadat pondered Mrs. Meir's position, the news leaked a fortnight later that the Nixon administration was preparing to supply Israel with another forty-eight Phantoms and thirty-six Skyhawks. It seemingly confirmed what Sadat had expected. Nixon—re-elected, confident of Brezhnev's need for détente, anxious to retain his domestic gains for the Republican party—was not going to lean on Israel.

At the end of March, Sadat gave an interview to Arnaud de Borchgrave of *Newsweek*. Sadat repeated that negotiations had now finally failed, and that war was necessary. After contacts with the world's major powers, there was only one conclusion: "If we don't take our case in our own hands, there will be no movement. . . . There is no sense turning the clock back. Everything I've done leads to pressures for more concessions. I was even told by Rogers that my initiative for a final peace agreement with Israel was very courageous and had transformed the situation. Every door I have opened has been slammed in my face—with American blessings."

"I can only conclude, from what you say," said De Borchgrave, "that you believe a resumption of hostilities is the only way out?"

"You are quite right. Everything in this country is now being mobilized in earnest for the resumption of the battle—which is now inevitable."

Sadat was determined to convince the West that, this time, he was not bluffing. He had "run out of ideas" for peace, he emphasized—and, if there was not to be peace, "this will be the nightmare to end all nightmares—and everybody will be losers." He complained to De Borchgrave: "Everyone has fallen asleep over the Mideast crisis. But they will soon wake up"; and Sadat made it clear that Egypt expected to have the hardware with which to fight, because the Soviets were now "providing us with everything that's possible to supply."

For the first time Sadat was prophesying war in earnest. "The decision on the war was made in April 1973," Sadat said afterward. The irony was that, at the time, virtually nobody believed him.

4. The Secret Preparations

When the Egyptian request reached the firm of Magirus Deutz in May 1972, it caused little surprise. Magirus Deutz Fire Protection Techniques Ltd., of Ulm in Bavaria, is one of the three big West German manufacturers of fire-fighting pumps. The Egyptians did not specify why they wanted to test two of Magirus' T.S.T. 40/7 pumps—powerful, turbine-driven machines, but handily portable. The most likely explanation, of course, was that Egypt was thinking of re-equipping its fire services.

In the construction of the Aswan Dam, though, the Egyptians had successfully used high-pressure water jets to strip away soil. Perhaps more work was needed on the dam? The T.S.T. 40/7, capable of pumping 1,000 U.S. gallons of water a minute, would rip away most soils with ease.

The two pumps were sent to Egypt for approval. And the Egyptians must have been pleased, because five months later, in October 1972, Magirus Deutz received an order from them for no fewer than 100 fire pumps of the T.S.T. 40/7 type. In May 1973, after lengthy haggling over price, the deal was finalized. The pumps, said the Egyptians, were needed as "fire brigade equipment." And they were needed with some urgency.

Why the re-equipping of Egypt's fire brigades should suddenly have assumed priority was unclear. And Magirus Deutz executives would have been puzzled had they learned that their consignments through that summer were unpacked not by Egyptian firemen but by soldiers of the Egyptian Army engineers corps.

The Egyptians did indeed have earth moving in mind—but not on the Aswan Dam. Work on the dam had been completed at the end of June 1970. Magirus Deutz was not to know that it had just supplied the Egyptian Army with the secret weapon which would enable it to cross the Suez Canal. But then, Israel did not suspect anything until it was too late either.

Israel's bloody failure to forecast the Yom Kippur War had four strategic causes, all but one of these deriving from failings in intelligence. Israeli intelligence is divided into five main branches. The oldest agency is the Mossad, the Secret Intelligence Service—as Israelis, following British usage, sometimes call it. Alongside this are military intelligence; the internal security and counter-espionage service, the Shabak; the Foreign Ministry research division; and a mysterious agency responsible for Jews in "countries of persecution." But in early 1969, another group was set up with the sole task of combating the Palestinian guerrillas—in particular, their network and operations outside the Middle East. The members of this group were drawn from the other agencies and the armed forces. But manpower was scarce. To staff it, Israel also withdrew, principally from Egypt, a considerable number of its most able intelligence personnel; after that, the quality of Israeli information from Cairo perceptibly declined. That was the first failure.

The second derived from the peculiarly unresolved and unhappy status of the Foreign Ministry within the Israeli Government. Nominally, it was the job of the Foreign Ministry research division to analyze Arab political thinking. But in the formation of foreign policy, Mrs. Meir virtually ignored the Foreign Ministry: Policy was in fact made by Mrs. Meir herself and a small group of her closest ministers. This downgrading of the ministry was reflected within the intelligence framework. The analyses of Arab intentions that were heeded came not from the experts of the Foreign Ministry research division, but from military intelligence. Yet this, as we shall see, was a failure of which Israel had already been warned.

A British diplomat precisely reversed the result of that bureaucratic confusion when he said afterward that the run-up to war was "a classic case of intelligence understanding the capabilities of an enemy but not his intentions." All intelligence analyses of Arab *intentions* were in fact based upon utterly mistaken assessment of their capabilities. That was the third failure; and it was the specific fault of Israeli military intelligence. Israel was convinced that its military superiority over the Arabs was so total—and so acknowledged by the Arabs themselves—

that Arab political intentions would prudently reflect that fact. Yet Israeli military intelligence knew the capabilities of the new Soviet weapons; had a good idea of the enormous quantities supplied; and even knew the lines on which Ismail was thinking. But their assessment never wavered: The Arabs could be crushed as swiftly as in 1967. The thinking of military intelligence on this point was so rigid that, within the intelligence services, it even had a name: "The Concept."

This deeper blindness again stemmed partly from the Israeli preoccupation—one senior Israeli intelligence officer called it an "obsession"—with the Palestinians. The Israelis were temperamentally unable to grasp that the Arabs might wage terrorism and conventional war. Israel's Defense Minister, Moshe Dayan, and successive chiefs of staff all reiterated their contemptuous conviction that the Arabs had been reduced to random terrorism precisely because they dared not face Israel in battle— and even the terrorists' cross-border raids had been wiped out. (And, militarily, this view was of course reinforced by the Israeli failure to appreciate what a savage blow to Arab fighting capacity in 1967 Israel's first strike had been.)

It was even the Palestinians who were responsible for the final and most ironic cause of Israel's failure. The Israeli Chief of Staff *did* predict war in 1973—but thought it was about to break out in May, as a result of Palestinian actions.

Distracted by the Palestinian bogey, Israel thus ignored through the early months of 1973 the accelerating pace of Arab preparations. For Sadat was now constructing the political framework for war. In March, he began to seek a common political strategy with Syria. Syria still challenged even the existence of a Jewish state: The most basic political decision that Egypt and Syria had to thrash out was thus what the war was to be about— the existence of Israel, or merely the recovery of the occupied lands? And since Jordan had, like Egypt and Syria, lost territory in 1967, it would be necessary to bring King Hussein back into the Arab fold. This was tricky: Neither Egypt nor Syria now had diplomatic relations with Amman.

But while the political talks began, the military consultations were farther advanced. On April 21–22, the Arab chiefs of staff met in Cairo to examine Israel's military situation. Elsewhere in Cairo, Egypt's War Minister, General Ismail, had already completed the same exercise. He later formulated his conclusions: "My appraisal was that [Israel] possessed four basic advantages: its air superiority; its technological skill; its minute and efficient training; and its reliance upon quick aid from the United States, which would ensure . . . a continuous flow of supplies. This enemy also had his basic disadvantages. His lines of communication were long and extended to several fronts, which made them difficult to defend. His manpower resources do not permit heavy losses of life. His economic resources prevent him from accepting a long war. He is, moreover, an enemy who suffers the evils of wanton conceit."

By April, Egyptian assessment of Israeli strategy—and how to counter it—was in fact a good deal more detailed than that. With the help of senior Egyptian officers, it is now possible to reconstruct in some detail the planning of the Yom Kippur War.

According to the Egyptian Chief of Staff, Shazli, no more than fourteen people ever knew the full plan as it evolved: seven members of the Egyptian high command; six of the Syrian; plus the Egyptian officer, Major General Bahi eddin Mohammed Nofal, seconded to run a "Federal Operational General Staff," set up at the end of January to coordinate Egyptian and Syrian planning. The others were, in each country, the Minister for War, the Chief of Staff, and the Chiefs of Operations, Intelligence, the Air Force, Air Defense (in Syria the latter pair were under the same command), and the Navy.

The plan grew from studies begun in late January in the compound of the Cairo defense headquarters—six studies in all: into Israeli strategic theory; into the temperament and thinking of the Israeli general staff; the collection of intelligence on Israeli forces and, particularly, the Bar-Lev Line; the reorganization of Egyptian forces to cope with the lessons of those studies; the choices for the date of attack; and the problem of ensuring surprise.

Of these, the fundamental study was of course the examination of Israeli strategy. The Egyptian planners concluded that it fell into three elements, each of which could be neutralized. Israeli military doctrine rested, first, upon a reliance upon "secure borders." On the Sinai front, this meant a daunting natural obstacle almost impossible to cross in force, the Suez Canal—defended in turn by the massive fortifications of the Bar-Lev Line, which at worst could be held by a minimum number of troops for long enough to enable Israeli reserves to be mobilized and rushed to the front.

But Israel, secondly, was determined never to allow the worst to happen. Israeli doctrine was that of the preemptive strike, using the fearsome long-range strike capacity of its Air Force. And to know when to strike, Israel relied upon its excellent intelligence services—with intensive assistance from the intelligence communities of the United States and elsewhere. Finally, even if Arab forces did cross into Sinai, Israel was confident that the hammer blows of its massed armor formations could swiftly destroy them.

Each of these tenets, however, could be overthrown by cunning and careful planning. If the Suez Canal could be crossed quickly —and that mysterious order for German pumps shows that the Egyptian engineers corps had been refining that part of the operation for almost a year—then the Bar-Lev defenses could be overwhelmed by sheer weight of numbers. A preemptive strike by the Israeli Air Force could be neutralized by surprise; by deployment of the latest Soviet missiles to inflict devastating losses upon the Israeli pilots; and by mounting an attack *along the length of the canal* to dilute Israeli air power against any single troop concentration or bridgehead.

As for Israel's belief in the destructive power of its tank crews, the Egyptians thought they knew how to cope with those too. The first necessity was to destroy as much of Israel's communications system in Sinai as possible with initial air strikes. The next phase depended upon turning every unit of infantry in the first waves across the canal into tank-destroyers, by equipping them with the latest Soviet antitank weapons. And after those first desperate hours, when the bridgeheads were at last established, then Egypt could impose its own pattern of battle upon Israel—a pattern that would neutralize the mobility and firepower of the Israeli tanks.

Slowly, through the early spring, the elements of this plan were pulled together. On March 10, War Minister Ismail—who seems to have seen the air strike against Israeli communications as his personal baby—had finished the study of that. On March 21, just under two months after planning had begun, Ismail called the first all-day conference of the full planning team. They looked at progress toward coordination with Syria; discussed likely Israeli reactions to an attack of the sort they were planning; and settled the first outlines of a complex military and political deception strategy by which Egypt might hope to achieve surprise.

It was at this meeting that the single most powerful factor working toward Egyptian surprise was identified: the simple, stark Israeli conviction that the Arabs could never achieve sufficient unity to attack on two fronts. And the first phase of the deception strategy, hinging upon the exploitation of that conviction, seems to have gone into operation almost at once. Because, according to high Egyptian officers, the outline of military cooperation between Egypt and Syria was agreed at a secret meeting of the Federal Operational General Staff on April 1. But, three weeks later, after that publicly announced chiefs of staff meeting in Cairo on April 21–22, Egyptian Chief of Staff Shazli was careful to announce gloomily that: "The presence of some political and military problems is still obstructing joint action."

It was ironic, though, that the next major secret meeting should have been held on May 2. That day, the Egypt and Syrian high commands met in force to discuss the possible dates and times of the assault; then, in the evening, to agree on the general plan of the combined air strike, including the target list. It was ironic because this leisurely planning was now interrupted by another, unplanned war. On May 2, savage fighting broke out between the Lebanese Army and Palestinian guerrillas.

An Israeli action sparked it. On April 10, in Beirut, Israeli commandos in civilian clothing assassinated three noted Palestinian leaders, as well as two women bystanders. The Lebanese Government promptly fell; and on May 2—basically because of bad feeling over the Army's inaction during the raid—a miniature civil war broke out in Lebanon. It lasted nine days. And Israeli Chief of Staff thought it was going to spread beyond Lebanon. Jittery over Arab speeches prophesying war, he was afraid that Syria was about to intervene on the guerrillas' behalf in Lebanon. And that, Balkan fashion, could have sucked into confrontation the other Arab states around Israel—a confrontation that would inevitably spill over into Israel itself. The Syrians certainly prepared. But the Israeli forces were put on alert—the May 7 military parade through Jerusalem to mark Israel's twenty-fifth anniversary was a good cover—and Israeli armor maneuvered conspicuously on the Golan Heights.

It was a false alarm. But it illuminates the problems that just four months later were to baffle the Israelis—because, according to the Israeli Chief of Staff, Lieutenant General David Elazar, that May alert was based upon far more convincing indications of Arab war preparations than were to be detected later in the summer. And the alert cost Israel ten million dollars that it could ill afford; that was to be a factor in Israel's reluctance to damage its economy by mobilizing the civilian reserves during the next wave of danger signals.

But the alert had another adverse consequence for Israel. The May crisis brought Chief of Staff Elazar into conflict with the analysts of Israeli military intelligence. Elazar prophesied war; the analysts disagreed. Elazar was proved wrong: The analysts were vindicated. The memory of that failure was to make the Chief of Staff much more cautious when the next crisis came.

Yet the Israeli Government was aware of the underlying, long term, dangers. Defense Minister Dayan was so impressed by Elazar's analysis of Sadat's likely strategy—even though the Chief of Staff had been proved wrong in this instance—that Dayan sent a firm directive to the Israeli General Staff in the wake of the crisis. "I speak now as a representative of the Cabinet and also on the basis of information," he wrote on May 21. "We, the Cabinet, say to the General Staff: Gentlemen, please prepare for war—those who are threatening to launch a war being Egypt and Syria." Dayan even forecast the date: "A renewal of war should be taken into account in the second half of this summer." Israel, seemingly, was alerted.

For Israel's ultimate guarantor, the United States, May was also a critical month in the run-up to war. The U.S. intelligence community comprises several independent, overlapping, and frequently warring agencies, of which the CIA is merely the best publicized. The smallest of these agencies is the State Department's own Intelligence and Research Bureau (INR). With access to the work of other agencies but without agents of its own, INR's function is analysis. And its track record is pretty good: It was a consistent and frequently lonely voice of pes-

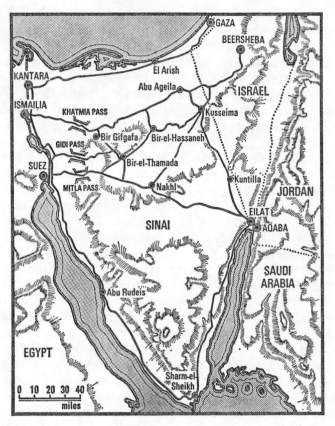

Map 3 The mountains that control Sinai strategy
The keys to Sinai are the three passes: Khatmia, Gidi, and Mitla. Southern Sinai
is impassable mountains. The Mediterranean strip is largely soft sand seas, which
so hem in the coast road through El Arish that tanks cannot maneuver in strength.
So an assault has to capture the passes through the Central Ridge, which control
the limited road network eastward to Israel's border. Since Israel captured Sinai
in the Six-Day War of 1967, its defensive strategy has been based on this, along
with the delaying role of the Bar-Lev Line of fortifications along the Suez Canal.

simism over Vietnam, for instance. Surveying the May crisis—
and the determined pattern of Sadat's actions—the bureau's
analysts produced a paper giving their long-range assessment of
the Middle East.

The paper was, according to one insider, "a rather sophisticated
analysis." It examined in somber terms the possibility of an

Egyptian-Syrian attack upon Israel. Its conclusion was that in the next six months, the chances were just less than even that there would be a war—"a 45 per cent chance," is how one Washingtonian recalled it. The second point that the paper made was that in the event of war, there could well be disruption of supplies—not because of a political combination of Arab states, which the analysts thought "unlikely"—but as a result of the inevitable anti-Americanism that a war would spark in the oil-producing countries.

That paper alone should have rung alarm bells all over Washington: A 45 per cent chance of war is, in intelligence forecasting, a very serious situation indeed. But worse was to come. Sometime in the latter half of May, one of the U.S. agencies picked up further evidence of Sadat's military planning. (Was it the same "information" that Dayan simultaneously mentioned?) It tipped the balance. In the last days of May, the INR director wrote a signed paper for Secretary of State Rogers saying that the odds had shifted—now, it was a better-than-even bet that there would be war in the Middle East by autumn. His precise phrase, as one analyst recalls it, was: "Contrary to previous general views, I think the chances are better than even." But there was a crucial caveat: This gloomy conclusion applied only *if* the Arabs could not make political progress meanwhile through the United Nations or the efforts of the superpowers. The analyst did not realize the degree to which Sadat has already lost faith in diplomacy.

And the CIA agreed with this reading though its dating was vaguer. Through the summer, both agencies repeated to the United States Government a generalized warning: The chances were that war in the Middle East was coming "sometime soon" unless there was political movement toward a settlement.

One factor behind these assessments seems to have been the sheer weight of weaponry that the Arabs—in particular Syria—were now getting from the Soviet Union. For these had an importance apart from their effectiveness as hardware: Possession of them would also alter the Arab's assessment of the feasibility of war as a policy option. The fresh shipments of the Soviets' latest T-62 tanks to Egypt and Syria need not have worried Israel. Trials of the two stolen T-62s had convinced Israel of their own

Centurions' superiority. If the odds were high, that was for Israel a traditional disparity. More worrying was the air defense system that Syria too was now getting. On May 3, 1973, President Hafez Asad of Syria made a twenty-four-hour trip to Moscow. He returned with a Soviet promise of a complete air defense system of SAM missiles plus another forty MiG-21 fighters. To supervise the arrangements for the SAMs, Asad returned from Moscow with the Soviet Air Force commander, Marshal Kotakhov. And for Syria's swelling tank forces, Asad got the help of the Chief of the Czechoslovak General Staff, Karel Rusov—intriguingly, an an expert in the *defensive* use of armor. In all, according to U.S. estimates, the Soviet Union supplied Syria through the first half of 1973 with $185 million worth of arms—$35 million more than the shipments through the whole of 1972. "These damned Syrians," grumbled the Soviet ambassador in Damascus, Nuritdin Mykhitdinov. "They will take anything except advice."

Virtually nobody in the top echelons of Washington listened to the intelligence warnings. Watergate had gripped the nation. There was no bureaucratic access to the White House whatever —"It was just closed off," one intelligence man said despairingly: Everyone had "hunkered down." And U.S. foreign policy was now rudderless as Secretary of State Rogers drifted through the dying days of his tenure of office—finally losing the job at the end of August. Only one man of any seniority in Washington appears to have taken the warnings seriously: the Deputy Secretary of State, Kenneth Rush. By himself, he could do nothing.

While Washington lay paralyzed, Sadat pressed ahead with his political negotiations to find a common strategy with the rearmed Syria. The problem was that, militarily, the joint planning had gotten a long way—though behind the so-called Federal Operational General Staff, most of the work was actually being done by the Egyptian planners under the Chief of Operations, Lieutenant General Abdel Ghani el Gamasy. But some political problems remained—still, principally, the need to persuade President Asad that a war of limited objectives was worthwhile at all. Through the late spring and early summer, the secret and public meetings between Egypt and Syria interwove:

May 9: Egyptian War Minister Ismail visits Damascus briefly on his way back from Iraq. (What support Egypt could expect from "second line" states like Iraq had preoccupied Ismail since early January, though he never told them the secret of the plan.)

May 19: Sadat visits Damascus for seven hours.

May 22: At a secret meeting of the Federal Operational General Staff, Ismail ran through the strategy of the entire war, as now planned. By this point, too, the planners were in a position to catalog the moves necessary on each front and the timing of these.

June 6: But problems still remained. A Syrian military delegation, led by Defense Minister Lieutenant General Mustafa Tlas, now arrived in Cairo. According to Egyptian sources, Ismail had to spend the whole of the next morning urging upon the Syrians the necessity of cooperating with Egypt—though whether this was to allay their fears that they were being asked to do too much, or whether they echoed President Asad's more fundamentalist doubts about the limited objectives, is unclear. Ismail must have succeeded, though, because later that day, June 7, Major General Nofal—heading up the Federal Operational General Staff—was apparently able to finalize the pattern of coordinated mobilization and preparation on both fronts.

June 12: Sadat flies to Damascus for final talks with Asad.

It was at this last meeting that Sadat finally persuaded Asad of the fact that, even with its Soviet equipment, Syria—its population only six million—could not hope to fight Israel except together with Egypt. Asad thus had no choice but to accept Sadat's objective—and limit Syria's war aims.

At last the Cairo planning staff could set a date for war. General Ismail later described, with no false modesty, the work his men did on timing the attack: "It was a great and scientific piece of work of the first order. When our documents are all laid out for historicial study, this work will certainly earn its full share of appreciation and will enter the scientific history of wars as a model of minute precision and genuine research."

Ismail has explained the reasoning behind the date: "There was the general consideration that the situation had to be activated when Arab and world support for us was at its highest. More particularly, we needed: first, a moonlit night with the moon rising at the right time; second, a night when the water current in the canal would be suitable for crossing operations; third, a night on which our actions would be far from the enemy's expectations; and fourth, a night on which the enemy himself would be unprepared. These particular considerations suggested October 6. On that day, astronomical calculations gave us the best times for moonrise and moonset. Our scientists examined the records of the old Suez Canal Company to assess the speed of the water currents, and that day was found most suitable. In addition, the Israelis would not expect any action from our side during the month of Ramadan. And for their part, they would be preoccupied by a number of events, including their forthcoming General Election."

In fact, the planning decision was even more complex than Ismail implies. The study of possible timings had been in train since January. There is dispute about its progress, though. Sadat has since said that the date for war was chosen in April; but this seems to be true only in the sense that a selection of dates, including that finally chosen, was compiled then. According to Chief of Staff Shazli, only in the middle of 1973 was the work done to refine this list.

The planners' skill lay in juggling the separate requirements which Ismail had sketched in outline. The first and trickiest proposition was the canal itself. Its current is always strong, but at certain times of year it can rip through the southern end of the canal at almost a hundred yards a minute—adding immensely to the problems of bridging the flow rapidly. On top of that, at certain phases of the moon the water level between high and low tide in the canal can rise and fall as much as six feet at the southern end. (And the tide is a six-hour cycle.) To keep bridges and landing stages for ferries operational, the planners would have to find times of least tidal variation.

Ismail then imposed the requirement of a long night, so that the Egyptian buildup on the east bank might have cover of darkness. But he also wanted a night when the moon shone through the first half and then set. The last bridges might have to be laid by moonlight, but the tanks could find their way across by starlight.

From the earliest studies, it was clear that this requirement meant an autumn attack. Only by September or October would there be ten or twelve hours of darkness. And the need to have moonlight—but not a full moon, because that would swell the ebb and flow of the tide—cut the possible dates in any one month to four or five days.

Further limitations were imposed by the Golan front. By November or December, there was a risk of snow on the Syrian plain, which would bog massed armored formations in a sea of mud.

All of which did not leave much choice. Even so, according to Egyptian military sources, the meeting to make that choice was one of the longest—and, necessarily, the most important—in the whole planning of the enterprise.

It was held at a military base in Alexandria in the first days of August. To it came all fourteen commanders who, according to Shazli, were the only group privy to the full plan. The specific purpose of the meeting was to fix the date of attack. And it was agreed that only the days pinpointed in September and October would work—and that the four days in October, two in the first half, two in the second, were the better choices. Beyond that, Ismail told the meeting, the selection must be a political decision.

Nominally, it was. But at a meeting a couple of days later of the Federal Operational General Staff, those four possible October dates were whittled down to one: October 6. And there was not really the slightest doubt that—if the war was on at all—Sadat and Asad would agree to it.

For October 6 also had a more atavistic appeal for the Arabs. In 1973, it would be the tenth day of Ramadan. On that day in the year 624, the Prophet Mohammed began preparations for the Battle of Badr, the first victory in the long campaign that culminated in 630 in his triumphant entry into Mecca—and the start of the spreading of Islam. It was a portent not to be missed. The military assault was code-named "Operation BADR." And in another code-word chosen by Ismail after Sadat's predictable approval, October 6 became "Y-DAY." (Y stands for *Yom*, meaning "day" in both Arabic and Hebrew.)

It was Ismail's first mistake—for October 6 that year would also be Yom Kippur in Israel, the Day of Atonement, the holiest of all Jewish festivals. Certainly, nobody in Israel thinks of war that day. But, more significantly, Yom Kippur is the one day of the year when the Israeli military know with 99 per cent certainty where every reservist in the country will be: at home or in the synagogue. And military traffic can speed along roads utterly deserted of civilian vehicles. More cunning calculation by Ismail might have suggested that an attack ten days earlier—over the Jewish New Year on September 27—would cause far greater chaos inside Israel. Over that holiday, everyone is out on picnics, visiting friends or relatives, clogging the roads with traffic, dispersed beyond recall. Since the most time-consuming phase of any mobilization is to locate and notify those being mobilized, Ismail —by planning to attack on Yom Kippur—was handing Israel a bonus of twelve hours or more in its potential response time. As he explained, behind his choice lay good technical reasons of moon and tide. But it was to provide a crucial margin for Israel.

5. Calculations of a Born Gambler

While military planning was that far advanced, however, Sadat had still to succeed in the other aim of his strategy: the re-activation of the threat to Israel across its eastern frontier, the river Jordan. The relationship forged to this end between Sadat and King Hussein of Jordan—the cementing of the uneasy alliance; the interplay of conflicting motives; the tantalizing combination of circumspection and frankness on either side—reveals a good deal of the cunning with which Sadat handled the rest of the Arab world through this critical period of preparation for war. And, throughout, the satisfactory part of the affair, from Sadat's point of view, was that the initiative came from Hussein.

To understand the chain of events that was to bring Hussein at last into the Yom Kippur War, it is necessary to grasp the dilemma that confronted him. With the final bloody onslaught through five days of July 1971 on the Palestinians' last enclaves among wooded hills half an hour's drive north of Amman, Hussein's army completed the destruction of the guerrillas' power in Jordan—a process begun by the near civil war in Amman in September 1970, the "Black September." The question was: what did Hussein do now?

The immediate answer, of course, was to concentrate upon attempting to rebuild an economy which—still badly scarred by the amputation of the West Bank in 1967—had taken further blows since: not merely the cost of the fighting itself, but the consequent loss of sixty million dollars in annual aid from Kuwait and Libya, both of whom disapproved of Hussein's attack on the Palestinians.

Yet even the future shape of Jordan's economy—and certainly Hussein's political strategy—depended upon another set of questions. Under what circumstances, if ever, would Hussein regain the West Bank? Would there be another war? Or would Sadat settle peacefully for a partial solution—concentrating merely upon retrieving most of Sinai? If he did that, how would Hussein's claims fare? While Hussein had to concentrate upon internal crises, those questions had been of secondary importance. But by the end of 1971, he could draw breath at last and contemplate them. And the fundamental answer pressed by his advisors was that Sadat was not proposing another war.

"Ironically," one of his closest advisors said afterward, "in reaching this conclusion we were heavily influenced by the Israelis. We looked at their conduct in the occupied territories, and it seemed to us that they would not be pursung the policies they were unless they thought they were going to be there for a long time. Well, we like everyone else shared the belief in the efficiency of Israeli intelligence. We reasoned that they must be confident that Sadat was not preparing a new war. So that persuaded us."

Jordan had no direct means of ascertaining Sadat's thinking. Since September 1970, relations with Egypt and Syria had steadily declined. But, the argument by Hussein's advisors ran, if there was no war, the political situation would stagnate. In that case, as the same advisor put it, "these so-called bad relations did not matter so long as the military/political situation did not change."

For, short of signing a separate peace with Israel—a scarcely thinkable act for Hussein—Jordan could take no individual initiative. Should a peaceful settlement slowly evolve, Jordan could presumably hope to share in it. Meanwhile, Hussein's best policy was to do nothing, except try to build up the East Bank as a prosperous economic entity on its own.

Opponents of this policy might have said that it regarded too equably the loss of the West Bank; that it placed too little stress upon the continuing problems of the Palestinians. It was certainly true that the main exponent of the "do nothing" policy was Hussein's Prime Minister through 1972, Wasfi Tell. Tell—a stocky, unyielding figure—had presided coldly over the final mopping up of the guerrillas. And within the spectrum of acceptable Jordanian politics, Tell was an "East-Banker," less concerned than many with the fate of the West Bank or its Palestinian inhabitants.

In fact, there was little or no criticism within the Jordanian political elite. Tell's orthodoxy prevailed. About the only protagonist of a different view was Zeid Rifai—and as Ambassador in London, his was a comparatively remote influence.

The Palestinians broke the mold. On November 28, 1971, as Wasfi Tell returned to his Cairo hotel from a day of talks, he was shot dead. His assassins announced themselves as "The Black Hand of September" (later shortened to "Black September") and they gathered round his body to lick blood from his wounds in an ecstasy of triumph at the death of the man whom they blamed for the killing of so many of their Palestinian comrades.

A month later, Zeid Rifai narrowly escaped death in London when a gunman emptied an entire magazine of automatic fire through the rear window of his ambassadorial car as it rounded a corner near the embassy. Rifai dived to the floor with a wound in his hand, and the chauffeur promptly stalled the car. But the gunman had fled.

In the reshuffle after Tell's death, Rifai was recalled to Amman. In March 1972, after three months' sick leave and a holiday, he took up a new job as political advisor to Hussein. At last, he had the ear of the king.

Zeid Rifai is a remarkable man. One of the three ruling families in Jordan who have served the Hashemite dynasty virtually since its establishment there, Rifai was born to political power. His father and his uncle were both prime ministers. To this lineage, Rifai added an education at Harvard and Columbia, and the life-long personal friendship of Hussein.

Together, Hussein and Rifai went as small boys to the Christian Missionary School in Amman. Almost all Rifai's adult life, he has worked close to Hussein—and shared the risks. When an Egyptian parcel bomb blew apart the then Prime Minister and surrounding officials in 1960, Rifai had left the room only minutes before. When the Palestinians tried to machine-gun Hussein in his car in July 1970, it was Rifai who lay on top of the king in the roadside ditch. And through the September crisis, Rifai was chief aide at the palace. (That was presumably why the Palestinians selected him as second target after Wasfi Tell.)

That Rifai has considerable ability, nobody has ever doubted. But it was a United States diplomat who pointed to his fundamental characteristic. "Rifai is a born gambler," he said. That is literally true. More than one stylish London gaming house lamented Rifai's departure. It is also the key to his political thinking. And as the thirty-five-year-old Rifai took up his new job at the palace, the gamble Jordan was embarked upon did not appeal to him. Because Rifai was convinced that there *would* be another war.

No specific facts drove him to this conclusion. He has since talked merely of "the logic of the situation." But his was, essentially, a gambler's calculation. Perhaps Tell had been correct. But what if he was wrong? Rifai remembered 1967 and pressed Hussein to do the same.

"In 1967," Rifai said crisply, "we sacrificed the West Bank to save the rest of the country." Hussein, in other words, had no choice but to go to war then—or risk overthrow by a popular rising. But Jordan had gone into battle against a background of bad relations with the other Arab combatants. There had been time neither to coordinate plans nor to make real preparation. The result had been disaster.

Rifai urged Hussein that Jordan's present policy risked a repetition of that. In a future war, Hussein would once again have no option but to join the battle. And the present policy would replicate the circumstances of 1967. But this time, who knew how much of the East Bank the Israelis would choose to take? For it was axiomatic in Rifai's thinking that Israel would swiftly win any future war. Where, after all, were the Arab preparations on a scale needed to put up a proper fight?

It seemed an insoluble dilemma. But Rifai spied the chance of a gambler's coup. Suppose Jordan could stay out of any new war *by agreement with the other Arab leaders?* If Sadat, for instance, were to declare publicly that he understood Jordan's position and agreed to a purely "defensive role"—or some such euphemism—that would for a time neutralize the political discontent that a new war would inevitably stir within Jordan. Provided a new war ended as quickly as the 1967 debacle, Hussein would be safe. To pull off that strategy, however, a restoration of relations with the likely Arab combatants, Egypt and Syria, was first priority.

Thus Rifai's argument reached its elegantly paradoxical conclusion. To ensure Jordan against the risk of war, it was necessary to improve relations with precisely those Arab states that might start one. After several weeks of discussions, Hussein saw the point. Sometime around the middle of 1972, Rifai was given a free hand to establish contact, covertly, with Presidents Sadat and Asad.

Precisely when Rifai contacted Sadat is unclear. But the intermediary was Rifai's uncle, Abdel Moneim Rifai, a former Prime Minister. He was a tactful choice. Abdel Moneim had a genuine sympathy for the Palestinian plight and, as Premier, he had spent months trying to patch up relations between Hussein and the guerrillas before resigning, in despair, on the eve of Black September. He was thus unstained by that bloodshed.

In the political wilderness through 1972, Abdel Moneim Rifai made two tours through Cairo, Damascus, and Riyadh—ostensibly as a private citizen but, latterly, carrying messages from his nephew. Finally, Sadat agreed to receive a more formal emissary from Hussein. According to diplomatic sources in Amman, it was at the beginning of December 1972 that Zeid Rifai at last flew secretly to Cairo. His gamble was under way.

Even this first, day-long, meeting with Sadat seemed to prove the validity of Rifai's thinking. For Sadat was seemingly frank. He told Rifai what he intended to do. He saw no way to move Israel, he said, or to reactivate what he called the "stagnant" political situation, other than by war. He even knew what sort of war. "I know I am not Tarzan," he said. "I recognize my limitations." All he proposed, Sadat told Rifai, was to cross the canal, seize a bridgehead, then trust to a swift Security Council call for a cease-fire—plus the threat of superpower intervention—to cement his victory. He did not want heavy Egyptian casualties; he had "strictly limited purposes."

Rifai flew back to Amman a very thoughtful man. He knew that Sadat had not told him anything like the whole truth. No date for war had been mentioned, for instance. (And Sadat gave Rifai the impression that the Soviets had gone for good—whereas, as we have seen, his need for new missiles had already forced Sadat toward reconciliation with them.) But Rifai realized that Sadat was serious.

In what followed, there were two strands to Jordanian policy: an attempt to stave off this coming war by persuading the United States to take diplomatic action in time; and a simultaneous race to carry through Rifai's insurance policy, in case that diplomacy failed.

The Jordanians contacted Kissinger in the new year of 1973. It was a calculated decision. The only member of the Nixon administration with the freedom and power to push through a realistic U. S. Middle East policy was the man in the White House basement, they reckoned. But they were surprised by Kissinger's response.

The Jordanians seem to have been fairly discreet, urging upon Kissinger the seriousness of the threat of war while not revealing Sadat's precise plans. (It occurred to some of Hussein's advisors, though, that Sadat had talked tough to Rifai precisely because he wanted the message to reach the West.) And Kissinger agreed. He had long thought, he said, that another war was coming. But he then spelled out his conditions for taking up the topic. He would do so in secret, he said, and at a time of his own choosing. His first moves would be to examine—by secret contacts—whether there did appear to be the possibility of diplomatic advance. If none emerged, he warned, he would abandon the quest. And should news of these first secret efforts leak, he would deny all knowledge of them—even perhaps abandon them. "Kissinger was very frank," one Jordanian recalled. "He said that he wished to preserve his reputation for success, which he regarded as his greatest political asset." He added, smiling: "But I think he has a certain personal liking for success as well."

There was nothing more that Jordan could do. (And, as we shall see, Kissinger did apparently contact an emissary from Sadat shortly after this warning.) Hussein and Rifai now turned their attention to cementing a relationship with Egypt and Syria.

Hussein wanted there to be no doubt what his terms were. On May 13, he circulated among his officers a memorandum. "It is clear today," he wrote, "that the Arab nations are preparing for a new war . . . The battle would be premature." Whatever the private purpose of Rifai's strategy, in other words, Hussein's public position was that he would only join an alliance for peace. With that clear, Rifai turned to Syria.

His approach to Damascus coincided with his further elevation. On May 26, Hussein appointed Rifai Prime Minister. He flew to Damascus two days later, on Monday, May 28.

However much the two quarrel in public, Jordan and Syria have always been closer at some levels than meets the eye. When Syria closed the frontier in 1972, for instance, Jordan's phosphate and vegetable lorries still in practice trundled across. More delicately, some sort of liaison persisted between the middle ranks of the armies. There was even fellow feeling with the Syrian Minister of Defense: Mustapha Tlas' wife is related to the late Wasfi Tell's family. Rifai's task in Damascus was not quite so hard as that in Cairo, therefore.

Nor, seemingly, did Asad echo Sadat's bleak options. Like Rifai, Asad thought that war was inevitable—and he admitted that he knew of Sadat's plans. But the Syrian president himself was not so specific. (How frank Asad was being is, of course, uncertain. As we have shown, the military discussions with Egypt were well advanced by late May. Perhaps Asad was prudently leaving to Sadat the decision how much to tell Jordan?)

If Rifai's meeting with Sadat had been simply to break the ice, that with Asad succeeded in its further purpose. Asad agreed to meet with Hussein and Sadat at a tripartite summit. The task now was to persuade Sadat of the same. The sequence of contacts between the Arab capitals indicates the maneuvers necessary to achieve this. Once again, the Prime Minister's uncle was the intermediary:

June 18: Abdel Moneim Rifai arrives in Cairo to see Sadat's ministers.

June 30: Rifai goes to Damascus, talking of the need to restore diplomatic relations.

July 19: Rifai is back in Cairo, with a message from Hussein to Sadat.

More secret were meetings that Premier Zeid Rifai had around this time: two with Sadat, one with Asad. The reason for the secrecy was that Abdel Moneim Rifai's mission was progressing only slowly.

Hussein was eager to meet Sadat—but without preconditions. Sadat, by contrast, wanted Hussein to give ground on three fronts. He wanted Hussein to renounce his plan for a federation of the East and West Banks of the Jordan (a plan which, ironically, Hussein had proposed as a way of appeasing Palestinian feeling); he wanted Hussein to make up his differences with the guerrillas; and, specifically, to allow their umbrella grouping, the Palestine Liberation Organization, to operate inside Jordan once more. All three conditions Hussein flatly rejected.

Sadat was persuaded to back down. And King Faisal of Saudi Arabia was an important intermediary. On July 28, Zeid Rifai went to talk with Faisal for twelve hours. To see why Sadat then listened to Faisal, it is necessary to plunge briefly into the subplot of Sadat, cash, and the Libyan connection. One of Sadat's early problems was how to pay for the war. Egypt, perennially strapped for cash, received significant subvention from Colonel Muammar el Qaddafi, the mercurial President of Libya. But Qaddafi's ideas of fitting Arab war aims were as gruesome as Asad's had been before Sadat talked him around.

How much Qaddafi knew of Sadat's war planning is hard to determine. Egyptian diplomatic sources claim convincingly, however, that Qaddafi had been told the broad strategy as early as the end of 1972. If that is so, the date can be fixed with some certainty as December 1972. On December 5, General Ismail arrived in the Libyan capital, Tripoli, for two days of talks on "military coordination." A week later, an unhappy meeting of the Arab chiefs of staff broke up in Cairo much faster than expected.

The reason for thinking that it was at these meetings that Qaddafi and his generals learned of Sadat's planning is that Qaddafi's public comments then altered significantly. On January 1, 1973, in his regular New Year's speech, the Libyan leader—reversing previous exhortations to an immediate call to arms on all fronts against Israel—now rejected precisely such hasty action. But he added, surely pointedly, that Egypt was mistaken in concentrating so heavily upon the recapture of Sinai, to the neglect of the Golan Heights. At the end of January, Qaddafi returned still more directly to the topic. An assault across the canal would be a tactical error, he said. He wanted the eastern front—by which he meant the forces of Syria—reactivated as well. It was, finally, Qaddafi who brought Sadat and Syrian President Asad together on February 5, 1973—"to discuss," it was reported later, "coordination for battle against Israel." Was it, then, Qaddafi who implanted in Sadat's mind the idea of a joint Egyptian-Syrian assault?

The evidence does no more than point that way. What is certain is that Sadat's war aims—however achieved—were vastly more muted than Qaddafi's. While Sadat from the start had limited objectives, Qaddafi was set upon nothing less than the destruction of Israel—"a holy march," he called it. If Sadat had to rely upon Qaddafi to bankroll Egypt's war expenditure, therefore, it took no political genius to see that Sadat's war aims could come under fierce pressure from the bloodthirsty Libyan. Egypt would need cash from elsewhere. King Faisal of Saudi Arabia stepped in.

In a compact finalized by Sadat on a secret flight in August 1973, first to the Saudi capital, Riyadh, and then on to the gulf state of Qatar, Sadat doubled his aid from Faisal, got another $500 million specifically for military spending, and picked up $650 million in long-term loans at trifling interest. Hearing rumors of the deal, Qaddafi angrily swept into Cairo unannounced. He was too late: Sadat was already in Riyadh. When Sadat returned —after Qaddafi had cooled his heels for three days—Sadat did consent to sign the long-awaited treaty signaling "the birth of a new unified state" of Libya-Egypt. Everyone knew it was mere theater. With Faisal's help, Egypt was free of Libya.

Why did Faisal do it? Bluntly, because—according to excellently placed Arab political sources—Sadat spun him a yarn. Sadat apparently represented to Faisal that he was desperate to sweep away the Socialist trappings of the Nasser era and revert to the path of a true, conservative Muslim—if only he had the cash. But how could he break free of a radical like Qaddafi when he needed Libya's subsidy? Faisal, of course, had seen Qaddafi as a pest ever since the colonel seized power. And historically, the Saudis have a "Cairo complex"—the belief that the fate of the Arab world revolves around Egypt. Sadat's pitch was thus precisely calculated to appeal to a reactionary old monarch like Faisal.

Sadat did also tell Faisal about his war plans—though apparently in general terms. Since just about the only opinion that Faisal shares with Qaddafi, apart from a mutual hatred of marxism, is a firm belief in the desirability of exterminating the Jews, Sadat had no problems getting all the cash he needed.

But Faisal's price was that Sadat re-establish relations with Hussein. Sadat agreed—and dropped his preconditions for a summit. Thus Hussein was swept to his objective, as it were, on the hem of Faisal's robe. On September 10, King Hussein and President Asad arrived in Cairo for a three-day meeting with Sadat.

The Cairo summit must qualify as one of the stranger diplomatic gatherings of recent years. For Hussein left afterward thinking that he had persuaded the other two to abandon thought of war in the near future; while Sadat and Asad in fact agreed privately at the summit to launch the assault before the end of the year. Hussein was doublecrossed.

The ostensible purpose of the Cairo summit was to finalize the restoration of relations between Jordan and her two "allies." The agenda comprised three items: the settling of all differences; the creation of a common military/political strategy; and the re-establishment of diplomatic relations. Inevitably, discussion centered on the military/political question.

Jordan's arguments against war were by now well known to Sadat. Zeid Rifai's basic contention had always been that Sadat's plan for a "limited" war was overoptimistic. "What makes you think that the Israelis will play the game by your rules?" Rifai apparently asked Sadat at their first meeting. To which Sadat replied by asking what alternative he had. Lacking Israel's *Blitzkrieg* capacity, Egypt's Army could not fight a mobile war across Sinai. The best it could hope to achieve was a limited, relatively static victory. Sadat was aware of the risk that the Israelis might expand the war in retaliation—perhaps by bombing his cities. In that case, he too would retaliate. He used the phrase "depth for depth."

Hussein had obviously to adopt fresh tactics at Cairo. So he *agreed* that war was necessary—but not yet. His mistake was to think that he persuaded Sadat of this.

How seriously Hussein believed his argument that diplomacy must be given a last chance is now hard to determine. After the war, Hussein said privately that he had not really had much faith in this. But through the summer the Jordanians had repeated more than once their warnings to Kissinger. And when, on August 23—just three weeks before the Cairo summit—President Nixon finally nominated Kissinger as his new Secretary of State, there was jubilation in Amman. Hussein has since said that this was his strongest positive argument at Cairo.

But the core of Hussein's thinking—the "neutrality by agreement" strategy—he necessarily advanced rather more circumspectly. Hussein said that the Arabs should only launch a war that they could win. That would require Jordanian participation on the eastern front. But Jordan could not afford another battle it might lose. "The first battle we lose will be our last," Hussein was fond of saying. To fight properly, Jordan needed equipment and time.

Whether Hussein actually took a shopping list to Cairo is disputed. He says he did not. But he certainly made it clear that Jordan lacked aircraft, air bases, and an air defense system. Unless other Arab nations rallied round, Jordan could never play its proper role in the battle. If and when Jordan was equipped, its forces would then need two years to train up to combat pitch on the new gear. But, Hussein concluded, the contribution Jordan could make was surely worth the delay.

Sadat fooled Hussein into thinking that he accepted these arguments. Hussein left Cairo in a state approaching euphoria. He had persuaded Sadat to give Kissinger a chance. And he was sure he could rely upon Sadat's help in persuading the richer Arab states to open their coffers for Jordan.

True, on the last evening of the summit, Sadat and Asad had suddenly raised the question of the Palestinians. Taking back the guerrillas, Hussein understood, might be the price for diplomatic relations. In a tense huddle with his advisors, Hussein almost acquiesced, but finally decided to stand firm. He marched back to the conference table and threatened to leave Cairo. Toughness paid. Sadat said that he thought they had made enough progress, even despite this, to warrant Egypt's restoring formal relations with Jordan. Asad did not commit himself, but Hussein was confident—correctly—that after a few days in which to juggle the factions in Damascus, Asad too would agree.

It seemed a triumph for Hussein. Of course, war had been discussed. Sadat and Asad both raised the possibility. Just in case something went wrong, they told Hussein, they understood that Jordan could do no more than play a defensive role. In the unlikely event of war, the three leaders agreed, Jordan would mass its forces in the north, in the lee of the Golan Heights, to deter

Israeli armor from striking up through Jordanian territory to take the Syrians on Golan in the rear.

Such things had to be talked about—just as a precaution. Hussein even revealed that his military commanders had a plan—more a "contingency idea" really—to move across the river Jordan just below Golan and Lake Tiberias to enter Israel itself. Nobody was clear what they would do once they got there. But perhaps a small slice of Israeli territory might be bargained for the return of east Jerusalem?

When Hussein returned to Amman from that summit, there is ample contemporaneous evidence—from diplomats to whom he spoke—that he really did believe that he had persuaded Sadat and Asad to seek a peaceful solution to the Middle East crisis.

Hussein was wrong. The extraordinary truth was that, in the intervals of their meetings with him, Sadat and Asad had been holding their own, far more private, summit. Together, they had finalized the details of war. The war aims they had agreed on were grandly simple: a final solution—ominous phrase—to the twenty-five-year confrontation with Israel. This was to be achieved not by extermination or genocide, but by sparking a crisis into which the superpowers would inevitably be drawn. Sadat's strategy was to force a superpower confrontation. If the superpowers then wanted to reassert détente, they would have to pay for it. They would have to cool the Middle East once more. And to do that, *they* would have to force concessions from Israel. Ismail had called the military plan "Operation BADR." This broader political strategy Sadat code-named "Operation SPARK."

Militarily, the objectives were the recapture of those parts of Syria, Egypt, and Jordan occupied by Israel. Even this was to be achieved in two phases, however. For while Syria might be able to regain its limited losses on Golan, Sadat had no intention of letting his army loose through the back of beyond in Sinai. Egypt's objective was thus the retaking of a slice of Sinai along the east bank of the Suez Canal. The rest of Sinai and the West Bank of the Jordan would come as Israeli concessions.

Sadat was confident of that, for the military strategy agreed on was brutally simple: Israel would be subjected to a war of attrition—the "meat grinder." If the superpowers failed, the Arabs would continue for weeks, even months, until Israel, through sheer exhaustion of money and lives, had to settle.

This strategy, of course, said nothing about the cause theoretically dearest to the Arab heart: the rights of nearly two million Palestinians or descendants of Palestinians dispossessed at the foundation of Israel. And, indeed, even while the summit was in progress, the Palestinians' radio station in Baghdad condemned the "series of basic retreats by certain Arab regimes. . . ." From the Palestinians' viewpoint, that was true enough: Egypt and Syria now accepted the existence of Israel. President Qaddafi had made the same point. But the stakes Sadat was playing for were too high to be left to guerrillas—or to Libyans. Besides, the leaders might reasonably argue that their strategy was likelier to win something for the Palestinians than anything the Palestinians could do themselves. (In the event, of course, the leaders did not bother to argue. Asad simply closed down the Palestinians' Damascus radio station, and Hussein tried to appease Sadat by releasing prisoners.)

Still, it was a successful—even momentous—summit. But when it ended on September 12 with a formal resumption of diplomatic relations between Jordan and the others, Sadat emerged with his options open. (Not even Asad knew the exact date of Y-Day.) The day after the summit dispersed, on September 13, Israel closed the options.

Israel may not have intended to pick a fight with Syria. The Israeli Chief of Staff insisted afterward that the battle "was not initiated by us," and that may well have been true. But why, then, were four Israeli fighters cruising along over the Mediterranean, temptingly near to, if not in, Syrian airspace? Israel said it was a routine patrol. On the other hand, it was a trick the Israeli Air Force had tried before. Either way, the Syrians fell for it. A force of MiGs was scrambled to intercept them. What happened next is again disputed. Israel claims it had to send up reinforcements. Other accounts hold that the reinforcements were already waiting—in ambush upsun. All that is certain is that in the ensuing *mêlée*, thirteen Syrian aircraft were shot down, for the loss of one Israeli. (The battle was tracked and the casualties logged on the radars of an American electronics intelligence vessel—a Mediterranean *Pueblo*—cruising in the area.)

If it were an Israeli ploy—just to remind the Arabs of Israeli power in the wake of the Cairo summit—it backfired appallingly. Western military attachés in the Middle East certainly took the incident to be an assertion of Israeli air superiority so over-whelming as to make war *less* likely. But excellent sources in Cairo claim, on the contrary, that it was after this battle that Asad telephoned Sadat to urged that the time had come to strike. Sadat agreed. He summoned his most senior military men: War Minister General Ahmed Ismail; Chief of Staff Lieutenant General Saad el Shazli; Director of Military Operations Lieutenant General Abdel Ghani el Gamasy; Director of Armaments and Organization Major General Omar Gohar; Commander of Air Defense Major General Mohammed Ali Fahmy; Air Force Commander Air Vice Marshal Mohammed Mubarak; and the commander of the Engineers Corps and the man who would have to construct the bridges across the canal, Major General Aly Mohammed. To these and about another ten officers present at the meeting, Sadat gave the order: Activate Operation BADR. From that moment, the countdown to war had begun. The most brilliant feature of the three weeks that followed was how completely the Arabs managed to disguise this.

6. Failures of Intelligence

When Egyptian armor began assembling on Friday, September 21, few Israelis were worried. For ten years past—save in 1967, when it was otherwise engaged—the Egyptian Army had held maneuvers every autumn. True, for the past two or three years, these maneuvers and other, more frequent, exercises had seemed to concentrate on the canal. But that was to be expected. Besides, even in the scattered strongpoints of the Bar-Lev Line, it was hard enough for the Israelis to remain efficient; and they had air conditioning and a four-to-six-week tour of duty. For the Egyptian conscript, his two *years* on the canal must have been a nightmare of tedium. So the Israelis dismissed the exercises— and the new embankments and fortifications the Egyptians had thrown up over the past nine months. They were just to keep the troops busy.

One oddity, though, Israel had passed to American intelligence. Each year, the Egyptian maneuvers got bigger. It was not Israel, however, that spotted the sinister difference this time. The first preparations that Egypt had made on September 21 had been normal enough precursors of an annual exercise. Some reservists were recalled. Some leaves were canceled, and so were a few training courses. Even at this earliest stage, though, two of the alert procedures seemed slightly unusual. Some of Egypt's crack commando units were quietly deployed to new bases. And communications to and from Cairo military headquarters suddenly switched from radio (which, of course, could be monitored) to land lines (which could not be overheard, or at least not until the lines were tapped).

Around September 24, the U. S. Central Intelligence Agency worked out further odd features. These were the first exercises in which the Egyptian Army had maneuvered in formations as big as a full division. The Egyptians were also stockpiling more ammunition than ever, assembling their most extensive logistics support yet seen—and, most disquieting of all, they were hooking up a vastly more complex field communications network than mere exercises could warrant. As soon as the CIA learned this, Israel was warned. Specifically, Washington intelligence sources now claim, Israel was asked "at very high level" whether this was not an indication of Arab preparations for the assault expected—by some of the American intelligence community, at least—since the spring. Israel rejected the fears.

Precisely as the Egyptian war planners had calculated, Israel was distracted. To its politicians, facing an October election, the most pressing battles were those of rival manifestos. On top of that the government faced serious domestic and international problems. In New York, a new session of the United Nations General Assembly had just opened; Israel was already aware that the new U. S. Secretary of State, Henry Kissinger, proposed to use it at least to make his first public steps toward a settlement in the Middle East.

Diplomatically, the failure of its African policy had left Israel isolated in the developing world. (Through the late 1960s, Israel had successfully sent technical advisers throughout Africa and enjoyed some prestige there. Under heavy Arab influence, more and more African states were now breaking those ties.) Increasingly worried by the foreseeable American oil shortage, Nixon seemed once again to be preparing to lean on Israel as part of the Kissinger Middle East initiative. More drastic still, Israel's appeal seemed to be fading even among the Diaspora. The key issue here was immigration. Immigrants to Israel are, mainly, either Sephardic Jews (originally from within the old Moorish Empire) or Ashkenazim (originally from Russia, now spread throughout the West). The nub of Israel's immigration policy has been to maintain a preponderance of Ashkenazim settlers (who are white) over Sephardic (who are brown). Yet immigration by Western Jews was now almost nil: For Ashkenazim, Israel was almost wholly dependent upon the flow of refugees from the Soviet Union. Meanwhile, even the financial aid from Western Jews—so lavish after the Six-Day War—was now dwindling below its monthly targets; and Israel depended upon this to balance its monstrous budget deficit. Yet the government's ability to tackle these problems was steadily waning as Mrs. Meir's coalition Cabinet, rickety at the best of times, began to split under pre-election pressures. It was a bad time. Even so, Israel's blindness to what followed is hard to explain.

The first Syrian moves also began around September 21. There was no dramatic dash for the front. Instead, slowly and methodically, infantry and artillery began to mass around the triple lines of Syrian defense constructed, with Soviet help, over the plain between Golan and Damascus. One element behind that first American alert to Israel was important new intelligence estimates that the CIA produced from Syria around September 23. One Washington source claims that the CIA spotted "something seriously suspicious about the nature of the Syrian deployments." Another U.S. source says that the Syrian information merely complemented what was known about Egyptian planning —and what was now being picked up from the Egyptian maneuvers. "Golan was the missing piece of the jigsaw," this source said. But, he added, although this increased the level of concern inside the agencies, "most people still generalized about the Egyptian tendency to bluster rather than act."

That—or something very like it—was also, disastrously, true in Tel Aviv. The Israeli General Staff holds its regular weekly meetings every Monday. The meeting on Monday, September 24, was thus crucial in determining Israel's responses in the fortnight ahead. It was the first General Staff meeting since the buildup across Israel's front lines had begun. It was at this meeting that Israel's attitudes to this development were set.

The commander of Israel's northern front, Major General Yizhak Hoffi, was worried. At the meeting, he pointed out that, while the Syrians had massed armor on previous occasions, this buildup would soon be unprecedented in scale. He also saw that the SAM batteries that the Syrians now deployed gave the buildup protection on an equally unprecedented scale. Combined, these two factors gave Hoffi cause for concern—whatever the over-all assessment might be of Syrian intentions. Hoffi was not alone: Chief of Staff Elazar echoed his fears. The head of Israeli military intelligence, Major General Eliahu Zeira, was wholly unruffled.

Zeira's role in what followed was decisive. There were several reasons for this, but the most fundamental arose from the structure of Israeli intelligence. In Israel, as in most western defense establishments, the collection of raw intelligence data is differentiated from their subsequent interpretation and evaluation. The purpose of this division is to ensure—at least in theory— that the agencies pass on *all* facts or clues they glean, rather than filtering out those which do not fit conceptions they themselves hold. In Israel, this safeguard had ceased to function. Of the three Israeli agencies with responsibility for collecting information from abroad—military intelligence, the Mossad or Secret Intelligence Service, and the Foreign Ministry research department—only military intelligence had the task of evaluating the facts thus collected.

For almost precisely a decade, Israel's politicians had known that this system was dangerously inflexible. At the end of 1963, a secret report to the Israeli Cabinet had pointed to the dangers inherent in reliance upon only one interpretation of intelligence data. The report—drawn up by some of Israel's most respected former military commanders—had suggested three remedies. The Mossad should be equipped to present its own evaluations in certain fields. The Foreign Ministry research department should present independent *political* evaluations— to assess, in other words, Arab intentions in the light of political rather than military developments. And the Prime Minister should appoint a personal intelligence advisor as a trouble shooter and devil's advocate, specifically to question agencies' evaluations and probe the evidence on which they were based.

None of these recommendations had been followed. Bureaucratic hostility ensured that no independent advisor was appointed. The Mossad had not been allowed to present its own assessments. And, under the premiership of Mrs. Meir, the weakening influence of Foreign Minister Abba Eban had led to a *cutback* in the staff and functions of his ministry's research department. Thus, at the worried General Staff meeting on September 24, Zeira—and Zeira alone—had the technical responsibility for gauging what the Arab buildup portended.

He was not well equipped to do so. Israeli military intelligence suffered from the faults that threaten to paralyze any bureaucracy. It was run on military, hierarchical lines—no civilians were employed, of course; and rank was meticulously observed. Some of its senior officers had been in one job for far too long—in several instances, as much as six or seven years. Moreover, no machinery existed within the agency for checking the evaluations handed up by the hierarchy. Whatever its technical expertise, in other words, Israeli military intelligence was classically vulnerable to mistakes derived from preconceptions or vested interests. That was precisely the trap into which it now fell.

Since 1967, military intelligence had been convinced that the lessons of that disaster must have imposed upon the Arabs two preconditions which they would infallibly observe before risking another war. The first was that Syria would not attack except in concert with Egypt. The second was that Egypt would not attack until its Air Force could neutralize Israel's. And since Nasser himself had said, shortly before his death, that Egypt's Air Force needed another five years to achieve that capability—itself an assessment regarded as wildly optimistic by most observers—the conclusion was the Egypt would not go to war, and neither would Syria. It was a powerful syllogism. And so generally was it held by military intelligence that it even had a name: "The Concept."

It has since been suggested inside Israel that had the two key men in military intelligence been different, some reconsideration of "the concept" might have been possible, even at the last minute. This is unlikely. But, certainly, they were an unfortunate combination.

Zeira—a man with a biting wit and a fondness for long cigarette holders—had a vast and usually justified confidence in his own abilities, and a considerable acquaintanceship among Israeli politicians. He had only been in the job since the spring of 1973—though with an earlier period as deputy head—and he had inherited "the concept" without questioning it very particularly. Indeed, given his temperament, it was predictable that, should anyone outside the agency question "the concept," Zeira would devote his considerable intellectual powers to a spirited defense of it. He was that sort of man.

A more dissenting view might have come from Zeira's assistant director, Brigadier Arie Shalev, head of the military intelligence research department—the evaluation section. Shalev did entertain doubts about "the concept" from time to time. In particular, he questioned its validity in the light of Egypt's new weaponry. But he had been in the job since the end of 1967—at least twice too long. It was unreasonable to think that, at a time of potential crisis, Shalev would or even could abandon the intellectual framework of six years.

Personalities apart, however, there were deeper reasons why military intelligence adhered so faithfully to "the concept." In a sense, it was merely the technical expression of the political orthodoxy expounded at all possible opportunities by Mrs. Meir and her Cabinet colleagues: that Israel's retention of its 1967 gains so increased the difficulties that the Arabs would face in going to war once more that the borders were themselves a deterrent. Thus, the political argument ran, Israel's unwillingness to cede this territory was not only in the name of Israeli security but also served the cause of peace and stability in the region. To explain this doctrine to foreign politicians visiting Israel, it was commonly officers of military intelligence who were responsible for the briefing sessions. Thus converted, by political will, from assessors into advocates, Israeli military intelligence was scarcely in the best mental state to question the technical expression of that doctrine of deterrence too closely.

Moreover, the decline in influence of the Foreign Ministry now meant that military intelligence had the task of weighing the political situation as well. In any circumstances, this would have been an ill-judged accretion of responsibility. In this case, it was wholly self-defeating. The military intelligence assessment of Arab political intentions was also subjugated to "the concept": Because the *military* assessment was that, without air superiority, the Arabs lacked the ability to go to war, therefore the Arabs' rational *political* intention must be to avoid war—whatever Arab politicians might say to the contrary.

That political moves in the Arab world for almost two years now had presented a consistent pattern of preparations for war; that Sadat, balancing internal pressures against the openings visible on the international diplomatic horizon, might see no political option but war; that, finally, the military "concept" itself might have been vitiated by technical developments—

none of these considerations, so far as it is now possible to ascertain, was rehearsed by Zeira at the worried meeting of the General Staff on Monday, September 24.

Instead, Zeira said two things. The assessment of military intelligence, he said, was that the Egyptian and Syrian deployments were unconnected. The Syrian buildup was taking defensive form—perhaps in expectation of some Israeli follow-up to the recent air combat over the Mediterranean. The Egyptian moves were preparations for a "multi-arm exercise"—that is, joint maneuvers by all branches of the armed services—similar to those held every autumn for some years past. Zeira then added a crucial reassurance. Should Arab intentions change, he said, military intelligence would have at least forty-eight hours' warning of the outbreak of war.

Zeira's confidence in this warning time never wavered in the days ahead. Why he was so sure is impossible to ascertain. Military intelligence undoubtedly did have access—as we shall see—to remarkable sources of information. Perhaps Zeira was relying on that. But there is another possibility. Perhaps Zeira supported the doctrine—propounded with vigor by its originator, Moshe Dayan—that there was such a thing as "strategic warning" of imminent war. The doctrine does not, in fact, mean anything. In practice, intelligence assessments are built up from the accumulation of tactical detail—rail movements, troop deployments, and such like—weighed against the political background. What strategic indicators might be is hard to see. It is, on the other hand, easy to see why Dayan—and perhaps Zeira—should have found such an idea attractive. If tactical indications of impending war were all that could be achieved, then Israel ought to mobilize every time the Arabs chose to mass any substantial body of armor on its borders. But in that event the burden on Israel's economy would rapidly prove intolerable. There had to be some subtler guide: hence the invention of "strategic warning."

As the General Staff meeting of September 24 broke up, Zeira's reassurances had had two consequences. They had not been enough to stifle all fears. Chief of Staff Elazar and Northern Commander Hoffi both communicated their concern to Defense Minister Dayan. But Zeira did, fatally, inhibit decisive action.

Two days after that General Staff meeting, Dayan became the first person in Israel publicly to admit concern. On September 26, the Minister of Defense—briefed on the General Staff's concern—inspected troops on Golan during his annual tour on the day before the Jewish New Year. "Stationed along the Syrian border," he told the troops and the Israeli public, "are hundreds of Syrian tanks and cannon within effective range, as well as an anti-aircraft system of a density similar to that of the Egyptians' along the Suez Canal." Publicly at least, Dayan professed to be worried less by this buildup than by the absence on Golan of the "buffer of natural obstacles" present on the Suez and Jordanian fronts. (The Golan Heights themselves had, of course, been a natural barrier to the Israelis—though not to the Syrians, who had lobbed shells down among the Jordan Valley settlements until Israel had captured the Heights in 1967. Once on top, however, the Golan plain contained no natural defenses.) Dayan talked that day of strengthening further the sixteen fortified settlements that Israel had established on Golan.

Dayan did not think that the Syrian buildup presaged a general war. But he did recall that a savaging of Syrian air power very like that which Israel had just inflicted had sparked the Six-Day War; and he anticipated a Syrian reprisal of some determination. He was thus sufficiently worried to do, in secret, two things. That same day, September 26, he put the Army on alert on both fronts. And sometime during the three days of the New Year holiday, he reinforced the single understrength armored brigade garrisoning Golan by bringing up Israel's crack tank unit, the 7th Armored Brigade. (It had been down at Armored Corps headquarters at Beersheba in southern Israel.) He also sent up reinforcements of artillery. It was perhaps the single most crucial Israeli decision of the war— yet it was done with no publicity at all.

It was as if Israel were wishing away unwelcome news. Dayan's warning of the Syrian buildup was barely reported. (There were no papers on the three days, September 27–29.) When news of the alert did leak after the holiday, it was soothed away as "standard practice during Israel's festive season"—with the added reassurance that tourists were still allowed on Golan. And Dayan himself did not quite have the courage of his convictions. The Army was put only on the lowest state of alert. And the 7th Armored

Brigade was sent to Golan understrength. It normally comprises four battalions plus a reconnaissance force again approaching battalion strength. Dayan sent three battalions. The remainder he allowed on maneuvers in the Negev desert.

Nor could U.S. intelligence persuade its political masters to take the threat seriously. On September 27, the day after Dayan's Golan visit, an Agena reconnaissance satellite was launched from Vandenberg Air Force Base, California. It was a routine launch—to the frustration of those in the U.S. intelligence community who wanted special surveillance of the Middle East buildup. But in 1973, for budgetary reasons, the Defense Department had cut back on satellite launchings. In 1973, the United States launched fewer than half the total of Soviet reconnaissance satellites and most of those it did put up concentrated on the Soviet Union and China. Moreover, while the polar orbit of the new Agena would enable it to cover the Middle East at intervals, the satellite would have to come down before its pictures could be examined. And no satellite was then ready to take its place. Normally, the United States would have had a Big Bird—a considerably more advanced surveillance platform—on global station; fortuitously, the latest was just about to land. Effectively, the United States was blind.

Not that a satellite was needed to pick up the next clue Sadat dropped. September 28 was the third anniversary of Nasser's death. His successor took advantage of the occasion to release from jail several politically deviant journalists and students. And Sadat ended his speech announcing the amnesty with a strange, foreboding passage. "Brothers and sisters," he said, "perhaps you have noticed there is a subject which I have not broached. This is the subject of battle. I have done this deliberately. We know our goal and we are determined to attain it. We shall spare no efforts or sacrifice to fulfill our objective. I promise nothing. I shall not discuss any details. However, I only say that the liberation of the land, as I have told you, is the first and main task facing us. God willing, we shall achieve this task. We shall realize it and we shall attain it. This is the will of the people. This is the will of our nation. It is even the will of God." Rarely had Sadat, in a major speech, discussed war in such a low-key, almost subdued, manner.

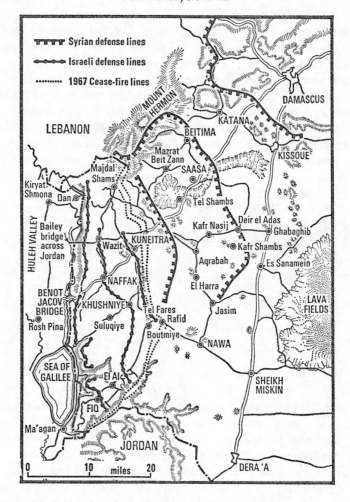

Map 4 The danger Israel faced on Golan

For Israel, Golan's danger was that it lacked natural defenses but was only seventeen miles deep from the 1967 lines to the Benot Jacov crossing. Three other roads led down the cliffs into Israel. To guard them, Israel had strengthened Syria's old lines, while its strongpoint on Mount Hermon overlooked the whole plateau. Eastward, Syria had now built three new defense lines to guard Damascus. The only natural barrier to an Israeli advance across the plain was the Saasa lava rock ridge astride the Damascus road.

Israeli military intelligence remained unworried. Sometime in or just after the New Year holiday—one source puts the meeting on September 28, New Year's Day itself, but others place it two days later, on September 30—there was a meeting of the small group at the very top of Israel's military hierarchy. Present were Chief of Staff Elazar; the Deputy Chief of Staff, Major General Israel Tal; the head of the secret service, the Mossad, Major General Zvi Zamir; and the head of military intelligence, Zeira. Surveying the evidence, the quartet was divided.

Zamir was the most worried: so far as we can ascertain, Mossad agents had obtained some approximation of Ismail's battle plan. The question was whether and, if so, when the Egyptians would implement it. Zeira remained confident: Military intelligence would infallibly obtain at least forty-eight hours' notice of an impending assault, he repeated; but the military assessment was still that the Arabs were conducting unrelated exercises. Just in case they were not, however, what more should Israel do? The Army was already on alert, and reinforcements were on their way to Golan. Deputy Chief of Staff Tal apparently wanted partial mobilization. He was especially worried about the Golan front. Elazar pointed in reply to three false alarms in the previous nine months, particularly the costly May alert. He had not forgotten the mistaken mobilization he had insisted on then. "But if it is the real thing this time?" Tal asked. Anxious not to waste money from a tight military budget, however, he did not press the point. The meeting broke up inconclusively.

What happened next was—perhaps—a stroke of bad luck. On September 28, two Arab gunmen identifying themselves merely as "Eagles of the Palestine Revolution" held up at the Austrian border a train carrying Soviet Jews from Moscow to Vienna. They took as hostages five Jews and an Austrian customs official, and demanded that Austria close a transit center in Vienna called Schonau Castle, which was used by Soviet Jews on their way to Israel. Austria's Chancellor Bruno Kreisky, himself a Jew, agreed to the demand—and let the gunmen go free. Israel was outraged.

But was Schonau really bad luck, or was it a cunning stroke of misdirection? The gunmen were members of a Palestinian organization called Sai'qa, which is based in Syria and controlled by the Syrian authorities to the extent that even Syrian Army officers are members. Only a week before Schonau, the Sai'qa leader, Zuhair Muhsen, had dismissed such exploits as "adolescent actions requiring no special courage and undertaken for fame and glory." What, or who, changed Muhsen's mind? Egypt's War Minister, Ismail, was certainly proud of his "decoy plan"—certain elements of which, he said later, had been "intended to distract attention from what we meant to do."

If it was misdirection, the Schonau raid succeeded. It is no exaggeration to say that from that day until the morning before war itself, Israel was obsessed by Schonau: demonstrations, petitions, public meetings, banner headlines, and pages of newsprint —all to the exclusion of the far graver threat massing on Israel's borders. News of such developments was tucked into paragraphs buried beneath Schonau coverage. More dangerously, the Israeli Government and its military and intelligence chiefs were equally absorbed—which was disastrous, because on September 30 the United States Government, in the plump shape of Secretary of State Henry Kissinger, finally became concerned by the Arab buildup. But what Kissinger was told by the U.S. intelligence community was now heavily influenced by the opinions of Israeli military intelligence.

Through this runup to war, the adequacy of Israeli and U.S. intelligence is clearly critical to any assessment of the political responses of their governments. Reconstructing what the agencies thought is made even harder than usual in this case because various politicians have since sought to explain their inaction by blaming the advice—inevitably and conveniently secret—that emanated from their intelligence services. The starkest accusation of failure has come from Kissinger: "We asked our own intelligence, as well as Israeli intelligence, on three separate occasions during the week prior to the outbreak of hostilities, to give us their assessment of what might happen. There was the unanimous view that hostilities were unlikely to the point of there being no chance of it happening." The reality was considerably more complex.

The first complexity was Kissinger himself—and his attitude toward intelligence. Kissinger had always been a believer in secret diplomacy. The only snag was that, during his time in the White House, he had extended this principle to mean secret even from his own bureaucracy. This might have been necessary on Vietnam and China—though, to judge from their receipt of filched White House documents, the Joint Chiefs of Staff did not think so. But when the habit of secrecy carried over into his running of the State Department, Kissinger just snarled up the machine. He sat in his paneled office on the seventh floor at Foggy Bottom; he was surrounded by a bodyguard of able young assistants, only one a career Foreign Service officer; on any problem, he would ask those involved to write everything they knew and send it up to this staff. Nobody outside the inner circle knew what Kissinger in the end saw. And there was no feedback at all. "Working for Kissinger is a one-way street," a senior State Department official said.

But intelligence, of all trades, has to be a circular process: The analyst is half blind without knowledge of his own government's policy concerns, objectives, and limitations. Less than a month after Kissinger took over at State, one of its most senior intelligence analysts warned him that he would have to open up in his working methods. Kissinger promised that he would. He didn't. To be fair, Kissinger was very new in the job: his working methods might improve in time. But for a crucial two weeks, his new subordinates were very unhappy.

Technically, U.S. and Israeli intelligence were excellent. To monitor Egyptian preparations, for instance, Israel had devices near the front line in Sinai—sophisticated electronic gear supplied by the United States. Back in Israel itself, manning the computers that unscrambled the findings, were ex-members of the United States' own electronic espionage establishment, the National Security Agency (NSA), working on swiftly supplied Israeli passports for double their American salaries. The NSA itself monitored Middle East radio traffic from a base in southern Iran, supplemented—because the atmospherics over the Persian Gulf gave reception problems—by spy ships in the Mediterranean. "Nobody made any mistake about the facts," Kissinger has said.

But after the facts comes their interpretation, and as Kissinger also said: "Facts are easier to come by than intentions." The failure was to divine Arab strategy. This has been denied. One of Israel's most distinguished soldiers, Lieutenant General Haim Bar-Lev—ex-Chief of Staff, Cabinet minister at the outbreak of war, and architect of the Bar-Lev Line—has claimed "no lack of knowledge" of Arab intentions. Another source close to the military establishment asserted that "Israel knew even the time of the attack." But a senior Israeli intelligence officer came much nearer the truth: "We were caught on the hop," he said.

Background briefings given to foreign correspondents in Israel during the ten days before war demonstrate the continuing power of "the concept" and the political belief in "deterrent" borders. Senior Israeli political figures stressed their conviction that the Arab leaders were not militarily ready for war. The Arabs might "miscalculate" and launch an attack, one such briefing admitted. But if so, they would doubtless be defeated. Israel, a senior politician giving one such briefing concluded with supreme overconfidence, was "not interested in war"; the Arabs, the implication ran, therefore would not be.

By a somewhat more empirical path, the U.S. intelligence community reached the same conclusion. On September 30, at Kissinger's request, one of his staff asked the State Department's own Intelligence and Research Bureau (INR) for an evaluation of the Syrian buildup on Golan. The INR's paper in reply went up the same day. So did a paper from the CIA. Neither was as blithe as Kissinger afterward claimed. INR's paper found the Syrian deployments, even viewed in conjunction with Egypt's moves, "inconclusive." But it was principally after surveying the political portents that the INR analysts, while not "optimistic" that there would be no attack, concluded that it was "dubious" whether there would be one "at this time"—a qualification that the analysts regarded as important.

The CIA's assessment was much the same: the Syrian buildup, in conjunction with the Egyptian maneuvers, was potentially "very ominous"; but the CIA's conclusion was "10 per cent less alarmist than INR," according to one of those who saw the papers. In reaching this conclusion, the CIA was heavily influenced by Israel's own confidence. "Our error was to accept Israeli reassurances about Arab intentions," we were told.

As further evidence of those intentions, however, the analysts looked closer to home: to the United Nations, where a new session of the General Assembly had just opened.

To the Arab and Israeli foreign ministers assembled for this opening, Kissinger—with all the hubris of a man about to accept the Nobel Peace Prize for "settling" Vietnam—announced that the United States was now anxious to assist "practical progress" toward a Middle East settlement. A lunch he had given for Arab envoys on September 25 was declared to have been his first diplomatic move. (He had, in fact, done considerable homework in private, as we shall see.) And in private talks in New York through the end of September, Kissinger did get somewhere. "The Arabs seemed more relaxed and self-confident than I have seen them for a long time," a senior UN official privy to these talks said later. The Israeli and Arab foreign ministers secretly agreed that sometime in November—the date to be fixed after the Israeli elections—they would meet under Kissinger's auspices to thrash out "a course of procedures" leading to substantive negotiations.

The intelligence analysts were fooled. The gloomy INR assessment back in May had, after all, attached great weight to progress at the UN. "The Arabs' interest in diplomacy seemed so great that we were misled," a Washington intelligence man said. "We had the right factors, but we didn't weigh their priorities correctly." Reading the intelligence assessments, Kissinger also thought the Arabs would give his particular brand of diplomacy a chance. (Since Sadat's original intention had been to back both the military and the parallel diplomatic initiatives, perhaps the most powerful of Kissinger's Arab contacts, Egyptian Foreign Minister Mohammed Zayyat, *was* desperately eager for last-minute progress—knowing in general terms what lay in store if he failed?) Whatever the motives, though, the effect was that, as the evidence of crisis mounted, Kissinger was—in the pithy phrase of a Washington columnist—"unusually ready to duck."

That day, September 30, as U.S. intelligence uneasily decided that war was unlikely, Egypt's War Minister Ismail sent a warning signal to his Syrian opposite number, Defense Minister Mustafa Tlas. The Syrians had still not been told the exact date of Y-Day. Now Ismail warned Tlas that his forces should be ready for action at any time within five days of dawn on October 1. The attack would be signaled, he said, by the cabling of the single code word "BADR."

In the early hours of Monday, October 1, Syrian tanks and heavy artillery began to move up from their rear positions to deploy opposite the Israeli outposts. Already installed to protect them were the missiles Dayan had warned about, now interlocked into a formidable air defense system the length of the Golan front. Simultaneously, along the Suez Canal the Egyptian "multi-arm exercise" at last got under way—at times even observed by the Israeli troops along the Bar-Lev Line (among them Avi Yaffe and his comrades opposite Ismailia). It was Y minus 5: The final countdown to war had begun.

Israel was unruffled. From their observation post high on the seven thousand-foot ridge of Mount Hermon, Israeli troops could scan eastward as far as Damascus and peer down on the Syrian armor marshaling unhurriedly across the rocky plain below. The Syrians exploited this: They mobilized in *defensive* formation. The Syrian tanks were positioned "hull down," dug in to resist an assault rather than to mount one. Their medium artillery was placed back, to cover not Israeli but Syrian territory—again apparently signifying defensive action. As Dayan admitted later, Israel was fooled.

Even some units that Syria had previously stationed on the Jordanian frontier had by now been moved to Golan. This "bolstering of forces," as Israeli "informed sources" tactfully phrased it, was merely a gesture of goodwill toward the Jordanians in the wake of the détente between the two countries. No Syrian "initiative" was expected. The next day, October 2—Y minus 4—Syria called up its reserves. And over the following twenty-four hours, United Nations observers on the Suez Canal saw Egyptian officers on the bank openly instructing their troops. At last the Egyptian division commanders were summoned to military headquarters in Cairo and told Operation BADR was on. It was Y minus 3.

That Wednesday morning, October 3, the Israeli Chief of Staff, Elazar, briefed Israeli newspaper editors on a tour of the Navy. For the first time, he revealed the extent of the Egyptian and Syrian concentrations along Israel's borders—"hundreds of thousands of troops, all fully equipped," one editor recalls him saying. Elazar added that the Syrians, at least, were drawn up in defensive formation. But the same editor recalls him warning that they could redeploy into offensive formation at any time. The Chief of Staff ended on an optimistic note, however: According to the concerted Israeli intelligence estimates, he said, the Arabs did not intend to start a war.

Elazar was wrong. One Israeli intelligence officer *had* spotted Egypt's real intentions. But Elazar could not possibly know that. The officer's conclusions had been suppressed by his superiors in military intelligence.

It was on Monday, October 1—the day when the Egyptian maneuvers at last began and when Syrian armor moved up to the Golan front—that Lieutenant Benjamin Siman-Tov, a young intelligence officer at Southern Command headquarters, prepared a paper entitled: "Movement in the Egyptian Army—the Possibility of a Resumption of Hostilities; October 1, 1973." Siman-Tov, whose responsibility was of course solely the Sinai front, summarized all that was known about the Egyptian preparations. What precisely swung his opinion has remained secret. But he seems to have spotted several facts that at least pointed to more serious Egyptian intent than mere maneuvers, and in some instances were actually incompatible with that interpretation. Siman-Tov concluded that the "multi-arm exercise" was a camouflage for Egyptian war preparations.

Having submitted that first paper, Siman-Tov was not unnaturally sufficiently concerned to continue working on the problem—now combing back through data gleaned even before the first Egyptian movements had begun on September 21. On Wednesday, October 3—at approximately the time when Chief of Staff Elazar was reassuring Israel's newspaper editors—Siman-Tov handed in a second paper: "Situation Report on the Egyptian Army; September 13–October 2, 1973." Basically, it was an expanded version of his first paper. But Siman-Tov guessed amazingly accurately. From September 13—which, as we have said, excellent sources in Cario now claim was the date on which Sadat and Asad decided on war—Siman-Tov detected a consistent pattern of activity in Egypt pointing to war preparations. His two reports were suppressed.

Siman-Tov's boss, the intelligence officer of Southern Command, Lieutenant Colonel David Gedaliah, found them simply heretical. The analysts of military intelligence research department at General Staff headquarters had decided that the Egyptians were engaged in an exercise. Siman-Tov's conclusions must therefore be

invalid. It was a vicious circle. Siman-Tov's papers would normally
have been distributed to headquarters. Gedaliah sat on them.

Not that Israel's politicians—or even the majority of its General
Staff—were any more skeptical. On that Wednesday afternoon, as
Gedaliah rejected Siman-Tov's frightening conclusions, Israel's top
leadership met.

In the Israeli Cabinet, as in any other, the doctrine of collective
responsibility glosses over the practical fact that some ministers
are more equal than others. This was especially true in Israel,
where the rival demands of factions within Mrs. Meir's rickety
Labor coalition had produced the absurdity of a Cabinet so big
that it contained rather more than a third of all the coalition's
members in the Knesset. The inner Cabinet that, inevitably, had
resulted—Mrs. Meir's "kitchen Cabinet," it was called—varied in
composition. But that afternoon, its most powerful members met:
Mrs. Meir herself; Deputy Premier Yigal Allon; Defense Minister
Dayan; and Minister without Portfolio Israel Galili, a man almost
unknown outside Israel but one of Mrs. Meir's closest political
confidants. The military contingent was Chief of Staff Elazar;
Zeira's assistant in military intelligence, Brigadier Arie Shalev
(Zeira was ill that day); and, on some accounts, the head of the
secret service, Zamir.

Dayan was worried. That was why he had asked Mrs. Meir to
call this special meeting. Elazar was worried too. So, apparently,
was Zamir. But calculation of the likelihood of war clearly hinged
upon the question whether the Syrian deployment was coordinated
with the Egyptian maneuvers. And on this point, Shalev—representing Israel's only intelligence evaluation unit—necessarily
presented the authoritative view. He said that the two movements
were unconnected, and he concluded his briefing with the words:
"The possibility of an Egyptian-Syrian attack is not, in my personal view, likely, because there has been no change in the Arabs'
assessment of the balance of forces in Sinai such that they could
go to war." In other words, the Egyptians could not believe that
they could win, therefore they would not try. It was "the concept"
in its purest form. And nobody at that meeting seriously challenged it. The military intelligence conclusion became that of the
meeting: The buildup across the canal was "an Egyptian exercise:
low probability of enemy-initiated war."

That still left open the question of what the Syrians were doing. Ironically, the Schonau raid provided one answer. Perhaps the Syrians, having known of the raid beforehand, had massed these forces to deter the almost inevitable Israeli retaliation? As for war, "the concept" held, of course, that Syria would not start one except in conjunction with Egypt. At the meeting, it was apparently the secret service chief Zamir who questioned at least that tenet. He had, he said, a suspicion that the Syrians meant business. But even Zamir did not dissent from the unanimous conclusion that the chances even of this were low.

Chief of Staff Elazar did raise the question of partial mobilization—just in case the Syrians meant business. He did not actually propose mobilization, just talked of it. The suggestion was thus turned down without its ever having been seriously discussed.

There was yet another meeting in Israel that Wednesday: an evening session of the full Cabinet. Those ministers not in the "kitchen Cabinet" were not even told of the Arab buildup. The meeting was devoted to Schonau. Mrs. Meir had just returned from Strasbourg—where she had torn up a scheduled speech to the Council of Europe on "Israel's disputes with the Arabs" and instead talked impromptu for 2½ hours on Schonau. She had then flown home via Vienna, in an abortive attempt to persuade Chancellor Kreisky to change his mind.

Israel's ambassador to France had, as protocol demanded, accompanied Mrs. Meir to Strasbourg. When she mentioned her desire to see Kreisky, he argued with her. Kreisky, he said, was too committed now to change his mind. And the diplomat knew, from his secret cables, of the Arab buildup. Her place, he told Mrs. Meir, was back home. She disagreed. "The Russian immigrants are so important to Israel," she said, "that if there is a 1 per cent, even half a per cent, chance of changing Kreisky's mind, I must try." The ambassador's son was one of the first Israeli soldiers to be killed on Golan. As one Israeli minister remarked afterward: "That week, you would have thought Israel's front line was not Suez but the Danube."

In Cairo, with appropriate symmetry, the Egyptian Cabinet too had its only meeting of the week on Wednesday—an innocuous discussion of the proposed Egypt-Libya merger. In Egypt, also, the momentous military news was kept from most of the Cabinet.

Moreover, when U.S. and Israel intelligence had found the Arab maneuvers "inconclusive," they had not realized how detailed was Egypt's deception strategy. "In every war, there are two plans," Ismail said later, "one an operations plan, the other a decoy plan. I believe we succeeded in planning our decoy plan at a strategic and at a mobilization level—and we fixed its timings to parallel the operations plan and its timings and movements." The CIA might have found the exercises more conclusive, for instance, had they known that Ismail was sending out a brigade in the morning but only bringing back a battalion, a third of the men, at night—"to give the enemy the impression that the force had been on training duty and come back after finishing it," Ismail explained. Two thirds of the men, in fact, remained in battle position. The Cairo paper, *Al Ahram*, announced that officers could take leave to perform the Moslem *omrah* (little pilgrimage). The *Al Ahram* editor, Mohammed Heikal, knew a good deal of the Egyptian plan: He agreed to run this decoy news, he later said, as "a patriotic duty."

"I also made a point," Ismail went on, "of delaying our crossing equipment as much as possible. Taking out such equipment from its depots at an earlier date would have been enough to alert the enemy to our intentions. We had even made special crates for some of this equipment so that nobody could detect that the huge trucks carrying them were engineer corps trucks. And when this equipment did finally come to the canal, by night, it was at once put into pits which had been specially dug for the purpose." The Egyptian Chief of Staff, Shazli, was surprised that these decoys succeeded so well: "The last three days were especially difficult, but we did not expect the enemy to be taken in as easily as he was."

According to Shazli, the decoy strategy hinged primarily upon repetition. Egyptian reservists had been called up and then demobilized, he claims, twenty-two times through the summer. So why should the twenty-third occasion, on September 27, excite the Israelis? Similarly, bridging equipment, he claims, had repeatedly been brought to the canal and taken away again—"Israel was used to its presence." And the buildup of key assault troops was disguised by random movements along the length of the canal.

Even so, according to Shazli, the plan envisaged that Israel might guess what was afoot three days before the planned assault. He refuses to say what the Egyptians thought would happen then. But according to other senior officers, the attack could have been launched by October 3. And, if it were discovered, the hope seems to have been that Israel would launch a preemptive air strike— during which the Israeli aircraft would be lured into prepared "destruction zones" of hidden missile batteries. (To conceal the most important of these camouflaged SAM sites, Shazli ordered that their radar be switched off, so that Israeli electronic reconnaissance should not pinpoint them.)

The most effective Egyptian camouflage was, like the Syrians', misdirection. Egypt, it was said as often as possible, feared an *Israeli* strike in retaliation for Schonau. Egypt wished to be ready: hence the preparations. The alibi was plausible. It may even have been true. There is some evidence that Israeli Chief of Staff Elazar, only four days before the war, was indeed occupied in planning a reprisal for Schonau. According to this information—from the Chief of Staff of a Western army close to the Israelis—the reprisal was to have been an air strike against the nation that bankrolled the guerrillas: Libya. If true, that would certainly have underlined Israel's proclaimed determination to strike at the guerrillas wherever they might be found. But it would have been exceedingly ironic. Sadat had still told Qaddafi nothing of the countdown to war.

But, however confident the politicians, by the next day—Thursday, October 4, Y minus 2—a pessimistic conviction was spreading among the active service units of the Israeli Army. At Bir Gifgafa, the main Israeli air base in Sinai, there was a lunch that day for senior officers of Southern Command. It was the custom for the guest of honor—on this occasion, one of their number who was retiring—to reply to the toast with platitudes. This lunchtime, the officer said simply that he did not, in fact, expect to be leaving: He thought war was about to break out.

In Washington, the mood was just as edgy but less decisive. That Thursday, the U.S. intelligence agencies had their last chance. Accounts of what happened differ. Once source claims that the agencies' main forum, the U. S. Intelligence Board, met that afternoon. Another source says it was just the normal weekly meeting of the board's "watch committee." Either way, it took place at the CIA headquarters, just outside Washington at Langley, Virginia. The main item on the agenda was the Middle East.

Since receiving the September 30 papers on the Syrian dispositions from INR and the CIA, Kissinger had asked no further specific questions about the progress of the buildup. He had gotten the daily INR bulletins as a matter of course. And Assistant Secretary Joseph Sisco, with day-to-day responsibility for Middle East affairs, had been briefed more than once by INR staffers—these informal views he had presumably relayed to Kissinger. But no other formal assessments had been drafted by INR or the CIA. On Thursday morning, Kissinger asked INR for another full-scale review.

As the agencies pooled their thoughts at the Langley meeting, however, they made little progress. The Soviet Union had just launched from its pads near Archangel a Cosmos satellite to orbit specifically over the Middle East. That proved they were worried too—and the U.S. intelligence men envied their satellite program. (Had the meeting known that this was only the first of six satellites that the Soviet Union would launch in the next three weeks, it might have reached a different conclusion. A satellite launch takes almost two weeks of preparation: The Soviet Union was getting ready for something altogether bigger than the U.S. analysts imagined.)

Ironically, Israel provided the crucial reassurance. Shortly before the meeting opened, the CIA had received from Israeli intelligence a fresh assessment of the Arab buildup. The Israelis outlined the most recent troop movements; detailed with some precision the battle order now massed along Israel's borders; and reported other news of the Arab logistics buildup at the rear. Reflecting the "kitchen Cabinet's" view of the day before, however, the assessment concluded that the chances of war breaking out were "low" to "remote."

Apart from the high regard in which Israeli intelligence is held in Washington, the Langley meeting seems to have felt that by virtue of the Israelis' position—they, after all, faced the grimmest penalties for failure—their opinions carried special weight. So although most of those at the meeting found the Israeli report a trifle insouciant, they were prepared to accept, broadly, its conclusion. Indeed, the group closest to the Israelis—the Pentagon's

Defense Intelligence Agency—still disputed even the threatening nature of the Arab buildup. (The three top men on that agency's Middle East desk were subsequently transferred.)

Late that Thursday afternoon, INR gave Kissinger its interim verdict: Though uneasy, it stopped well short of predicting war. Given the six-hour time lag between Washington and the Middle East, that assessment was delivered at approximately the moment when Thursday turned to Friday in the Middle East—and the imminence of war was further confirmed. Late on Thursday night in Cairo, roadblocks were set up around the pleasant suburb of Zamalek, the Nile island that is the favored home of foreign diplomats. In convoys of official cars, the families of Egypt's Soviet advisors drove to the airport and began to evacuate. The Soviet airlift out of Damascus began a few hours later. Meanwhile, through the early hours of Friday, the Syrians redeployed—into offensive formation. The heavy artillery, previously grouped in the northernmost sector of the Syrian line, now moved south to cover the length of the Israeli front. Ismail had sent Defense Minister Tlas the long-awaited signal: BADR. It was Y minus 1.

7. Mrs. Meir Takes a Risk

The last thirty hours to war are the most critical and the most mysterious period so far as Israel is concerned: critical because decisions the Israeli Government made or did not make then conditioned its Army's responses through the first five days of war; mysterious because strangely little has emerged about those decisions. As we write, major questions remain unanswered: It may be a long time before the pressures of Israeli politics bring all the facts to light.

By Friday morning, new information had come in from two, perhaps three, sources. At last light on the day before, the Israeli Air Force had carried out its most detailed and extensive reconnaissance flights over the canal front so far. There is some evidence that the Air Force did this on its own initiative. According to Western intelligence officers who were briefed after the war—and it is confirmed by Shazli—the Air Force had run more frequent but essentially normal reconnaissance flights from mid-September to Wednesday, October 3. At that point, the Air Force apparently became really worried by what the flights were recording: hence the special effort late the next day, Thursday, October 4. The examination of the films from this latest survey went on all through Thursday night. But before midnight, the Air Force had become convinced that war was now imminent. The new films revealed that the Egyptians were moving up bridge-laying and water-crossing equipment once again.

Around breakfast on Friday, October 5, these pictures were shown to the head of military intelligence, Zeira—now recovered from his illness. Meanwhile, the first reports had come in of the evacuation of Soviet personnel. And it looked as if, at first light on that Friday morning, the Soviet naval contingents at Port Said and Alexandria had also set sail. One well-informed Israeli source also claims that, late the day before, a specific warning of the danger of war had reached Israel from a foreign and "highly reliable" source. What this source was—if it existed—we do not know.

Zeira relayed all this to Chief of Staff Elazar, who as promptly told Dayan. Hurriedly, the Defense Minister and the Chief of Staff met. Dayan had by now swung to a suspicion that some sort of attack was indeed imminent. But would it be a limited Egyptian raid to capture perhaps a few Bar-Lev forts, with perhaps the accompaniment of a Syrian artillery barrage? Or would it be a full-scale war?

These were questions that Dayan and Elazar could not decide on their own. Shortly after 11 A.M., Dayan, Elazar, and Zeira trooped into Mrs. Meir's office to discuss the new turn in the crisis with her. In the short interval between the two meetings, Elazar had already ordered further military precautions.

The Army had been on low alert since Dayan's warning on Golan nine days before. Now—around 11 A.M., according to his own account—Elazar had put the Army on "the highest state of military preparedness." (This is not quite correct. Elazar put the forces on Alert State 3, the most intense alert since the ending of the War of Attrition, but not the highest possible.) He had also canceled the leave of those serving soldiers due to go home for Yom Kippur—though that was too late. By the time the order got to the front line, most of them had already set off. And Elazar had warned his logistics teams that a callup of reservists was possible. In fact, the Air Force—with a far smaller proportion of reservists than the Army—had been so alarmed that it had discreetly called its own up, by telephone, the day before.

Elazar told the meeting in Mrs. Meir's office what he had ordered. Thus reassured, the four participants reverted to the basic question: would there be an attack? At this point, there was a mysterious misunderstanding. Dayan turned to Zeira and asked if military intelligence were using "every possible source" of intelligence. Zeira replied that it was. This was incorrect. Zeira was not utilizing one possible means of obtaining information. What this was the Israelis have contrived to keep extremely secret. All that is known is that these "additional measures" were at Zeira's disposal; that they might have revealed "important complementary information"; that Zeira's rejection of these means was "a most important operational decision"—and one on which he should have consulted Elazar. Elazar knew nothing of what Zeira had done.

But Zeira then further reassured Dayan. He agreed that the information so far looked ominous. But he reported that he expected further information from another important source in a few hours. For his part, Zeira concluded, he still thought that war was of "low probability"—even "lower than low."

Elazar apparently agreed. The Chief of Staff seems to have accepted that some limited Egyptian attack probably would take place. But in that event, he assured the meeting, the regular forces already in Sinai could hold their own until the arrival of the reserves. On that, he reported that senior reservists in the armored corps were already being called in and briefed. But he concluded: "The mobilization of reserves and additional measures are being held back until there are further indications"—presumably those Zeira was expecting to receive.

Clearly somewhat nonplused by the evident impossibility of reaching any firm conclusion—and needing Cabinet approval of any decision on mobilization—Mrs. Meir now decided to hold a full Cabinet meeting. It was too late. Several ministers—including such heavyweights as Deputy Premier Allon and Finance Minister Pinhas Sapir—had already dispersed to the country in preparation for Yom Kippur next day. Mrs. Meir decided to go ahead with whichever ministers could be rounded up in time. Around noon on Friday, this final meeting began. As well as Dayan, Galili, and Elazar, there were the ex-Chief of Staff, Lieutenant General Haim Bar-Lev, now Minister of Commerce, and Shimon Peres, Minister of Transport and Communications. They met in Mrs. Meir's office in the old government compound in Tel Aviv. According to Peres: "It was the shortest discussion I can recall. We were unanimous in our decision not to mobilize."

But the meeting was unhappier than that. Elazar related what he had done: the imposition of Alert State 3; the briefing of those reservists who were commanders of armored units; the cancellation of leave; and the readying of the Air Force. But the intelligence picture was still hazy. The assessment Elazar gave the meeting was almost precisely that which INR had given Kissinger a week before: While not confident that there would not be a war, Elazar was just as uncertain whether there would be one.

Against that background, it was a delicate question whether to disrupt the hallowed calm of Yom Kippur by calling up the reserves. A decision was taken against this. The official version—repeated, properly, by Peres—is that nobody dissented. The truth is that Elazar was overruled, but did not protest. Afterward, Elazar barely attempted to conceal this. Had the reserves been called up "twenty-four or forty-eight hours earlier," he said on November 11, the war would have "undoubtedly looked different." He added the explosive point that casualties would also have been fewer. But, he said, the decision was taken at "the highest political-military level." "We will never know whether the war would have broken out had we called up the reserves," he concluded. Barring quite improbable self-abnegation, Elazar was putting the boot in. But why he had now changed his mind, to favor at least partial mobilization, is unclear.

Dayan's role was crucial to the decision against it. Mrs. Meir hinted as much on Israeli television on November 16: "When somebody who was authorized to propose mobilization came, I agreed at once." The authorized person was the Minister of Defense. Dayan later sought to defend himself, in front of a tense meeting of officers on November 14, by saying that on Friday he did not think there would be war—"I was not the only one to think so, and I did not hear anyone say that war was about to break out that day."

This was correct. Remarkably, the meeting was still worried less by the Arab buildup itself than by the Soviet advisors' departure—and even this, they thought, had its hopeful aspect. "It was clear that the Russians had no intention of taking part in what was to happen," one source close to the meeting said after the war. "This was an encouragement and a worry at the same time." (It should also be recorded that in Washington various CIA personnel were awakened early that Friday with news of the Soviet departure; they dismissed its significance.) Elazar had been suggesting precautionary measures only.

Still, Mrs. Meir did plan for trouble in one respect. As the meeting broke up and the ministers prepared to disperse throughout Israel, she instructed Cabinet Secretary Michael Arnon to find out how every Cabinet Minister could be contacted, if necessary, over the holiday. Then the meeting dispersed—to prepare for Yom Kippur.

Down through the Israeli Army Elazar's alert had already passed. Some senior reservists had been called in. The briefing of "Arik" Sharon was fortunately untypical. But, then, so was Sharon. Until his retirement from the Army three months before, Sharon had become—through twenty-six years of intermittent warfare—undoubtedly the most popular military leader among the Israeli Army rank and file. Yet the Army's upper echelons found him undisciplined and incautious; and it surprised few but himself when he was passed over as a potential chief of staff. Disappointed, Sharon had decided to quit the Army and run for the Knesset; since then he had energetically set about welding together the Likud, a coalition of right-wing opposition parties. Now, at 11:30 A.M. that Friday morning, Sharon had been summoned from his ranch outside Beersheba to Southern Command headquarters, to be shown the latest air reconnaissance pictures, with their signs of a big buildup of water-crossing and bridging equipment. Sharon, according to his later account, told his division officers: "I think there is going to be war in one or two days."

He was so sure of this that he wanted to mobilize his reserve division at once. But the Southern commander, Major General Gorodish "Shmuel" Gonen, had no orders to permit that. It was difficult for Gonen. Only four months before, Sharon had been Southern commander and Gonen his subordinate. Nor did Sharon now hide his opinion that he should be promptly reinstated. As Gonen overruled Sharon's desire to get moving at once, there was a tense clash of wills. The scene was set for worse confrontations to come.

If most briefings were mercifully smoother than that, there were still bad hiccups in the alert procedure: Israeli commanders as senior as brigadier were somehow never warned. Much farther down the line, though, old sweats like tank sergeants got to know what was afoot. As one tankman told the Jerusalem *Post* on the first day of fighting: "We were told before Yom Kippur that we could expect something big."

But how big? A further indication of what was in store now reached Elazar. In that flap early on Friday when the reconnaissance pictures were first scanned, Elazar had ordered military intelligence to prepare another full-scale assessment of the situation on both fronts. The analysts had worked flat out. By 1:35 P.M. the summary was ready. The section detailing the Syrian buildup was remarkably inconclusive. But the Egyptian section was hair-raising. Prepared by the Egyptian desk of the research department under Lieutenant Colonel Yona Bendman, the Egyptian section contained forty paragraphs. The first thirty-nine spelled out, in great detail, what Bendman himself later admitted were "all the signs you could wish for indicating offensive intentions." But Bendman's conclusion, in paragraph 40, read: "Though the actual taking up of emergency positions on the canal appears to contain indications testifying to an [Egyptian] offensive initiative, according to our best evaluation no change has occurred in the Egyptian assessment of the balance of power between their forces and the I.D.F. [Israel Defense Forces]. Therefore, the probability that the Egyptians intend to resume hostilities is low." It was, yet again, "the concept" in full bloom.

Shortly after 2 P.M., Elazar was telephoned at home. The report was read over to him. By now thoroughly alarmed, Elazar telephoned the Air Force commander, Major General Benjamin Peled. What happened next is the subject of some dispute. Sources close to Elazar say that the conversation went like this:

Elazar: "Benny, how long would it take you to get into a state of readiness for a quick strike?"

Peled: "If the order were given now, we could be in full operational readiness by tomorrow morning."

Elazar: "I give that order. Put the Air Force on a war footing."

But sources close to Peled report a different version. They claim that Peled already had put the Air Force on to a war footing. They claim that, as soon as he had heard Elazar's account of the latest intelligence summary, Peled wanted to prepare a preemptive strike at once. Elazar, it is claimed, turned the request down flat. But he did apparently allow Peled to prepare to launch a preemptive strike the next day, should the signs of Egyptian preparation for war have by then become conclusive. Elazar, it is said, was heavily swayed by the continuing confidence of military intelligence.

We have not been able to decide between those versions. But

a sliver of evidence in favor of the latter is perhaps contained in the opinion, attributed by excellent sources to the Israeli judicial commission of inquiry into the war, that Bendman's paragraph of conclusion was responsible for deterring several of Israel's top military and political leadership from decisions they would otherwise have agreed to.

Bendman's conclusion had one final consequence. At 5:30 P.M. —as dusk fell and across the land the Kol Nidre service signaled the start of Yom Kippur—one Western military attaché was still contemplating with something like incredulity a cable he had just dispatched to his own government. It reported the result of a top-level briefing he had just been given on the military situation. The latest authoritative view, he cabled, was that the chances of war were just 2 per cent.

In New York that Friday evening, Kissinger completed the last of a two-day round of talks with the Middle Eastern foreign ministers gathered at the United Nations. And the final phase of Ismail's decoy plan worked perfectly. Everyone knew of the Arab buildup. But everyone also knew that the Cairo daily *Al Ahram* was headlining the news that Egypt was preparing *defenses* against an Israeli retaliation for Schonau. And this was believed. Even the Israeli Foreign Minister, Eban, told Kissinger that the Arab moves were "defensive." So unconcerned was the mood that Kissinger's top aides in New York—Sisco and his senior press spokesman, Robert McCloskey—volunteered to cancel their scheduled flights back to Washington and instead to stay on and help Kissinger prepare a speech he had to deliver the next week. In Washington, the INR had still not quite completed the full-scale assessment of the Middle East situation that Kissinger wanted. But hearing of the trio's decision to stay on in New York, the analysts relaxed: They would finish it in the morning. Apart from working on that speech, Kissinger aimed to have a quiet weekend in Manhattan, broken by nothing more taxing than a couple of parties. Around Friday midnight, he settled down in his thirty-fifth floor suite at the Waldorf Towers. In Israel, it was 6 A.M. on Saturday, and over Sinai the sky was already paling. It was Y-Day.

For Israel, the crisis had already begun—with one or possibly two telephone calls. Around 4:30 A.M. on Saturday, Chief of Staff Elazar was woken by the military intelligence chief, Zeira. One of the Mossad agents had finally obtained the Arab plan. Egypt and Syria would strike at 6 P.M., Elazar was told. The attack would be simultaneous on both fronts.

Elazar telephoned Dayan. At this point the mystery of the second telephone call remains. According to by far the best-informed version of events yet published in Hebrew (*Hamechdal*, by seven Israeli journalists), Dayan already knew, having himself been telephoned at almost the same moment as Elazar by an informant in an unspecified country overseas.

Even at this early stage, the arguments now began. Elazar wanted immediate full mobilization and a preemptive air strike at least against the Syrians—the Golan front being the more vulnerable. Dayan replied that they could issue neither order without Mrs. Meir's authority, and that he was against both. He telephoned Mrs. Meir and woke her with the news.

Such contradictory timings have been offered of the events that followed that the only firm conclusion is that, predictably, none of the participants kept an eye on the clock. Our timings represent the most plausible compromise between such conflicts.

Sometime approaching 6 A.M. Dayan and Elazar arrived at Military headquarters in Tel Aviv. It looked as if the secret service might be right. Over the past hour or so, Israeli monitors had picked up from Syria the unmistakable radio traffic patterns of units preparing. Mysteriously, the Egyptian front was still quiet. Israel was not to know—until interrogation of prisoners revealed it in the war—that in Egypt the secret of Y-Day was so tightly kept that even brigade commanders were not told until 4 A.M. that Saturday morning, and battalion commanders not until 9 A.M. But Ismail had been right not to trust Syrian security. It later emerged that the Israelis—by means not disclosed—had managed to hear quite junior Syrian officers phoning relatives in Lebanon in the dawn hours of Saturday, warning them not to come to Syria that weekend.

After listening to the reports coming in for about forty minutes, Elazar was convinced that Israel faced a major assault on both fronts. He had already put in hand the preliminary stages of Israeli mobilization. But Elazar and Dayan could still not agree on what scale the mobilization should be. A difference of objective defined the dispute. Elazar was sufficiently alarmed by what he now reckoned was the likely scale of the assault to believe that full mobilization—or something approaching it—would be necessary. He foresaw that Israel would give ground in the first stages of the assault and would have to counterattack later. For that phase, Israel would need all its reserves.

Dayan disagreed. He thought that the forces Israel already had on its front lines could hold the enemy until the reserves had arrived. No major counterattack phase would be needed. The only reserves that should be mobilized, therefore, were the minimum necessary to mop up any pockets of trouble. Dayan suggested the calling up of two armored brigades, according to *Hamechdal*. Elazar promptly appealed to Mrs. Meir. It was now 7 A.M.

Dayan and Elazar set off to Mrs. Meir's home shortly after 8 A.M. Mrs. Meir had already summoned her indispensable advisor, the minister without Portfolio, Israel Galili; he arrived shortly after the other two. Last of all came the ex-Chief of Staff, Bar-Lev.

By now, the desert sky was fully light. Elazar was desperate to launch his preemptive strike while the pilots would still have some advantage of early surprise. With Dayan's backing, Mrs. Meir vetoed the plan. "How many friends would we have left if we did that?" she asked Elazar. Her Chief of Staff—and perhaps Bar-Lev—argued back emotionally. "Every time we decide to take into account the opinions of others, we have to pay for it in blood," one Israeli source quotes them as saying. Mrs. Meir pressed the counterargument. If Israel struck first, she would have to persuade a remarkably skeptical world that this was not simply a rerun of 1967. How could she *prove* that the Arabs had been planning to attack? It was an indication of how shaken Mrs. Meir had been by the spasmodic toughness of Nixon and Rogers—and of how little faith she placed in the new Secretary of State, Henry Kissinger.

Dayan produced technical arguments against. Given its likely political damage, a first strike was only worthwhile if it could inflict irreparable damage on the Arabs. That had been achieved in 1967. But the Egyptian Air Force had been lined up on the runways then. Now Egypt's aircraft were hidden either in underground hangars or—the combat-ready formations—under specially-built concrete "hangarettes" of Soviet design, affording almost total protection from aerial attack. And to knock out the Syrian Air Force did not need a preemptive strike.

As for a first strike against the assembled armor and artillery, Dayan argued that, at best, Israel could only hope to disrupt the Arab preparations for a few hours. And the pilots would be flying against an alert enemy protected by a lethal missile screen. For an uncertain gain, the losses Israel might suffer could affect her air-strike capability through the rest of the war. (As we have said, that seems to have been precisely what the Egyptians had calculated.)

Thus forbidden by Mrs. Meir to order a first strike, Elazar was then—to his despair—forbidden to order full mobilization either. Again, Dayan was his opponent.

Contingency plans exist for three methods of mobilization in Israel. Each strikes a different balance between secrecy and speed. The slowest but most secret is mobilization by letter. Next comes callup by courier—in which one man contacts ten, ten contact a hundred, and so on. The last, swiftest, but least secret method is to mobilize by means of code words broadcast over Israeli radio. Dayan pointed out that a general mobilization, such as Elazar wanted, would now have to be by this third, broadcast method. But the Arabs would learn of Israel's intention at once. Supposing *they* then struck—and claimed afterward that they had done this only because Israel's sudden mobilization proved that it was about to be done to them? We have already noted that an element of paranoia is understandable in Israeli thinking.

Moreover, Dayan remained confident that the troops already in position could hold their ground against the first assault. He thought the policy Elazar had put in train on Friday—briefing the reserve armor commanders—would suffice. Israel need only mobilize its tank crews, Dayan said. So, arguing fiercely, Elazar got permission only for partial mobilization. (Loyal in the midst of war, Elazar defended the decision later that day at a private briefing of Israeli newspaper editors. "I accepted it," he said, "not only because I as an officer carry out the policies of the civilian government, but also because I was persuaded that full mobilization would be a blunder." In fact, Elazar secretly took it upon himself to call up more reserves than the morning decision had specified.) At 9:05 A.M. Elazar telephoned the callup orders from

Mrs. Meir's house. Mobilization was to begin at 10 A.M.—the interval allowing the necessary preparations: the opening of ammunition stores and so on.

For most of the civilian population of Israel, the realization that this was to be no ordinary Day of Atonement had already dawned. At 7 A.M., a Phantom roared low over Jerusalem heading north to survey the Golan. (Other flights headed across to scan Suez.) At the Wailing Wall, relic of the ancient temple in Jerusalem, early worshipers looked up, shocked and frightened. To break Yom Kippur in that fashion was unthinkable—unless the unthinkable were about to happen. Rumor spawned rumor throughout Israel in the hours ahead, until anxiety was like a smell seeping through the air.

The tight handful who shared the secret knowledge had now gathered in Mrs. Meir's office in Tel Aviv. With military preparations under way, the problem they confronted was political. If Israel was not to strike first, how could they ensure the international diplomatic advantages they hoped this would confer? Shortly after 8 A.M., Mrs. Meir had telephoned the U.S. ambassador in Israel, Kenneth Keating. Could he please come to her office in Tel Aviv? Keating had not been long in the job and was thus not yet as trusted as his predecessor, who had been in Israel for so many years as to have gone virtually native. But Keating had for almost twenty years represented New York in Congress—and New York, as the joke ran, had more Jews than Israel. He was thus in a position to talk frankly to Mrs. Meir.

Both the American and Israeli governments have kept very quiet about what followed. But it looks as if a simple but deadly threat was relayed to Mrs. Meir by Keating. Mrs. Meir told him that Israel had "proof" that Egypt and Syria were planning to attack at 6 P.M. "Are you going to strike first?" Keating asked. "Emphatically not," Mrs. Meir replied. But as Keating explored the topic, Mrs. Meir did not hide that her military were unhappy with this decision. (According to one Israeli military source, Elazar still hoped that—should the Arab preparations continue—he might get permission for a strike at 1 P.M.)

According to political and military sources in both Israel and the United States, Keating warned Mrs. Meir that if Israel did strike first, the United States would feel unable to supply fresh equipment. It was put diplomatically: "If Israel refrained from a preemptive strike, allowing the Arabs to provide irrefutable proof that they were the aggressors, *then* America would feel morally obliged to help," was how one source described Keating's message. The threat was the same.

Behind this *démarche*, two strands of American thinking are apparent. The first was simply that the United States was as we have seen, skeptical about Arab intentions—and Keating reflected that doubt. As one Israeli source, describing those last hours, blandly put it: "Not everybody agreed with Israel's assessment of the situation." The United States was the only party whose agreement mattered. Second, the United States hoped that if it was clear that, this time, the Arabs were the aggressors, world opinion would prevent a shutdown of Arab oil to Israel's allies.

So Keating fell in with Mrs. Meir's next suggestion. Perhaps, after all, the Arab story was true. Perhaps—as *Al Ahram* had been headlining—the Egyptians were convinced that Israel was about to strike in retaliation for Schonau. In that case, Mrs. Meir would reassure them. Or, if they were contemplating war on their own initiative, Mrs. Meir would warn them. She requested Keating to pass an urgent message to Nixon and Kissinger for them, in turn, to pass to the Arabs and to the Soviet Union. Israel did not intend to strike first. On the other hand, Israel knew all about the Arab plan to attack at 6 P.M. Israel was prepared. Keating went back to his embassy to send the message. It was Mrs. Meir's gamble for peace. Having made it, Mrs. Meir relented on the question of reserves: Elazar at last got permission for full mobilization.

(When the full Israeli Cabinet finally convened at noon—to be told not only that mobilization was under way and a war was imminent, but that the inner circle of ministers had known for days of the growing threat—the rest of the government was too stunned to do other than acquiesce in Mrs. Meir's policies.) It was her early decision that Mrs. Meir hinted at on Israeli television on November 16 when she said: "I think that so far as everything that happened—including the need for equipment and the obtaining of equipment—had the situation not been clear beyond the shadow of a doubt regarding who began hostilities, I doubt whether the vital equipment received in the course of time would have flowed in as it did, as it still continues to do . . ." But if

Mrs. Meir really had any hopes that Kissinger could save the situation, she was disappointed.

By now it was past 10 A.M. Deputy Premier Allon had arrived back in Tel Aviv, summoned by Mrs. Meir's staff. Israel could now gear its government for war. There was no question who the ruling *troika* would be: Mrs. Meir, Galili, and Allon. Nor was there much question what areas of responsibility each would cover. Galili already acted as Mrs. Meir's personal foreign policy advisor: He took charge of that field. Allon—a veteran of the first, illegal, Jewish militia in British-run Palestine and commander of its striking arm, the Palmach, at independence—took direction of military affairs. Both reported to Mrs. Meir. (Allon was still bitterly resentful that he had been told nothing of the impending crisis until October 3. For three days before that, while Mrs. Meir had been at Strasbourg and Vienna, Allon had been Acting Premier. But Dayan had kept the secret of the Arab preparations so tightly guarded that, even then, Allon was not put on the circulation list of the daily military intelligence summaries. Thus the most senior politician then in Israel had known little more than the lowliest newspaper reader.)

The first task the *troika* now set in hand was to alert Israel's representatives in the United States. Israel would need not only political but also financial support. And in the unlikely event of the war not ending with an Israeli victory within a week, Israel would also need to pursue Keating's implicit promise of war materiel.

At 10:30 A.M. Dayan telexed the Israeli military attaché in Washington, Major General Mordechai Gur, warning him of an expected Arab attack at dusk. It was a few minutes after 5 A.M. in Washington when the message arrived. It threw the embassy into something approaching panic—heightened by the mischance that the ambassador, Simcha Dinitz, was in Israel for the funeral of his father.

But the embassy had at least kept in touch with the Arab build-up. (The Israeli intelligence reports to the CIA seem to have passed through their hands.) Israel's foreign minister, Eban, on the other hand, had been out of Israel for ten days—mainly at the United Nations—and, like Allon, he too had been told nothing of the mounting crisis. Now Galili had to contact Eban, asleep in the

Plaza Hotel in Manhattan, through the New York office of the Israeli consul-general. Galili's message told Eban of the likelihood of an attack and asked him to get Kissinger to soothe the Arabs. When Eban was awakened and handed this telex by one of his aides, it dumfounded him. "Get me Kissinger," he said. But it was now after 6:30 A.M. in New York. Kissinger already knew.

At 6 A.M.—noon in Israel—Kissinger was awakened at the Waldorf Towers by Assistant Secretary Joseph Sisco and told, as Kissinger later recalled, that "a war might be imminent." But who had told Sisco? One Israeli source claims that Gur had phoned him but Washington sources say Sisco was awakened by the State Department Operations Room. But what happened to Keating's cable passing on Mrs. Meir's plea? Recounting his 6 A.M. awakening, Kissinger referred obliquely to this cable at a press conference on October 12: "We were informed *somewhat earlier* [our italics] that Israel did not intend to attack herself, but that did not indicate to us necessarily that an Arab attack was imminent." Thus Kissinger implicitly differentiated between the Keating cable and the message that led to his waking. (And Keating's message cannot have arrived later than 5:15 A.M.) But Kissinger's comment that the message "did not indicate to us necessarily that an Arab attack was imminent" cannot be correct. One strand of Mrs. Meir's message to Keating had been her assertion of Israeli "proof" of an Arab attack plan.

In effect, Kissinger was saying that Washington was skeptical of Mrs. Meir's warning. He gave two explanations for this. The first was his accusation of a major failure in intelligence—and we have shown that he somewhat exaggerated the extent of this failure. But as his second reason Kissinger added, a trifle plaintively: "Nor was the possibility of hostilities raised in any of the discussions with either of the parties that took place at the United Nations during the last week [before war]." It looks very much as if Kissinger's confidence that he had struck up a relationship with the Arabs strongly colored the American response to those first intimations of crisis.

Once alerted by Sisco, however, Kissinger did get busy. According to what he later told the editor of *Al Ahram*, Kissinger first telephoned the CIA—to learn that they too had just picked up information that led them to expect war. Then, around 6:07

A.M., Kissinger phoned President Nixon at the Florida White House.

But did some crannies of Washington have many hours' more warning of the crisis? There is the mystery of Dayan's 4 A.M. phone call. There is no reason to doubt that it existed. The Israeli authors of *Hamechdal* first reported it. Our own inquiries have since confirmed it. So, independently, did work by Eric Rouleau, the distinguished Middle East correspondent of *Le Monde*. Rouleau felt able to state definitely what everyone else was told but had been unable to prove: that the call came from "a high CIA official." Rouleau will now specify only that his source was "very highly placed"—but, perhaps significantly, his articles after the war were extremely well informed about Allon's view of these early events. Rouleau does add, however, that his source might not have been aware of the existence of, say, the DIA—the Pentagon's Defense Intelligence Agency—besides the CIA. So confusion is possible there. But that the call came from Washington, no inquirers in Israel now doubt. Yet 4 A.M. in Israel that Saturday, when the call came, was of course 10 P.M. on Friday night in Washington. Kissinger's aides insist, however, that he, at least, had no intimation of danger until he was awakened by Sisco. Was there a serious failure of communication in Washington? And, if not, who did call Dayan?

It is doubtful, of course, whether Kissinger could have staved off war even with an extra six hours to parlay in. Still, he tried. When Sisco and McCloskey reached the Waldorf Towers just after 7 A.M., Kissinger was still barefoot. He had only bothered to don shirt and trousers before making his first calls. One of them was to the Soviet ambassador, Anatoly Dobrynin. The Soviet was stunned—he had not even known of the departure of the Soviet advisors. He promised to pass the message from Israel to the Arabs through whatever channels the Soviet Union had—and so keen was he to contact Moscow fast that Kissinger laid on a special telephone linkup for him. But Dobrynin scoffed at the idea of direct Soviet involvement in the conflict. Kissinger was still on the telephone at 9 A.M. when the CIA reported that fighting had been in progress for an hour.

But who had started the fighting? Israeli intelligence itself had spoken of an Arab plan to attack at 6 P.M. The war had started at

2 P.M. The inference was clear. Kissinger phoned Eban. According to the authors of *Hamechdal,* there ensued the following memorable exchange. "Mr. Eban," Kissinger said, "this minute I got a message from the CIA to say that war has begun and that battles are raging on the Suez Canal front. I suppose it wasn't you who began it?" Eban: "I do hope there was no irresponsible action . . ."

For some hours, at least, Kissinger was convinced that the Israelis had mounted another preemptive strike—as a witty fragment of evidence demonstrates. Late on Saturday, Riyadh radio broadcast the text of King Faisal's reply to the cable Kissinger had sent him, asking for Saudi Arabia's good offices to persuade Sadat and Asad to stop fighting. Faisal took the chance to repeat the guts of Kissinger's message: "I have received a message sent by Your Excellency," Faisal wrote, "which says that, on the strength of a report emanating from Israel to the effect that Egyptian and Syrian forces had been planning to launch a coordinated attack on the Israeli forces, Your Excellency became certain when land and air clashes actually took place between the Egyptian and Syrian forces on the one hand and the Israeli forces on the other, that it was Israel which started the attack . . ." Faisal, quite aware of the truth, must have had a lot of pleasure reading that cable from Kissinger.

With tragic irony, the Israeli secret service had been too good— and not quite good enough. Until four days before the war, Ismail's plan had indeed been to attack at 6 P.M. Then the plan changed. "For several reasons," Ismail said later, "most important of which was to have the sun in the eyes of the enemy, the Syrians preferred to begin at the first light of dawn. But for several reasons also—not only the direction of the sun, but the necessity of setting up bridges and moving tanks across the canal under cover of night—we [Egypt] preferred to act at sunset." On Tuesday, October 2—Y minus 4—Ismail had flown to Damascus to reach a compromise. Both sides settled on 2 P.M. So Israel's intelligence was three days out of date. And as a result the Israelis stood to lose, in the eyes of their most crucial ally, the hoped-for political gains from abandoning a first strike. Kissinger did not believe them.

Watchtower
Firing position 3
Firing position 4
Mortar position 3a
Suez Canal
Dining room
Store
Command bunker
Disused bunker
Men's sleeping quarters
Showers
Firing position 2
Gate
Blast wall destroyed by shelling
Firing position 1
Israeli armored personnel carriers destroyed by shelling

1. Artist's reconstruction of the bunker where Avi Yaffe and his colleagues were surrounded for sixty hours.

2. Avi Yaffe with his portable tape recorder pictured after his escape from the surrounded bunker in the Bar-Lev Line.

3. June 1973: President Sadat visits the canal and takes a long look at the Israeli positions. He had already decided on war. Behind him is General Ismail, planning the attack of four months later.

4. Hussein, Asad, and Sadat at the Arab summit on September 10, at which differences were settled and the objectives of war were determined.

5. Golda Meir on a prewar visit to the canal. With her is General Bar-Lev, creator of Israel's canalside defensive line.

6. In the elaborate underground command center from which Egypt ran the war: Sadat with Generals Shazli (left) and Ismail (right).

7. Scattered over the arid, undulating wastes of the Sinai, between the ridge and the canal, Israeli tanks await the start of massive battles. On the horizon, toward the canal, smoke rises from unceasing bombardments.

9. Egyptians march from their canal bridge into Sinai. The gaps in the massive sand ramparts were blasted by water cannon smuggled in from Europe.

8. Short-lived moment of joy for Egyptian troops when they first crossed over to Sinai. Israel's failure to prepare for war, and the profusion of Egypt's new weapons, destroyed Israeli defense plans.

10. Meanwhile, 250 miles to the north, the Israeli tank crews held out in the grim battle for Golan.

11. A Skyhawk over Golan. The Israeli Air Force was decisive in blunting the Syrian attack, but a high price was paid against the SAMs.

12 and 13. The appalling toll of the Golan fighting: seven Israeli Centurions knocked out on a single road, and the common graveyard of three Syrian T-62s.

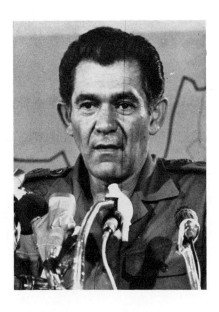

14, 15, and 16. The morale battle: General Elazar makes his "break their bones" speech and the opposing Chief of Staff, General Shazli. Moshe Dayan, Israel's Defense Minister, tours the Golan front.

17. Machine gun guard over Kuneitra, center of the Syrian assault.

18. Egyptian troops storm through the Bar-Lev fortifications on the first day of war.

19. The Israeli infantry begin a counterattack over the salt marsh by Kantara.

20. After an Israeli naval strike on the Syrian port of Latakia—the listing Japanese cargo ship was one of the victims.

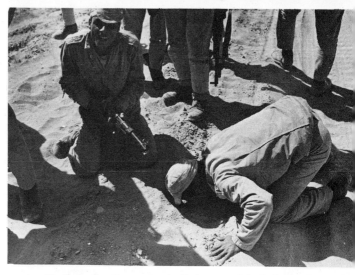

21. Kissing Egypt's recaptured soil: the apex of the Arab triumph.

22. A briefing in Golan: The Israeli officer is using a carefully hand-drawn, though not very accurate, map of the Damascus plain.

23. A small column of Israeli tanks, part of Sharon's task force, drives toward the canal, where they would lead the most daring stroke of the war, the crossing into the Egyptian heartland.

24. Death of a tank commander hit by an infantry-launched Syrian missile.

25, 26, 27, and 28. In the lull of war: A brief respite before battle in a shelter improvised from pipeline sections; a briefing interrupts an improvised shower; a religious service in the desert; and—as the situation eases in Golan—a girl entertainer gives a concert for an Israeli armored unit behind the front line.

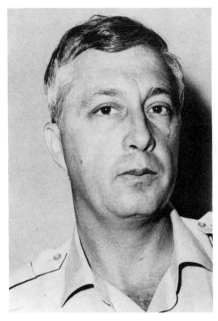

29. General "Arik" Sharon quarreled with his commander. "If they fire me," he said, "I'll join up under another name."

30. Israeli troops and Egyptian prisoners under fire near the canal.

31. At last the tanks roll freely across the canal bridge at Deversoir, belatedly established by Sharon's task force.

32. Attack on the seven thousand-foot stronghold on Mount Hermon, the key observation post overlooking the Golan plateau and Damascus.

33. Men of the Israeli Golani Brigade wave triumphantly after winning the epic battle to recapture Mount Hermon, the highest peak of Golan, just eight hours before the cease-fire.

34. Aftermath of the bloody Mount Hermon battle. The body of a Syrian soldier lies in the wreckage of the Mount Hermon ski lift.

TWO

THE NEW ARAB GOES
TO WAR

1. The Y-Day Onslaught

The first casualties in the fourth Arab-Israeli war were not, so far as we can trace, any of Avi's fellow Israelis along the Bar-Lev Line stunned by the sudden Egyptian assault across the Suez Canal. They were Arab villagers, among them a mother and child. And they were casualties of the coordinated Syrian assault on Israel launched over the Golan plain just two minutes before the attack by Egypt began.

At 1:58 P.M. on the afternoon of Saturday, October 6, five Syrian MiG-17 fighters skimmed into attack low over the Israeli positions along the northernmost sector of the Golan lines. It was cool and cloudy, and the Israeli tanks were unmanned, their crews chatting beside them, the more religious reciting the Yom Kippur afternoon prayer. As the fighters opened up with cannon and rockets and the crews leaped into their tanks and hurriedly revved up, it crossed their minds that this was not a particularly impressive first strike by Syria. But at the northern end of their strafing run, the MiGs, their cannons still firing, curved away over the Druze village of Majdal Shams in the Mount Hermon foothills. A young mother, who had run out of her house to stare up in surprise at the sound of gunfire, was killed by a cannon shell, which also smashed the legs of the eight-month-old baby she was carrying. Several other villagers were killed or wounded.

As another wave of fifteen to twenty MiGs—part of the initial strike by 100 aircraft—swooped over the Israeli positions, Syrian fighter-bombers made low-level attacks on the Israeli brigade headquarters 10 miles behind the front line at Naffak. (That was its Arab name; Israel had "Hebraicized" it to Nafad.) Then, at precisely 12:05 P.M.—at the moment when, 250 miles to the southwest, Egyptian commandos were scrambling down the Suez banks to launch their rubber assault dinghies—a barrage of artillery fire crashed down from the Syrian batteries massed on the Golan plain. Now the extent of the crisis facing Israel became brutally clear. The Syrian gunners were "walking" the curtain of fire toward the squadrons of Israeli tanks hastily assembling at their firing stations. And through the continuous explosions flung up by the shells, the Israeli tank commanders peering over their turrets could see a rolling dust cloud, in the middle of which they faintly discerned the outlines of hundreds upon hundreds of advancing Syrian tanks.

Plumb in the middle of the Golan cease-fire strip, just north of Kuneitra, was Observation Post "Winter," one of the string of United Nations bunkers stretching down the Golan front. Incredulously, the UN observer in Winter, an Australian, watched a formation of 300 Syrian tanks roll toward him. They were in 4 columns, 2 each side of the road, their turret hatches open and their commanders proudly at attention. "It wasn't like an attack," said the awed observer later, "it was like a parade ground demonstration." As it approached his bunker, the column divided and, like a tide, flowed past his bunker on either side—one fork heading north of Kuneitra, the other south. As they approached the Israelis, it seems likely that one waiting tank commander's recollection of those minutes was echoed by all: "I never knew there were so many tanks in all the world."

At least 700 Syrian tanks went into action along Golan in that first wave: 300 in the thrust down toward Kuneitra, another 400 rolling in an equally daunting display from the south, up the long and utterly exposed road from Sheikh Miskin to Rafid—in all, 2 Syrian armored divisions. Facing them were precisely 176 Israeli tanks—2 armored brigades, both understrength.

What followed will surely, whatever the political consequences of the October war, become an epic in military history; for the United Nations observer—trapped for days in his bunker while the battle raged around him—saw barely a handful of those Syrian tanks return. After 5 days of the most desperate and unrelenting battle since the war that had heralded Israel's birth 25 years before, the Israeli forces had destroyed that Syrian armor and advanced eastward over the Syrians' own defense lines toward Damascus.

The Golan battle was one of the two most critical actions of the war, and it made possible the other, which was Sharon's crossing of the Suez Canal in the second week to disrupt the Egyptian assaults—and ultimately, to encircle one of their armies. While the Syrian armor so urgently threatened its northern front, Israel had not the resources to gamble on an assault like that in Sinai.

In the first phase of the war, therefore, the stories of the two fronts are very different. In Sinai, while isolated bunkers such as Avi's held out—one for as long as eight days—the Egyptians consolidated their hold over virtually the whole east bank of the canal. In practice, Israel had no choice but to let them do so. Its canal defenses were overwhelmed by the weight of the Egyptian attack. Two armored and two infantry divisions crossed the canal in the initial wave. But in Sinai, geography favored Israel. The 125 miles of desert between the canal and the heartland of Israel presented the Israelis with a simple defensive equation: Give ground to gain time.

So in Sinai—after the first terrible forty-eight hours, when the overconfident Israelis learned, first, that this time there would be no dashing victories and then struggled to recover their balance from the Egyptian blows—Israel's initial strategy was to fight a rearguard action as cheaply as possible. In this aim, their greatest allies were paradoxically the Egyptians themselves, who—seemingly startled by their own swift successes and inhibited by a battle plan of inflexible caution—frittered these gains away by waiting far too long to launch the second phase of Ismail's strategy.

On Israel's northern front, however, the geography of Golan presented its forces with none of the options of Sinai. From the front line to the cliffs overlooking Israel, Golan is just seventeen miles deep: To hold it the Israelis had to fight virtually where they stood. This they did, with extreme courage and skill. But Golan presented other—and in the final outcome, more damaging —problems for the Syrians too. While the Suez Canal supplied the Egyptians with a natural defense upon which they could group their successful assault forces on the east bank, Golan was bare of natural features for the Syrians to exploit as fixed strategic positions. To succeed, the Syrians had to fight a war of continuing movement and unceasing assault. That was precisely the warfare at which the Israeli tank crews excelled—as Syria was once more to learn at terrible cost. But the price Israel paid in this war was also high. And the first shattering blow was the collapse of the Sinai defenses.

The battle for Sinai was heralded by four crashing waves of artillery fire from two thousand howitzers and heavy mortars concealed among the dunes behind the west bank of the canal. The assault that followed was concentrated along three stretches: below Kantara in the north; around Ismailia in the center; and, south of the Bitter lakes, from Shalufa to El Kubri (see map, page 138). Amazingly, it achieved almost total surprise. The Israeli Chief of Staff, Elazar, later ascribed this unreadiness to "a serious failure in observing the order for full battle alert at some of the lower echelons." Nobody seems to have told the men on the front line of the imminence of war.

The extent of Israel's unreadiness is more simply illustrated. To man the thirty-one strongpoints and twenty rear posts of the Bar-Lev Line to planned operational strength required at least a brigade of infantry—roughly four thousand men. On October 6, the line was in fact manned by less then one battalion: according to Mrs. Meir, fewer than six hundred men. They were reservists of the 52nd Battalion, 16th Brigade—known officially as the Etzioni Brigade, more commonly as the Jerusalem. Most of them were middle-aged businessmen, many on their last tour before retiring from the reserves. (In view of the bravery with which these men fought, it is a hard—but nevertheless inescapable, and unsurprising—verdict that their training was distinctly rusty.) They had been sent into the line for their annual month's callup, while the regular garrison went on maneuvers in the Negev. But even the 52nd Battalion was understrength: Two hundred of its eight hundred men had been given leave for Yom Kippur. Elazar's order canceling this had, as we said, come too late.

When the assault came, many were, like Avi, washing their clothes—presumably taking advantage of Yom Kippur's break from more martial chores. Others were at prayer. One, Private Unsdorfer, was in a squad so religious that the majority assumed the sudden barrage was some transient local incident and, dashing to their battle stations, continued their service. "We said our Minha prayers in our positions," Unsdorfer recalled. "And when we recited the Shma—'Hear, O Israel'—everybody, even the nonobservant, joined in with great fervor." Indeed, they might have.

In the first assault wave alone, eight thousand Egyptian infantry slithered down the sandy banks and scudded in rubber dinghies over the water toward the waiting Israelis.

Even in crossing the canal, unimpeded by anything worse than small-arms fire, the Egyptians had scored a notable victory—yet the Israelis did not know it. The secret weapon of the Bar-Lev Line was a device to transform the canal into a moat of fire. In the early hours of Saturday, Egyptian commandos had slipped across the water and sabotaged it.

The device was simple. Beneath main Bar-Lev strongpoints was a series of underground oil storage tanks, pipes interconnecting them and finally leading to wide nozzles down by the water's edge. A switch in each strongpoint started pumps to spray the oil over the surface of the canal in a thin film—which a Thermite bomb would then ignite. The blaze would have incinerated any Egyptian assault force.

Egyptian planning to neutralize this had been typically thorough. Reconnaissance patrols had slipped across the canal and discovered the pipes. "Our first problem," the Egyptian Chief of Staff, Shazli, said later, "was to cope with the prospect of the canal turning into an inferno as soon as the crossing started. Experiments we made showed that attempting to extinguish such blazes would require at least half an hour, even supposing no further inflammable material was thrown in." But each Bar-Lev strongpoint could pump two hundred *tons* of oil.

The Egyptians thought of blowing up the tanks, but dropped the idea. "Reconnaissance showed that the enemy stored the material sufficiently underground as a protection against artillery fire." The Egyptian solution was simple. The system was most vulnerable, they decided, at its canal outlets. "Our plan," Shazli revealed, "was to send teams to block these pipes with cement." War Minister Ismail adds that the commando groups slipped over on Friday—probably Friday night. "Our men," Ismail said, "cut off these pipes without the enemy realizing that this was part of a wider plan." (Shazli said afterward that the sabotage squads had also hammered custom-made wooden bungs down the pipes. As an added precaution, the initial assault routes were also chosen *upstream* of those strongpoints equipped with the fire-weapon.)

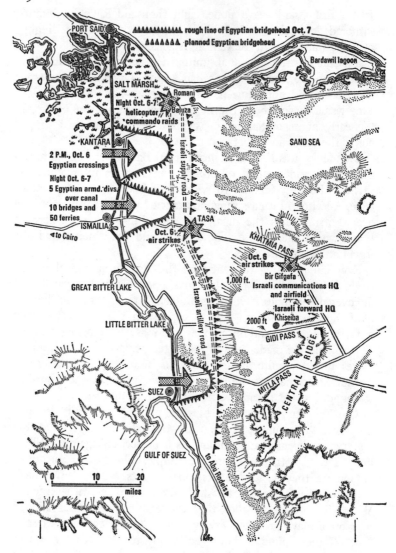

PORT SAID

▲▲▲▲▲▲▲▲▲▲▲▲ rough line of Egyptian bridgehead Oct. 7
▲▲▲▲▲▲▲ planned Egyptian bridgehead

Bardawil lagoon

SALT MARSH

Romani
Night Oct. 6-7
helicopter
commando raids

Baluza

SAND SEA

KANTARA

2 P.M., Oct. 6
Egyptian crossings

Night Oct. 6-7
5 Egyptian armd. divs.
over canal
10 bridges and
50 ferries

Israeli supply road

ISMAILIA

◄ to Cairo

TASA

Oct. 6
air strikes

KHATMIA PASS

Oct. 6
air strikes

1,000 ft.

Bir Gifgafa
Israeli communications HQ
and airfield

Israeli forward HQ
Khiseiba

2000 ft

GREAT BITTER LAKE

Israeli artillery road

LITTLE BITTER LAKE

GIDI PASS

CENTRAL RIDGE

SUEZ

MITLA PASS

GULF OF SUEZ

to Abu Rodeis ►

0   10   20
miles

Map 5 Egypt's assault and objective: October 6–7

But it was not, in practice, the blow that the Egyptians imagined. After the war, the Israelis—embarrassed by the revelation of this device—claimed, first, that the scheme had been tried in 1970 but found impractical and, then, that it had been installed at one point but that all the other outlets were dummies. The truth, according to an Israeli military expert, is that the Israelis did install the complete system, but abandoned it for political reasons. Israel knew that Egypt had gas shells; the Israeli high command was afraid that if Israel used the fire device, Egypt would shell its Sinai positions with gas. So the device was allowed to run down. The Egyptian neutralizing of it stands, however, as an example of their thoroughness and ingenuity.

The main obstacle, of course, was the Bar-Lev Line itself. After the disaster, the soothing Israeli alibi was that the Bar-Lev Line was only intended as a "tripwire"—"simply a forward screen to delay the Egyptian advance," said the ambassador to Britain, Michael Comay. The truth—as proud Israeli officers had told journalists on tours of Sinai before the war—was that the Bar-Lev Line and its associated defenses had been reckoned impregnable. The reason was one of timing, as the Egyptian Chief of Staff, Shazli, later explained: "The Suez Canal is a unique water barrier," he said, "due to the steepness of the banks and their irregularity, which prevent amphibious vehicles from descending into or ascending out of the canal without a way being prepared—a feature shared only by the Panama Canal. In addition, the enemy had piled up a sand embankment thirty to sixty feet high, as well as his defenses of the Bar-Lev Line . . ."

Facing those obstacles, Dayan had predicted any Egyptian attack across the canal would be finished in twenty-four hours. Shazli saw why Dayan believed that. "Dayan made his statement, I believe," he said, "on the basis of calculations that our engineers would need twenty-four hours to establish bridges and that heavy equipment [such as a substantial Egyptian tank force] could not be got across the canal inside forty-eight hours—allowing enough time for the arrival at the front of the Israeli armored reserves." Dayan's timing was in fact faster than Shazli had thought. "I had a theory that it would take them all night to set up the bridges," Dayan said, "and that we would be able to prevent this with our armor." In six swift and brilliant hours on

October 6, Egypt showed how ingenuity plus modern weapons could destroy that Israeli strategy.

To the puzzlement of the Israelis in the Bar-Lev bunkers, almost every man who came scrambling up the rope and bamboo ladders, thrown over the Israeli sand ramparts by the first assault wave, was carrying unusually shaped equipment. Some had tubes over their shoulders; others were carrying canvas-covered "suitcases" either in their hands or strapped to their backs. (According to Shazli, they were each laden with sixty to seventy-five pounds of equipment.) These first troops did not try to capture the bunkers themselves—that was the task of the second wave. Instead, while sappers at once reinforced the blocking of the oil nozzles, the main task of the first assault was to destroy the Israeli tanks positioned along the Bar-Lev Line.

But the positioning of their tanks was the greatest Israeli blunder on that first day in Sinai; for the Bar-Lev defenses were founded upon the idea that each strongpoint would be backed by a formation of tanks, dug in every hundred yards and firing straight across the canal at any assault force bringing up crossing or bridging equipment. But when the attack came, the Israeli armor was not in position. The Bar-Lev Line was stripped of its crucial firepower.

On October 6, Israel had 240 tanks in Sinai, mostly American-built M-48 Pattons. The main unit was the 100 tanks of the 14th Brigade—like the 7th Brigade on Golan, a training unit of skilled regulars. In support were the cadre elements of two other brigades (which Elazar was supposed by now to have reinforced with the earliest reserves). The plan was for the 14th Brigade and one of these other brigades to be up by the Bar-Lev bunkers, while the third brigade remained in the rear—ready to move up when the main axis of any Egyptian thrust became clear.

But when the Egyptian assault came, the Israeli deployment was in fact precisely the reverse of that planned. The 14th Brigade was alone at the front—and barely half of *its* tanks were actually by the canal; the remainder were about five miles behind the bunkers. And the two cadre brigades were still in the rear, only a few miles in front of the mountain passes.

The reasons for this blunder are disputed. The commander of the Southern front, Major General Shmuel Gonen, was certainly responsible. According to Israeli military sources, Gonen had deliberately held his main tank force back from the canal on the morning of Y-Day. He was planning to move them up only at 4 P.M., two hours before the expected attack. When the assault was actually launched, therefore—four hours before Israeli intelligence had predicted it—the order to move had not even been given to the Israeli tank crews. But why did Gonen delay in this fashion? There seems to have been a straightforward military reason: Egyptian howitzers now massed along their bank of the canal could have caused havoc among Israeli armor massed prematurely. But the fundamental reason—at least, according to defenders of Gonen—was political. These sources claim that, anxious to avoid the slightest provocation that might give the Arabs an excuse to attack, Dayan had made it clear to the Israeli military that all overt preparations for war should be carried out only at the last minute. And that, it is claimed, was why Gonen delayed bringing up his armor.

Ironically, the failure was to Israel's advantage. A few tanks were permanently stationed around the bunkers. And in the opening minutes of the new war, they were the first to discover the devastating effectiveness of the strange weapons the Egyptian assault troops carried.

The tubes were the launchers of an advanced Soviet-built bazooka called RPG-7 (literally, Rocket-Propelled Grenade). But the suitcases contained a considerably more sophisticated device: a Soviet antitank guided-missile code-named "Sagger"—directed all the way to its target by signals the soldier firing it transmitted down hair-fine wires unreeling behind the missile in flight (see pictorial essay, The Missile War). Abdul Alati was one of the first Egyptian troops across. He was twenty-three, and before he joined the Army in 1969 he had been a student at an agricultural school. Now he was in charge of an antitank missile unit. According to his account later in the Cairo newspaper *Al Gomhouria*, his unit destroyed eight Israeli M-60 tanks on the Bar-Lev Line within ten minutes. "The tanks accelerated to their maximum speed to avoid our rockets," Alati said. "But we could hit them in their weakest spots as long as they remained in range. Every Egyptian missile was worth an Israeli tank." (Alati pardonably exaggerated: The tanks must have been the less modern M-48s.)

The Israeli tanks were already under a barrage from Egyptian tanks firing from sand ramps on the west bank of the canal. Now, too late, the Israelis realized the point of all that Egyptian building activity—not just to keep troops busy but, as Ismail later revealed, to raise fortifications "capable of detecting enemy positions and controlling the eastern bank as well as the western." The combination of this artillery barrage with the missile attack by the first assault was deadly: Within minutes, the bulk of the Israeli tanks were silenced. As Dayan said later: "Our effort to bring up tanks to the canal to prevent the erection of the bridges cost us very dear. We hadn't anticipated that."

One twenty-two-year-old sergeant, a red-haired tank gunner, was a typical Israeli casualty. He was in the lead tank as his unit frantically drove toward the canal. About half a mile from the water's edge, a shot from an Egyptian tank perched on the opposite ramparts killed his tank commander in the turret and slightly wounded him. He escaped, to take the place of a badly wounded man in another tank. This tank, too, was then hit by three rockets simultaneously. Terribly burned, the sergeant managed to crawl out as the ammunition began to explode.

At 2:07 P.M., Cairo radio announced: "Communiqué 5: Our forces have succeeded in overrunning the Suez Canal in several sectors, seized enemy strongpoints in these sectors, and the Egyptian flag has been raised on the east bank of the canal . . ." (The first four communiqués had dealt with the outbreak of fighting, embroidering a specious claim that Israel had started it.) In fact a whole forest of flags were being raised on the canal bank: Each unit had been issued one to raise when its crossing was accomplished.

Methodically, the Egyptian missile troops now set about their second task. What Shazli called "small buggies, which the soldiers could use to carry awkward or heavier equipment" had by now been ferried across the canal. While the second wave—crossing under heavy fire from the Israelis in their strongpoints—began the assault on the Bar-Lev bunkers with grenades, smoke, submachine guns, and savage hand-to-hand fighting, the missile-troops loaded up their "golf trolleys" and fanned into the desert for nine or ten miles. There they dug in, reassembled their antitank missiles—and produced the third, and most sophisticated, of all their new infantry weapons: the portable Soviet antiaircraft missile, SAM-7. The task of the missile infantry was now, said Shazli, "to hold the ground against counterattack by tanks and aircraft for a period of from twelve to twenty-four hours while we got our tanks and heavy weapons across."

This was the phase Dayan was relying on to delay the Egyptians enough to enable Israel's reserves to intervene. But the Egyptian corps of engineers, under Major General Aly Mohammed, cut Dayan's timing by more than half. Shazli explained how: "The problem was the sand barrier. To make a single hole about 20 feet across in the barrier [the minimum to get tanks through easily] would, we calculated, mean removing about fifteen hundred cubic yards of sand. And we needed to open sixty such holes on the east bank—ninety thousand cubic yards of sand. You must also remember that we ourselves had built a sand embankment over the past six years to guard against a surprise enemy attack. This doubled our problem.

"Our first idea was to use explosives," Shazli said. Ismail adds the detail: "In the course of our experiments for breaking down these barriers we had tried guns of all calibers but we did not get what we hoped for." Shazli continued: "We stuck to explosives until mid-1971, when a young officer in the engineers suggested that we use water under great pressure. This proved to be a superior method, making it possible for us to open holes in a period of three to five hours."

That was the secret background to the Egyptian order for two powerful fire pumps from the West German firm of Magirus Deutz in May 1972. And it was after tests by the Egyptian Army engineers corps that Egypt followed this up with the order for 100 more. It was such a big order that Magirus Deutz quoted the Egyptians the mass-production price: 30,000 Deutschmarks (about $12,500) a pump. As secret weapons go, this one was pretty cheap.

It was also a staggering advance: Shazli does not say, but with bulldozers or explosives the reduction of the sand ramparts would have taken twice as long. But until the fire hoses—fed from pumps floated on pontoons to the middle of the canal—actually began to rip away their sand ramparts, Israel had never taken into account this simple device. Ismail revealed: "We did not bring up the equipment necessary for this until the last moment, so that our secret weapon could remain strictly guarded." (For all Shazli's account of the bright young engineer officer, however, it is hard to believe that his staff did not simply consult the engineers of the Suez Canal administration—the world's greatest experts on sand removal. They had been using pressure jets for years.)

As the hoses bored away the ramparts, Shazli explained, "we had, meanwhile, to trim the banks with explosives and other methods [presumably bulldozer tanks] to make possible the fastening of the bridges." And here too the Egyptian engineers—with the help of Soviet know-how—destroyed Israeli calculations. Old fashioned military bridge-laying is a cumbersome process of bringing alloy pontoons to the bank, floating them into the water, and then marshaling them into a long line with the aid of barges. By rule of thumb, that sort of bridge can be laid at the rate of perhaps six feet a minute: To bridge the canal that way would have taken the Egyptians about two hours. But the Soviets, facing several rivers should they ever decide to invade Western Europe, have a new device. The crossing of the Suez Canal was the first time it had ever been used in combat. The PMP bridge, as it is called, is a series of box-shaped pontoons, each carried on a lorry. The vehicles form a line along the bank and slide their pontoon sections into the water—where they are unfolded to their full width and clipped together, still floating in a line alongside the water's edge. The completed bridge is then swung across the river. As the few Israelis still surviving in their bunkers reported: "It grew across the water like an extending arm." The PMP can be laid at about twenty-one feet a minute, so the engineers could bridge the canal in roughly half an hour. Egypt was heading for a military triumph.

The Egyptian "Operations Command Center" is buried deep underground. This is an eyewitness account: "A military Jeep goes up and down the rugged land. A halt before a sand dune. An opening in the sand dune. At the end, a heavy steel door, like the door of a huge safe. Behind it a long passage. Then staircases going down and down. Another steel door and another long corridor, at the end of which stands a third steel door. Behind it, all of a sudden, the place becomes vastly wide: meeting rooms, operations rooms, communication centers, corridors, map rooms, offices . . ." (The sand dune is, perhaps, dramatic license: The command center is, in fact, just on the outskirts of Cairo.)

To this center, War Minister Ismail had come immediately on his return on October 2 from settling with the Syrians the 2 P.M. timing of Operation BADR. He did not see daylight again for fourteen days. Ismail's office was small, on its door the sign MINISTER OF WAR AND GENERAL COMMANDER. In the corridor opposite his office was a door leading to the main operations room.

The eyewitness, Mohammed Heikal, editor of *Al Ahram*, was stunned: "A big hall it was . . . bright lights . . . the vivid colors of maps . . . maps not merely colors but showing movements too. Around the room stood groups representing the commands of each branch of the armed forces. Behind each group stood its maps and in front its communications links with every front. In the main body of the hall stood a dais for the general command personnel: the Minister of War and Commander in Chief [Ismail]; the Chief of Staff [Shazli]; and the Director of Operations [Lieutenant General Abdel Ghani el Gamasy]. Facing the dais, on the opposite wall, were the main maps showing the situation as a whole. Drawn on large glass panels running the width of the entire hall, they displayed the situation on land; the situation in the air; the situation at sea; the situation on the Syrian front. Minute by minute, as the situations changed, fresh colored touches would be added to the maps. All the time, the sound of communications machines [telex and telephone] clattering and ringing. Voices in hasty discussion. The issuing of orders fraught with important consequences for Egypt . . ."

It was a magnificent center for conducting a set-piece battle—and during the meticulously preplanned crossing of the canal it worked superbly. It was only in the later, more fluid stages of the war that the disadvantages of this overcentralized, Dr. Strangelove command structure began to appear.

"You should have seen this room on Y-Day," Ismail said. "You would have felt then that this room symbolized not only this age but the entire history of Egypt. . . . We were all at our seats. The whole sequence of operations we had planned was displayed in front of us. As messages came from the front, we could see the operations progressing before our eyes: Such-and-such a task has started, such-and-such a task has been fulfilled. . . . From two o'clock the scene in this room was exciting to the limit. The work was carried on with more precision than anybody could have imagined—efficiently and daringly. There were moments when feelings were shaken to the core, but we did not allow ourselves to be swept by emotion. . . . Our nerves had to remain cool and intact. Any confusion at headquarters would unbalance the entire operation."

President Sadat was also in the command center as Operation BADR unfolded. "For the first three hours," he said, "I was under terrific tension, frozen. We didn't know what the Israelis had in store. What new weapons did they have? But after three hours it was clear that the Israelis had not mobilized and had been totally surprised. Our troops made their crossing over the steep canal sides . . ."

Laying its bridges for the northern assaults between Ismailia and Kantara, Egypt's Second Army was on schedule. But, in the south, the Third Army hit trouble. The hosed sand turned to mud; the pontoons could not be anchored firmly; and the first tanks across bogged down. By 5 P.M. the Third Army was stuck. Ismail took drastic action: "I sent the commander of the engineers himself [Major General Aly Mohammed] to positions on the bridgehead of the Third Army and instructed him to have the job completed at any cost. The job was completed, although his deputy commander was killed over on one of the bridges." An Israeli air strike hit him. The Third Army's tanks, meanwhile, had to cross at Ismailia, and scurry forty miles south through Israeli-held Sinai to cover these bridging operations.

Even without that crisis, the engineers' achievement would have been extraordinary. "In a period of between six and nine hours," according to Shazli, "our engineering corps carved out sixty holes, established ten bridges, and set up fifty ferries." This was not as many bridges as Ismail had wanted—he did not think ten gave him enough insurance against damage from Israeli air or artillery bombardment—but by dusk on Saturday, it was clear that the missile infantry was holding off the first Israeli counterattacks. "Dayan really miscalculated the ability of infantry to fight off tanks and low-flying aircraft and to hold onto territory for long periods without heavy equipment," Shazli remarked later. The way was clear for the crossing of the Egyptian armor.

This phase, too, had been meticulously prepared. Shazli again: "Signal cables had been strung across the canal from the very first moments of the assault. Different colors were used to indicate each unit's route, and our forces had been trained in these details before the operation." Under cover of darkness, Egyptian tanks and missiles began to pour across the canal. By midnight Saturday, after ten hours of war, Egypt had assembled on the east bank of the Suez Canal five hundred tanks and a forward missile defense system. "The whole operation," Shazli said, "was a magnificent symphony played by tens of thousands of men." In less grandiose terms, it was the high point of Egypt's military achievement in the war.

2. The Citizen Army Musters

For Israelis at home, the nightmare began with an air raid warning just after 2 P.M. As sirens wailed over every city and settlement, people halted, almost involuntarily looked up at the clear blue sky, then ran to the nearest radio set. Israeli radio does not broadcast on Yom Kippur, but at 2:40 P.M. the Home Service broke its silence: "The IDF [Israeli Defense Forces] spokesman says that at about 1400 today Egyptian and Syrian forces launched an attack in Sinai and the Golan Heights. Our forces are taking action against the attackers. Because of Syrian aircraft activity in the Golan Heights sector, sirens can be heard all over the country. These are genuine sirens. . . . Orders have been given for the partial mobilization of reserves . . . necessary emergency orders . . . in view of the state of emergency, everyone who has no need to move on the roads, should refrain from doing so . . ." Then there was classical music, with a promise of further bulletins every fifteen minutes. All morning, there had been rumor, anxiety; everyone knew someone who knew someone who had been just called up, but nobody knew why. (In the first phase even of that morning's partial mobilization, the logistics teams are called up first; they in turn supervise the later phases of the operation.) News, any news, was now almost a relief. Nobody in Israel will ever forget the hours that followed.

Shalom, a twenty-five-year-old studying for a Ph.D. at Hebrew University in Jerusalem, was visiting friends with his fiancée, Sara. "A neighbor ran down the stairs, shouting 'It's war.' Almost immediately, before we could react, the air raid sirens started. We went down into the street. There were lots of people around but nobody knew what was happening. I think like me they were stunned, couldn't believe it. . . ." Shalom went home. He was a lieutenant in the reserves and knew he would be called.

Israel had no need to keep its callup secret now. The radio began to blare the code words of units being mobilized: "Sea wolf, Sea wolf . . . Stewpot, Stewpot . . . Meat pie, Meat pie . . ." Shuki, a twenty-three-year-old trainee architect, was with friends in the center of Tel Aviv when the sirens went: "I ran all the way home, about a mile and a half. I arrived just in time to hear my unit's callup sign broadcast." The courier system was still in operation too, for who hears the radio in a synagogue? In the residential quarters of Israel's cities, military Jeeps growled to a halt as couriers got out to scan house numbers. All over Israel, services were interrupted as men in military uniform appeared at the synagogue door with lists in their hands. In the synagogue of Beit Hakerem, a suburb of Jerusalem, the sexton called for silence to read the list of names handed him. One was that of his own son. In the Sephardi Synagogue in Jerusalem, a young man rose from his place when his name was shouted from the door. His father, sitting next to him, embraced him, refused to let him go. The rabbi unclasped the father's arms and tried to comfort the weeping man. "His place is not here today," he said. Young men set off hitchhiking to their bases, leaving their fathers to clear the junk from the air-raid shelters. Shuki in Tel Aviv was frantic to obey his callup: "But my mother was bustling around preparing food for me to take and she wouldn't let me go until it was ready. There was enough food for a small army."

Motley attempts at uniforms flourished: a major in full service dress except for pink suede boots; an artillery sergeant in a T-shirt proclaiming "Let's go Mets," the fans' chant for the New York baseball team. Everyone tried to cobble up a facsimile of uniform: The Army outfitters were notorious—it was said they only had one size of trousers. Nobody wanted to go into battle in that sort of discomfort.

Family men took their wives and children to stay with relatives. Farewells were carefully phrased—not goodbye, but *lehitraot* (*au revoir*). Those not called up were impatient. Many drove to their units without being asked. Others were like Shuki's father: "He is also a reservist but his code word had not yet come over the radio. I think he was upset that I was going to war before him. He telephoned one of the officers in his unit but was told to wait at home until he got the call. He drove me to the main road where I thought I could hitch a lift."

Outside the country, Israelis and Jews besieged El Al ticket desks at airports. But the El Al fleet was grounded in Israel for Yom Kippur and, anyway, Lod Airport had just been closed until further notice. (When, next day, flights did restart, reservists had priority, then doctors, then journalists and television crews.) Perhaps the most remarkable callup was that of a man charged with forgery, who had skipped bail and fled from Israel earlier in the year. He was a lieutenant in the reserves and, overcome by patriotism—and possibly reasoning that, if convicted, he would certainly get a reduced sentence in consequence—he flew back to Israel. The immigration authorities arrested him at once, but the magistrate was so impressed that he accepted the man's own surety and sent him to join his unit—to stand trial, if he lived, when the war was over.

As Israel drove to war through the gathering dusk that Saturday afternoon, it looked like some "transport through the ages" tableau: commandeered private cars; aging buses; bread vans; removal trucks; the large open vans known as Tnuva trucks, after the dairy organization that runs them. Men drove themselves to the front: One of the *Sunday Times* reporters on Golan later saw an abandoned Dormobile with a cello in the back—its owner had been playing in a symphony concert away from home and drove straight to his unit. The roads began to jam with traffic. The Arab service stations in east Jerusalem—open as usual on Yom Kippur—did a roaring trade. By the roadside, soldiers were thumbing lifts, the more devout still wearing their prayer caps and shawls and clutching packets of sandwiches to eat when the fast of Yom Kippur ended—though the rabbis had hastily blessed food and transport for the war effort.

Ambulances began clearing the hospitals, ferrying the noncritical cases back to their homes. Doctors rushed to report to emergency military medical units. The civil defense authorities warned everyone to stick tape across their windows and observe blackout precautions. By dusk, pavement cafes had reopened; and knots of customers sat and talked in the gathering darkness.

As the blasts of the ram's horn *shofar* signaled the end of Yom Kippur at sunset, groups of young teen-agers and old people still worshiping at the Wailing Wall broke into a *hora* dance. A police loudspeaker halted them. "Please disperse immediately to your homes. Happy New Year and good health to you and your families," said the officer. Suddenly, the streets were deserted of young men. "A war has begun," said the rabbi at Katamon; "let us pray for our soldiers, may God give them courage and protect them."

At that moment, Israel's reservists were battling with their own Army more than with the Arabs. Despite ten days of supposed alert, preparations for the mobilization were chaotic. Not only were 10 per cent or more of Israel's tanks being serviced, that is routine maintenance loss, though an alert is supposed to override standard checks—but even the serviceable tanks in the vehicle parks at Beersheba were, in fact, unusable. Their gun barrels had not been cleaned of the grease applied in storage to protect them from desert grit. Ammunition posed as bad a problem: Stocks were low, and its storage was too concentrated. Israel, with the third-largest tank force in the Western world, had about the same number of ammunition depots as, say, Portugal. Long lines of trucks filed outside the store gates. Some tanks drove into battle with half loads of ammunition. When the tanks were loaded and fueled, transporting them posed further problems. In civilian guise, Israel's tank transporters carry phosphate from the Dead Sea quarries. Not all of them had been called up. Anyway, Israel had only the standard ratio of about one transporter for every three tanks. As for Israel's boast—"nobody in this Army walks"— one infantry unit drove across Sinai on a milk float.

Sharon's experiences capture the frantic atmosphere of those first terrible hours. At 9:30 A.M. on Saturday—half an hour before the callup began in earnest—Southern Command HQ telephoned Sharon at his ranch once again, this time with the order to mobilize that he had sought in vain the day before. "My uniform was still in the back of the car," he said, "so I put it on and rushed to HQ." But when the order to head for the canal finally came at 2:00 P.M., Sharon's tanks—the first were by now ready to roll— were stranded by the shortage of tank transporters. His division, Israel's vital reserves in Sinai, had to set off across the desert roads on the tracks, grinding forward—damaging the tanks and exhausting their crews—at a painful average of twelve miles an hour.

Sharon himself headed down later that day in a civilian pickup truck driven by a journalist drafted as a war correspondent.

In part, such shortcomings were inevitable in an Army in which the front-line forces so outweigh the backup infrastructure. As its tiny population dictates, Israel's Army is all teeth and no tail: The price is paid precisely in such emergencies. But if there were avoidable failures too, the single stark fact that Israel could not escape was that, even with the broadcast method of mobilization at last adopted, there was no way of bringing a significant proportion of reserves into battle in less than twenty-four hours. Israel was trapped without its citizen Army.

By 6:15 P.M., Israel's leaders should have known the war was going badly. Understandably, Mrs. Meir, speaking on radio and television, glossed over the shambles of unpreparedness: "Citizens of Israel, at around 1400 today the armies of Egypt and Syria launched an offensive against Israel. . . . The IDF is fighting back and repulsing the attack. The enemy has suffered serious losses. . . . They hoped to surprise the citizens of Israel on the Day of Atonement while many were praying in the synagogues. . . . But we were not surprised. . . . A few days ago the Israeli intelligence service learned that the armies of Egypt and Syria were deployed for a coordinated attack. . . . Our forces were deployed as necessary to meet the danger. We have no doubt about our victory but we consider the resumption of the Egyptian-Syrian aggression as tantamount to an act of madness. . . .

Equally predictably, Mrs. Meir did not question what the war was about: "Citizens of Israel: This is not the first time that we are facing the test of a war imposed on us. We must all be prepared for every burden and sacrifice demanded for the defense of our very existence, freedom and independence. . . . The victory of the IDF is the guarantee for life and peace."

Israeli morale was further bolstered by Moshe Dayan who, single eye glaring into the cameras, radiated aggressive confidence: "In the Golan Heights, perhaps a number of Syrian tanks penetrated across our line and perhaps they have achieved here and there some occupation, but no significant occupation. . . . Although we had a number of losses and hits here and there, the situation in the Golan Heights is relatively satisfactory, more or less, in my opinion. In Sinai, on the canal, there were many more Egyptian forces, and the problem there is different altogether. . . . This is a large area. . . . There is no chance whatsoever of protecting every meter. . . . Since they began the war they succeeded in crossing the canal. . . . We are prepared for such a situation tomorrow. . . ."

But it was Dayan's peroration that was to do most damage to his reputation. "We should know that this is a war and we are prepared for the transition period, which is relatively short and then to rely on our forces . . . so that the Egyptian action of crossing the canal and north of the canal will end as a very, very dangerous adventure for them. . . . We had losses but, relatively speaking, this was more or less what we estimated to be [likely in] the first day of fighting—which will end with victory in the coming few days. Thank you."

Dayan and Mrs. Meir should have known by then how critical Israel's plight was. Dayan, as we shall see, must have had some idea. Yet the extraordinary fact is that none of the Israeli leaders yet fully grasped the magnitude of the military crisis. The high command had always envisaged that, in the opening phases of any new war, the small regular Army would have a tough rearguard action on its hands until the reserves arrived. Had Israel's leaders yet realized the scale of the Arabs' assault—or the deadly effectiveness of their new weaponry—the truth might have dawned earlier. But that first evening, Mrs. Meir and Dayan really thought that Israel's position was about par for the course so far. The reality was that, in Sinai, the Egyptians held the initiative and were in a position to dominate the battlefield—even to take the crucial passes—by morning. And on Golan the Syrians had broken through. There was nothing to stop them from crossing the Jordan.

3. No Ground to Give

As they crashed through the high wire fences of the cease-fire line, the first Syrian tanks did not pause by the bunkers, where unbelieving Israeli infantry clutched their inadequate weapons. The opening artillery barrage was drowned by the roar and screech of the tanks' engines and tracks. Days later one Israeli officer still recalled the onslaught in shocked tones: "They flowed in like water, finding their way wherever they had the chance."

The coordinated Syrian armored thrusts struck across the Golan lines at two separate places—one thrust spearing southwestward along the Kuneitra road; the other scything northwest from Rafid toward Khusniye (see map, page 157). Then both thrusts divided. The attack on Kuneitra separated into the classic pincer movement that so impressed the UN observer in Observation Post Winter. The other attack separated even more sharply: Two hundred tanks wheeled southward along the Golan border, where cliffs drop steeply down to the Yarmouk River; the other two hundred continued straight on through Khusniye toward Naffak. For both main thrusts, Naffak was a key objective. It was the headquarters of the two defending Israeli brigades. It also controlled the main route from Golan into Israel—the historic trade route, in fact, from ancient Damascus to Cairo.

The terrain of Golan, as it slopes to the Damascus plain, is flat, gray and barren—a basalt plateau littered with rocks of lava ranging in size from tennis balls to huge boulders. The desolate landscape is punctuated by conical hills, a few hundred feet high —still recognizable but long extinct volcano cones. Goatherds roam the plateau from the Druze villages on the lower slopes of Mount Hermon; other farming had been abandoned, with only crumbling walls of lava rocks faintly outlining former plots. A dry wind fans steadily across.

Over the plateau, the hamlets that once housed thriving Arab communities were deserted in 1967—when only the Druzes, a distinctive people with a lofty disdain for the rest of the Arab world, remained on Golan. Now the Arab villages, like their fields, were mostly derelict. Kuneitra had survived after a fashion—the 1967 rubble adorned with barbed wire and tank traps by the Israeli military garrison. Naffak had become no more than an underground command post amid sandbagged bunkers. Only the minaret of Khusniye—its slender form, leaning slightly, a honeycomb of bullet scars—survived to remind prying tourists of the lives that 1967 destroyed.

Four routes give entry into Israel. To the north a road twists down from the foothills of Mount Hermon to the kibbutz of Dan, at the head of the Jordan Valley. In the extreme southwest of Golan, where a high tongue of fertile land ends in cliffs over Lake Tiberias (Sea of Galilee), another road winds down into Israel. Only at two more places does the rugged western edge of the Golan plateau soften enough to allow passable roads to descend. An ugly girder contraption across the river Jordan—with the incongruously beautiful name of Gesher Benot Yacov (the Bridge of the Daughters of Jacob)—carries the main road from Kuneitra and Naffak. And the fourth and last exit is a little to the north, over a Bailey bridge below Wazit.

The Syrian objective had to be the capture of at least two of these four crossings—and one of them had to be Benot Yacov, the main military supply route from Israel. That was clearly the joint objective of the left-hand fork of the Kuneitra column and the column pressing northwest from Rafid. As the remainder of the Rafid column veered left, it became clear that the other route the Syrians were trying to take was the southerly road at the tip of Lake Tiberias.

The first Israeli defenses to collapse were its fortified settlements, which had been the keys to Israel's hold over the occupied territories since 1967. The role of the settlements—apart from straightforward colonization—had been to deter the infiltration of Palestinian guerrillas. The settlements had watchtowers and rudimentary defenses of barbed wire and a few sandbagged firing posts, and their settlers were organized into vigilante patrol groups. But against a full-scale armored assault, they were indefensible.

And as one of the geniuses of armored warfare, Rommel, had written in 1942 in the essay, "The Rules of Desert Warfare": "Against a motorized and armored enemy, nonmotorized divisions are of value only in prepared positions. Once such positions have been pierced or outflanked . . . they become helpless victims . . . and motorized formations have to be employed to gain time to extricate them." That, indeed, became a priority task for the outnumbered Israeli tanks, which had to be diverted to rescue some of the settlements.

It was an indication of how scornfully Israel had rated the Syrian armor that the civilians on Golan were not evacuated until after the battle had begun. At the settlement of Ramat Magshimim for example, a Syrian artillery shell hit the bus into which the women and children of the settlement were just about to be shepherded. And the men of the settlement were not evacuated until Syrian tanks were actually in view. So, reopening old memories, many Jews once more became refugees, confronted again with situations as pitifully trivial as the old man from Giv'at kibbutz, inconsolable in the relative safety of the Jordan Valley because he had abandoned two pet goats and a parrot in a hut on Golan. "The line of settlements contributed nothing to halt the Syrian attack. In fact, the ones which fell to the Syrians served them as solid bases for continuing their attack," one Israeli postmortem on the assault concluded.

The Israeli tank crews realized they were not to be reinforced immediately. "The troops knew from the very beginning that they were to act as advance forces to stay the invasion of the Syrian Army," an Israeli communiqué said later. It would be at least thirty hours before any of the reserves called up that morning could trundle along the winding road from Rosh Pina down over the river Jordan and then up the steep ascent to Golan. In the meantime, two Israeli tank brigades—both three-quarter strength —had to keep this overwhelming weight of Syrian armor from crashing a mere seventeen miles down into Israel.

The two brigades covered different sectors of the Golan front. In the north, defending the narrowest—therefore, the Israeli Northern Command had reasoned, the most vulnerable—strip of Golan, was the 7th Armored Brigade: one hundred tanks under a brilliant commander known to his devoted crews simply as

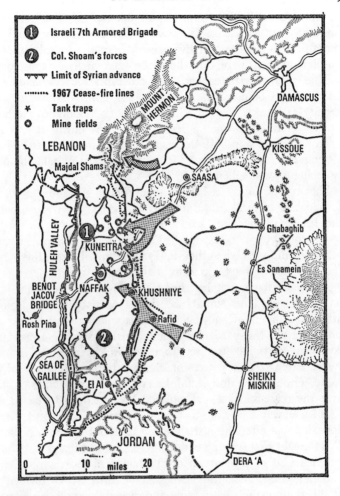

Map 6 How Syria's tanks overwhelmed Israel
The Syrian thrusts were intended first to cut Golan in half down the main Kunei-tra-to-Naffak road, and simultaneously to take the southernmost route down to Israel through El Al. To overwhelm the Israelis' 176 defending tanks, the 700 Syrian tanks in the first wave divided. Shoam's tank force was quickly scattered and destroyed; but the 7th Brigade, behind better defenses, fought in formations. Syria's early airborne capture of Mount Hermon deprived the Israeli brigades of gunnery spotting but enabled the Syrians to range their artillery onto Israeli positions.

"Colonel Janos." (The names of commanders below field rank are military secrets in Israel: We have been unable to discover Janos' surname.) Janos was a native Israeli, born of central European immigrants: In his off-duty hours he was chiefly famous for his skill as a Hungarian dancer. The other brigade commander on Golan was Colonel Ben Shoam, a less flamboyant figure. His seventy-six tanks covered the central and southern sectors— roughly from the Kuneitra-Benot Yacov axis down. It was thus Shoam's task to stop both thrusts of the Syrian column from Rafid —one now pressing northwest to cut the plateau in half, the other sweeping toward Tiberias.

Shoam's brigade faced horrendous odds: An average of five to one, and in local confrontations as great as twelve to one. As the Israelis opened fire, scores of Syrian tanks were hit. Others broke down, their tracks smashed by the rocky terrain. But more came on; and even when their tanks were immobilized, the Syrians fought on, using the tanks as fixed artillery.

A young Israeli captain named Yossi commanded seven tanks on Golan, until his throat was ripped open by a shell splinter after three hours of fighting. (Hideous wounds to the head and shoulders are the particular occupational hazard of Israeli tank commanders, trained to direct their battles looking out of an open turret hatch.) Yossi's account conveys the noisy horror of the scene. Through the dust cloud, he saw three Syrian tanks crashing over the cease-fire line and wheeled his squadron to face them. "All three were hit by our first shells. I aimed at a fourth tank that appeared and after the first shot saw its turret flying into the air. We thought that was the end of the battle. But it was just the beginning. Out of the curtain of dust emerged dozens more tanks, tank-bulldozers, and armored personnel carriers. We divided the attackers among our seven tanks and picked them off one after the other . . . but before we could catch our breath, another wave moved toward us."

Facing gunners as highly trained as the Israelis, the Syrian assault was bound to be mauled. Against the first waves, the Israeli tanks could fire—as Captain Yossi did—from prepared positions, with guns ranged-in to cover the likely lines of advance, each tank's field of fire interlocking with its neighbor's. The Syrian lead tanks were heading into fire traps of devastating intensity. Walking over the first few hundred yards of the assault route from Rafid, a *Sunday Times* reporter counted thirteen Syrian tanks in perfect line-ahead, their guns pointing toward Israel, all blown apart by the Israeli gunners. But the two-pronged course of that thrust finally told against Shoam's men. Having broken through the defenses, the Syrian tanks fanned into line abreast. To avoid being outflanked and swamped, the Israeli tanks —many by now almost out of ammunition—had to abandon their prepared positions and begin a fighting retreat. Once dispersed, the tanks could be picked off one by one. Shoam's brigade began to suffer heavily. They fought with suicidal bravery: Finding himself alone and facing an overwhelming force of Syrian tanks advancing only 200 yards away, the commander of one of the tank battalions in Shoam's brigade radioed the Israeli artillery to pour fire on to his own tank and the surrounding terrain. The Syrian formation was shattered. The Israeli commander and two of his crew managed to escape from their own burning tank, all badly wounded. But despite such bravery, sheer weight of numbers had to tell against the Israelis. As dusk fell they had virtually lost the battle for southern Golan.

The southernmost thrust of the Syrian armor—heading straight toward Lake Tiberias—halted its advance that first night at El Al. The crews did so because, at their dawn briefings, El Al had been given as their first night's objective. In fact, nothing could have stopped them had they pressed on. Shoam's brigade was still just a coherent unit—but certainly without the force to counterattack. Ironically, it may even have been this absence of opposition that deterred the Syrians from proceeding: Surely it must be a trap? It was no trap. Israel had all but lost southern Golan.

Against the pincer movement round Kuneitra in the north, Colonel Janos' 7th Armored Brigade was, amazingly, faring better. One of his officers later stressed how difficult the Golan terrain was to fight in. Hills, rocks, small groves of scrubby trees, low bushes, and the ruins of deserted villages all obstructed the defenders' field of vision. "You never know what's behind the next turn in the roads," he said. "It's not like the desert, where the whole battlefield is visible."

But, to the Syrians, the whole battlefield of Golan ought now to have been visible. At 4:20 P.M. on the first day, Damascus radio announced: "Our forces have liberated certain positions, one of which is the Mount Hermon position." The broadcast was slightly premature: Their final capture of Hermon seems only to have come on Sunday. But not for ten days would Israel admit this loss; it was, potentially, a disaster comparable to the loss of the Bar-Lev Line in Sinai. For whoever controlled the observation point seven thousand feet up on the Mount Hermon ridge could scan all Golan. In a helicopter assault, Syrian commandos captured the Israeli fortress. If the Syrians could now contrive an efficient system of artillery spotting, they could direct devastating fire from the Syrian defense lines onto Colonel Janos' tank formations far below.

Down on the dusty plain, the achievement of the 7th Brigade in those first hours was remarkable. The thrust north of Kuneitra was halted in its tracks; and the division of Syrian tanks forking south of Kuneitra had been savagely mauled as dusk approached.

We will explore later the details of Janos' tactics; but the key, as one of the Israeli commanders later said, was coordination of three elements: tanks, infantry, and aircraft. The defenses in the northern sector of Golan were certainly more intricate than those protecting Shoam's brigade to the south. North of Kuneitra was a patchwork of antitank obstacles, mine fields, and a wide antitank canal. The Syrians had anticipated these, and the northern-most attack was spearheaded by bulldozer tanks to thrust aside the obstacles, flail tanks to beat a path through the mine fields, and bridging tanks to surmount the ditch. But they were easy targerts for Janos' marksmen, and the triangle running from Kuneitra north to the cease-fire line was soon so choked with the smoldering wrecks of the Syrian vanguard that the Israeli tank crews' radio chat began to give the area a special name: "the graveyard."

The Syrian tactics allowed even the Israeli infantry to inflict significant damage. Scattered outposts—ten to fifteen men in a bunker—held out on the Israeli front lines as the Syrian armor washed over them. Nor did the Syrians try in any very determined fashion to reduce these outposts: The Syrian goal was to capture ground before nightfall. The infantry and artillery in these bunkers were thus able to "take potshots at everything moving past them," as an Israeli put it. One outpost, on the crossroads in front of Kuneitra, is said to have accounted for more than a dozen tanks.

But inevitably, from the early minutes of the battle, the real edge of the Syrian attack was blunted by Israel's classic weapon, the air strike. The A-4 Skyhawks played the heaviest ground-attack role, with Phantoms and Mirages giving air cover. The Israelis' targeting was so precise that tank commanders could call down air strikes only a few yards from their positions. But losses were heavy. The Israeli aircraft had the ECM capacity to jam the Syrians' SAM-2 missiles—while helicopter crews hovered dauntingly close to the Golan front lines, operating more powerful ECM as back-up. But among the defense screen that the Syrians had moved up to their Golan lines was the latest Soviet mobile antiaircraft missile, the SAM-6. And Israel had no counter to this: It had never been seen in combat anywhere in the world before. In the first afternoon, Israel lost thirty Skyhawks and about ten Phantoms over Golan, all to SAM-6s or the devastating flak of the mobile ZSU-23 antiaircraft batteries (also Soviet) which chewed up the Skyhawks if their pilots dropped to deck level in an effort to beat the SAMS. There were rarely any parachutes. A Dutch Army missile specialist, trapped on Golan as a UN observer, reckoned that through this first afternoon the Israelis were losing three out of every five aircraft they sent over. That scale of losses was so clearly insupportable that in midafternoon, Chief of Staff Elazer actually abandoned air strikes over Golan. (Dayan knew of this decision —and the losses that led to it—when he gave his overconfident appraisal on TV.)

But without air strikes, there was no hope of salvaging the Golan front: After a couple of hours they had to resume. The Israeli pilots switched tactics. As dusk fell, the *Sunday Times* Amman correspondent, John Bonar, watched from the roof of a farmhouse in the lee of the Golan cliffs in northern Jordan as pairs of Israeli aircraft, silver in the halflight, skimmed in a low northward curve over Jordanian territory, hugging the contours until they rocketed up and over the Golan plateau to take the Syrian armor in the flank and then curve away west of Mount Hermon—hopefully without ever passing over the deadly SAM sites. It was partially successful: The loss rate dropped; but it was still worrying.

As night fell, the Golan plateau was a confused world of

individual tank battles and ferocious hand-to-hand infantry fighting, as the Israeli defenders slowly retreated. The Israeli commander of the northern front, Major General Yizhak Hoffi, had now decided to place the defense of Golan in the hands of one man, Brigadier Rafael Eytan. The man matched the hour.

It is recounted that after the Israeli commando raid that destroyed thirteen aircraft at Beirut Airport on December 28, 1968, Eytan, in charge of the operation, strolled into the transit lounge and ordered a black coffee. As the terrified barman hastened to obey, others of Eytan's men ordered drinks. Eytan pulled from his pocket an Israeli ten-pound note—worth just over two dollars —signed it, and put it on the counter, saying that if ever the barman got to Israel, he would pay in full for the drinks consumed that night.

Eytan is a man of few words. Born on a farm in northern Israel, he is stocky with huge hands; and he is, quite simply, reckoned one of the best fighters in the Israeli Army—even too courageous for the good of his men. Yet Eytan, trained as a paratrooper, once left the Army in the early 1950s and returned to the land. The story goes that, in the 1956 campaign, a friend still in the Army reproached him with this. "They are killing Jews and you are milking cows," he is supposed to have said. Eytan returned to the Army—and stayed. His actions in the Six-Day War of 1967 were "commended," high praise in an army without medals.

Among his fellow officers, Eytan was considered no strategic genius. A bullet went through his head in 1967, and the army joke was that this proved he had no brains. (It was a glancing wound: An arrowhead scar across Eytan's forehead marks the bullet's path.) And, taciturn, Eytan has few close friends. His heroes are both dead: On the wall in his office—where most officers might have pictures of Mrs. Meir or Dayan—Eytan has a photograph of a lieutenant killed in a savage battle precipitated by Sharon in the Mitla Pass in 1956, and another of a captain killed by the Palestinian guerrillas near the river Jordan during the War of Attrition.

But the northern commander, Hoffi, had long admired Eytan. They had been paratroopers together; and Hoffi had often told Eytan's detractors that, beneath his silence, Eytan had an unusual and subtle intelligence. His opinion was dismissed as mere solidarity. It was thus against some opposition that Hoffi gave Eytan charge of the Golan front at the height of the battle. But Hoffi could not control the sector from his northern headquarters at Safed; the commander had to be on the spot, and Eytan was in the underground command bunker at Naffak. So Hoffi had his way—and he was right. Eytan proved to possess exactly the qualities needed for the defense of Golan: courage, resource in a desperate situation, a temperament so mulish that had he been ordered to retreat he would probably not have done so—and, as Hoffi had discerned, a rare and precise tactical skill. As the first phase of the battle ebbed at nightfall, the newly appointed Eytan set about organizing his defenses and tactics for the next day. The critical question was: How soon could the reserves come?

4. Egypt's First Failure

The deployment of reserves, however, depended in part upon the situation in Sinai. The early Israeli counterattacks there had been flustered and reckless—individual tank squadrons gallantly rolling forward, only to be blown apart, sometimes by several missiles simultaneously. With professional detachment, the Egyptian Chief of Staff, Shazli, later observed that "the element of surprise was clearly manifested in the lack of coordination and response on the part of the enemy for at least two days." The Israelis were more bitter about it. In those early hours there was an almost total breakdown of coordination—"not one but several Israeli armies," one very senior officer said later, "each doing its own thing." A lot of Israeli lives were lost unnecessarily. As Dayan observed bitterly of the Egyptian tactics: "They just lie in the sand dunes and every tank that comes close is hit by these personal antitank missiles." He added: "The war is now more against this Soviet equipment than against the Egyptians." But Israel's problems went deeper than that.

It was as Ismail had calculated. The cleverness of his plan lay in its combining of two distinct elements of warfare in a way not seen before. The single massive stride across the canal was, strategically, an offensive of the most aggressive sort. But Ismail then consolidated this by *defensive* tactics. The Egyptian soldiers just dug in with their missiles. The combination brilliantly exploited the strength of the Egyptian Army—which has always been its tenacious defensive ability—while avoiding its weakness, an equally persistent inability to conduct a war of movement. At the same time, Ismail's plan capitalized upon Israel's greatest tactical weakness: the belief, carefully instilled into every rising young tank commander, that the only fit way to conduct a battle was to charge. An Israeli tank lieutenant described the conse-

quences: "Our tactic the first two days was, as usual, to move
forward, move forward. But we hit a wall of tank missiles and
heavy guns. There were heavy casualties on both sides. . . ." Another Israeli put it with more succinct bitterness: "They charged
like Zulus up against machine guns." After the war, Sharon said
that the Israeli high command had "ceased to be brilliant and
substituted for military thought, initiative, and intelligence a
blind belief in quantities of steel." There was truth in that; but
it derived less from a belief in numbers than from an unreflecting
faith in Israeli combat superiority. That faith was to be justified
once again; but it could not, in the short term, compensate for
the numbers and technology that the Egyptians now deployed in
Sinai.

Yet the Israeli Army was damaged in those first days of war by
deeper failures. The irony was that these were rooted precisely
in the dazzling success that Israel's forces had won in 1967. For
the basic geographical fact was that in overrunning Sinai in 1967,
Israel had destroyed the buffer which had previously separated it
from its main opponent, Egypt. For the twenty years before that,
Egypt's inability to mobilize and sustain massive forces in Sinai
had produced *de facto* disengagement. So completely was this
acknowledged, indeed, that when the Egyptians did at last manage to mass forces in Sinai, in 1967, the Israelis had taken that as
a *casus belli* and launched a preemptive strike. But now, with
its forces fronting the canal, it was Israel that faced the logistical
problems of Sinai, while Egypt—with short, internal lines of communication—could menace Israel's new "border," the east bank
of the canal, any time it wished.

The first consequence of this had been, of course, that retention
of their 1967 gains posed for the Israelis the choice of remaining
in a state of almost permanent alert—or taking a continual risk.
And on October 6, they finally gambled wrong.

But the Israeli Army's tactical response to the post-1967 borders
was equally unsettled. Since the formation of the state, the overriding Israeli military strategy had been that of the preemptive
strike: The war must always be taken into the enemy's own
territory. That made sense in the first twenty years of Israeli's
existence. And Yizhak Rabin, Chief of Staff in the Six-Day War,
had expanded the concept: The aim of Israel's battle plan was not

merely victory, but a rout of the enemy. The 1967 Sinai campaign achieved just that.

But it was scarcely possible now. After 1967, Israel could only have taken war into Egyptian territory by crossing the canal. And after 1970—if not before—it was an assumption of Israeli policy that this would provoke Soviet intervention. For the first time in their history, therefore, the Israeli strategy had to be *defensive*.

But how could this be integrated with the Israelis' tactical emphasis upon *offense*? The Israelis thus faced the mirror image of the problem confronting General Ismail—and it has to be said that they did not solve it with the elegance of the Egyptian strategist.

Rabin's successor as Chief of Staff, General Haim Bar-Lev, had produced one answer: the Bar-Lev Line. But the arguments among the Israeli military establishment as to the merits of this raged through 1968—until, ironically, Nasser settled the matter by launching the War of Attrition in September of that year. At that point, the Israeli Government decided that its troops could not be seen to be pulling back from the canal under pressure from Egypt. Yet if they stayed they would need protection. Construction of the Bar-Lev Line became settled political policy.

The unhappy paradox was that the forts—and the immobile defensive strategy they enshrined—reached completion precisely at the time when "Arik" Sharon was promoted to run the Southern Command at the end of 1968. Sharon disapproved of the Bar-Lev's whole concept, and so did powerful groups within the General Staff. Sharon did not want bunkers in Sinai. He wanted roads—and spent millions of dollars building them. Sharon's proposed strategy was to let the Egyptians into Sinai and destroy them there. With a road network across Sinai, he held, Israel could revert to its old tactic, a war of mobility.

Sharon, indeed, was so against the defensive strategy represented by the Bar-Lev Line that by the time he finally handed over the Southern Command to Shmuel Gonen only four months before the Yom Kippur War, Sharon had actually *closed* half the forts of the Bar-Lev Line. His regret was that he had not been able to close them all. Gonen, in his short time in command, had simply never had the manpower to open those forts again. That was the main reason why the Bar-Lev Line was so sparsely manned when the Egyptian assault came.

Sharon's doctrine depended, however, upon swift and massive response by Israeli armor to an Egyptian incursion into Sinai. And Israel's failure to mobilize its reserves—compounded by Gonen's decision not to move up the bulk of his armor in time—undercut that option as well. Thus, Israel faced the first hours of the war in Sinai with the Bar-Lev defensive strategy in ruins, and the opposing Sharon concept of a mobile offensive unworkable. In this confusion, the achievement of the Israeli tank crews in those first hours of battle in Sinai was all the more remarkable.

The first Egyptian air strikes—two hundred aircraft, according to Ismail—had hit Israel's main airfields and communications centers at Bir Gifgafa, Bir el Thamada, and the forward sector headquarters at Tasa (though the facilities there were deeply buried and escaped intact). Until the damage to runways was repaired, Israeli counterstrikes—the few that could be diverted from the defense of Golan—had to operate mostly from bases back inside Israel, which cut their frequency still further. The Egyptians did not achieve this without loss. During the first hours of the war, President Sadat's half brother, Adel Sadat, a twenty-two-year-old Air Force captain, was shot down in his MiG over Sinai. But even the sparse Israeli counterstrikes hit touble. Early targets were, obviously, the bridges being constructed over the canal, but the Egyptian infantry's portable antiaircraft missiles were already in action. According to Shazli: "The enemy tried extreme low-flying tactics to get at the bridges but the SAM-7 rockets proved a magnificent success in bringing down the attackers." Shazli exaggerated: The infantry-borne heat-seeking SAM-7s homed unerringly on a lot of Israeli aircraft tail pipes. But their explosive charges were too small to down many of them. It was the more formidable track-mounted SAM-6s and the ZSU-23 batteries that, as on Golan, took the toll.

The Air Force's concentration upon Golan, however, meant that the containment of the Egyptian attack had to be by Israeli armor largely unaided—the 240 tanks in Sinai, of which the core was the 14th Armored Brigade under a burly, mustachioed extrovert, Colonel Amnon Reshef. But more than half Reshef's tanks had been stationed by the Bar-Lev Line, the cadre on garrison duty—as it turned out, not enough to do much good, but enough to make the early losses to Egyptian missiles a significant blow. And the initial Egyptian assault penetrated considerably farther than the Bar-Lev Line. By the early hours of Sunday, with 500 tanks massed in Sinai, Egypt was threatening Israel's second line of defense as well.

Israel had spent almost $90 million on the construction of the Bar-Lev Line. (It is alleged that when its creator approached Mrs. Meir's predecessor, Levi Eshkol, for more cash, Chief of Staff Bar-Lev explained that one costly item was the piping of fresh water. Eshkol looked puzzled. "Surely," he asked, "they can drink the water in the canal?") And, at Sharon's insistence, Israel had spent at least another $150 million constructing roads, with yet more expenditure on airstrips, bases, and strongpoints throughout Sinai. The most important of the roads were a pair running north to south parallel to the canal—one about 15 miles (maximum) from it, the other about 18 miles back and running through the forward sector headquarters at Tasa. The Israeli defense plan had always been to use the forward road for its 155mm and 175mm heavy artillery, with the road just behind carrying ammunition supplies and reserves of armor. The range of the artillery was such that, from the safety of this forward road, it could bombard enemy concentrations even on the west bank of the canal. The Egyptian advance through the early hours of Sunday disrupted this tidy design.

In the first place, Israel had few heavy guns. Its tanks were expected to serve as artillery. Moreover, the initial Egyptian air strikes knocked out almost 40 per cent of what guns Israel did possess. Finally, the effectiveness of the surviving artillery was further reduced by the overrunning of the Bar-Lev Line, after which only ten or so of the Israeli bunkers still held out; for a crucial task of the Bar-Lev forces had always been to act as spotters for the Israeli gunners. Even heavier, therefore, was the burden on Reshef and his tank crews.

As in Golan, the fighting that followed was governed by geography. Southern Sinai (see map, page 70) is a lunar landscape of parched, impassable mountains. But to the north, these narrow to a central ridge, which tails away in the sand seas bordering the Mediterranean. Through this ridge run three passes: the Mitla

Pass in the south, the Gidi Pass in the center, and the Khatmia Pass farther north. Apart from the passes, the only other way across Sinai is by the coast road, and the Mediterranean on one side and the soft sand sea on the other virtually rule that out for tank formations.

To advance across Sinai, the Egyptians thus had to capture at least one pass. According to military sources in Cairo, Ismail's objective in the first phase of Operation BADR was the establishment of a bridgehead to serve as the springboard for his second phase, the capture of all the passes. The first bridgehead he had planned was to be twenty miles into Sinai—just beyond the rear Israeli support road—at which depth a chain of sand ridges would, Ismail thought, provide an intermittent but serviceable defense line. Ismail's campaign—and the Israelis' desperate struggle to smash it—thus took place entirely between the canal and the central mountain ridge.

It is a triangle of land, roughly sixty-five miles from north to south, at its widest only forty miles deep and narrowing opposite the southernmost Mitla Pass to a mere twenty miles. The terrain is a complex tangle of scrub and dunes, sudden sand ridges and wide plateaus, with scattered waterholes and treacherous pans of soft, impassable sand. Here, on the first night of the war, the outnumbered Israeli tank crews won a remarkable victory.

From their northern and central bridgeheads, the Egyptian tanks overran the artillery road in places, but the Israelis destroyed the advance before the rear supply road fell. From the southern bridgehead, the Egyptian objective, the sand ridge almost twenty miles into Sinai, was effectively at the mouth of the Mitla Pass itself. They got ten miles before the Israelis managed to stop them.

Egypt, meanwhile, tried to disrupt the Israeli attacks from the rear. Taking advantage of the early moonset, which had been one of General Ismail's requirements for the night of Y-Day, helicopters ferried Egyptian commandos on raiding expeditions deep behind the Israeli positions—tactics reminiscent of the deep Israeli strikes in 1967. Egypt's twenty commando battalions were its toughest troops—and Chief of Staff Shazli, himself a paratrooper, took a personal pride in them: For him, they were symbols of the revival of Egyptian arms. But in combat, they were not very effective: Israeli antiaircraft fire downed several helicopters with total loss of life. One was shot down far away from the main area of battle, near Ras Sudar, on the east bank of the Gulf of Suez. Perhaps the targets were the oil rigs of Ras Sudar and Abu Rodeis themselves; perhaps the commandos were intending to swing in a southward curve to disrupt the Israeli reinforcements grinding toward the Mitla Pass.

Some commandos did get through. Sixty flew over the coastal salt marsh to attack the Israelis' northern forward command post at Baluza. But the Israelis had built a floating road into the marsh, and could deploy to drive them off with heavy Egyptian loss of life. Other raiding parties, landed near Bir Gifgafa and at Sharm el Sheikh, did survive—despite confident Israeli propaganda. But they were never more than a nuisance.

The decisive battle was the armored clash. It was, as Wellington remarked of Waterloo, a damned close-run thing. Two reporters on the London *Sunday Telegraph*, Christopher Dobson and Ronald Payne, penetrated Israeli security in Sinai after the war to talk with Reshef about that battle. "It did not seem to matter how many we killed," he said, "they kept coming on." All that first night, the attack was unceasing, Reshef said: "I had few tanks left. By now many of my units were down to two or three tanks." An Israeli armored company comprises ten tanks: Reshef had lost as many as four out of five. "A situation arose where two Israeli tanks faced fifty Egyptian tanks supported by infantry. I had to rearm and refuel my formations three times while actually engaged with the enemy." And from a hospital bed in Cairo, an Israeli lieutenant wounded in the battle still remembered that Egyptian infantry support with amazement: "Ordinarily, an infantry platoon would be equipped with one big antitank weapon and two smaller ones. But every third Egyptian seemed to be carrying one, and they were the most sophisticated things I've ever seen."

There is also considerable evidence that the Egyptians knew far too well where to point them. With considerable precision, the Egyptian infantry aimed their missiles at the weak points in the Israeli tanks' armor. The most modern tank the Israelis possessed —the American-built M-60—proved exceedingly vulnerable in two respects. Unlike the British Centurion, which revolves its turret and elevates or depresses its gun by means of an electric motor, the M-60 relies for these functions upon a system of hydraulics.

Not only did this system prove to be inadequately protected at certain points on the M-60 turret. The fluid in the hydraulic system also proved to have a flash-point so low that it would explode into flame from the heat even of a missile impact which otherwise might not have killed the tank's occupants.

Many Israeli crews were incinerated in their M-60s as a result of this and one other design flaw. The ammunition and fuel on an M-60 are stored closer together than in several other models of tank. And under the impact even of a missile whose charge did not penetrate the tank's armor the fuel and ammunition would commonly explode, blasting inward, not outward—again killing the crew.

Examining the wreckage of their tanks after the war, the Israeli Ordnance Corps acknowledged that the penetrative power of the Sagger missile and the RPG-7 made all existing tanks to some extent vulnerable: No tank had armor thick enough at all points to resist the missile. What perturbed the Ordnance Corps, however, was that—particularly in respect of the M-60—the Egyptians knew precisely where to aim. The conclusions, admittedly disputed, which several Israeli experts have since come to is that Soviet intelligence has been able to analyze so minutely the weak spots of the M-60 that a major Western security failure is indicated.

In those first desperate hours in Sinai, however, the sheer intensity of the Egyptian missile fire was the most potent factor. The savagery of the battle is conveyed by the incident later recounted by a twenty-year-old Israeli tank lieutenant from another hospital bed. As he led a squadron of three tanks toward the canal around midnight that first night, his lead tank had been hit by an RPG: "The tank was disabled but I managed to put the fire out. The Egyptians fired a flare and I saw the enemy soldiers. There were lots of them, I'd say a company, lying in line in front of low sand dunes." His tank's armaments were still working, and he opened fire from three hundred yards. Then, when his No. 2 tank drew level, he changed places with its commander and ordered the driver to charge directly at the Egyptians while his other tanks gave covering fire. As he reached the enemy line, his new tank was also hit—this time by four RPGs simultaneously. The lieutenant, standing exposed in the turret, fell wounded into the body of the tank. As he slid down, he shouted to the driver to wheel left and run along the enemy line: "Crush them, crush them," he shouted.

By dawn on Sunday, the crisis was over—though not until noon did the fury of the Egyptian assault finally begin to ebb away. By then, Israel's citizen army was at last arriving—in the first wave, no more than 50 tanks but with about 20,000 infantry in 5 divisions, plus artillery. At 5:00 A.M. on Sunday morning, Sharon had set up between Tasa and the canal his forward command post, a group of five armored personnel carriers afforested with aerials. By early afternoon, Sharon's painfully assembled reserve division was also beginning to deploy in the central sector in front of the Mitla and Gidi passes. The regulars had held on for the vital 24 hours. The cost had been high. No more than 90 of Reshef's original 240 tanks had survived. Reshef himself had seen 2 groups of staff officers killed around him. But the Egyptians had penetrated no farther than 8 to 10 miles into Sinai. Ismail's strategy had suffered its first—and ultimately fatal—setback.

That was not quite how it seemed to the isolated pockets of resistance still holding out by the side of the canal—among them Avi Yaffe and his fellow warriors still in their beleaguered fort in the Bar-Lev Line. Egyptians, in attempting now to consolidate the position rather than continue to press fruitlessly forward, were about to open an artillery barrage on the fort. Again Avi had his tape recorder switched on.

MEYERKE (as the shelling begins): Shuki! Go take a jump to Outpost 3 [one of the firing positions], and report when you're there. Signalman Shlomo [Avi's assistant] will run with you. Wait a moment. I want somebody in the northern outpost. They'll attack us from the north, possibly. Give me Position 4.
AVI: You're connected to it.
MEYERKE: Hello! Hello! . . . Avi, they don't answer there.
AVI (on the loudspeaker): Position 4. Pick up your phone.
MEYERKE (on phone): Who's that? Dubbele [nickname of lookout called Mordecai Eichebaum]. Bless ye the Lord every day [facetious greeting]. . . . How are you? [powerful explosion].

Where did it hit? In the bunker? . . . O.K., but every now and again you have to poke your head out afterward because they might come from the north. You understand? . . . I should know what's going to happen! We'll soon see. I don't know where they're hitting us from.

Now a heavy mortar bombardment ranges onto the fort.

AVI (reporting to Meyerke): They say the shells are falling by the gate of the fort.
MEYERKE (to gate position): Pay attention the whole time. Lie down low and the moment there's any sort of letup put your head outside right after the shell and watch the gate. O.K.?

Two direct explosions on the fort.

AVI: Shuki doesn't reply. . . .
MEYERKE (snatching phone): Shuki . . . Shuki . . . Perhaps he went to Position 3?

The shelling is increasing, and now almost every shot is on target. There are earthfalls in the trenches and bunkers. Some of the telephone lines between positions are cut, and the radio antennae are destroyed. Avi and Shlomo, the two signalmen, go out, exposed to the fire, to replace them.

MEYERKE: Give me headquarters. . . . hello, Yigal, listen: They're hitting us hard. Artillery, perhaps also tanks. It's falling directly on me, I don't know where from. The tanks I think are shooting from the other side. A shell lands every minute. That's it.
DUBBELE (on phone): Moment. Shuki is in the bunker, Position 4.
MEYERKE: Certain? Good. Are you looking out on that side? O.K.?

More shells and mortar bombs. Direct hits.

DUBBELE: Exchange. Exchange. The trench to Positions 3 and 3A is blocked.

SHUKI (on loudspeaker): The trenches to 3 and 3A are blocked.
MEYERKE (to Shuki): You'll stay in 4. O.K.?

Sergeant Baruch appears in Meyerke's command bunker, bleeding from the head. Shrapnel has torn his helmet, and is still lodged in the side of his head. His ear is cut and bleeding.

BARUCH: Give me some help, boys, give me some help.

The medic and the doctor take over. The shrapnel is extricated and a sedative injection is given. Baruch falls asleep on the doctor's bed. The shelling continues.

AVI: We should explain to headquarters things are getting serious.
SOLDIER: Tell them we have casualties. That's it.
MEYERKE: So what if there are?
SOLDIER: So they should hurry.
MEYERKE (to headquarters): They're shelling us. I don't know where from.
AVI: Don't make things too easy for them.
MEYERKE: What should I do? I've said they're shelling. So what?
AVI: Exaggerate a little bit. Put some spirit in it.
MEYERKE: I have exaggerated, so? (To headquarters): Where from? I should know where they're firing from. They're firing at us and that's that. (To Avi): Give me Shuki in Bunker 4.
AVI: I think the line's been cut.
SHLOMO (on the loudspeaker): Shuki. Lift the phone.
MEYERKE: Give me headquarters again. . . . (Breaking off for the phone): Shuki, where are you?
SHUKI: Bunker 4. It's impossible to be outside. Everything's exploding.
MEYERKE: But someone should always be jumping up to see what's happening to the north. . . . [Breaks off again to try to get headquarters.]
AVI: Headquarters doesn't answer. I'm trying the whole time. They have all the time in the world, those guys at headquarters.
SHUKI (on the loudspeaker after another explosion): Bunker No. 4 is blocked off. I'm stuck here. Can't get back. Somebody should go out near the gate. . . .

MEYERKE (finally getting through to headquarters): Now listen a moment. Yigal, Yigal . . .

HEADQUARTERS: Hello, you'll get it right away.

MEYERKE: Get what?

HEADQUARTERS: Artillery.

MEYERKE: On what? I want to tell you on what. . . . I want it like this. They should give artillery on the tank park. . . .

SHUKI (on the phone): What's happening? They're still shelling. I left the bunker. It's blocked between all the trenches to 3 and 3A. I'm in 4 at the moment, completely buried, trying to get out. Maybe something will work.

By now it is dark. Another powerful explosion is heard.

MEYERKE: What's that?

SHUKI: It's still falling on me. . . . I can't see. I think the shell fell in the middle of the fort. What shells, honey! The trench in Position 4 has also had it. Everything on top's collapsed on me.

Shuki asks for someone to be sent to clear the entrance to Bunker 4, but he digs out an opening before this is done.

SHLOMO: Position A say they can hear armor. They don't know from where. And there are halftracks on the canal road opposite us.

MEYERKE: Give me headquarters. . . . Headquarters, listen, the fort again. We can see lights on the canal road. . . .

HEADQUARTERS: Instead of talking give me targets.

MEYERKE (amid more explosions): I gave you the targets. First of all the canal road. All of it. Halftracks are moving on it. The question is whether ours or theirs. I don't know, can't see in the dark. Second thing: I understand you have lots of artillery, so if you can hit right away, do you hear, because they are wiping us out here. Our main positions we can't get to them because they are blocked. So I want as follows: Shells on Concentration Point G [a coded map reference]. After that I want fire by the church in Ismailia. There's a tank position there. You'll see it on the map between the church and the mosque. Then in the tank park. Also to the north, 200 northeast . . . [another gigantic explosion]

. . . Oh-oh. All the bunkers are collapsing. . . . I want rapid fire now.

SOLDIER: Can't they send some sort of vehicle to take us away?

MEYERKE: Here? During the shelling? We'd get killed outside. Tanks would just get knocked up in a shelling.

SHUKI (phoning from ruins of Bunker 4): We've just caught a whopper. We're completely covered in sand.

MEYERKE (voice choking with dust): We can't see a thing. We're choking here. The ventilator has bust . . .

The shock from the last shell has broken the ventilation pumping machinery. It is, however, the last Egyptian salvo. The barrage subsides almost as abruptly as it began. The tape picks up the squeak of the ventilator as a soldier cranks it by hand, but otherwise quiet returns. Avi starts to speak a private message to his wife into the microphone: "Dassy, do you hear me? I feel like talking to you. . . ." But he breaks off dispiritedly and switches off his tape recorder until the following morning.

5. Choreography of a Tank Battle

On Golan, too, Sunday was the hardest day for the Israelis. In the Israeli newspaper *Ha'aretz,* military correspondent Zeev Schiff wrote: "The Israelis at home never knew or felt how great was the danger nor how bloody the battle. Eight hundred tanks had broken onto the heights. . . . The pride of the Syrian armor was only a few miles from the Benot Yacov bridge." Late on Sunday afternoon, the Israelis thought for two hours that they had lost the battle.

In the southern sector, the Syrians had bedded down through Saturday night. They had gotten to their first objective, El Al, and were awaiting further orders. Besides, around El Al there were no Israeli tanks left to shoot at. So Colonel Shoam had been able to use the respite of darkness to regroup the battered remnants of his brigade—he had already lost about half by nightfall on Saturday.

But in the northern sector, Colonel Janos' 7th Brigade had no respite. They had been able to prevent the Syrians from consolidating their hold on their first night's objective in that sector—a defile through which the road ran just beyond Naffak on the route down to the Benot Yacov bridge. So the Syrians fought on through the night. In an extraordinary partnership, Eytan and Janos managed to hold on.

Janos' tactics were the reverse of Shoam's. Instead of dispersing his tanks to prepared positions and trying to fight the Syrians to a standstill, Janos kept his tanks in formation. He split them into two combat teams—initially, about fifty tanks apiece. And while the Syrians, after the initial assault wave, largely confined themselves to Golan's limited road network, Janos took to the surrounding terrain. The most evocative military comparison is perhaps with the German U-boat tactics of World War II. Janos marshaled his combat teams as the U-boat packs had maneuvered in the Atlantic, continuously striking at the flanks of the doggedly moving convoys.

Janos' objective was simple: If he could not hold territory, he could still inflict crippling damage—provided he kept moving. So his teams wheeled across the northern sector, now cutting into that Syrian formation, now retreating in a cloud of dust, now darting in again on some other suddenly exposed flank. A lone Israeli tank would appear around a hillock, enticingly vulnerable. A Syrian detachment would chase it—and as the "lone" Israeli retreated, an ambush closed in from the side.

Where there was no natural cover, Janos created it. He had a squad of bulldozers; they threw up earth ramparts for his tanks to hide behind. After the battle, one such rampart outside Kuneitra bore mute witness to the intensity of the struggle: Behind it were four burned-out Israeli tanks; in front of it were twenty-six shattered Syrian ones.

Where the terrian was too rough or too rocky, Janos simply made new tracks—again, with his bulldozers. Janos' combat teams were frequently crossing from north to south and back over roads clogged with Syrian tanks heading from east to west.

Where he could choose, Janos fought and withdrew, fought and withdrew, rather than seeking duels to the death. He could not always choose. We have said that the triangle of roads between Kuneitra and the border became known to Israeli crews as "the graveyard." There, the Israeli tanks had not been able to withdraw. Trapped by the terrain, they had to stand their ground— though, in the end, Janos did manage to bring up other tanks to give covering fire while the surviving Israelis escaped. By then, more than forty Syrian tanks had been destroyed for the loss of half a dozen Israeli. Nor was that ratio unusual. The Battle of Golan passed, swiftly and inevitably, into Israeli folk myth; but this statistic at least is accurate: A single company of the 7th Brigade—ten tanks—destroyed more than one hundred Syrian machines.

Coordinating this extraordinary battle, choreographing it, was Rafael Eytan, trapped in his underground bunker at Naffak—surrounded all that first night by Syrian tanks, the nearest thirty yards away. Eytan was one of only two senior Israeli officers promoted in the war. One reason was that in this siege, he did not, unlike colleagues in Sinai, revert to a role more suited to a lieutenant than a general and dash about with a submachine gun and grenades. While his subordinates defended the position —destroying more than forty tanks—Eytan remained underground, coolly directing Janos' wider battle with map and stopwatch.

Janos' tactics—to abandon territory in order to inflict damage —necessarily had to be modified at critical moments when particular Syrian formations, having broken through, were in a position to spill over the ridge and down the road to the Benot Yacov bridge. At such crises, Janos' men had no choice but to hold ground until they had destroyed that Syrian formation or had themselves been destroyed.

Eytan's cleverness—the subtlety that Hoffi had discerned—lay in his second-by-second management of those confrontations. When one of the Israeli infantry posts was about to be overrun, Eytan would detach four or five of Janos' tanks for a rescue operation. The task done, the squadron would rejoin its combat team. In the same way, Eytan would time the Syrian advances down the road from Naffak to the ridge and, at the last moment, bring up tanks in devastating ambush, while other units moved to block the road ahead. Before the ambushers could in turn be mauled by Syrian reinforcements, Eytan—still timing immaculately—would shift them to new and unexpected positions from which to catch the Syrians again unawares. With that crisis past, that Syrian formation destroyed, back the Israelis went once more to Janos' constantly moving combat teams. All through the night, in carefully timed sequence, groups of Israeli tanks slipped back to Naffak to break through the blockading Syrians and refuel and rearm while the crews showered and snatched a meal. Then back to battle, back to the roadblocks, the split-second ambushes, the desperate rescues, the wolf-pack harrying of Janos' outnumbered combat teams. . . . And so it continued for thirty-six hours.

It does not seem to have occurred to the Syrians to adopt fresh tactics: to concentrate on destroying Janos' tanks *before* capturing ground. Even the Syrian battle formations remained unchanged. Using the infrared night vision equipment with which many of their Soviet tanks are equipped, they redeployed through the night and at sunrise on Sunday were waiting to attack once more in a long line abreast down the axis of the roads—"Not regarded as a classic tactic these days, but perhaps that's what the Russians teach them," observed one Israeli commander. At first light, the long line advanced. But now, in one sector of the battle, they faced the first Israeli reserves.

Through Saturday night and the dark hours of Sunday morning, a steady trickle of tanks with hastily assembled scratch crews had driven over the Benot Yacov bridge on to Golan. One of the clichés of the war was that they were "flung into battle." Quite to the contrary, Eytan positioned these fragmentary reinforcements with extreme precision: constructing a defensive position here, an ambush there, gradually adding one tank to another until he had built up a group to be wielded at last as a viable new force.

Most of those early reinforcements Eytan had to deploy on the northern sector. But by Sunday dawn, the first substantial group of reserve tanks was on its way. Eytan sent these to relieve the pressure on the survivors of Shoam's brigade on southern Golan. Behind this decision was not merely the calculation that with daylight the situation was now toughest there; it was yet again a question of timing. The farther north the reinforcements had to drive, the later they would arrive. Eytan brought the reinforcements up to Golan by the most southerly route possible: by the cliff road south of Lake Tiberias.

The first reservists who drove up that road were operating Israel's weakest tanks. They were World War II Shermans, which, though they had mostly been modernized with 105mm guns, were by modern standards hopelessly weak in armor plate (some, indeed, had only 75mm guns). Ranged against them were large numbers of Soviet T-54 and T-55 tanks—dating from the fifties and sixties—and even some of the latest T-62s. Several of these T-62s, the Israelis found later, had only 50 kilometers on the clock. They had been driven off the tank transporters straight into battle. "They're all modern, freshly painted and with the smell of fresh rubber," was one Israeli report—with the bitter comment: "Everything Russian except the food; that's Arabic." (And, instead of the green and brown which are Syrian camouflage colors, many were still painted dark brown—the Red Army camouflage.) Yet amazingly, in this unequal confrontation, the Israeli reservists won.

In part, this was a product more of Eytan's cunning than of their fighting skill. Those first reserves Eytan largely used as decoys, tempting out the Syrian tanks into ambushes by Israeli infantry armed with SS-11 antitank missiles. Yet there were also tank-to-tank combats.

Lieutenant Dov, a twenty-eight-year-old civil servant working on the West Bank, was commander of one of those first Shermans. His signalman-loader was twenty-nine-year-old David Elimelech. When Elimelech heard from their tank squadron commander, Captain Gadi, that they could expect to face seventy to eighty Soviet tanks, a shiver literally ran down his spine. It was shortly before midmorning when they approached the Syrian formations, carefully deployed around El Al. Lieutenant Dov said later that he was almost in a state of shock: "We went into El Al in such a hellish noise of exploding shells." He weaved his tank between the shellbursts, heading for the nearest cover. He could not believe his eyes when he saw the size of the Syrian columns. "Only when I saw our guys beginning to shoot at them did I grasp what was happening." The squadron commander, Gadi, gave them a target; Elimelech loaded, and Dov's tank too opened up on the Syrians.

Some of the ensuing battle was fought at such close range that on one occasion a T-55 blundered into the midst of the halftracks carrying the reservists' headquarters company. "Most uncomfortable," the operations officer, Major Itzik, recalled. Nobody knew quite what to do. It was clearly unwise to provoke the tank, which could have obliterated them all, so none of the Israelis fired. Fortunately, the Syian tank crew were as puzzled: The T-55 wheeled around and left without firing a shot.

It was no easy Israeli victory. As an Israeli gunner from Scotland observed of his Syrian opponents: "They hit things; the days when they couldn't shoot straight are over." While the reservists halted the southernmost Syrian thrust, the destruction of Colonel Shoam's brigade continued. At noon on Sunday, Shoam himself was killed. He had climbed one of the old volcano cones to reconnoiter: The Syrian artillery got him. His second-in-command took over what was left of the brigade. That was not much: The Israelis have not released precise totals, but so far as we can work out, by 5 P.M. on Sunday, nearly 150 of Shoam's brigade had been killed. On the Israeli rule of thumb that the dead roughly equal the crew of every other tank hit, Shoam's brigade was virtually wiped out.

It was at 5 P.M. that the Syrians made their last attempt to destroy the 7th Armored Brigade as well. Over the cease-fire line rolled the main Syrian reserve force, 300 T-62s of the crack armored division commanded by Rifad Asad, brother of the Syrian President. "The next two hours, from five to seven, were the most crucial in the whole battle," an Israeli officer said afterward.

The weight of the new Syrian assault was unstoppable. By dusk on Sunday, the lead tanks had chopped down the Kuneitra road, past Naffak, to the Old Customs House at the top of the ridge above the Jordan. Less than five miles down the road ahead lay the Benot Yacov bridge. All that lay between were scattered squadrons of reserves coming up the road toward them—"We could not wait to group our reserves," an Israeli officer in Northern Command headquarters said later. "As fast as we got them, we sent them up the road to stop the Syrians." It seems inconceivable that a determined Syrian push could not have demolished these uncoordinated units in the hours ahead. Yet the Syrian advance got no farther.

There is some evidence that the Syrian advance just ran out of steam. The few UN observers, still trapped in their bunkers on the cease-fire line, for instance, saw little fuel or ammunition coming up behind the armor. The Israeli Air Force had destroyed it. The Syrians did not dare to bring up their convoys of ammunition trucks and fuel tankers by day. But as Saturday night fell, the roads behind the Syrian lines were jammed with these vulnerable convoys. They became the priority targets for the Israeli Skyhawks.

In a sense, Israel had no choice. After the terrible first hours, even the Air Force's reduced loss rate was running at about one Skyhawk down in every twelve sorties. The brutal economics of warfare dictated that unless they attacked the most vulnerable targets on Golan, Israel would be coming off worse in terms of attrition. And while the Skyhawks' 30-millimeter Defa cannon proved to be able to smash through the armor of a T-62, the Syrian tanks were tougher to destroy than the soft-topped Syrian supply convoys. Besides, the elimination of supplies was as effective a way as any of stranding the Syrian assault. So, through Saturday night, the Skyhawks had lit up the sky over the Golan plain with magnesium flares and dived in to savage the convoys. The Syrian missiles and antiaircraft guns exacted a persistent price. But the Israelis found later that a quarter of all the Syrian tanks abandoned on Golan had simply run out of fuel.

It was also the Israeli pilots who supplied the other most plausible cause of the Syrian failure to advance over the crest of Golan on Sunday evening. Phantoms and Skyhawks used the last minutes of light to make hair-raisingly low-level runs across the Jordan Valley and up over the Golan ridge to strafe the advancing tank formations. One observer later saw an entire file of Syrian tanks obliterated outside Naffak by those air strikes. And the long swathes of burned earth testified that napalm was used. "It was the supreme effort of our Air Force," an Israeli commentator wrote afterward.

It was the turning point of the Golan battle. By dawn on Monday Israeli reserves were choking the roads up to the plateau. Around noon, reinforcements finally reached Colonel Janos' brigade. By that time, the 7th Armored had lost 100 dead. Half its tanks had been destroyed. In all, by mid-Monday—forty-eight hours after war began—Israel had lost 250 dead in Golan, and the same number in Sinai. On both fronts, the immediate crisis was now past. But at that price in dead—with at least 1,000 wounded —Israel could not afford to keep fighting at this intensity. (That, at least, was the view taken by the Israeli Cabinet and by the General Staff; whether a more cold-blooded acceptance of losses would have brought a swifter victory is debatable.) The urgent necessity to limit casualties was to be one of the major factors governing Israel's strategy through the rest of the first week.

6. The Rain of Missiles

By Monday the casualties that most concerned the Israeli high command were their pilots; for it had become clear during the first two days of war that, in combating two deadly types of antiaircraft missile deployed by the Arab armies, Israel's Air Force faced potential losses as harrowing as those already inflicted on Israel's armor. In the Six-Day War, Israeli losses had been four aircraft per one hundred sorties. In the first two days of this new war, the losses of Skyhawks were running at up to twice that rate.

The Israelis knew what these missiles were: the SAM-6 (NATO code name "Gainful") and the SAM-7 (generally known by its Soviet name of "Strela"). But the Israeli pilots were encountering both for the first time. They had some forewarning about the SAM-7, which had been used in Vietnam: a highly mobile short-range missile, used against low-flying aircraft. The SAM-6 was in action for the first time and still largely an unknown quantity: It proved to be devastatingly effective at both high and low altitudes.

The first confirmed victim of this new weaponry was a Phantom coming in low over the desert to bomb the Egyptian bridgehead only a couple of hours after the crossing. After the first wave of strikes against the Egyptian bridges, however, the Israeli high command had decided that the priority task for its Air Force was to crush the Golan advance. And here the aircraft had been caught by the Syrians' cunningly deployed SAM-6 batteries, interlaced with ZSU-23 AA guns (spewing a thousand shells a minute from each of four barrels).

The Israeli pilots, in fact, found themselves facing on Golan the first integrated missile system ever seen in combat. From ground level to more than 70,000 feet, the Syrian armor was covered: by the SAM-6s, SAM-7s, and ZSU-23 antiaircraft guns at low-level, by SAM-3s at low to medium altitude, and with SAM-2s on top.

Over the first week, Israel lost 78 aircraft, two thirds over Golan —and virtually all to SAM-6s and ZSU-23s as they flew ground-attack missions. (The Israelis, indeed, claim that only 5 of the 115 aircraft they lost throughout the war were downed in aerial combat.) As the Israelis caught their breath on Monday, with the immediate disaster of Golan momentarily resolved, the grim task ahead of the Air Force was the destruction of these missile defenses.

The first problem was the missiles' mobility. The cumbersome SAM-2 and SAM-3 missiles were essentially designed for fixed or semipermanent sites (it takes at least six hours to dismantle and relocate one). Both the new SAMs, by contrast, could be shuttled around the war zones with bewildering speed. The SAM-6s were mounted in threes on a tracked launching vehicle that could travel over sand: The launcher and its accompanying radar vehicle could drive to new positions immediately after firing a missile. Camouflage and concealment were relatively easy—and the Syrians, in particular, exploited this cleverly. (They had moved their SAM-6s, for instance, after the Israeli reconnaissance flights on the eve of battle but before the actual assault.) For most Israeli pilots, the first sign of danger was the thin white smoke trail of a SAM-6 as it climbed toward them in a shallow curve at almost three times the speed of sound. By the time the Israelis—the pilot if he survived, or the watching ground forces if he did not —could call down artillery fire or bring in support aircraft, the launcher and radar vehicle had disappeared elsewhere.

The SAM-7 was even more mobile. Apart from the infantry-carried version—so light that it could be fired from the shoulder —the Israeli pilots realized by the second week of war that they were also confronted by SAM-7s in a different mode. The Egyptians and Syrians put into action new vehicle-mounted launchers, capable of firing salvos of four or eight Strelas simultaneously—reducing the possibilities of evasive maneuvers. There were many hits by SAM-7s, on the Israeli Skyhawks—though these proved tough enough to stagger back to base mostly. The Phantoms were safe; the SAM-7s could not catch them.

These missile defenses had to to be destroyed before the Israelis could hope to roll back the armor facing them on either front. In Sinai, the Egyptian bridgeheads now comprised three methodically organized lines of defense: infantry dug in with Sagger and RPG-7 antitank missiles; then tanks; and behind them batteries of SAM-6 missiles brought over the canal even before the Egyptians had moved up their armor. And over Golan, the Syrian missile screen made it prohibitively costly for the Israelis to adopt, as a consistent tactic, the close coordination of tanks and air strikes that was the core of their armored thinking. Somehow, the SAM missiles had to be outwitted by Israeli countermeasures or tactics before they—and the armor they protected—could be smashed.

In Vietnam, a good deal had been learned about the guidance system of the older SAM-2—and the SAM-3 had largely the same electronics—and the Israeli Phantoms and Skyhawks had been equipped by the Americans with elaborate systems of electronic countermeasures (ECM). An early-warning alarm—called by pilots the "Sam Song"—sounded in the cockpit as soon as the missiles' ground radar began tracking an aircraft; another ECM device then jammed the missiles' guidance system by sending out rival transmissions on the same frequency. But, as the electronic conflicts of the 1969-70 War of Attrition had shown, missile technology and the means to counter it proceed not in smooth tandem but rather by leapfrog: now an advance in missile capability, now a breakthrough in ECM response. And the new war found Egypt and Syria with missiles that Israel could not counter. Soviet technology had achieved a temporarily decisive jump ahead.

The SAM-7—and the SAM-6 in its homing phase—operate on new principles that made Israel's existing ECM devices irrelevant. Instead of being guided by radar, these two SAMs "home" onto aircraft by heat-seeking infrared sensors that guide the missile to the exhaust from the plane's jet engines. The early part of the SAM-6 flight is controlled by radar, but even here the Israelis found their existing ECMs ineffective. The SAM-6 radar ranged —at different stages of search, acquisition, tracking, and guidance —over three separate frequencies, together adding up to a far wider frequency band than any Soviet missile had used before. And while U.S. electronic intelligence had picked up each phase of the SAM-6 system, monitoring test launches in Egypt from early 1973, not enough was known about the precise signals or about the missile's ability to switch among different frequencies while in flight to throw off jamming transmissions. The result was that the

Israeli pilot had no "Sam Song" warning of a SAM-6 launch: If he did not spot that telltale puff of white smoke, his only other hope of warning was if his existing ECM pods were by chance tuned to the frequency that this particular SAM-6 happened to be operating on. Even if he was lucky in that—which was unusual —the missile was by now closing with his aircraft at about Mach 2.7 and he had only a few seconds left in which to try anything. (The SAM-6 radar—NATO code name "Straight Flush"—could pick up a low-flying aircraft fifteen to twenty miles away, a high-altitude target at fifty miles; at twenty-mile range, launch to impact took the SAM-6 just forty seconds.)

The Americans, as much with their own interests in mind as the Israelis', launched an intensive program early in the war to find out more about the SAM-6 electronics. Their electronic detection satellites orbiting over the Middle East were no doubt used in this: the method being to fly over a high-altitude reconnaissance plane to trigger a SAM-6 launch at a time synchronized with the passing of the satellite. This way, the technicians in the United States could get an almost immediate readout from the satellite of the transmissions from the missile's tracking and guidance systems. It was, however, a hazardous business for the pilot. It was not until the last days of the war that any modified ECMs on the Israeli planes showed signs of being effective. In the meantime, Israel's pilots could rely only on much cruder devices.

One of them, extensively used, was to pour out of the aircraft showers of "chaff"—thin metallized strips that blur the plane's radar image. The Israelis did not have big enough chaff dispensers, so they took to stuffing chaff into the air brake cavities of their aircraft. By momentarily applying the brakes, the pilot could then disperse a cloud of strips in his slipstream. But in order to be fully effective, the length of the strips must be "tuned" to a multiple of the radar's wavelength. So, until the SAM-6s wavelengths were known, this method was of questionable value. The other common device, developed in Vietnam, of dropping high-heat-intensity flares from the aircraft as decoys to confuse the missiles' heat-seeking sensors, was also used against both SAM-6 and SAM-7. Here, too, the Israeli Air Force was in for a shock. The Soviets had developed the "countercounter measure" of equipping the sensors with filters that could distinguish between the infrared frequency from jet exhausts and the lower frequency of the flares.

The Israelis also had small stocks of remote-controlled jet "drones"—two sorts, both obtained from the United States in the later phases of the War of Attrition for use in high-altitude photo-reconnaissance missions. These were now converted into decoys to distract the SAMs not only by their presence but also by the chaff they could be signaled to dump at the critical moment of a nearby Skyhawk attack. These drones were fairly successful—while they survived.

There was one other—last resort—counter to the SAM-6s: violent evasive action. After the first few days, Israeli pilots were using a prearranged evasive maneuver known as the "split-S roll"—turning violently into and across the missile's path—in hope of breaking its homing lock. In some cases, to give the pilot more time, helicopters were used to spot the puff of white smoke that signaled a missile launch; even then, pilots had only a few seconds to react. (And Israel lost half a dozen helicopters.)

Over Golan on the first Wednesday of the war, October 10, *Sunday Times* reporter Philip Jacobson saw five Israeli planes— three Skyhawks and two Mirages—hit by missiles in the space of an hour near Kuneitra. A Skyhawk pilot who had bailed out safely landed nearby. "Once that thing gets behind you, it's all over," he observed while waiting for a rescue helicopter. "We have orders to eject as soon as it locks onto our exhaust." Israel faced, as we shall see, enough problems ensuring replacement simply of its aircraft; its pilots were even more precious.

After the war, a question inevitably prompted by these Israeli experiences was whether the new antitank or antiaircraft missiles had changed the nature of likely combat elsewhere in the world— in the apocalyptic event of a NATO-Warsaw Pact clash, for example. And the impact of the cheap and simple Sagger and RPG-7 antitank weapons certainly warrants a rethinking of armored doctrines. But in its air war, Israel faced SAM-6s fired at a density almost certainly unattainable in any larger conflict. Technically, the SAM-6 is an ingenious weapon—though to what extent its undoubted qualities have been amplified by the U. S. Defense Department in the interests of securing larger appropriations for American missilery is uncertain. But the deadliest element in the SAM-6's success was simply the profligacy with which it was flung at the Israeli aircraft—and even so, its success was apparently considerably lower than the 97 per cent kill rate promised the Egyptians by the Soviets. Dayan put his finger on the key point when he told a private briefing of Israeli newspaper editors midway through the first week: "I doubt whether there is another place in the entire world that is protected by such a dense array of modern missiles. I doubt whether there is a place in Russia or Vietnam that is equipped like the Arab front—and, chiefly, the Egyptian front at the canal."

Syria deployed thirty-two SAM-6 batteries; Egypt had forty-six —each battery having four launchers, each launcher three missiles. The canal defenses were denser than the Soviet missile screen around Moscow. As for profligacy: In the first three days of this geographically confined war, the number of surface-to-air missiles fired roughly equaled the total NATO stocks in Europe. Those are considerably larger than the 1,000 or so surface-to-air missiles that are deployed in the continental United States, if nowhere near Soviet stocks. Even by Soviet standards, though the Arab missile density was unrepeatable. The Soviet Union—which plumped for missile defense while the United States concentrated upon the strategic bomber—now has around 10,000 missiles to protect the whole of Soviet airspace and, presumably, provide air cover for any incursion into Western Europe. Deploying all those missiles simultaneously would still not give the Soviet Union a missile screen of a density approaching that which it provided for Egypt and the Syrians.

The Israeli pilots, in other words, faced unique and probably unrepeatable odds. And against this massive Egyptian missile presence in Sinai, it indeed looked by the third day of the war as if Israeli counterattacks were going to be costly in both aircraft and armor. Amazingly, not until Monday evening did the Israeli high command realize the magnitude of the problem it faced in Sinai.

7. Morale Collapses in Sinai

At a press conference that Monday evening, the Israeli Chief of Staff, David Elazar, echoed Dayan's brand of barely qualified confidence: "This morning we embarked on a counterattack simultaneously on both fronts. . . . I am happy to tell you it is succeeding. . . . We have begun to destroy the Egyptian Army. In some places we have returned to the canal and in others our counterattack is still under way. . . . We are advancing on all fronts. . . . This war is serious, the fighting is serious. But I am happy to tell you that we are already at the turning point, that we are already moving forward." He even dropped heavy hints of further Israeli expansion: "I have to remind you that the cease-fire lines are not marked on the terrain. . . . We are moving wherever it is possible, and we shall destroy him wherever it is possible. We shall strike them, we shall beat them, we shall break their bones."

Elazar had made a terrible mistake. To cover it up, the explanation was put about next day that his clearly inaccurate prophecies had been designed to bolster the morale of the reservists now going into battle.

There is an element of truth in this. Elazar's briefing to Israeli newspaper editors barely half an hour before had been considerably less blithe. Elazar said afterward that he had been on his way to the press conference when he realized that the broadcast of his words would be heard by troops about to go into action—and by neighboring Arab states still on the sidelines, such as Jordan and Iraq. "I wanted them to hear that Israel was not too worried," he said, "and that I was confident that we could defeat the enemy, so that they would sit tight and not join the battle." But there was another reason that Elazar has not mentioned.

Elazar, as he spoke that evening, thought Israeli forces were once more reaching, perhaps even crossing the Suez Canal. Only as he finished his confident address could an aide tell him the news: So many Israeli tanks had been blown apart by Egyptian missiles that the attack had swiftly to be abandoned.

As the Sinai campaign had opened in earnest, it was not merely the reservists whose morale had needed bolstering. Shortly before dawn on Sunday, the Sinai commander, Major General Shmuel Gonen, had moved from Beersheba to his forward headquarters at Khiseiba, twenty-three miles from the canal on a hill guarding Gidi Pass. Here the atmosphere was little short of despairing. Reshef's men were beating off the Egyptian thrusts for the time being; and the Israeli reserves were on their way. But if the Egyptians chose to press on, it did not look as if Israel—even with its reserves—would be able to do other than fight a continuing rearguard action. The Israeli tank crews were becoming unnerved by the "creeping, crawling" techniques of the Egyptian missile infantry and the seeming inability of the dashing Israeli tactics of the past to cope with their endless ambushes. A few tank crews even deserted. (Israeli tanks, of course, were loaded with armor-piercing shells—fine against enemy armor, but useless against infantry. It was already clear that antipersonnel ammunition would be one of Israel's earliest shortages.)

Sharon was rude to Gonen when he helicoptered down from Tasa to Khiseiba at 9 P.M. on Sunday. "It was a terrible situation," Sharon said afterward. "We were being made to dance to the Egyptian tune; and nothing was being done to change the tune." Sharon held two people responsible: the Southern Commander, Gonen, and Major General Avraham "Albert" Mendler. Mendler commanded both the armored forces in Sinai and the Suez Canal sector—in effect, the front line. Sharon blamed both for not realizing rapidly enough the scale of the Egyptian assault; they had deployed as if against an altogether smaller operation, he said. This was unfair. The crucial failure had been to deprive the Bar-Lev Line of its tanks. But that seems to have stemmed from Gonen's interpretation of the concern felt at the highest *political* level that the Israelis were not to move forward until the last minute. And the war had certainly not taken Mendler by surprise: He had been the guest of honor at the officers' lunch in Bir Gifgafa on the Thursday before the war who prophesied quietly that he would not be leaving Sinai because fighting was about to begin.

It was true, though, that the setbacks of the first terrible twelve hours had shaken Gonen's nerve. He was new to the job: He had held it since May. And he had a distinguished record. In 1956 he had commanded the first tank unit to reach the Suez Canal; he had then gone to Britain to train at Camberley Staff College in the use of Centurion tanks; and in 1967 he commanded the crack 7th Armored Brigade—in that war fighting in Sinai— to brilliant effect. But Gonen, now forty-three years old—he had come to Israel from Lithuania as a baby—was not the sort of leader to raise morale in a tough situation by sheer imposition of personality. Physically slight, intensely religious, slightly fussy —he hated his officers to smoke, for instance—Gonen was, however personally brave and technically competent, a less than charismatic figure in an army overly impressed by *machismo*. Dayan and Elazar had to spend much of Sunday in Sinai trying to restore morale.

There was, of course, much to be shaken by. Israel, according to a NATO paper filed in Washington, had reckoned it had the resources to fight a thirty-day war. Israeli military sources explain the timing of this as follows: one week for the reduction of the Syrian Army; three weeks to beat Egypt. But this convenient belief in Israel's ability to fight on one front at a time hinged upon the role of the Bar-Lev defenses in fatally impeding an Egyptian buildup in Sinai. By Sunday evening, that strategy was in ruins: Egypt had six hundred tanks across the canal, with perhaps five divisions of infantry.

Nor did there seem to be any way of really denting the Egyptian buildup. Apart from close ground-support in Golan, the priority for the Israeli Air Force through Sunday and Monday was the destruction of the pontoons over the canal. It was a costly failure. The attacks took a steady toll of gallant pilots; and the Egyptian Chief of Staff, Shazli, later explained why they were unsuccessful: "The enemy air attacks were severe and sustained. They did hit some points. But military bridges [Shazli meant the new PMP pontoons] are built from linked sections which are replaceable. Repairing a bridge usually took from half an hour to an hour. We also moved our bridges from one location to another, to confuse pilots who were working from reconnaissance information. And we put up heavy smokescreens to make aiming more difficult for them, while dense anti-aircraft fire added to these difficulties."

The only hope of sustained damage to the bridgeheads was from the Israeli 155mm and 175mm guns, ranging in from the relative safety of the road fifteen miles back from the canal. But, for reasons already outlined, the effectiveness of that artillery had been sharply reduced. There is also evidence—from a source close to the commission of inquiry set up after the war by Mrs. Meir—of a further, inexplicable factor behind the relative failure of the Israeli artillery. The gunners were totally dependent on forward spotters—tank crews, and the last surviving Bar-Lev strongholds such as Meyerke's. The postwar inquiry found such evidence of confusion in the use of coded map references by the spotters —"Concentration Point G," and so on—that it seems the artillery in some cases may have been using different maps or codes from the spotters. There were even incidents when the Israeli artillery hit their own side in Sinai, including one reported shelling of an Israeli tank unit that resulted in the deaths of the crew of the command tank and possibly of two other tanks. (All Israeli radio exchanges in Sinai were automatically recorded at forward headquarters; the tapes formed important evidence at the subsequent inquiry, though their transcription was a harrowing experience.)

To break out of this seemingly inexorable spiral to defeat, the Israelis on Monday essayed a typically dramatic counterstroke. They tried to destroy the Third Army's main bridgehead by armored assault. While one division attacked Egypt's Second Army head-on in the north, Sharon's division set off to cut through the Third Army far to the south. But did the Israelis plan to cross the canal? Sharon has said that his plan that day was to "strike at the canal with a crossing to the other side, in order to destroy the self-confidence of the Egyptians." But other military sources in Israel claim that Gonen's plan was *not* to cross the canal, but merely to destroy one of the bridgeheads, and then, by advancing up the *east* bank of the canal, to cut off Egyptian supply routes, to attack the Sinai forces in the rear, and to bombard the west bank.

The attack began midway through Monday afternoon. Sharon had argued for a start at 5 A.M. Monday, but Gonen rejected this—adding to Sharon's disgust. It was sensible, though: By noon on Monday, Sharon's division was still only 90 per cent ready; and his tanks crews, the late-comers still exhausted by the drive across Sinai, needed as much rest as possible. More controversially, Gonen rejected Sharon's plea to make the frontal assault himself.

The long-standing Israeli contingency plan for the defense of Sinai called for roughly four divisions to range from north to south between the canal and the passes. In the north, by Kantara, the defenders would be a division primarily of infantry. So would the division be in the south, opposite Suez. But to hold the central sector in front of the Gidi and Khatmia passes, the contingency plan deployed two "strike divisions": the tank forces that would not only provide armored backup in the defensive phase of a new war, but would also then spearhead an Israeli counterattack.

Gonen had stuck to this plan. Sharon's was one of the strike divisions. The other was commanded by Major General Avraham "Bren" Adan, one of Israel's foremost tank tacticians. It was largely Adan who had devised Israel's response to the antitank missile. Israel had acquired back in 1955 its first such missiles, French SS-10s—crude, first-generation weapons, but still lethal enough to force a review of tactics. The response of the Israeli armored corps had been to group its tanks in ever-larger formations. The tactic that the Israelis practiced on maneuver was to charge the "enemy" missile infantry with a phalanx of tanks several hundred yards wide, careering forward at top speed, laying down smoke as well as throwing up a blinding dust cloud. The idea was that the missiles might pick off a few tanks on the edges, but that the main body would crash through. And protected in the center of the formation were armored personnel carriers of infantry, who would then mop up the stranded missile defenders from the rear. It seemed so obvious that, in fact, the Israelis did not practice the maneuver very often—missiles were too costly. But Adan was in every respect the logical choice to make the frontal assault on the Egyptians on Monday afternoon, while Sharon set off to the south.

Adan's assault was a disastrous failure. The theory behind the massed charge of missiles was fine: As Pythagoras could have pointed out to any ancient Greek tankman, quadrupling the tanks in a phalanx only doubles the number exposed at its edges. What went wrong that Monday was that Adan did not have enough tanks. He had at most a hundred, which meant that roughly a third were exposed to fire. The Egyptian missile infantry were numerous enough—and brave enough—to pick off as many tanks as they could see.

"We were advancing," one of Adan's officers recalled, "and in the distance I saw specks dotted on the sand dunes. I couldn't make out what they were. As we got closer, I thought they looked like tree stumps. They were motionless and scattered across the terrain ahead of us. I got on the intercom and asked the tanks ahead what they made of it. One of my tank commanders radioed back: 'My God, they're not tree stumps. They're men!' For a moment I couldn't understand. What were men doing standing out there—quite still—when we were advancing in our tanks toward them? Suddenly all hell broke loose. A barrage of missiles was being fired at us. Many of our tanks were hit. We had never come up against anything like this before. . . ."

What happened to Sharon is as disputed as the plan of attack itself. Sharon gave his version of events to several people, one the columnist Joseph Kraft: "At the last minute I was ordered not to move. My force was held in reserve. The task was given to another commander. I watched and saw his force slaughtered. The attack failed because of a lack of tanks. If we had all gone together, it would have succeeded." Other Israeli sources—including officers close to Sharon—tell a vastly different tale. All agree that Sharon was actually on his way south with his division when the first ferocious losses in Adan's attack revealed the impossibility of the plan. Sharon was summoned to return north as swiftly as possible—if necessary, to extricate Adan. Sharon obeyed, but apparently with extreme reluctance. Indeed, Gonen subsequently formally charged that Sharon had disobeyed orders; to which Sharon replied that the orders had been contradictory and confused.

Thus, in a welter of blood, confusion, and recrimination, the first Israeli counterattack collapsed. It was the final undermining of Gonen's morale. While Israeli Chief of Staff Elazar and Defense Minister Dayan now began hurried attempts to reconstruct the command hierarchy in Sinai, Egypt took advantage of the Israeli confusion to attack once more.

The northern Egyptian bridgehead at Kantara had—because of the soft and marshy terrain—relied upon infantry more than the others. But on Monday night, after the slaughter of Adan's tanks, an armored brigade of the Egyptian Second Army secured Kantara East. (The veracity of Egyptian communiqués sagged a bit the next day, however, when they talked of its Arab inhabitants thronging to greet the liberators. Kantara East had been a ghost town since 1968, when Israel evacuated its inhabitants a hundred miles eastward to El Arish.)

Farther south, around the Ismailia and Suez bridgeheads, the Egyptians now steadily, methodically, expanded sideways— "stretching their elbows in areas where they have been successful," was one Israeli military euphemism. The blunter truth was that the Egyptian bridgeheads were consolidating into an unbroken front the length of the canal. And through all the battles of Monday, their efforts to wipe out the last Israeli bunkers on the canal had not slackened. Late on Monday morning, in fact, Avi and his colleagues had faced their greatest crisis, as the Egyptians tried at last to capture their battered outpost. . . .

The doctor is being kept busy. Sergeant Baruch, wounded the day before, walks around carrying his infusion bag. Soldiers come in with backaches. They haven't urinated for two days. They are ordered to drink lots of water.

MEYERKE (suddenly): Armored troop carriers are moving up.
DOCTOR (over loudspeaker): Back to your positions. Get back to your positions.
MEYERKE: They're advancing on us, do you understand?
SHUKI: What about the mortar and bazooka?
MEYERKE: Mortar, mortar. What bazooka? Honest! Let them hit with the artillery. (To Avi): Tell the artillery they're advancing on us and entering Positions A and B. They should send some planes here.
HEADQUARTERS: One moment.
AVI: That one moment of theirs!

MEYERKE (impatiently): Eight armored personnel carriers are firing on us.

Sound of shots. A plane is heard.

DOCTOR (excitedly): Excellent!
HEADQUARTERS: Are they attacking yet?
MEYERKE (with emphasis): Yes! But the plane is bombing. . . .

A bomb falls between the fort and the Egyptians. The Israeli troops' rejoicing ends abruptly as they realize the plane isn't one of theirs. Automatic fire is heard. The Egyptians fan out from their APCs but don't attack. Hand-to-hand combat is expected. Everyone grabs his personal weapon.

MEDIC: Avi, is that your Uzi [submachine gun]?
AVI: I don't know.
DOCTOR: It's mine.
MEDIC: So I don't have one.
AVI: Who took my Uzi, Don't take my Uzi.

The telephone rings.

HEADQUARTERS: What's your problem?
MEYERKE: What's our problem! Ten APCs facing us. Soldiers moving toward us. Aside from that, their planes dropping on us. And you ask what is our problem?
HEADQUARTERS: Great, guys. Just keep beating into them as hard as you can.
MEYERKE: We're shooting at them. But where's your artillery?
HEADQUARTERS: O.K. I'm already sending it.
MEYERKE: Yes, yes, immediately.

Small-arms firing is heard from the soldiers in the fort, but no artillery. The Egyptians eventually retire to the junction on the canal road, leaving casualties.

HEADQUARTERS: Did we score any hits?
MEYERKE: You haven't even been firing!

HEADQUARTERS: Hell! Look, there'll be some artillery soon. We're a little short. Be patient, everything will be fixed.

MEYERKE (ironically): Sure, sure we'll be patient.

HEADQUARTERS (a few minutes later): What's the situation now? In order?

MEYERKE: *In'alrabak!* [Good God Almighty!] What should be in order? The APCs that were on the road turned around and dropped off men and left markers. Markers where to attack from. They're probably planning another attack, in the afternoon or tonight. Now they've gone to the north. . . .

The Egyptian assault switches to the fort to the north. On the radio, Avi and Meyerke—the tape machine still recording—listen to increasingly desperate interchanges between the commander of the northern front and headquarters as the assault develops. Eventually, repeated calls from headquarters fail to get a reply: The northern fort has been wiped out. Meanwhile the situation in isolated forts to the south is deteriorating. The commander of the next main fort, by the Bitter Lakes, radios that hundreds of Egyptians are attacking with tank support and he can hold out no longer. Forty-two men in Fort "Mezakh," at the extreme south of the Bar-Lev Line by Port Tewfik, are still bravely holding on—and would continue to do so for four more days, before a highly publicized, televised surrender. (Only one fort, code-named "Budapest," and at the northernmost point of the Bar-Lev Line in the coastal salt marsh, actually held out until the Israelis relieved it.)

Terrifyingly, over the loudspeaker-telephone that linked together all the forts of the Bar-Lev Line, Meyerke and his men now begin to hear the screams of men being roasted alive in their underground bunkers by Egyptian tanks mounted with flamethrowers. They know their luck cannot last. That night they decide on an escape plan.

8. Escalation Against Syria

The lack of Israeli resources to help the beleaguered Bar-Lev fort stemmed, partly, from the fact that on the other front, Golan, they were having a much tougher time than they had bargained for. By Monday, the tide of battle was turning for Israel in Golan—but far too slowly for comfort. "Good starters, bad finishers," a British diplomat in Amman called the Syrians, prophesying that their advance, its momentum slowed, would now quickly crumble. The Israeli reinforcements going up to Golan thought the same. "In the last analysis, they're chicken," an Israeli officer on Golan said. Yet the Syrians did not crumble. Instead, they fought back with tenacity and skill.

Why the Israelis so despised the Syrians is hard to fathom. Chief of Staff Elazar, of all people, had cause to know that the taking of Golan in 1967 had been no walkover: As a brigadier he had commanded the northern front in that war, marshaling the forces for the battle. (The commander of the actual assault had been Yizhak Hoffi, northern commander in this new war.) The Syrians fought well before collapsing under pressure. "We just pounded them continuously," said the then Air Force commander, Major General Mordechai Hod. "After twenty-seven hours they broke and ran." (Hod's memory speeded the sequence: Most of the Syrian line held for about thirty-six hours.) Israeli intelligence must surely since have learned that one reason for that Syrian collapse had been the corrosion of its command structure by "political" officers. Most officers in 1967 had been members of the Alawite Muslim sect; under heavy fire they simply deserted their men, mainly of the Shi'ite sect. Where officers and men stuck together, they had done rather well.

But presumably the Israelis had discounted that. And, to a people seeking bravura in their military leaders, the Syrian Army commander, General Mustafa Tlas, must have cut a dispiriting figure in Israeli eyes. A former law student, Tlas had been just another "political" officer when he first emerged in the Syrian Army in 1964 as president of the Damascus military tribunal. He saw no action in 1967—he was commanding the 5th Division at Homs—yet was elevated to Chief of Staff in 1968. Tlas, now forty-five years old, was certainly politically shrewd: When the military-civilian split in Syria's ruling Baathist party came, he backed his fellow soldier Hafez Asad—and collected the Ministry of Defense as a reward. But Tlas was also militarily capable: His book on guerrilla war is reckoned first-rate. And the first days of war showed that he and his Chief of Staff, Yusif Shakkour, were considerably more determined than the Israelis had thought. It looked, for instance, as if those rumors around the beginning of 1972 that President Asad had been persuaded to purge incompetent "political" officers from the forces had been true. Certainly, there was nothing incompetent about the Syrian defense of their gains in Golan. (Another possible reason for the Syrian improvement was advanced by an Israeli lieutenant—one-armed, it should be noted—midway through the Golan battle: "You play good chess players," he said, "you get better at chess.")

To Syrians who recalled the humiliations of 1967, merely to have an army now capable of standing up to the Israelis was a victory. But the Syrian armor did much better than that. By Tuesday, the pattern of the Israeli assault was established. Israeli pilots would launch ferocious air strikes against the Syrian formations. Israeli artillery would then open fire. Finally, Israeli tanks would attack head-on. It was war reduced to a slugging match—"Not our sort of war," a tank commander on Golan said with a shrug, "but what else can we do? We are used to taking the initiative, but this time the Syrians beat us to it."

It was brave, but it was all taking Israel too long—and costing too much. For twenty-four hours, Israeli pilots had been trying to knock out the Syrian SAM-6 batteries to open up the Syrian tanks and artillery to the full weight of Israeli air power. In the chilling euphemism of the Israeli military spokesman: "Our Air Force suffered losses to establish its supremacy." Yet despite optimistic Israeli statements about the "destruction of the central sector" of the Syrian advance, the Israeli tanks had barely managed by Monday to consolidate their hold upon their first objective, which was their own brigade headquarters at Naffak. The Syrian headquarters set up at Khusniye in southeastern Golan remained the hub of a solidly entrenched Syrian tank force of close to a division.

During the early hours of Tuesday morning, the Syrians even launched a series of determined and coordinated counterattacks. Simultaneously, a division broke into the Israeli lines in front of Kuneitra while another formation drove in by Khusniye on the southern sector. Only at 4 A.M. Tuesday did the Kuneitra action ebb away as the Syrians retreated once. Three hours later, farther north, another formation—this time mainly of the Syrians' most modern tanks, the T-62—thrust several miles into the Israeli front consolidating north of Kuneitra, on the 7th Armored Brigade's old territory. By Tuesday midmorning, that assault too had been broken, with eighty more Syrian tanks burning in the "graveyard" of the Kuneitra triangle. But the battle to contain the southernmost Syrian counterattack, near Khusniye, took longer. A large part of that Syrian column had been cut off during the early hours of Tuesday: At dawn the Israelis called in air strikes to destroy the clustered Syrian formations of tanks, mobile guns, and armored personnel carriers. By dusk, the Syrian formations were smoking wreckage. But Golan was still absorbing most of the Israeli Air Force's depleted resources.

So ended the last major Syrian counteroffensive. As the last bitter fighting continued into Tuesday night, however, Israel could not know that. And even at its end, Northern Command estimated that Syria still had in reserve another four hundred tanks—"More than enough to make a good fight of it in the days to come," one of Hoffi's headquarters staff commented gloomily.

Somehow, Syria had to be crushed swiftly. On this fourth day of fighting—Tuesday, October 9—Israel embarked upon a calculated escalation of the war. Its Air Force bombed the Syrian capital, Damascus, and then proceeded to destroy in the days ahead as much of Syria's heavy industry as it could.

There was an immediate cause for this. Shortly before sunrise on Tuesday, a Soviet "Frog" rocket launched from Syria had landed amid the buildings of Kibbutz Gevat, near Nazareth in central northern Israel. The resulting explosion wrecked twelve buildings and caused $250,000 worth of damage. Some of the buildings were dormitories for 270 children of the kibbutz. The children were sleeping in underground shelters, as were most of the adults, so nobody was hurt. But it was a horrifying indication of how vulnerable Israel's civilian population was to rocket warfare.

The "Frog-7" is the latest of a series of Soviet battlefield missiles, launched from a wheeled vehicle. Even with a range of less than forty miles, it could be lobbed from the Syrian lines into the center of northern Israel. This the Syrians had been doing each night of the war.

At 8 A.M. on Tuesday, Israeli radio announced: "In the past two days, the Syrians launched some twenty Frog missiles on civilian settlements in northern Israel. . . ." (The Syrians had in fact launched sixteen Frogs: three on Sunday, seven on Monday and now six this Tuesday. The attacks had come as a nasty surprise: the Syrians had been reckoned to have only ten Frogs, but the Soviets shipped in at least another twenty just before war broke out.) At 9:06 A.M. the Syrians—no doubt appreciating what was in store—broadcast back: "Our forces shelled Ramat Airport and other military targets in the area and . . . did not attack any civilian target." But while it may, just, have been true that the Syrians were aiming the unguided Frogs at the network of military bases in northern Israel—Dayan, at least, accepted that they were—their impact had consistently been upon civilian targets. Israeli retribution was now inevitable.

At 12:10 P.M. six Israeli Phantoms approached Damascus, flying low and fast over the desert south of the town. In three waves little more than a minute apart, the Phantoms opened up with rocket and cannon on the buildings of the Syrian Air Force headquarters and the Ministry of Defense, wreaking havoc inside both. One of the strikes badly overshot. The Air Force headquarters backs on to the ancient fairgrounds of Damascus. But the Ministry of Defense stands in Omayad Square, and a couple of miles behind it lie the quiet and pleasant streets of the Abu Rummaneh residential and diplomatic quarter. As the rockets and cannon shells of one strike overshot, they destroyed almost a whole street of houses in Abu Rummaneh. A senior Western diplomat in Damascus later gave *Sunday Times* reporter Brian Moynahan his estimate that two hundred people died in that strike. Among them were women of the Indian community, holding a coffee party for a visiting Indian singer; a rocket penetrated the house, killing four and injuring sixteen.

A Norwegian United Nations official, his wife, and their eight-year-old daughter also died. Presumably spotting the aircraft lining up far off on their approach run, he had hustled his family into the basement of their home. The Israelis were using delayed-fuse rockets to penetrate the military buildings: A rocket made a neat hole in his roof and exploded in the basement. The Damascus radio station and the Soviet cultural center were also hit. So was a hospital.

Israel claimed to have hit only "strategic targets." And through the days ahead, its strikes on Syria became even bolder. Not merely did the bombing continue of obvious tactical targets such as airfields—that had begun on the second day of the war. A sizable part of Syria's heavy industry was also shattered. Two oil refineries at Homs were hit; so were fuel tanks at Adra and Latakia worth five million dollars. More oil tanks at the port of Tartous were destroyed, together with their loading terminal. Power stations at Damascus and Homs were bombed. (The Homs station alone had supplied one fifth of Syria's electricity.) The costliest blow of all was to Banias, the Mediterranean terminal for Iraqi crude oil: It was devastated. The Banias installation had been earning royalties for Syria of fifty-five million dollars a year, and the Banias and Homs refineries together had employed thirty-four hundred people—a lot for a small, poor country. In 1972 Syria's growth rate had been 12 per cent: The Israeli bombing was a massive setback to future hopes.

That was the point. Certainly, Israel also had an immediate tactical objective in widening the war. Its Air Force was finding the battle against the Syrian SAM-6s too costly. But at least they had now found a way of hitting the batteries. The Soviets had not supplied Syria with all possible radar gear. In particular, the omission of the surveillance radar that NATO code-named "Long Track"—used by the Soviet Union in connection with another missile, the SAM-4—meant that the Syrian radar cover had somewhat weakened altitude discrimination. And the SAMs also took off in a shallow curve, steepening as they climbed. To exploit these flaws, the Israelis took to dive-bombing tactics; approaching very high and then swooping down on the batteries as steeply as possible. It confused the SAMs—some of the time.

By Tuesday evening, after almost forty-eight hours of effort, Israeli Skyhawks had destroyed more than half the batteries around Golan. Meanwhile, Israeli Phantoms and Mirages, giving cover, tangled with scores of Syrian fighters sent to interdict the Skyhawks. The Israelis shot down twenty-seven MiGs in one day over Golan.

But the Syrians had still more SAMs in reserve. If they were brought up to Golan, the Israelis would have to begin this destruction of the Syrian armor's air cover over again. They did not have the resources to do it. The decision to bomb important targets throughout Syria was thus, in part, an Israeli attempt to force the Syrians to dilute their air defenses over the battlefield by deploying the available SAMs around strategic industrial targets.

The scheme was partially successful. In the eight hours after the first round of antimissile strikes, Israel lost only one aircraft over Golan. Through Tuesday morning, no SAMs were fired on Golan at all—either, as Dayan grimly said, "because they had been destroyed or because the Syrians ran away." But the Syrians did then move up other batteries, and Israeli losses began to climb again. More than half the surviving SAMs were, however, deployed not on Golan but around Damascus and the Syrian ports.

But the punishment of Syria had a more strategic purpose too. Elazar's seeming bombast about "breaking the bones" of the Arab armies *was* Israel's strategy. Syria had to be subdued not merely rapidly, but also in sufficiently exemplary fashion to deter other contenders from entering the fray—most particularly, Iraq and Jordan. Israel was uncomfortably aware that the longer the war continued on two fronts, the more likely it was that Arab political pressure would force King Hussein—whatever his military weakness—to open up a third. Israel knew that the United States was using all the leverage that its massive aid program gave it to vehemently counsel Hussein to stay out of the conflict. But Hussein was, after all, an Arab and a proud one. The taunts of

President Qaddafi—who, himself keeping Libya safely on the sidelines, had taken to calling Hussein a coward—might be ludicrously inapposite, but they presumably stung just the same. More ominous was the possibility of Iraq's entry into the war: Unlike Jordan, Iraq had considerable military resources; hence the decision to demonstrate the vulnerability of Syria's economic infrastructure. Also as a warning to other neighbors, Israel on Tuesday bombed Lebanon's most powerful radar station on Jebel el Baroukh, a mountain ridge southeast of Beirut, which it claimed was tracking aircraft movements in northern Israel.

9. "No Easy and Elegant Victories"

If the Israeli plan to repeat on Golan the Hod strategy of 1967 and "pound the Syrians into cracking"—as the Jerusalem *Post* now confidently put it—was having only slow success, Tuesday, October 9, brought further disaster to Israel's campaign in Sinai. Sharon tried to emulate Adan's assault of the day before—and his tanks too were massacred.

The Southern commander, Shmuel Gonen, carried the can for the debacle. His critics back in Tel Aviv were not slow to tell the New York *Times*, for example, that the attack had been made "without sufficient preparation and with insufficient strength." But it is questionable whether Gonen was responsible. Loss of control is, of course, as much a reflection upon a commander as military misjudgment. But it does seem that by Tuesday, Gonen's position was impossible. All four division commanders nominally subordinate to him now disputed his orders. Sharon was the most recalcitrant. "If I were still in command, you wouldn't have much to do in this war," he told Gonen contemptuously. (Dayan and Elazar had spent all Monday night down at Khiseiba HQ, trying to patch up relations—Dayan at the same time decreeing that Israel must go on to the defensive in Sinai until the Syrians were beaten. The pair did not leave Sinai till 5 A.M. on Tuesday, exhausted.)

It was against this background that, according to an official complaint subsequently filed by Gonen, Sharon launched his Tuesday attack against orders. Sharon's version is that Gonen's headquarters did not know what was happening in the field, lost an opportunity to reach the canal, and failed to back up his assault for personal reasons. Israel has been at some pains to cloak the entire Sinai campaign, and this mess in particular; but the sequence of events, so far as we can unravel it, seems to have run like this:

Sharon's brief was to relieve a couple of the more desperate outposts still beleaguered on the Bar-Lev Line—in particular, a couple of forts north of Avi's bunker by Ismailia. The attack was spearheaded by the 190th Armored Battalion, under Colonel Assaf Yagouri. And when the 190th ran into severe trouble, it is correct that Gonen, while sending in air strikes, did not push up reinforcements of armor. But his reasons were simple: Gonen could not spare them; and Sharon apparently wanted to expand his already abortive rescue operation into a crossing of the canal.

Sharon was so furious at Gonen's refusal that first Elazar and then Dayan had to intervene. To Elazar, Sharon raged: "Has everyone gone mad? I am certain I can do it. All I need is forty-eight hours to destroy the enemy." More to the point, however, he needed extra tanks and infantry. "This would be the way to throw the Egyptians off balance," he told Dayan. But Dayan pointed to Israel's desperate shortage of armor in Sinai while the Golan battle sapped its resources. The only spare unit, Dayan said, was a brigade of paratroopers below the Mitla Pass, covering a potential Egyptian breakout down the coast road toward the oilfields of Abu Rodeis. (Already, the Israeli Air Force had only just managed to smash one Egyptian column of fifty vehicles—mostly tanks— that had headed south from Port Suez toward Abu Rodeis. It was uncertain whether air power alone could do this a second time.) According to the plausible account of Payne and Dobson in the London *Sunday Telegraph,* Dayan told Sharon: "You might succeed; but if you fail there is nothing left in Sinai. And the state would be endangered." Sharon reluctantly acquiesced. The 190th Armored Battalion was lost.

Its commander, Colonel Yagouri, survived—humiliatingly—to answer questions on Cairo television. Yagouri clearly found his defeat difficult to fathom. All he seemed to know was that he and many other tanks had suddenly been hit, that his tank had caught fire, and that he had no choice but to surrender. But the men who destroyed the 190th were the forward troops in the central sector of the Egyptian Second Army, just north of Ismailia. And their commander, forty-three-year-old Brigadier General Hassan Abu A'Saada, later explained—in excellent English—where Yagouri had gone wrong.

"Yagouri made several tactical mistakes," he said. "There had been information of an impending Israeli attack, so our troops and tanks were well dug in. Yagouri sent out ten tanks, and we destroyed seven. Then he sent out thirteen and we destroyed four. By this time I had made a decision to accept penetration of our position for up to five hundred yards. When Yagouri's main force charged us quite suddenly at high speed, about 30 mph, we had been able to set up the ambush and they fell into the trap. It was men against tanks—infantrymen with RPGs, Saggers, and hand grenades. Frequently they were knocking out a tank from the rear after it had gone by. That takes courage and determination. They were wiped out in three minutes, having scarcely fired a shot. Yagouri's tank was hit while trying to escape and fell into a gully." Israeli sources say twenty tanks were lost in Sharon's attack; A'Saada claims thirty-five knocked out and seventeen captured. A'Saada claims, in fact, that Yagouri's command was a *brigade*.

As if to emphasize their reserves of power, the Second Army now followed up that success by finally capturing the site of Israel's central sector advanced headquarters. This was a concrete blockhouse dug into the side of what the Egyptians called "Triangle 100," the 577-foot hill of Katib el Kheil, west of Tasa. Israel was not, in fact, using the blockhouse as a headquarters. Sharon and Adan both preferred mobile bases. But the hill itself dominated the surrounding terrain—an ideal vantage point for artillery spotting and, although surrounded, its Israeli defenders had held out. The Egyptians overran them in a night attack on Tuesday. A series of Israeli counterattacks through Wednesday were beaten off with considerable Israeli losses.

So when Haim Herzog, the retired general used through the war as the official Israeli military commentator, disavowed Elazar's previous optimism, only the Israeli military then knew how accurate his warning was. "I have no doubt that the struggle facing us will not be an easy one," Herzog told Israeli television viewers on Tuesday. "I would not say we have moved over to a major offensive yet."

Naturally, Herzog did not talk of successive Sinai counterattacks running into trouble. But it was still a far cry from Elazar's "offensive on all fronts." "So far," Herzog said, "We have been consolidating, deploying, and seizing the initiative." And he was frank enough to make the central point: "I would not be lulled into believing this can be an easy and very rapid operation." This time, he warned, there would be "no easy and elegant victories." Israel had finally gotten the message.

It was through these Tuesday Sinai tank battles that Meyerke and his men, unescorted and on foot, were to march to safety. The decision had been taken during the night, after another armored personnel carrier had penetrated the gate of the fort and left a flashing marker, presumably to guide flame-throwing tanks in a night assault. (As it was doing so, the men had debated whether to try the desperate tactic of capturing the APC intact and riding to freedom on that.)

The preparations for departure are again recorded on Avi's tape, and the men subsequently recalled details of their escape in other tape recordings.

MEYERKE (after the debate about the APC): Boys, we're leaving this place on foot, tonight. [There is a brief argument, which Meyerke firmly settles.] We're leaving tonight. . . . But we have to ask for formal permission. After all, this isn't a *bardak* [Russian for brothel].

HEADQUARTERS (after Meyerke submits his request): It'll work out O.K. if you stay.

MEYERKE: I don't want any more promises. . . . I want a reply within ten minutes.

The commanding officer, Sharon, comes personally on the line. Meyerke explains the plan.

SHARON: You haven't got much of a chance. We can't come out to help you.

MEYERKE: We're leaving anyway.

SHARON: Well, if you think it will work, do it.

MEYERKE: We'll report again next time when we're back there.

SHARON: Take care of yourselves.

The men, who have now gone sixty hours without sleep, get ready. Meyerke makes them all eat. They fill water flasks, put on heavy flak jackets, and assemble their weapons—Uzis, two grenades each, a bazooka, and six machine guns, with ammunition and flares. They destroy other equipment and documents, except for the main radio set, which is left in use until the last minute so as not to arouse Egyptian suspicions.

MEYERKE (giving his final briefing): Our aim is to get back safely, with a minimum of casualties. The main thing is to keep moving forward and not to get delayed. If we get fired on, try to fight, charge the enemy, and move forward quickly.

Avi bundles up the tapes he has made and puts a new battery into his portable radio equipment. They wait into the early hours for the setting of the moon, and start out in pitch darkness. Outside they split into two groups, Meyerke and Avi heading one, Shuki and Shlomo the other. They go separately but in the same general direction: three kilometers southward along a strip of sand parallel to the canal, then the risky crossing eastward over the canal road followed by a long, thirteen-kilometer march to the northeast over sand dunes. Barbed wire is in their way, and the dunes are pockmarked with craters. They are worried mainly about the two wounded, Marciano and Baruch, but both make their way without help. Flares flicker in the sky. The men freeze until the light goes out.

At five-thirty dawn breaks, and Meyerke changes direction into the rising sun. They take off their heavy, cumbersome flak jackets and bury them in the sand. At six o'clock a large tank battle starts up and the men find themselves trapped between the opposing armored forces. They take cover in a dip in the dunes. Avi can't hear base on his radio because of his low position. He climbs to the top of the dune and makes contact again. Two MiGs are shot down and their pilots parachute to the desert nearby. The men debate whether to try to take them prisoner, but decide not to complicate matters. As the sun gets up, and the heat of day begins, they spot another group of men a kilometer away. It is Shuki's group. They join up in the same dip in the sand and excitedly compare experiences.

Avi discovers that one of the soldiers, a mortarman called Meir Orenstein, has strictly against orders rescued a small battery-powered tape recorder from the fort. Avi is annoyed with him for breaking orders and carrying excess weight. But with his unfaltering sense of occasion he borrows the machine and, as they shelter from the tank battle, records one of his by now quite practiced commentaries. He also passes the recorder around for the other men to describe their experiences of the night.

MARCIANO: When we passed through them in the night, we actually heard them shouting. Enough to make you feel faint. All the way we kept seeing tanks, but when the Phantoms came . . .
DOCTOR: That made us feel good.
MEYERKE: When I set out I wasn't scared. And when we passed by them I wasn't scared. You know when I began to worry? You didn't even notice it. There was this embankment of sand and all sorts of guys lying in foxholes. I thought we were coming on the Egyptians so I got hold of that one who speaks Arabic—where is he—that's you, Roni. I told him mutter something aloud in Arabic about wanting to get there quickly to smash those Jews . . .
BARUCH: You know he came to Israel after the Six-Day War . . .
MEYERKE (astonished): Is that so?

Others join in and the recording ends incongruously—against the continuing background of the tank battle—with a discussion between Avi and Baruch about the cost of hi-fi equipment.

Burning tanks are now scattered in all directions, but Meyerke encourages the men to press on. They come under machine-gun fire. Avi calls base on the radio. "We're sending a tank to rescue you," he is told. Meyerke says he will fire a green flare for identification. A classic rescue operation follows. Armored infantry in halftracks suddenly appear over the dunes fighting a quick, angry battle against the Egyptian infantry positions. Two tanks, one giving cover, are approaching. Marciano fires the green flare. Almost simultaneously, a green flare is fired from an Egyptian position too. (Has the radio conversation been overheard?) Avi hastily radios a caution for the tank commanders, and Marciano sends up another flare.

As the tank arrives the thirty-three men clamber all over it holding onto anything available, even the gun barrel. Exposed to fire, the tank zigzags at full speed to where a halftrack is waiting. The military road that they reach, just a little way farther, is still under full Israeli control.

The nearest the Israelis got to the old "quick and elegant victories" of which General Herzog had wistfully reminded his televiewers came on Wednesday. They were won by the service Israel had always regarded as something of a poor relation, its Navy. And, as an additional irony, they came because the Navy, at least, had recognized that missiles revolutionized warfare.

The Israeli Navy's attention to missiles is readily understandable: On October 21, 1967, its destroyer *Eilat* was sunk off Port Said by a Styx missile launched from a Soviet-built Komar class missile boat of the Egyptian Navy. Israel's immediate retaliation had been to destroy Egypt's Port Suez oil refineries. But, as a longer-term response, Israel built up its own fleet of a dozen fast missile boats—five of them smuggled out of their French constructors' dockyard at Cherbourg on Christmas Day, 1969, in defiance of De Gaulle's embargo on arms sales to Israel. These "Saar" boats, plus two homemade models named *Reshef*, are armed with a missile designed and manufactured by Israel itself, the Gabriel. This has a range of only twelve miles—half that of the Styx missiles used by the combined Egyptian and Syrian missile fleets of twenty-eight boats. But its guidance system is highly sophisticated. And while Styx missiles curve up and over in a normal trajectory—and are thus exposed to jamming—the Gabriel skims almost level, low over the waves, its approach masked by the clutter of surface reflections picked up on enemy radar screens.

Certainly from the first day of the war—when Israel wiped out four Syrian craft, mostly with the Gabriel—the Israeli Navy had the battle all their own way. On the first Wednesday, October 10, three Egyptian missile boats were sunk near Port Said and, in a more controversial action, Israel tackled Syrian missile boats actually in harbor—sinking four but contriving to damage Greek, Soviet, and Japanese cargo vessels in the port at the same time.

From then on, Israel had the run of the coastlines. Its boats were out twenty-four hours a day, rocketing and shooting up anything that moved. And their 76mm guns played a part in the destruction of the Syrian coastal oil installations, as well as damaging several radar stations, military complexes, and supply depots on both the Syrian and the Egyptian coasts. According to one Israeli source, the Navy even tackled some of Egypt's most northerly SAM sites.

In return, Israel admits to a shrapnel hole in one Saar and the loss of a couple of other light craft in Red Sea engagements. Inside Israel, the impact of the Navy's victories far outweighed their actual significance. Depending as they did upon superb maneuverability and handling to dash well inside the Styx range before they could launch their own Gabriels, the Israeli boats were solitary and morale-boosting reminders of the heady days of 1967.

In the absence of such consolations on land, what was Israel to do now? The facts of Israel's plight—any clues to what Mrs. Meir and her ministers were trying to achieve—were carefully concealed during the war. But it is now possible to know how Dayan, at least, saw the war by late Tuesday. That afternoon, he gave a confidential briefing to Israeli newspaper editors; and, after the war, a transcript of this became available. It was a long, at times rambling, account, but it boiled down to four themes.

First, Syria: "We want," Dayan said, "to make a supreme, productive, and effective effort to get Syria out of the war. I don't know whether we can get the Syrians to ask for a cease-fire. I do believe and hope that we can bring Syria to a situation where it will in fact cease firing and will not have effective fire power . . . We very much want to silence the Syrian front. It was first priority . . . In order to achieve this, we want to hit them at two levels: first of all, to destroy the forces they sent here—and I think we are not far from that. . . . Destroying them costs us dearly, since destroying a tank is not like crushing a flower. But they are stubborn and there is no other way. We are not far from the point where their entire force will indeed be crushed. . . .

"The second part concerns Syria itself . . . the war should cost Syria so dearly that they will regret what they did. . . . If there is a war, then the Syrians must pay a heavy price for it. We did it today, hitting Syria itself—economic and military targets, power stations, oil installations, army camps, air fields, and also civilian economic targets. If one has to hit their Air Force headquarters, Army headquarters, and the Defense Ministry, this means attacking Damascus. . . ."

"There were very basic considerations whether to take action against Damascus or not. We did it for the first time, and I don't know what the American reaction will be like. And their reaction is very important to us at all times and especially in this situation. There were two considerations: one of which was the use of the Frog missiles—because once the use of ground-to-ground missiles starts [to raise the possibility of civilian deaths] then Damascus is on the list of targets. But this was not the main consideration, which is [to hurt Syria severely]. . . .

"We cannot do this every day, not because of military problems, but because of political difficulties. One can do it once, in the present situation, but it would be very difficult to make Damascus a permanent target. It was decided to do it now, as part of the over-all, supreme effort to get Syria out of the war. . . ."

Dayan was optimistic about the Golan front: "I'm delighted with the way we've handled the Syrians. . . . I do believe we've got the Syrian thing behind us . . . I believe we will finish off the Syrians. And then the Jordanians will not enter the war, neither will the Iraqis . . . I think we will achieve this within a few days. . . ."

But Dayan then turned to Sinai—and detonated what one of the appalled editors called "an earthquake." "The situation is different with regards to Egypt," Dayan began. "First of all, I want to state in the clearest manner that we do not now have the strength to throw the Egyptians back across the canal. We cannot do these things [fight on two fronts] without exhausting our forces almost completely . . . The situation is that the Egyptians have more tanks on the east bank of the canal than we have there. In addition, their tanks are supported by artillery, missile batteries, and infantry equipped with antitank weapons. Our superiority is in the air . . . But our planes have difficulties operating there because of the missiles. . . .

"We realized this after the first stage—bringing our forces down to the canal area—when we tried to throw the Egyptians back to the west bank of the canal. Had we persisted in that, we would have lost our forces and left Israel without any power, because we would have been engaged in a battle for which we did not have sufficient strength. . . . Therefore, we have given up at this stage [that] objective . . . and our forces are along a line parallel to the canal, a few kilometers outside of effective [Egyptian] firing range. Our forces are deployed there defensively, and are putting up a line to contain the Egyptians, until the situation changes. . . . The view is that we should not allow our forces to be worn down. That would be futile. We must redeploy and establish defense lines. . . .

"This has many implications . . . if we cannot throw the Egyptians back, they will continue to assemble their forces. And they have tanks on this side of the canal. And the question is: What will come next? . . .

"I have absolutely no doubt that if indeed the Egyptians launch an attack with their maximum force—though I am not certain that they will—we will have to deploy our forces along new lines closer, or farther away from the canal. I do not say that the situation will end with our not being able to throw them back, and our having to redeploy along other lines. It is possible that we will have to find ourselves shorter and more convenient lines with topographical obstacles which we can hold better. These lines could be somewhere in the area between what is called the Mitla Pass and the Suez Canal.

"This is the general picture . . . What we cannot do now is to throw the Egyptians back and defeat them. I put the emphasis on now. . . . It is possible that, within a short time, opportunities will be afforded and it will be worth our while to cross the canal, either along its length or at a part of it, to deal with the Egyptian forces. . . . It is also possible that such an opportunity will not arise, and that in time we shall have to establish this or that line. I want to reiterate that it is my personal assessment that we shall form a line somewhere between the canal and the mountain tops in that third of Sinai, which the Egyptians will be unable to cross."

Militarily, Dayan was not too unhappy about this: "If the canal is gone, let's do without the canal. I like the canal. But, after all, it isn't the Jezreel Valley. The canal is only a line." Nor was he at all sure that Israel should even try to recapture the lost ground: "We will be able [after the breaking of the Syrians] to concentrate our whole Air Force on the southern front and transfer armor there. I don't know whether it is worthwhile doing that now, when we are not holding the [Bar-Lev] line of strongholds, as a result of which it would be costly for us [to hold the canal] . . . When we consider what it would cost and what we could gain: If it were Degania that was involved, we would make the effort; but for the Bitter Lake, no. It isn't worthwhile wrecking ourselves in an effort to throw them back for that . . . If what is involved is not fifty kilometers [of territory] that count with respect to holding the line [around the heartland of Israel], I can tolerate it. . . ."

In the calmness with which he contemplated this, Dayan was certainly at odds with many, perhaps most, of his Cabinet colleagues—who refused to contemplate any Israeli losses at all. Dayan was also at odds with his colleagues in a more immediate respect too. He wanted to tell the Israeli people the truth.

He had personal motives in this: "The matter of the [Bar-Lev] strongholds will become known. Another two or three days will have passed and we will not have expelled the Egyptians. We are at war, and everybody is saying 'Well?' I want to be able to look people in the eye. I don't want to be suspected—neither as an individual nor as Defense Minister—of deceit, of trying to gloss over things." He added, nevertheless: "I will try to say it all elegantly."

Dayan's fundamental reason for wanting to speak out, however, was that he agreed with the assessment of Gershom Schocken, editor of Ha'aretz, who said: "If you say on television tonight what you have told us, that will be like an earthquake for the consciousness of the Israeli nation, the Jewish people, and the Arab nations. . . ." Dayan was thinking of the long term. He saw the fundamental implications of what had happened: "It revealed to the entire world that we are not stronger than the Egyptians. The halo of superiority, the political and military principle that Israel is stronger than the Arabs, and that if they dared to start a war they would be defeated, has not been sustained here. One way or another, we will have to tell people the truth. I have to appear on television tonight, and I want to tell the truth—in a more carefully worded style. We cannot have this gap between us and the public. We have to live with the true facts of life with our own people, with the American public, with the world, and with the Arabs. We won't gain anything from trying to cover up the truth."

Mrs. Meir did not agree. As the meeting broke up, one of the editors telephoned her to report Dayan's intention. Mrs. Meir promptly forbade her Defense Minister to appear on television. That evening, the nightly statement was delivered instead by one of Mrs. Meir's trusted military men, the ex-chief of military intelligence, Major-General Aharon Yariv. (He was in line for a Cabinet post should Labor win the now-delayed elections.) Yariv struck a somber note, repeating Herzog's warning against banking on a "short war." But he revealed nothing of the facts that Dayan had intended to confess. The Israeli public—and the world —were left in ignorance.

THREE

THE VICTORY EGYPT
THREW AWAY

1. Ismail vs. Shazli

Yet Dayan's facts, however concealed, now ruled the battlefield. By Wednesday, October 10, Syrian tanks in Golan still held a substantial pocket around Khusniye. And Egypt was steadily adding to the seven hundred tanks massed on the east bank of the Suez Canal, with an intact missile defense system to back them. As Dayan had implied, the crucial question was: What did Egypt intend to do now?

"To me," General Ismail said afterward, "rigidity was better than looseness, especially if it was a matter related to war." Specifically, he was rejecting criticism of tight-mouthed Egyptian war communiqués. But as War Minister and Commander-in-Chief, Ahmed Ismail was not merely overlord of the Egyptian planning of the assault; he directed the campaign itself. And "rigidity" was its hallmark throughout. As Henry Tanner, the New York *Times* Cairo correspondent, wrote: "The Egyptian Army has doggedly adhered to a comprehensive, preconceived strategic and tactical plan. Military spokesmen insist that there have been no departures from the plan, no improvisations and no unauthorized initiatives by local commanders." That was Ismail's doing. "Wars," he said lyrically, "are a dialogue between one plan and another. . . ."

Partly, this mystical faith in planning was a product of Ismail's temperament. Now aged fifty-five, he was, as one description put it, "a brilliant classroom soldier." In 1950, already a highly experienced officer, he had graduated top of his year from the Cairo Military Staff Academy; in 1965, he was first again on graduation from the Nasser Military Academy for senior officers. In 1957—in the wake of Nasser's rupture with the West after the Aswan Dam-Suez War debacle—Ismail had been one of the first officers chosen for training in the Soviet Union. Nor was Ismail short of practical experience. He had been through four wars: starting as an intelligence officer in the North Africa campaign in World War II; and an infantry commander through the 1948, 1956, and 1967 Arab-Israeli wars. It was Ismail's memories of 1967 that along with his belief in planning, exerted the most potent influence upon his conduct of the October war.

In July 1967—barely a month after Egypt's shattering defeat—President Nasser had appointed Ismail to command the Suez front. Years later, Ismail recalled the moment in moving terms in a long interview in *Al Ahram*: "My memory still carries the picture of the situation then. There was no front. . . . There was no Army either. . . . Everything had been smashed into fragments and lay broken in ruins. We had to prepare for the stage of steadfastness, as Gamal Abdel Nasser called it."

That time haunted Ismail—just as, through World War II, British commanders were haunted by the losses of thirty years before on the Somme. With genuine passion, Ismail tried to explain: "The safety of my forces was my first preoccupation throughout the new war. . . ." He knew he would be criticized: "There are those perhaps who think we should have taken greater risks. I was ready for any risks and for any sacrifices. But I had resolutely set my mind on one target, which I kept all the time before my eyes, which I felt to the depths of my conscience: to preserve the safety of my forces."

Ismail, who was close to President Sadat, knew the strain that "no war, no peace" imposed upon the Egyptian economy. He knew that Sadat saw this war as the decisive catalyst, making possible a political settlement in the Middle East—the final desperate effort to rid Egypt of a military incubus so monstrous that to keep its Army in being and then prepare it for this new war had cost more than enough to build *two* new Aswan dams. "I was aware," Ismail said, "of the effort which Egypt had exerted to rebuild its Army. I had to reconcile my knowledge of the magnitude of this effort—which can never be repeated so easily —with the fulfillment of my military objective. I knew what losing our Army once more would mean. It would have meant Egypt's surrender. And for Egypt to surrender would have meant its complete defeat for this generation and for generations to come."

It was the thinking of a humane and sensible man. And those

qualities served Ismail brilliantly during the preparations for war. After his 1967 appointment, Ismail had supervised the construction of the Egyptian lines along the Suez Canal—"Egypt's Bar-Lev," he was called. He was appointed Chief of Staff in March 1969 after his predecessor had been killed in an artillery duel across the canal at the beginning of the 1969–70 War of Attrition. But he did not get on with Nasser—Ismail has since hinted that Nasser's grandiloquence grated on him—and he was swiftly sacked, to re-emerge only with the succession of Sadat in October 1970. Ismail became War Minister in October 1972.

With some introspection, Ismail explained the task as he saw it then: "The problem was our own forces. Circumstances had forced them to remain for six or seven years on the defensive—most of this being static defense. Under those conditions, forces —any forces in the world—would be exposed to what we in the military profession call 'trench disease.' We had to dispel the effects of this.

"I concentrated at the time on a number of essentials, without which I believed we could do nothing, nothing at all. The first of these was that our forces should be convinced that fighting was inevitable—and that there could be no solution without fighting. . . . I visited the armed forces, in their positions, and I explained the circumstances to them, saying that the existing situation had to be changed—and that, if we did not change it, the enemy might force a change upon us . . . because for neither of us could the conditions of 'no war, no peace' continue indefinitely.

"The second essential was that our men should have faith in their arms. I wanted to change the concept that arms make the man. It is man who makes the arms. Unless our men were confident of themselves, their arms would never protect them. If, on the other hand, they did have confidence in themselves, then any arms in their hands would protect them."

Clearly, Ismail was exaggerating. The infantry he sent across the canal on October 6 were armed with some of the most formidable personal weapons yet devised. But there was validity still in Ismail's insistence upon the importance of the individual soldier. Ground missiles demanded courage of their operators. The RPG-7 (rocket-propelled grenade) is best fired at little more than 100 yards—and it takes considerable nerve to let an enemy tank get that close. (Even if the tank is then disabled, its crew tend to survive, to machine-gun the infantryman.) The Sagger wire-guided missile is calibrated to a range of 1.8 miles, though most effective at about 1 mile. At those ranges, the missile is in readily visible flight—like a high-speed model aircraft—for up to 30 seconds, a long time in battle when you are exposed and at risk of being machine-gunned. Yet, throughout, the operator must coolly pilot the missile, keeping his sight fixed on the target by means of a small joystick. The Israelis were certainly not expecting the new confidence of the average Egyptian soldier.

In part, that was a tribute to Ismail's "third essential"—intensive training—and to his fourth and last stipulation, that this should be under realistic conditions "to get our forces to see plainly what we would have to face in the future and to remove any fear from it. I therefore began to select training grounds which bore as much resemblance as possible to the conditions and nature of the task which our forces would have to discharge later." The training was meticulous. The commander of the engineers, Major General Aly Mohammed, later revealed that his men had practiced assaults on an accurate mockup of the Bar-Lev Line no fewer than three hundred times. Ismail adds: "There were water currents in our training ground which had the same velocity as the currents in the Suez Canal."

They even practiced the crossing on the canal itself—at El-Ballah, north of Ismailia, where the canal forks for a few miles into two channels. Egypt still held both banks of the western channel, so that stretch became a training ground. Even in training, however, the emphasis was heavily on Soviet-style set-piece battles. In a land 90 per cent of which is shifting sand, the mock battlefield at the Egyptian military training college was constructed of concrete.

By the fifth day of war—Wednesday, October 10—Ismail's planning had worked superbly. Operation BADR had overwhelmed the Israeli defenses and thrown the whole Israeli strategy out of gear; and the Egyptian bridgehead extended virtually the length of the canal from Port Said to Port Suez—with Egyptian armor pressing to fill the few remaining gaps. In creating this long front, Ismail's strategy was deliberate: "The enemy would have

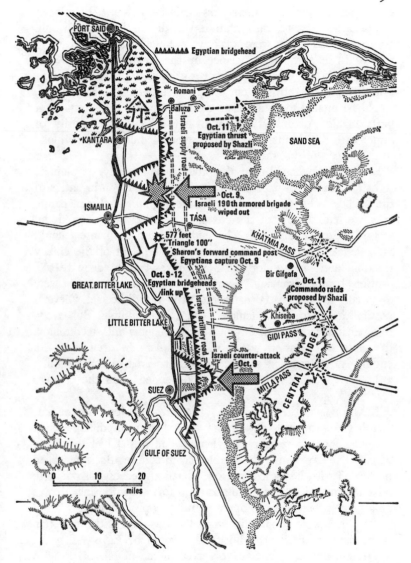

Map 7 Egypt consolidates its hold: October 9–12

to disperse his aerial counterstrikes against our forces. In view of the extensive area of confrontation, this dispersal of effort would ensure that his strikes were weak everywhere." Israel's land forces too would be thrown off balance by the length of front: "The enemy would not be able to discover at any early stage the direction of the main thrust of our attacking forces and, consequently, would be unable to concentrate on it." Adan and Sharon—their units mauled because they could not achieve the density of armor to break through the missile screen—could testify in blood to the success of that tactic.

But what did Ismail plan after that? Paradoxically, he planned to halt, consolidate—and hand Egypt's brilliantly won initiative to the Israelis. "Our original plan envisaged a 'mobilizational pause' after we had completed the crossing operation and ensured the security of our bridgeheads," he said. "During the pause I could make a re-evaluation of the situation in the light of the enemy reaction, and prepare for the next move—taking adequate precautions before advancing." Ismail's ideas on what to do next were essentially responsive. "What comes after that?" he said. "Several possibilities. We had calculated them all minutely. But everything ultimately depended upon what the enemy did. Accordingly, the crossing operation was a plan complete in itself, with an ending. What came after that was also covered by our planning although the choice of possibilities depended upon the enemy's reaction."

It was when this phase had been reached on Wednesday, October 10—the fifth day of the war—that major differences of opinion opened up between Ismail and his Chief of Staff, Shazli. The day before, the second Israeli counterattack had been beaten off with heavy losses. Now, Shazli argued, Egypt ought to seize the initiative once more and press forward into Sinai. It was an argument between two opposing military philosophies.

"If Shazli weren't so deliberately low-key—and if the Egyptian Army had any flair for publicity—he would be Egypt's Dayan," a Western diplomat in Cairo observed in the middle of the war. If Shazli never sought that mythopoeic status, he was nevertheless a hero to the Egyptian public even before the October war—a model of the "new Egyptian officer." It was scarcely overnight

35. An Israeli Centurion under bombardment from a Sukhoi-7 near Saasa.

36. Suez city under fire during the battles of October 22 after the "cease-fire." During this day, Egypt's Third Army was encircled.

37. An Israeli rabbi tags the dead. The rate of deaths was even heavier per day than in the War of Independence of 1948–49.

38. Egyptian prisoners of war packed 140 to a truck after the fighting around Suez city on "cease-fire" day.

fame: Since World War II, Shazli had stood out as perhaps Egypt's most aggressive field commander.

Saad el Shazli was born in 1922, the eleventh of thirteen children in a land-owning family on the Nile Delta. He graduated from the Egyptian military academy in 1940, and according to Egyptian sources, first came to notice as an eighteen-year-old lieutenant in the Western Desert, when his post near Mersa Matruh was apparently overrun by the Germans. Ordered to evacuate, Shazli is said to have stayed behind until all the equipment had been removed. It was the start of a continuing reputation for bravery. In the Arab-Israeli wars, however, Shazli's career is undisputed. In 1948, he commanded an infantry platoon; in 1950, by now regarded as one of Egypt's brightest young officers, he went to the Staff Academy; three years later, he transferred to the arm that had since proved his greatest military interest: the paratroop special forces.

He was excellently trained in this, by courtesy of the United States Government at Fort Benning, Georgia, in 1953. In the 1960s, Shazli took a training course in the Soviet Union too. And his personal life also reflected a certain internationalism: A student of British politics, he was prone to cross-question visitors on the troubles in Northern Ireland. (Like Tlas, Shazli was interested in irregular warfare: His study of the "Black September" 1970 clash between Hussein's men and the Palestinians is a minor classic.) One of his three daughters is married to an American in Hawaii, and his niece is the wife of a British journalist. Shazli himself lives with his wife in a modest bungalow in a Cairo suburb.

A friend, asked whether a theme ran through Shazli's life, paused and then said: "Unlike many of his colleagues, Shazli always thought Egypt could win." The friend recalled Shazli saying during the 1956 war: "Why are we despairing? We can beat them." And the hectic pace of Shazli's career in the wake of the 1956 humiliation suggests the deliberate grooming of a man on whose skills Egypt already knew it would one day call.

In 1960, he commanded the Egyptian paratroop units sent to the Congo as part of the United Nations force. In 1961 he went to London as military attaché—where he became rather too close to the handful of British fascist groups campaigning against Jews and Israel. Returning to Egypt, he was one of the few officers whose reputation survived Nasser's ill-fated Yemen campaign of the early 1960s—in Yemen, Shazli put into practice his ideas on long-range helicopter-borne penetration by commando units.

He was then one of even fewer officers to gain credit from the 1967 disaster. Shazli's division in eastern Sinai was surrounded, but he got his men back over the canal in good order. The incident has become encrusted with legend. One story holds that he slipped into disguise; another that he was surrounded by the Israelis, but had himself already captured prisoners, so bargained his way out. The simpler truth is that Sharon was given the job of cutting off Shazli's retreat but missed him in the dark. Whatever the circumstances, mere survival with dignity set the seal on Shazli's reputation—though critical Israeli tacticians have since noted that a bolder commander in Shazli's position in 1967 might have pressed eastward, taken Israel's southern port of Eilat, and thrown part of the Israeli offensive seriously off-balance. Given his reputation, however, Shazli's appointment as Chief of Staff in 1971 caused little surprise—even though Sadat plucked him from his relatively junior place at thirtieth in the ranking of major generals.

It was a shrewd appointment; for Shazli brought to the post not only military talent—and a flinty determination to beat the Israelis—but a care for his men unusual among his contemporaries. The Egyptian Army has always been cursed by a gulf between officers and men—the officers regarding themselves as a privileged elite and their men as peasants. Shazli, by contrast, was close to his troops. Instead of the medals and gold braid he could affect, he wore the standard beret, jump boots, and camouflage smock of a paratrooper. (Although balding and on the short side, Shazli—a keep-fit enthusiast—looked younger than his fifty-one years.) In May 1972, he inaugurated an armed forces blood bank with a pint of his own blood—a simple enough gesture, but in that army a brilliant common touch. And although himself a stern disciplinarian, he stood up fiercely for those in his command: His almost legendary popularity inside the forces was finally cemented in 1972, after a public slanging match in which Shazli bawled out the head of the Soviet military mission for claiming, in a tactless moment, that Egyptians were "untrainable." (The Soviet soldier was sent home—which, of course, might have been his purpose.)

By Wednesday, October 10, few would still have delivered that verdict on the Egyptian soldier. But the irony was that although the Egyptian Army's brilliant success was popularly ascribed in Cairo to "the Shazli plan," the strategy so far had more nearly been Ismail's. By Wednesday, in fact, Shazli was vigorously trying to persuade Ismail to switch from his methodical set-piece approach to a more mobile exploitation of the Egyptian successes. He was unsuccessful.

Ismail and Shazli had first met in the 1960 Congo operation, when Ismail tried to take over Shazli's role. The two men had not gotten on then, and according to Cairo sources, had never gotten on since. Given their different backgrounds, it is not hard to see why. Nor is it hard to understand why the two should by Wednesday have differed so strongly. Shazli, the more aggressive field commander, wanted to follow up the Israeli defeat with a decisive switch to a more mobile and adventurous strategy. He is thought to have advocated another round of helicopter-borne commando raids to strike at the eastern ends of the passes and to destroy Israeli supply dumps and communications centers throughout the area. One source in Cairo reports that Shazli also wanted an armored thrust along the northern coastal road. That was certainly logical. Dayan's confidence that Israel could hold the passes was almost certainly justified. The coast road was the only route open.

Ismail vetoed Shazli's plan. Defensively, Ismail later sought to explain his reasons: "Were we unable to see the chance available to us? For me, the question was not one of chance but a matter of calculation. Whatever chances presented themselves to us it was my duty not to run risks. . . ." And he produced strong technical justification for this decision: "We had begun the operation under the protection of our famous missile screen. If I had to advance after that, I was determined to wait—whether there was a chance which someone else could see or whether I saw it myself —until I had made sure that my forces had adequate backing. I had to give time for my armor and my antiaircraft missiles to cross."

From which it seems fairly clear that Ismail questioned even the existence of the "chance" Shazli and the others saw. And Ismail's plea that by Wednesday he had still not gotten as much equipment as he wanted onto the east bank tends to confirm persistent reports in Cairo that in its later phases the Egyptian buildup was hitting severe logistical problems. Shortage of ammunition seems to have been one. Egyptian fire control in the early days of the war was apparently poor: They just blazed away. An oblique reference by Ismail also supports allegations that there were shortages of more basic stores such as gasoline, water, and even food. "There was a time," he said, "when we had soldiers who lived on half their food rations and yet their fighting ability was not in the least affected." Some Cairo sources also think that by the middle of the first week the Egyptian missile forces' enthusiastic salvos of SAM-6s had severely depleted stocks of those too.

But the strongest reason for Ismail's alleged shortage of equipment on the east bank was that he had deliberately kept half his tanks on the west bank. By the end of Wednesday, Egypt had pushed more than seven hundred tanks over into Sinai (though many of these had already been destroyed, of course). But another seven hundred still remained as reserves west of the canal. Ismail was keeping them to defend the homeland against the possibility of an Israeli airborne assault from the rear or against an attempted Israeli crossing—both possibilities that the Egyptians had studied in detail. Although Egypt had numerical superiority of armor in Sinai, its advantage was nothing like enough to ensure success in a conventional assault.

Ismail could, and did, claim that he alone understood what Sadat wanted—and that was a more complex and subtle outcome than straightforward military victory. Sadat's strategy had not altered since the Cairo summit of September 10: to use the war as a means of sparking an international crisis sufficiently serious to persuade the superpowers that the Middle East situation was too dangerous to remain unresolved any longer. To achieve that, Ismail saw no need to pursue Israel across Sinai: His own, more cautious plan would suffice.

Yet it is hard not to think that Ismail's temperamental differences with Shazli were the critical factors in his rejection of Shazli's plan. "Those who had heard me speak to the forces," Ismail said later, "knew that I feared nothing more than that we should be conventional. I did not want to be conventional. But at the same time I did not want us to be adventurers." Pointedly, he added: "Wars are a much more momentous issue than adventures. . . ."

Ismail was right to reject Shazli's plan—not least because it was based upon an exaggerated assessment of what the Egyptian Army could do. Shazli, the new model soldier, evidently believed that the Egyptians could now take on the Israelis at their own specialty: mobile warfare. This was singularly ill-advised, as events were to prove. Mobile warfare demands a level of initiative among junior officers, a level of confidence in senior ones, and the willingness of both to communicate, that the Egyptian Army simply did not possess yet. At a more technical level, few Egyptian officers had even practiced the swift deployment of large formations: Those final maneuvers that were a cloak for Ismail's war preparations were the first to involve units in division strength.

Ismail's plan, in contrast to Shazli's, took account of these continuing weaknesses. His brilliant combination—strategic offensive, tactical defensive—was designed precisely to avoid taking on the Israelis at their own game. With his slow advance by "creeping, crawling" missile infantry, Ismail had changed the name of the game—to the Israelis' discomfort. Shazli, the first to reject *Blitzkrieg* in favor of a "meat grinder" war, should have seen this. Ironically, failure to do so, while militarily stupid, was to his personal credit. Shazli had unbounded faith in his fellow soldiers. Ismail did not. And Ismail was right.

But Ismail went farther than mere rejection of Shazli's dashing proposals. As he told *Al Ahram* editor Heikal, he was not ready to move at all. That was disastrous. The critical failure of the first phase of Operation BADR was already clear: Egyptian armor had not penetrated Sinai as far as planned. Instead of reaching the sand ridges twenty miles in, Egyptian tanks had gotten at most sixteen miles, and in most places little more than twelve. And in repulsing the Israeli assaults since then, Egypt had given still more ground. By Wednesday, therefore, their bridgehead stretched impressively the length of the canal. But it was only ten miles deep —half what it should have been. It thus presented one potentially fatal weakness. It was not deep enough to allow resilient defense against a determined Israeli thrust concentrated on a narrow front. That was precisely the flaw that had already sparked among Israel's generals an argument paralleling the Ismail-Shazli debate.

2. *Sharon vs. Almost Everybody*

The Israeli regular Army is small, only 11,500 men (omitting conscripts); and most of its senior commanders have fought together in 4 campaigns: as adolescents in guerrilla actions against British and Arabs alike in Palestine before the British withdrew; then rising in rank together through the wars of 1948–49, 1956, and 1967. The strengths and weaknesses, failures and achievements, of each man are thus intimately known to his contemporaries. This has not left over-much reverence within the high command. Equally inevitably, there is a tendency to magnify the exploits of previous commanders to the disadvantage of the present generation. These stresses are reinforced by the straightforward bureaucratic point that the small scale of the Army interweaves its officers' careers to a remarkable degree. Factions coalesce—one officer advancing as the protégé of this commander, another owing allegiance to that. And in the six years since the Six-Day War, a growing connection between the Army and politics—officers had to retire around forty, and several had chosen to go into politics—was an additional source of potential friction. The Israeli Army is thus not easy to run—as its new Chief of Staff, Lieutenant General David Elazar, had already found by October 6.

David Elazar's career encapsulated the story of Israel's Army. He was born in 1925 in the Yugoslav town of Sarajevo—where his father, a former major in Tito's army, still lives. But in 1940, aged fifteen, Elazar emigrated to Palestine—joining his boyhood friend, Haim Bar-Lev, who had arrived from Yugoslavia the year before. Elazar first went into a kibbutz, where he met his future wife. But the cast of his life was set in 1946, when he joined the Palmach, the striking force of the illegal Jewish militia, the Haganah, which was then in open revolt against British rule and fighting a savage war of terror and counterterror against the

Palestinian Arabs. In the full-scale combat that followed the British withdrawal, the Palmach was regularized as the commando arm of the Jewish forces. And it was the attempt by two platoons of the Palmach to relieve the heavily outnumbered defenders of the Jewish quarter of Jerusalem in May 1948 that first brought Elazar to his seniors' notice. Elazar, newly commissioned, commanded one of the platoons. The Palmach had to withdraw, but it was a gallant effort, and Elazar afterward rose swiftly.

The War of Independence, as the Israelis came to call it, was an infantry affair: The Israelis did have a few run-down tanks, but by far the most important vehicle was the Jeep. And until the 1956 campaign Israel concentrated on its infantry, with paratroops as the elite strike force. Elazar rose to direct the School of Infantry in 1956 and, in the brief Sinai campaign that year, commanded an infantry brigade in the Gaza Strip. Israel's most feared weapon in those days was the mortar. It was equipment suited to a small, poor country: powerful, easy to make—Israel designed its own, superlative model—and, above all, cheap. "Cheap and clever was the doctrine then," one Israeli military analyst recalled with perceptible nostalgia.

But Israel did have a few tanks. And it was their relative failure in 1956—and the realization by the Israeli General Staff that, had they not attacked the Egyptian armor from the rear while it was facing the British and French, they might have suffered heavy casualties—that forced a rethink. Israel decided that it too needed armor. The task of building it up was given to Haim Bar-Lev—from 1957, commander of the armored corps. Elazar joined him in the tank corps. (Their lifelong habit of slipping in the middle of discussions into their boyhood language, Serbo-Croatian, irritated more than one of their colleagues.) Elazar had comparatively little hand in the molding of Israel's distinctive armored strategy: mobility and deep penetration as the riposte to massive but static Arab tank formations. That was initially the contribution of Yizhak Rabin, later Chief of Staff during the Six-Day War; and further work was then done on the techniques of large-scale tank maneuvers by two other tankmen, Israel Tal and "Bren" Adan. But it was the soft-spoken, level-headed, unflamboyant Elazar who succeeded Bar-Lev in 1961 as commander of Israel's armor. (Afterward, Elazar always wore the tankman's black beret.)

And it was Elazar who fostered among tankmen—as before he had fostered among paratroopers—a conscious elitism. He devised a Wagnerian commissioning ceremony for young tank lieutenants: the midnight swearing of an oath of loyalty in a ring of flaming torches on top of the Masada plateau by the Dead Sea—scene of the Jews' last bloody stand against the Romans nineteen hundred years before.

In 1967, Brigadier Elazar held the Northern Command—the Syrian front—and directed the successful assault on the Golan Heights. It was not, perhaps, an overimaginative battle: With two possible plans of attack, Elazar chose the more straightforward and, some observers think, lost more men than necessary. Still, he won—and in sufficiently dramatic fashion to gain public acclaim.

The 1967 war also saw Moshe Dayan back in the Ministry of Defense, after some years of comparative political eclipse. Promptly, Dayan scooped the credit for the victories of that war—though he had, in fact, little or no hand in their devising. The career of one of Dayan's favored officers, Haim Bar-Lev—who since 1961 had also been in eclipse—was now prospering too. He was Deputy Chief of Staff during the 1967 war and became Chief of Staff in January 1968. Elazar took over as Bar-Lev's deputy.

Elazar's elevation came not without dissent. Two candidates might have been groomed to succeed Bar-Lev: Elazar or Yeshayahu Gavish, one of the key generals in Sinai during the Six-Day War. Gavish was Dayan's candidate; Elazar was Bar-Lev's. Within the contest were complex political strains—going back to the roots of independent Israel—between the men of the Haganah-Palmach (Bar-Lev/Elazar) and the supporters of Israel's first leader, David Ben-Gurion (Dayan/Gavish). Ultimately, though, Gavish was beaten by the cult of youth. The 1967 commander, Yizhak Rabin, had been the first Chief of Staff to get the job when more than forty: He was forty-one; and Ben-Gurion, just retired, did not hide his amazement. If Gavish were now to be named Bar-Lev's heir apparent, he would be in his late forties before he in turn became Chief of Staff. By the margin of a couple of years, Elazar won.

Bar-Lev saw Israel through the 1969–70 War of Attrition, most of his attention going on the construction of the canalside fortifications that bore his name—and that enshrined Israel's new defensive strategy. Elazar looked after Israel's armor—for the tank

corps' success in 1967 had ensured their place as the keystone of
Israel's tactical thinking. But the Bar-Lev/Elazar strategy, as we
have said, divided the Israeli Army, and even the General Staff.
In the field, the commander of Israel's most important front,
"Arik" Sharon in Sinai, was bitterly opposed to the scheme. And
inside the General Staff, the thinking was equally criticized even
by the head of the General Staff development branch, Israel Tal
—joint creator with "Bren" Adan of Israeli armored tactics in
their most sophisticated form. When Bar-Lev retired as Chief of
Staff, therefore, the question of his successor was effectively also
a question whether Bar-Lev's defensive strategy would be continued. Orthodoxy won. Elazar took over as Chief of Staff on
January 1, 1972. His first initiative was to endeavor to heal the
rift: As Deputy Chief of Staff, Elazar chose Israel Tal.

Elazar was the safe choice, even if his tactical limitations were
known. "Elazar has the bulldog technique of taking a big bite
and then hanging on," one Israeli journalist said. And he was popular: At forty-eight, a stocky, darkly handsome figure, he was
chosen in a poll just before the war by readers of the Israeli
women's magazine *At* as their ideal husband.

In the months that followed Elazar's appointment, every single
top Israeli commander was due for replacement. It was the most
sweeping reallocation of jobs the armed forces had seen. Most of
Elazar's new commanders—including the head of military intelligence, Major General Eliahu Zeira—had been installed only in
the spring of 1973. The GOC of Central Command—the Jordan
front—had held his post for just six days when war began. Elazar
—himself with barely eighteen months in which to adjust to his
job—thus faced the war with an untried, unsettled team.

Midway through the first week of war, the most unsettled team
of all was clearly the unhappy Gonen and his unruly commanders
in Sinai. After the failure of Adan's attack on Monday had further
damaged Gonen's morale, it was clear that he would need command support. After the Tuesday failure of Sharon's initiative,
Gonen himself brought matters to a head. He formally requested
Chief of Staff Elazar to strip Sharon of his command—allegedly
for disobedience, a charge Sharon denied. This posed problems of
the utmost delicacy—and not merely military ones. Apart from
the imprudence of dispensing with Sharon's unquestioned abilities

at this critical stage, there was the political problem that he was the most prominent field commander identified with the opposition parties in the Knesset. It was already clear that there would be, after the war, a political storm of no mean intensity over the government's apparent lack of preparedness. To fire potentially the most outspoken military contributor to that debate would be asking for trouble. Elazar referred the problem to Dayan.

Dayan, to his credit, looked simply at the military needs. Whatever the facts in the Gonen-Sharon dispute, he told Elazar, it was clear that the one could not command the other. He advised Elazar to displace Gonen and restore Sharon to his old job as Southern commander. Elazar toyed with the idea. Mrs. Meir vetoed it: To replace a government-appointed commander by the head of an opposition party would be a major political defeat. Gonen had to stay.

Late on Tuesday, Elazar helicoptered down once more to Khiseiba to patch up relations between the generals. He stayed an hour. The dispute had gone too far to be resolved. Two hours after Elazar had flown back to Tel Aviv, Sinai had a new commander—in fact, though not in name. Officially, Lieutenant General Haim Bar-Lev—sometime Chief of Staff, Minister of Commerce, and one of the inner Cabinet during the runup to war—took up "special duties at the request of the Chief of Staff." In fact, Bar-Lev now became the power behind the throne—in this case, Gonen's folding canvas chair—in Sinai.

It was an ingenious solution. And the government seized the chance to announce next day—Wednesday, October 10—that five other newly retired generals were also to be called up, all for "special duties." This was tactful camouflage of the fact that several of those nominally summoned had in fact called themselves up—in some cases, just donning their uniforms and driving out to their old commands, where, naturally enough, nobody had the nerve to challenge their presence.

But at least they were able and bore reassuring names. Apart from Bar-Lev, there was, for example, Aharon Yariv, for nine years head of military intelligence and one of the sharpest brains in Israel; Yeshayahu Gavish, sometime commander in Sinai and Elazar's rival for Chief of Staff; and Mordechai Hod, commander of the Air Force in its finest hour in 1967. (Hod's name had not been wholly free of controversy since. The talk of Israel before the October war had been Dayan's installation of him as chairman of Israel Aircraft Industries—an appointment vigorously denounced by that firm's president with much talk of "cronyism" and even "the military-industrial complex.") But while the resurrection of "the old war-horses," as Elazar called them, did reassure the public and genuinely take a burden off the shoulders of their successors—Hod, for example, was already running the air battle over Golan—it did not significantly ease the political problems in Sinai.

The thirty-six hours from the morning of Wednesday, October 10, to the evening of Thursday, October 11, were as critical for Israel as the start of the war had been; for when Mrs. Meir's ministers met on Wednesday morning—for the eighth time since war began—Israel's ability to fight on was in grave doubt. The failure of successive counterattacks had demonstrated Israel's weakness in Sinai—which Egypt must surely exploit—while Golan drained Israel's resources. Other Arab nations would soon enter the fray. (Later on Wednesday, Iraq did proclaim its entry into the war. Its pilots had been fighting over Golan, in fact, for twenty-four hours. But Israel still had a couple of days' grace before Iraqi land forces could actually deploy along the front. In Jordan, Hussein ordered mobilization on Wednesday, but did not yet commit himself.)

The critical development, however, was the growing likelihood that the Soviet Union was preparing to restock the Arab arsenals. Further supplies of SAM-6s to Syria would overturn the careful balance the Israeli Air Force had achieved: so many Skyhawks sacrificed to destroy so many SAM batteries. Israel was physically unable to start that cycle over again. But without this new and hard-won ability to call down air strikes on the Syrian armor at will, it was doubtful if Israel's tanks could smash through the Syrian lines fast enough or cheaply enough to enable Israel to switch its attention to Sinai in time. Israel's juggling act was becoming impossible.

Its mounting losses had finally locked Israel into playing the game Ismail's way. The classic Israeli move at this point in the war—the move Sharon advocated—would be some dashing, unexpected thrust. But the Israelis had lost the capacity to take that sort of gamble. By Wednesday, they still—just—had the resources to mount twin assaults in Golan and Sinai. But any setbacks—such as a repeat of the 190th disaster—would effectively leave Israel bare of reserves. Resupply by the United States would then be the only way in which Israel could continue the war. Mrs. Meir's ministers surmised, however, what Kissinger would want in return for a promise of arms: Israel's agreement to a cease-fire. And the only realistic terms for that would leave the Arabs in possession of their new gains.

Israel, at least if Dayan had his way, could bear the loss of a strip of Sinai. In the United Nations, its foreign minister, Abba Eban, was already talking semipublicly of "concessions" amounting to withdrawal from most of Sinai. But Israeli pride and military security forbade any Syrian gains on Golan. Before Israel lost so much material as to have no choice but to accept the likely American terms, therefore, the Syrians must be driven from their last remaining pockets of armor around Khusniye and Kuneitra. That was the decision of Mrs. Meir's ministers on Wednesday morning. By Wednesday evening, the job was done.

The battle for Khusniye was the harder. Here, as elsewhere in their fighting retreat across Golan, the Syrians used antitank missiles in almost the profusion of the Sinai campaign. The low rock walls of the abandoned fields on Golan provided excellent cover for Syrians armed with RPG-7s: More than one Israeli tank commander was killed as he peered out of his turret during this counterattack phase. Dug into the fortified rubble of Khusniye behind weapons like those, the Syrians seemed impregnable. And, indeed, the Israeli forces in the end not so much captured Khusniye as overwhelmed it. On Wednesday evening, they charged the Syrian defenses in a frontal attack. Again, it was a battle that cost a lot of tanks and men.

By contrast, the assault on Kuneitra began late on Wednesday afternoon and was over in an hour. This pile of rubble was taken in the same fashion as Khusniye. After a perfunctory barrage, Israeli tanks simply charged up the main road from Narrak and into what had once been the center of the town—relieving the Israeli garrison surrounded since the first night of the war. The Syrians had fallen back in the face of the Israeli charge, but a few terrified prisoners were hustled away. The garrison was unruffled: "We

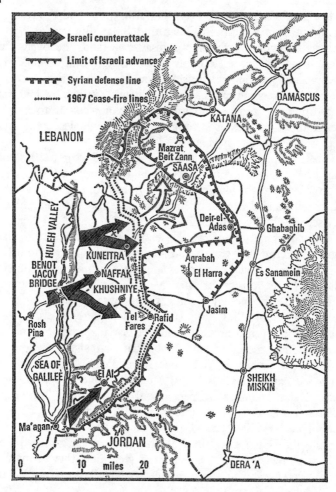

Map 8 Israel's hard slog toward Damascus

Having broken the Syrian armor on Golan, Israel thrust down the road to Damascus. But Syria's second line of defense held; Israel was pushed back from Saasa; and the Moroccan troops along Mount Hermon's lower ridge threatened Israel's flank. Jordanian and Iraqi armor attacked the Israeli advance from the south. The Iraqis, mauled, were chased back to Deir-el-Adas. Jordan's brigade headed up toward Kuneitra but, their attack unsupported by the Syrians, they had to retreat to Jasim.

never worried when the Syrians came through," a nineteen-year-old Israeli infantry captain, late of Brooklyn, said. "We shot them up as they went through the first time and we shot them up when they came running back."

It was a bloody affair, though. Israeli air strikes caught the retreating Syrian column on the road back home about two miles northeast of Kuneitra. The road was cluttered with the ruins of their tanks. Two men from one T-54 had tried to run for it when the planes swooped down: Their corpses lay as they had been hit, both staring back over their shoulders. Beside another tank, the driver lay beneath a blanket as if asleep, his head on a pillow. Perhaps he had been exhausted and trying to snatch a fifteen-minute doze? His face was quite relaxed: He must have died in his sleep as the Israeli fighters' cannons blew off both his legs.

By nightfall, Israel had recaptured Golan. Its infantry were cautiously probing the outposts of the first Syrian defense works on the other side of the erstwhile cease-fire line. It was clear that by the morning of the next day, Thursday, Israel would be in a position to attack into Syria. The only question Israeli military analysts thought it worth raising was whether Israel would now strike due east, heading across the plain to threaten Damascus from the South, or whether the tanks would just spear northeast up the main road to Damascus. Just in case the Jordanians had not gotten the point, the Jerusalem *Post* reported that Israel "will not be cowed into blind respect for the armistice lines."

Syria fought back still. The dawn of Thursday, October 11, brought death to four helicopterloads of Syrian commandos, ambushed as they tried to land behind Israeli lines. The Israelis had been monitoring the Syrian radio nets and an Arabic-speaking officer had listened to the planning of the raid. Syria threw in more armor, too, in a counterattack on Thursday morning in the northern sector, straddling the Kuneitra-to-Damascus road. But it was the last effort; that the Syrians attacked at all came as an unpleasant surprise to the battered Israelis, but this last effort did not compare in intensity to the earlier Syrian struggles. Indeed, this attack precipitated the actual Israeli crossing into Syria: In a looping southward curve, the Israelis swung through the line of Syrian tanks to take them from the rear—and found themselves behind the first of the Syrian defense lines. "My unit achieved the breakthrough without a single casualty," Eytan said later. "We achieved our target objectives within three hours. The actual breakthrough only took thirty minutes." By Thursday evening, Israeli armor was six miles into Syria, pressing northeast up the road to Damascus.

The wrong side of the cease-fire lines on Golan, Syria had left more than six hundred tanks blown up or burned out, and another five hundred simply abandoned, more than a hundred for lack of fuel. A subsequent estimate by the U. S. Defense Department was that Syria might also have lost eight thousand of its soldiers there—a handful captured, the overwhelming proportion killed. Touring the scene in a helicopter, Dayan now announced that the Syrians were to be taught that "the road which leads from Damascus to Tel Aviv leads also from Tel Aviv to Damascus."

But if Dayan, despite his good resolutions, found it hard even now, after the debacle of the first five days, to distinguish publicly between confidence and hubris, other military men were willing to murmur the truth: which was that Israel had barely reached the end of the first phase of the war; that on the Syrian front it still faced an exhausting slog toward Damascus; that the worst Sinai battles were yet to come; and that Israel's equipment was by now in terrible shape. By Friday morning, as the Syrians fought back in a relatively orderly retreat, cheerful Israeli promises about "downhill to Damascus" were silenced. As he had done to Elazar's blithe boast of "breaking the bones" of the Arab armies, General Herzog now publicly punctured Dayan's facile optimism. "Smashing such defense lines [as Syria's] cannot be done quickly," he said. "The defense is not a single line which we broke through yesterday, but a defense network which continues deep into the country and over very difficult terrain which is not ideal ground for a tank battle."

But at least by Thursday evening, the transfer could begin of some Israeli armor from Golan to Sinai. With more immediate impact, Israel's overworked and battered Air Force could now concentrate its efforts against the Egyptians. Just as the question of what Egypt should do next had split its high command on

Wednesday, so Israel's growing capabilities in Sinai fomented on Thursday the sharpest disagreement yet among the Israeli generals.

After the war, the fullest Israeli discussion of these, albeit still guarded in tone, came in the Hebrew magazine *Haolam Hazeh*, run by Uri Avneri, a millionaire, then a member of the Knesset, and the most outspoken critic of what he saw as Israel's drift toward militarism: "Political figures who played key roles in the election campaign were suddenly compelled to cooperate in the battlefields. It was impossible to erase all at once the personal and ideological rivalry between them or the difference in their political perceptions and outlook. The belief which prevailed at the outbreak that this would be a swift war, at the end of which it would be necessary to return immediately to the election struggle, contributed its share to the creation of this intolerable situation. The fact that the war also led at once to an ideological debate about the validity of the various political views on peace and security—secure borders, strategic buffers and the deterrent power of Israel's forces—aided in fostering the political differences."

Down in Israel's Sinai headquarters, that first Thursday of the war, Sharon put the charge more pithily: "Bar-Lev," he shouted, "since you arrived the day before yesterday, you have been thinking only about elections." Even after the war, Sharon smoldered over Bar-Lev's insertion into Sinai. "Bar-Lev was a political opportunist," Sharon told Joseph Kraft, "put in place by the government to justify past actions and deny credit to any other officers." The truth was that, without Bar-Lev, the Sinai command would have degenerated into anarchy. And on Thursday, Bar-Lev tried to have Sharon removed from his command.

The focus of the row was Sharon's continued confidence that, given the resources, he could cross the canal—and his anger at being forbidden to do so. The military arguments were finely balanced. Strategically, as Sharon put it: "Our aim was to check them in Sinai while we attended to the Syrians. I personally thought that this was a mistake and expressed my views several times. I saw that we did not have unlimited time. I saw that the Egyptians were not pressing forward, but were digging in; and that a cease-fire would see them strongly entrenched." But Sharon was overruled, first by Gonen and then by Bar-Lev and Dayan.

Again in Sharon's words: "For the first week the concept was to hold against the Egyptian attacks and try to destroy as many of their tanks as possible while we were in defense."

The principal reason for this was, as we have said, the stark fact that Israel did not have the resources to risk failure. Another factor, though, was the need to cut the casualty rate. (In this, the Israeli commanders were successful. After the first desperate 2 days of fighting, the toll of Israeli dead mounted at less than a third of the initial rate of 250 a day.)

But Thursday morning brought a decisive change in Egyptian deployment. Ismail now began to bring into Sinai most of the 700 tanks he had held on the west bank of the canal to protect the rear of his armies. In Egypt, Ismail has since been savagely criticized for thus committing Egypt's main reserves. Sadat knew of the decision, however, and could have vetoed it. And Ismail did it reluctantly. But Egypt was under intense pressure from Syria to take some of the Israeli weight off Golan. President Asad was threatening to denounce Sadat's "betrayal" of the Arab cause unless Egypt attacked once more. Politically, Ismail had little choice but to prepare for a fresh assault in Sinai. The arguments that followed between the Israeli generals on Thursday, October 11, at the Ministry of Defense in Tel Aviv and in Gonen's Sinai headquarters were about how Israel could best take advantage of Ismail's unexpected move. Sharon, more vehemently than ever, wanted to cross the canal.

In his four years as GOC Southern Command, Sharon had found ample time to study—even to prepare—potential crossing points. And his argument for doing so was straightforward: Israel should strike first, and the west bank offered better chances for traditional Israeli tactics. "By carrying the war to the west bank, we would be in our element," he said, "fast-moving armor in open, classic tank country." Sharon, of course, was not a tankman —and he had been advancing the same argument since the first Monday of the war. Now, however, he got powerful support inside the Ministry of Defense from Brigadier Abrasha Tamir—at forty-nine, regarded as one of the two or three cleverest men in the Israeli Army, though one of the least known. Tamir, backed by several other officers—on one account, even by some major generals—urged a swift canal crossing on the grounds that an attack now, while the bulk of the Third Army was redeploying from the west bank to the east, would catch its armor unprepared and with its rear unprotected by the antitank missile screen in Sinai. Gonen's view earlier in the week—before the first Monday counterattack—that Israel's capture of a corridor along the east bank of the canal would prove the less expensive option was now, Tamir argued, superseded by Ismail's transfer of his reserves.

Tamir commanded respect. (He was subsequently promoted to major general—with Eytan's, one of the only two Israeli senior promotions in this war—and put in charge of a new army planning branch, answering to the Deputy Chief of Staff.) But he was reckoned short of combat experience. The Tamir-Sharon plan was overruled at the highest level: by the triumvirate of Dayan, Elazar, and Bar-Lev. They decided to wait. Each succeeding day now would see more Israeli armor and air power concentrating in Sinai—improving the chances of a later assault. If the Egyptian eastward buildup continued, the succeeding days would also see ever fewer tanks remaining on the west bank of the canal—enhancing the chances of any Israeli force that might finally cross. As for the expected Egyptian assault, it seems to have been the abused Sinai commander, Gonen, who saw that this could provide the decisive opportunity for Israeli tanks to destroy the Egyptian armor—because the Egyptians, in advancing, would have to leave the protection of their infantry-borne missile screen. Bar-Lev's support of this appreciation was decisive in the rejection of a swift crossing—as Sharon realized: "Bar-Lev said that we should wait and repel their armored attacks. I believe that we should have crossed the canal and that we wasted several days. . . . But in an army you obey orders." Bar-Lev's verdict on the argument is indicated by the fact that on Thursday he advised Dayan that Sharon should be removed from his command. For the reasons that had led to the rejection of Gonen's earlier and similar request, Bar-Lev's conclusion was turned down.

Behind this tactical argument, however, there was an underlying strategic reason for the rejection of Sharon's plan. It was one over which Israel itself had no control. By Thursday, a Soviet airlift to resupply Syria—and to a lesser extent, Egypt—was in full swing. But the United States was making no similar effort to re-equip Israel. Dayan, Elazar, and Bar-Lev were thus acutely conscious that the Israeli Army was now not in a position to risk the losses that even a successful assault would bring. Israel's ability to do other than accept the Egyptian gains in Sinai, in other words, now depended on what terms Kissinger required of them in exchange for arms.

3. Statesman with a Hangup

On the surface, the first week of war seethed with momentous diplomatic and political effort: at the United Nations, attempts to secure a Security Council resolution calling for a cease-fire; in Washington, agonized discussions whether to resupply Israel; and most dramatic of all, a massive Soviet airlift to the Arabs. The reality was less frenetic but somewhat more chilling. The reality was the activity of Henry Kissinger.

At midday on Sunday, October 7, with the war just twenty-two hours old, the British ambassador to Egypt, Sir Philip Adams, was driven in his Rolls-Royce, Union Jack fluttering, to see President Sadat at his wartime residence, Tahra Palace. Sadat had moved to the palace, in the Cairo suburb of Heliopolis, to be close to the "Operations Command Center" deep underground nearby. Adams arrived just as a meeting of Egyptian generals was breaking up. Two chairs were hastily drawn up, and Sadat and Adams sat looking out of the big window over the palace gardens. Sadat, puffing on his pipe, made a casual remark about the view. There was a pause, which Sadat finally broke. "Well," he said cheerfully, "what's going on?" Adams had rarely seen him so relaxed.

Back in the British Embassy lay a confetti of deciphered cables, briefing the ambassador of the urgent international efforts to get a cease-fire. At the United Nations, the British representative, Sir Donald Maitland, was urging anyone who would listen—and many who would not—to support a meeting of the Security Council. The United States had also called for one; and Maitland, by virtue of Britain's status as author of Resolution 242, was thought to have the best chance of cajoling the Arab states into accepting the necessity for a cease-fire. The British Foreign Secretary, Sir Alec Douglas-Home, was ready to fly to New York. Everything was set. Now, sitting comfortably opposite the man at whom all this activity was directed, Adams cautiously raised the critical question: Would Sadat be interested in a Security Council resolution calling for a cease-fire? The Egyptian leader was brusque, almost angry. It was out of the question. In a few pithy sentences the President spelled out that this time the only cease-fire Egypt would consider was one inseparably linked to a long-term settlement. And the only acceptable basis for that would be Israel's implementation of Resolution 242—the Arab interpretation of 242. Then Sadat dismissed the topic.

The lobbies of the United Nations hummed for the rest of the week with the sound of diplomats rehearsing the well-worn peripheries of the problem. Was there any way of redefining 242's crucial vagueness on the extent of Israeli withdrawal so that it would be both precise enough to satisfy the Arabs yet still offer a negotiating position to Israel? Would India and Yugoslavia make an acceptable peace-keeping force? Would Israel settle for international assurances of security; and, if so, what sort: a joint superpower guarantee; a defense treaty with the United States? But unspoken at the heart of the debate was the crucial question: How could Israel be pressured into accepting the substance of 242? And that in turn depended on a single issue: Would the United States resupply Israel?

As Nixon's national security advisor at the White House, Henry Kissinger had kept well clear of the Middle East. He was, after all, busy elsewhere: Vietnam, détente, and China all, naturally enough, figured higher on his list of priorities than the Middle East. Nixon, Secretary of State Rogers, and Assistant Secretary Sisco had handled that part of the world. But there were deeper reasons for Kissinger's avoidance of the subject. He is a Jew, and proud of that cultural heritage. Emotionally, he had supported, after the horrors of World War II, the idea of a Jewish national home. But as a foreign policy theorist, he came to believe that American support for the creation of that home in the Middle East had been inimical to the United States' long-term interests, which necessarily centered on Arab oil. Israel having been established, however, he now held that the United States could not allow its destruction—certainly not by force of Soviet-supplied arms. Finally, Kissinger was deterred from taking a public stand on the Israel-Arab debate in Washington for fear of arousing anti-Semitism inside the United States. That fear might be irrational. (Or, of course, it might not.) Irrational or not, it was readily understandable in someone whose early adolescence had been cauterized by the nightmare of Nazism in southern Germany, from which his family fled only in 1938.

All this added up, as Joseph Kraft later put it in the New York *Times*, to "a severe hangup" on the question of Israel. When Mrs. Golda Meir had first come to see Nixon at the White House, Kissinger had not even met the Israeli Prime Minister; he sent one of his deputies instead.

Not that there was any pressure on Kissinger to become involved. When Sadat said despairingly: "Everyone has fallen asleep over the Mideast crisis," he was very nearly correct. From March 1971, when the efforts of Rogers and the UN intermediary Jarring effectively collapsed, the Middle East did indeed seem to fall asleep. A British diplomat later ticked off the symptoms of apparent torpor: "Détente; the Russians out of Egypt; the conservative forces, principally Kings Hussein and Faisal, stronger than ever; and Israel's success at continuing fairly normal life in, and bringing prosperity to, the occupied territories—'creating facts' as the Israelis called it."

Kissinger was, in fact, one of the few who did not believe that it was possible to put the Middle East to sleep. He consistently said so to those who asked. One who did was an Israeli friend of his, Brigadier Uzi Narkiss. Narkiss had come to one of the international seminars that Kissinger ran at Harvard. In return, as head of the Israeli Defense College, Narkiss had twice brought Kissinger to lecture in Israel. In the Six-Day War, Narkiss headed the Central Command: His troops captured Jerusalem. So it was against a background of old acquaintance and military success that, in the summer of 1969, Narkiss dropped in on Kissinger at the White House. And he agreed that a *Life* correspondent, David Niven, then engaged on a profile of Kissinger, could sit in on their conversation:

" 'Henry,' Narkiss said, 'the big thing that we have learned is that there are many problems that have no solution, that people must live with. The Middle East is such a problem.'

" 'Yes,' Kissinger said, 'but that does not mean that what is without a solution will remain unchanged. . . .'

" 'Of course,' Narkiss said, 'but Israel will stay a long time in the territories that it has taken. It will stay as long as it likes.'

" 'No. For a while, yes; for a year or two . . .'

" 'Fifteen years.'

" 'Oh, I doubt it. I think the world climate will not permit it.' Kissinger paused. The sun was pouring in his windows. There were prints on the wall, and the furniture, though new, looked pedestrian and uncomfortable. Narkiss was frowning, but Kissinger's face was calm and inscrutable as he went on.

" 'The issue here is to be sure that the United States and Israel do not find themselves against the world and that a general world war does not result. The question before Israel is whether it can trade some of its physical superiority for some political legitimacy. . . .' "

After the Yom Kippur War, Narkiss recalled more of that conversation: "Kissinger's point was that the time might come when the Middle East situation might lead to a world conflict, or at least to a confrontation between the United States and Russia. . . . If war started, the two superpowers would face each other on behalf of their friends. . . .

"But I said I doubted whether the Soviet Union would interfere actively on behalf of the Arabs, unless Israel crossed the canal or threatened Cairo. He agreed that the Soviet Union wouldn't enter a war directly unless we crossed the canal. But he said that the present situation couldn't be allowed to persist—the potential danger was too great. . . ."

Kissinger continued to avoid the problem, however, until, at the end of 1972, there were at last domestic reasons why he should involve himself. The first fuel crisis had hit the United States. Whether the shortage of central-heating oil that winter was the result of a plot by the major oil companies to drive the small independents out of business; or whether it was, as the oil majors claim, merely the first flake of the blizzard to come, is irrelevant. Nor is it necessary, at this point, to examine the reality of the United States oil problem. What matters were the consequences. The claim by John Ehrlichman, then Nixon's chief advisor on domestic affairs, that energy was a "front-burner project" at the White House by December 1972 is a considerable exaggeration. The White House was already almost paralyzed by Watergate. But

Kissinger, still insulated in his semibasement from the repercussions of that scandal—his role in telephone tapping had not yet surfaced—did begin preliminary work on the options for U.S. policy in the Middle East.

This switch to activism was a response not merely to the objective facts of the situation. True, Kissinger was scratching around for "themes" for Nixon's second term of office: The Middle East was a logical one. And examined calmly, Sadat, Hussein, and Mrs. Meir did also seem prepared now to discuss less than their maximum demands. So the situation did perhaps permit flexibility. And there was the Jordanians' warning.

On all counts, however, Kissinger had to tread carefully. In consequence, according to an ex-colleague of this period, one of Kissinger's first moves was to open secret diplomatic contact with Egypt. According to the source, Kissinger did this during the visit to Washington early in 1973 of Sadat's personal representative and national security advisor, Hafez Ismail. (Ismail's visit, as we have related, was Sadat's last effort to cajole the U.S. toward a diplomatic solution.) The source maintains that, during this visit, Ismail met Kissinger in extreme secrecy. The State Department now claims to know nothing about this meeting "as it happened too long ago." But the story is plausible. Ismail met President Nixon and Secretary of State Rogers on February 23, and UN Secretary General Waldheim on February 24. But Ismail did not arrive at his next stop, Bonn, until February 28.

Meanwhile, as a more overt approach to the problem, Kissinger had instructed his National Security Council staff to prepare a "study memorandum" on the problem and the options. These memoranda are a standard device for floating policy ideas around Washington: In replying to them, all the agencies involved have a chance to put up their rival schemes; the council staff supposedly digest the results into more or less agreed policy choices. More often, of course, the memoranda merely furnish further examples of the traditional bureaucratic ploy of collecting so many opinions that they all cancel out, so the original ideas emerge unscathed. The initial conclusions of this memorandum were certainly gloomy. By late January 1973, Kissinger's staff had sketched the outline of the U.S. dilemma:

The sheer cost of rising oil imports would within a decade

quadruple the U.S. foreign payments burden—even if the unit cost of oil rose only slowly. The consequences of this currency drain upon other areas of American overseas spending—its ability to afford foreign bases, for example—was another potential problem. As important, however, was Kissinger's judgment that the fuel shortage had sufficiently alarmed the American public that they might, for the first time, be willing to think hard about the realities of U.S. interests in the Middle East. Previously, it had been axiomatic that U.S. interests were enshrined in, inseparable from, those of Israel. Now the first forebodings of an oil problem might bring a fresh perspective to public view, might reveal the reality: which was that the relationship between the United States and Israel was not symmetrical. Israel's interests might indeed be bounded by the importance of its American ties. But U.S. interests in the Middle East ran far wider than Israel—and might even at times be inimical to those of Israel.

Kissinger had always sought to operate foreign policy independent of domestic concerns. Where this had not been possible, he had endeavored to fit the complex interactions between these two strands of government into a somewhat mechanistic framework. It had been, arguably, one of his wider blind spots. Yet now he was well aware of the domestic dangers involved in remodeling U.S. policy in the Middle East: not merely his long-standing fear of stirring possible anti-Semitism, but more practical concerns, such as the extraordinary power of the Jewish lobby in Congress; Nixon's new-found desire in the wake of his 1972 victory to cement a large segment of the traditionally Democratic Jewish vote into a new Republican coalition; and the straightforward bureaucratic point that Rogers and Sisco were still very much in charge of Middle East policy.

But the Western alliance could be severely tested. The United States' allies were considerably more dependent upon imported oil than was the United States. The rising cost and growing scarcity of this oil could debilitate their economies and might lead to a damaging scramble for resources.

The potential contradiction between U.S. support for Israel and its growing dependence on Arab oil had not been posed in stark terms yet—not for any reasons of American cunning, but because the main Arab oil producer, King Faisal of Saudi Arabia, had so far rejected all pleas from other Arabs to transform oil into a weapon against Israel. But would this self-restraint persist? As the study was being drafted, one of Kissinger's staff put the dilemma crisply: "The question is: Can we still import in the 1980s if there is no resolution of the Arab-Israeli dispute by then?"

The memorandum floated around Washington through the late spring and early summer of 1973. The conclusions did not perceptibly brighten. If the United States wanted to avoid a choice between Israel and oil, the Middle East crisis had to be solved soon.

None of this thinking was particularly new. Less clearly formulated, it had been the spur to Rogers' efforts since 1969. But, after the shock of the fuel shortage, Kissinger enjoyed greater domestic freedom than Rogers had; and, in the afterglow of Vietnam and China, he shone with incomparably greater international luster. His entry as new Secretary of State into the mine field of Middle East diplomacy—with the intensive talks we have already recounted at the United Nations just two weeks before war began—thus not only came against a background of considerably greater study than Kissinger admitted, but seemingly had better prospects than any previous initiative. (Though, to be fair, Kissinger still saw Europe as his most immediate foreign policy problem.)

In these circumstances, Kissinger's response to the news—relayed to him at 9 A.M. on the morning of Saturday, October 6—that another Arab-Israeli war had begun, was pardonably egocentric. He described this reaction to Sadat after the war was over: As recalled later by the Egyptian President, Kissinger said: "I had been planning to move toward a settlement perhaps by late in 1974. I did not think the time would be ripe until then. So when I first heard the news, I thought: 'The Arabs are going to get another bloody nose. And that will end the chances of getting anywhere in the life of this Administration.' I saw my last chance fade of pulling off a settlement."

4. Kissinger's Secret Plan

On what little he knew, Kissinger—surveying the Middle East scene from the thirty-fifth floor of the Waldorf Towers that first Saturday morning of war—had good reason for gloom. The one assumption consistent to every recent U.S. intelligence assessment of the prospects in the Middle East had been that Israel could demolish the Arabs forces at will. And now, because of that discrepancy between Israeli intelligence of an Arab attack at 6 P.M. and the actual start of the fighting at 2 P.M., it looked as if the Israelis had ensured their victory by a preemptive strike.

It is impossible to understand American actions in the days that followed, without knowledge of the secret but central aim of Kissinger's policy. Kissinger himself subsequently explained it, though in tactful terms: "Throughout the crisis, the President was convinced that we had two major problems—first, to end hostilities as quickly as possible; but, secondly, to end hostilities in a manner that would enable us to make a major contribution to removing the conditions that have produced four wars between Arabs and Israelis in the last twenty-five years." In blunter terms, Kissinger wanted a limited Israeli defeat. The nicety lay in calculating the optimum scale of his defeat: big enough to satisfy the Arabs; modest enough to preclude a propaganda triumph for the Soviets; sobering enough to bring Israel to the conference table to negotiate almost total withdrawal from its 1967 gains; modest enough to avoid the collapse of Mrs. Meir's government and its replacement by right-wing intransigents. Balanced up, those considerations indicated very clearly what military outcome would be politically optimal: a stalemate in Sinai, with Egypt victoriously across the canal and Israel secure but battered astride the vital passes. In pursuit of this objective, Kissinger refused arms supplies to Israel.

That was Kissinger's over-all policy. But in the first hours of war that Saturday, the question of arms supply had not yet been raised by Israel; and the possibility of an Israeli defeat never occurred to anyone. The immediate problem, as Kissinger saw it then, was how to prevent another crushing *Arab* defeat. After a few hours of further fruitless telephoning in New York, Kissinger flew down to Washington on Saturday afternoon. By now, he knew what to do: Get a Security Council resolution calling for an immediate cease-fire. From Washington, he phoned the representatives and then the home governments of every member of the Security Council. That was how the plan for a British-sponsored cease-fire resolution was put together.

The urgency of this was still posited on the necessity to stave off the expected Arab defeat. Kissinger, talking after the war to Heikal of *Al Ahram*, gave a plausible account of his thinking at that point: "I imagined then that this [cease-fire proposal] would be more in your interest than in Israel's. Let me put it another way. If I told you that I was thinking of your interests alone I would be deceiving you. My thoughts ran at the time along these lines: The Egyptians have embarked upon a serious major initiative—probably driven to it by despair. But Israel's military might will now descend on them with the utmost ferocity. What will happen then? Egypt will turn to the Soviet Union for its rescue. At that point there would be two possibilities:

"One, either the Soviet Union will intervene in such a way as to make it incumbent upon the United States to intervene as well, which would have confronted both us and them with a fearful situation. Or, two, the Soviets would not intervene directly, but would so increase their presence in Egypt as never to come out of it again. That was another exigency which we did not desire. The whole business was not primarily for the sake of Egypt. The whole thing was primarily a desire to observe the facts and balances of power in this age."

It was an assessment that at least the Western members of the Security Council were willing to accept. By Saturday evening, Britain's UN representative, Sir Donald Maitland, had begun to put together the nuts and bolts of a cease-fire resolution.

The first break in this sequence should have come that Saturday evening. In the Situation Room at the White House, Kissinger chaired the first crisis meeting of the Washington Special Action Group. WASHAC, as it is called, is the compact heart of the obese National Security Council. Throughout the war, it was WASHAC—not the National Security Council as a whole—that functioned as the central forum of U.S. policy-making. Staffed by the normal NSC bureaucracy, WASHAC's actual participants varied from time to time; but the representation remained constant, top-level, and tight: State Department, Defense, the CIA, the NSC machine itself.

The new fact that this first WASHAC meeting had to contend with was that Israel had clearly not, as Kissinger had feared, mounted a preemptive strike. (By now, Kissinger had been briefed by Keating on the warning he had given to Mrs. Meir.) The Arab assault had been launched as planned, and was obviously determined both in planning and execution. So, contrary to expectation, Israel had decisively lost the initiative. WASHAC's views were not swayed by the news, however. As Kissinger told editor Heikal later: "When the war did break out, it became clear that our calculations were wrong. Yet we continued to believe that our assessment of the outcome was still correct." WASHAC did not doubt that Israel would swiftly get on top.

Specifically, WASHAC had reassurance of this from two sources. The chairman of the Joint Chiefs of Staff, Admiral Thomas Moorer, retailed to WASHAC the Pentagon's unwavering confidence in a smashing Israeli triumph. And, shortly before the meeting opened, Kissinger had telephoned the Israeli Foreign Minister, Eban, to get his views. Eban, still in New York at the United Nations, knew nothing beyond what he was being told in cables from Galili, the minister who had taken over direction of foreign affairs in Israel's war leadership. And Galili, in turn, reproduced the optimism that still permeated that leadership. His cables talked of the halting of the Arab thrusts, of the Israeli counterattacks beginning—precisely the picture that Mrs. Meir and Dayan had just given to Israeli television viewers. Eban relayed the good news to Kissinger. Some slight loss of initiative had always been expected during the mobilization phase, he said, but Israel was in no trouble and would wrap up the war in four or five days. He even added that Israel was vehemently opposed to a cease-fire proposal: It would merely deprive its forces of an inevitable victory.

But the next day, Sunday, October 7, Kissinger allowed the U.S. cease-fire proposal to become public. The proposition—requesting, in effect, a unilateral Arab withdrawal—was so ludicrous that it could only have been founded, as indeed it was, upon a total misunderstanding of the progress of the war. In the circumstances, Sadat's decision was as predictable as Israel's. When London relayed to Washington at around Sunday lunchtime (Washington time) the Egyptian leader's frosty dismissal of the proposal, the second WASHAC meeting—early that Sunday afternoon—had two choices: to press on with the resolution regardless of Arab hostility, or to accept the impasse. Kissinger swiftly chose the latter: "Let the boys play awhile," he reportedly remarked. If Sadat was sufficiently confident to reject his proposal, perhaps there was a chance that the war would be more than a rerun of 1967. Britain was told to halt its work toward a cease-fire—which Whitehall, discouraged by Sadat, itself wanted to do. Less to London's liking, it was also intimated that Britain should make no further independent efforts to achieve a cease-fire: Kissinger would handle everything.

If the swift Israeli victory was proving slower than expected, Kissinger's basic policy nevertheless held: Israel should not be provided with the supplies to augment the scale of this coming victory. According to an Israeli account, it was on Sunday evening that the first formal Israeli request for arms was made in Washington. The Israeli ambassador, Simcha Dinitz, was still somewhere in midair between Tel Aviv and Washington, hastily returning from his father's funeral. Thus, according to this account, it was Dinitz's deputy at the embassy, the minister Mordechai Shalev, who that Sunday evening called on Kissinger's Assistant Secretary for Near East Affairs, Joseph Sisco. Shalev apparently wanted to know the outcome of the WASHAC meeting. He also made a formal request for U.S. military supplies. Elsewhere in Washington, however, the same request had already been received. The Israeli military attaché, Major General Mordechai Gur, had been cabled by Dayan on Saturday evening to begin negotiations for supplies. Presumably, Gur contacted the Pentagon on Sunday morning. That is unclear. What is certain is that at 2:20 P.M. on Sunday afternoon, the Israeli military procurement group attached to the consul-general's office in New York received a coded telex from its embassy in Washington. The U.S. response to the first Israeli request for arms, this said, was "negative."

Kissinger had embarked upon a very dangerous game. It was dangerous for two reasons. The first was that he was running head-on into the considerable might of the Jewish lobby in Washington. The second was that, as he later indicated to Heikal, he was doing this in pursuit of détente. He was gambling a certainty against at best a sporting chance.

Kissinger got on well with the long-time Soviet ambassador in Washington, Anatoly Dobrynin. When war broke out Dobrynin was a few weeks short of fifty-four years old—and he was the principal Soviet specialist on the United States. He had first come to Washington in the hysterical years of the early 1950s. And as he had risen in the Soviet diplomatic service in the intervening twenty years—concentrating upon the United States or the United Nations—Dobrynin had come to have not only a considerable regard for the United States, but also a shrewd understanding of it. Within the Kremlin, Dobrynin—a member of the party central committee—was heard with attention. He was just the sort of person Kissinger liked to deal with. And during the long and secret Vietnam negotiations, the two had established a personal rapport. Dobrynin once gave Kissinger a cartoon: "Henry, take it easy," the caption read. Virtually all major U.S.-Soviet relations were conducted through Dobrynin: the U. S. Embassy in Moscow was—except for its functions as a listening and trading post—a consular formality.

Before the war, Dobrynin told Kissinger that American anti-Sovietism was stronger now than at any time since the "Cold War years" when he had first come to Washington. Kissinger later repeated the remark with a half-despairing gesture. He, too, was very worried that détente had not been widely accepted in the United States. In fact, Nixon's rapprochement with Brezhnev had had the effect of making anticommunism fashionable again among American liberals. As a result, traditional conservative "cold warriors" had been joined by these liberal Democrats to form something of an unholy alliance against the Nixon-Kissinger policy. The two men who got these disparate Washington comrades together were the distinguished Soviet physicist and dissenter, Andrei Sakharov, and the senator from Washington, Henry "Scoop" Jackson.

Sakharov's role was important in part because he had changed his mind. Until recently he had supported the concept of détente, arguing that it would force the Soviet Union to open up: to allow a greater exchange of information, ideas, perhaps even people. Back in 1970, he wrote that a modern economy demanded "the creative participation of millions of people at all levels of the economic system . . . and a broad exchange of information and ideas." Some liberals now held that, on the contrary, détente as conceived by Nixon and Brezhnev was actually a device to enable the Kremlin to perpetuate its control over its society—courtesy of technology provided by willing American businessmen and paid for with credits funded by the American taxpayer. Sakharov's present opposition to détente reinforced this. So did the reason Sakharov had swung around: the fact that the first three years of détente had seen an unprecedented KGB crackdown on Soviet civil rights groups, Samizdat movements, and all the flowering expressions of dissent half tolerated in the late 1960s.

The issue that had sharpened opposition to détente into a potent political weapon—and welded a coalition between the Jewish lobby in Congress and the anti-Soviet lobby—was forged from the coincidence of Nixon's foreign trade bill and an upsurge of public interest in the plight of Soviet Jews. The bill sought to grant the Soviet Union "most favored nation" trading status— whipped away during the Korean War—plus vast financial credits to enable Moscow to buy American technology. Liberal cynics saw Nixon's promise to Brezhnev as the *quid pro quo* for Soviet help in getting Hanoi to agree to "peace with honor." And they suspected that a scandalously cheap grain sale to Moscow had been just the first payment. Opposing the granting of further credits were such motley bedfellows as Jackson, Professors Hans Morgenthau, and Arthur Schlesinger, Jr., Tom Wicker, William F. Buckley, Jr., the AFL-CIO, the Americans for Democratic Action, and many more. Supporting Kissinger were few more than Senator William F. Fulbright, George Kennan, and the National Association of Manufacturers—whose members, of course, stood to make a killing out of the deal.

Kissinger, indeed, might have been forgiven for echoing the old Sicilian prayer: "I can deal with my enemies, but God protect me from my friends." Every patient explanation he gave that détente did not imply approval of the Soviet system, merely recognized the realities of the nuclear age, was undercut by men like Armand Hammer, chairman of Occidental Oil, saying that Brezhnev was "a most humane person"; or Donald Kendall, Nixon's friend and contributor and chairman of Pepsico, declaring: "The selling of Pepsico to the Soviet Union and Stolichnaya Vodka in the United States is another sign of progress, bringing our countries together so there will be peace in the world." Kendall even described Brezhnev as "warmhearted"—which, however true, massively missed the point.

The point, so far as the American public was concerned, was that Jews wishing to emigrate to Israel had a hard time at the hands of the Soviet authorities. In fact, by the time U.S. attention was stirred, the worst was over: The treatment of putative emigrants had been much worse at the end of the 1960s; but their present treatment was still far from good. From the right, Senator Henry Jackson—an ardent supporter of Israel and an equally ardent hawk on all matters connected with the Soviet Union—saw in the plight of these Jews an excellent way of beating old enemies while solidifying old friendships. He had appended to Nixon's foreign trade bill an amendment that read: "To prohibit most favored nation treatment and commercial and guarantee agreements with respect to any nonmarket economy country which denies to its citizens the right to emigrate or which imposes more than nominal fees upon its citizens as a condition to emigration." By the outbreak of war, he had seventy-six senators behind him. And Sakharov was publicly asking that more join. The fact that, presumably in response to this pressure, the Kremlin had already dropped its huge exit tax on Jews and allowed more emigration than ever—even throughout the war the flow continued—did not lessen the damage that this campaign was doing to the prospects for détente.

5. Nixon and the Jews

It was a measure of Kissinger's conviction of the necessity for détente that, against this background, he was willing to run the risks inherent in his Middle East policy. Should the Soviets let him down—even by so little as, say, overly enthusiastic but all too predictable rhetoric on such lines as "the just struggle against Zionist oppression"—Kissinger could find himself singularly exposed. For, if that was a risk, and worth a gamble, it was a certainty that Kissinger was going to run into fire on the other flank —from the Jewish lobby. And that was a formidable threat.

"There is probably no issue in America, foreign or domestic, on which there is such consensus as Israel—amongst Northerners and Southerners, liberals and conservatives, Democrats and Republicans," said Hyman Bookbinder, Washington representative of the American Jewish committee. Senator Fulbright, chairman of the Senate Foreign Relations Committee, put the point another way at the beginning of the war: "Israelis control the Congress," he said simply. Fulbright's statement was not far from the truth, because Bookbinder's was also not far from the truth. The Israeli lobby in Washington was effective not so much because it was very well organized and rich—though it was both—but because it had an extraordinarily broad consensus of public support behind it.

There are 5.9 million Jews in America—60 per cent in and around New York; 3 million are potential voters; and the vast majority—at least 80 per cent—had from Roosevelt's New Deal days until 1972 voted unwaveringly Democrat. Behind this powerfully cohesive voting bloc, an extraordinary range of political organizations has grown up. There were, at last count, 31 major Jewish organizations in the United States, running the gamut from orthodox to reform to revisionist. The most important are

B'nai B'rith/the Anti-Defamation League, since its birth 70 years ago the watchdog against anti-Semitism in the United States; the American Jewish Congress, which promotes fraternal Jewish participation in public affairs and, if it has a political coloration, is to the left; the American Jewish Committee, organized at the time of the pogroms in Russia early in this century, and now with a more conservative complexion—it supports an excellent political and literary magazine, *Commentary*; and, finally, the American Israel Public Affairs Committee, a propaganda and political lobby organization for Israel.

These organizations are not necessarily all Zionist. But they are all pro-Israel. As Bookbinder of the American Jewish Congress would point out, thirty years ago most American Jews were non-Zionist: "Settled here, they saw little need for a state. But once Israel became a fact they naturally supported it fully." (In domestic politics, Bookbinder's view parodied Henry Ford's: "What's better for America is better for Jews, and vice versa." His committee's other job, as he saw it, was "to help prevent any situation in which Jews could be scapegoated.")

In the context of the Yom Kippur War, there could be no doubt that all these organizations would now endeavor to put the maximum possible pressure on Congress and the Administration. Since 1954 that sort of pressure has been channeled through I. L "Si" Kenen, the short, soft-spoken, straightforward executive vice chairman of the American Israel Public Affairs Committee (AIPAC). Si Kenen is certainly among the most successful lobbyists on the Hill—perhaps the *most* successful. He is the umbrella man for all American Jewish organizations. (AIPAC has an annual budget of about two hundred thousand dollars, all raised in the United States.) Born in Toronto, Kenen was a journalist in Cleveland until he involved himself in Zionist affairs in 1943. Now sixty-eight, he has been lobbying for Israel in Congress since 1951.

It is Kenen who coordinates the power of the American Jewish community for Israel. "He tells us what Israel's needs are and how to get public support," Bookbinder said. But his success on the Hill is at least as much due to his own personality and work-style as to the support he can summon. Kenen's operation is low-key, subtle, totally nonpartisan, and very, very knowledgeable. Kenen is never too busy to help a congressman of either party write a speech or draft a resolution. And it pays off. The Senate minority leader, Senator Hugh Scott, once asked an aide for a statement on the Middle East. "This looks like what we need," said Scott when it was ready. "But, just in case, why don't you check it out with Si." A lobbyist can have no greater "in" than that. And Kenen's ties to the Israeli Embassy and even directly to the Israeli Government are equally close. He is, in sum, a superb soft salesman. His job is to get money, materiel, and moral support for Israel both in Congress and in the country. And his operation has continued largely unchanged since Eisenhower.

In some ways, of course, it had not been hard. Congress had been sympathetic to Israel ever since it approved the Balfour Declaration. It had been giving economic aid to Israel since a Taft-Douglas amendment to the foreign aid program in 1951. But, until Nixon, the amount of U.S. military aid to Israel had not been as large as Kenen considered necessary. "From 1945–70 the United States gave away fifty-five billion dollars' worth of arms and none of them went to Israel," he said. Still, Congress had been trying hard since. In fiscal year 1972, Congress began earmarking aid funds for Israel; when war broke out, three hundred million dollars in aid was earmarked for Israel in both the Senate and House versions of the 1974 foreign military aid bill, then in conference.

Nor, as Kissinger realized, would it be hard for Kenen to muster the political clout to persuade Congress to increase that aid to Israel once the war had begun. In 1972, John Richardson, executive director of American Near East Refugee Aid, Inc., had contended that "most senators have a kind of knee-jerk pro-Israeli reaction." He was right. "I rarely go to the Hill," Kenen explained. "There's so much support for Israel that I don't have to."

There is a definable, hard-core, pro-Israel group in the Senate: Jackson; Scott; Edward Kennedy; Edward Brooke, also of Massachusetts; Robert Dole of Kansas; Edward Gurney of Florida; Jacob Javits of New York; Gale McGee of Wyoming; Abraham Ribicoff of Connecticut; Stuart Symington of Missouri; Herman Talmadge of Georgia; Charles Percy of Illinois: six Democrats and six Republicans, only two of them Jews. These twelve can be counted on by Kenen in almost any situation. But, as the war was soon to demonstrate, support for Israel is far more widespread than they. As Fulbright, one of the four or so senators consistently anti-Israel, said: "The emotional and political ties are too strong. . . . On every test on anything the Israelis are interested in, in the Senate . . . the Israelis have seventy-five to eighty votes."

Kenen considered that almost all congressman were sympathetic because Israel "has demonstrated it can do for itself. The country doesn't require American boys to fight for its causes." But ideology played its part. Conservatives saw Israel as "a source of strength against Communist-backed Arab regimes and a bulwark against the totalitarian possibility," he said. Liberals, on the other hand, "point to the democratic way of life in Israel." Pressed, Kenen would agree that Jewish campaign contributions might play a part in securing this affection; but he stressed that AIPAC was carefully nonpartisan—and would politely refuse to discuss Watergate.

Kenen, of course, maintained that the pressure was not all one way. According to him, AIPAC had to spend a lot of its time counteracting propaganda from the "petroleum-diplomatic complex," which he defined as "a coalition of oil lobbyists, diplomats, and educators with cultural and theological interests in the Arab world." But the propaganda battle, at least, between Jews and Arabs in the United States was hardly an equal one. Against the 5.9 million Jews in America there are around 1 million to 1.5 million Arabs. And as Charles Alawan, leader of Detroit's Arab community of 85,000, plaintively said: "Somebody told us this country was a melting pot. Unfortunately we melted. We don't have the same nationalist ties to the Arab countries as do our counterparts to Israel." Yet there was resentment. Helen Haje, executive secretary of the National Association of Arab-Americans, would ask: "What makes us so wrong and the Jews so right? We're American citizens too. We don't go out begging for money." When the Arab community did try to raise funds during the war, one of the speakers acknowledged wryly: "We have to try harder. We're No. 22." Paradoxically, the American public automatically attached the epithet "oil-rich" to the word "Arab"—without ever reflecting that, if this were true, then U.S. policy might be a trifle imprudent.

Unscathed by such forebodings, the Jewish American community thus affected U.S. policy in two ways. First, they provided the grass-roots political muscle to give Kenen the ability to push through Congress virtually any policy the Israeli Government wished. Second, their community leaders themselves had direct access to the White House. Under J.F.K. and L.B.J., there was always a middle-ranking White House official—first Meyer Feldman and then Harry McPherson—who had what was known as the "Jewish portfolio," whose job was to be always accessible to these community leaders. The community in turn had its own links with Israel apart from Si Kenen—especially with Foreign Minister Eban. So there were two interlocking levers on U.S. power: the community leaders directly on the White House; and Kenen, with the community behind him, on Congress and on the public. Nixon changed all that.

Nixon once told a state governor: "I owe nothing to the American Jewish community, but I'm not going to let that affect my support for Israel." In a sense, that was true: There was never any doubt that Nixon supported Israel. But, as we have recounted, Nixon was able to use his freedom from Jewish ties after 1968 to lean much harder on Israel than his predecessors had done.

And, domestically, Nixon did cut back the influence of the leaders of the American Jewish community. He did not give anyone the "Jewish portfolio"; instead, he dealt exclusively with the Embassy, or even with Mrs. Meir. Instead of a Feldman or a McPherson, Nixon had one of his White House counsel, Len Garment, working part-time on American Jewish matters. (He did at first also use one Jewish leader, his friend Max Fisher, as a liaison with Jewish groups. Fisher was a Detroit financier, with money in oil and real estate, who gave over one hundred thousand dollars to the Republicans in 1968. "Nixon's Jew," one Israeli journalist in Washington called him.)

Even before he was drowned by Watergate, Garment had a hard time. In 1970, for example, he tried unsuccessfully to stop a group of Jewish veterans demonstrating outside the Waldorf-Astoria in Manhattan against President Pompidou, in protest against France's sale of 110 Mirage fighter-bombers to Libya. Garment invoked the help of the Israeli Embassy, and Nixon flew to New York to accompany Pompidou. The demonstration was not called off: Nixon was furious. For some time, all routine presidential messages to the Jewish community simply ceased.

Nixon's chief of staff at the White House, Bob Haldeman, thought that American Jewry was not worth bothering about at all—it would never pay Nixon dividends. Haldeman was wrong in one sense, right in another. In 1968, Nixon had won only about 15 per cent of the Jewish vote. But we have detailed how, after the collapse of Rogers' peace-making efforts, Nixon had re-armed Israel on an unprecedented scale through the end of 1971. In 1972, perhaps 40 per cent of the Jewish vote went to him. Whatever support Nixon gained from the Jewish community, therefore, was because of what he did for Israel, not for them.

This gulf between the American-Jewish domestic lobby and real power over U.S. relations with Israel had been accentuated by the Israelis' own actions. When the Israeli Chief of Staff during the Six-Day War, Yizhak Rabin, became ambassador in Washington at the beginning of 1968, he broke new ground. Previous ambassadors—including Abba Eban, now Foreign Minister—had tended to rely for contact with the White House upon intermediaries in the American Jewish community using their channel to Feldman or McPherson. Rabin cut through that. He went straight to the White House—at top level. And he possessed the tanklike determination and the political power back home to pull off this upgrading of the Embassy's influence. But that, in turn, brought other problems: notably, the final castration of the Israeli foreign ministry.

Rabin reported not to Foreign Minister Eban but directly to Mrs. Meir. Reportedly, Eban at times did not even see copies of Rabin's cables. That scarcely made for the orderly formation of Israeli foreign policy—but then, arguably, Israel did not have a policy apart from the American relationship. Inside the United States, it was equally destructive. Traditionally, and for obvious geographical reasons, the Israeli consulate-general in New York had been the focus of Israel's contacts with the American Jewish community. But the post of consul-general—which carried ambassadorial rank—was in Eban's gift. The result was that both consuls-general during Rabin's term as ambassador were effectively frozen out of policy-making. The domestic American Jews were even further cut off.

Rabin's replacement, Simcha Dinitz, was in some respects an improvement. He was, for a start, easier to get along with than the dour, abrasive Rabin. And he did try to re-establish relations with Eban's New York empire and with domestic Jewry. At a personal level, he also struck up a relationship with Kissinger— "They have similarly heavy senses of humor," one Israeli in Washington said. But Dinitz was very much Mrs. Meir's creature: He had headed her private office; he had gotten the Washington job only at her unbudging insistence; he had no diplomatic experience. And against ex-Chief of Staff Rabin, Dinitz could only appear lightweight in a war situation.

6. Hanging on for Peace

So while the group that on Sunday, October 7, gathered in Si Kenen's office at AIPAC, three blocks from the White House, undoubtedly constituted a "Jewish lobby," it was considerably less monolithic and less certain of its hold upon real power in this crisis than its participants would have admitted publicly. Representatives of almost all the major Jewish groups in Washington were there. But none of them knew what was going on. The embassy could relay nothing more precise than second-hand optimism about the course of the fighting. Nobody knew what Kissinger was up to. Some of those at the meeting called up congressional aides to find out what was afoot. Not even they seemed to know. As a holding operation, Kenen sent a telegram to every senator: "Once again Arab states . . . have launched aggression against Israel. . . . We urge you to support Israel in her resistance to aggression and in her struggle for negotiations which will end bloodshed and bring about a genuine peace. . . ." Several senators—including George McGovern and Kennedy—immediately issued statements attacking the Arabs and backing Israel more or less fervently. On "Face the Nation," Fulbright made the bleak comment that the United States was in no position to cut assistance to Israel because "Israelis control the Congress." But Kenen had been shrewder than that. His telegram had carefully not asked for aid. And while Israelis might control the Congress, it was by no means certain who or what controlled Henry Kissinger.

The answer is that, once he realized that the war was not to be decided in a matter of hours, Kissinger—as he later indicated to Heikal—was preoccupied with the task of preserving the détente with the Soviet Union. And he was hopeful of his chances.

When the Egyptian assault was launched, the assumption

adopted almost automatically in the West was that Sadat must have planned the war in conjunction with the Soviet Union. Clearly, to the extent that the Soviet Union had supplied Egypt's weapons, it was an accomplice. But had the relationship been closer than that? Viewed from Washington, the evidence was contradictory. The last-minute evacuation of Soviet personnel could be interpreted as evidence of scant warning. More worrying was the launching, on October 6 itself, of a second Soviet COSMOS reconnaissance satellite: That did indicate suspicious prescience. Most worrying of all, preliminary analysis of Soviet merchant traffic passing through the Dardanelles from the Black Sea suggested an increase in the flow—which might indicate that a Soviet resupply effort was already under way.

But on balance—and with the benefit of a certain amount of intelligence information on the topic—Kissinger's staff was not convinced that the Soviets had learned of Sadat's precise intentions more than two days before the war: in other words, on Thursday October 4. (In this, we now know, they were somewhat generous to the Soviet Union. Egyptian sources in the Soviet capital now claim that Moscow was told on October 1 or October 2, while Sadat himself has claimed privately that he informed the Soviets on October 3—and that their immediate reaction was to inform him, very coldly, that they proposed to withdraw all their personnel as soon as possible.)

Whatever the precise date, of course, the terms of détente—as represented by the agreements reached at Nixon's meetings in Moscow—required the Soviet leadership to share this knowledge with Washington. Realistically, Kissinger was not overly surprised that this had not happened. Instead, during the first forty-eight hours of war, Kissinger assumed that self-interest—the Soviet desire to prevent what Washington still predicted would be an inevitable Arab defeat—would drive the Soviets to attempt to procure a cease-fire. And the Soviet Union did indeed attempt this—in a secret, clumsy, but unmistakably serious fashion. And Kissinger was one of the few people who knew of this.

After the war, President Sadat—still angry over the episode—recalled it in detail: "At 8 P.M. on October 6, only six hours after the war had started, I was in the Operations Room. I was informed that the Soviet Ambassador [Vladimir Vinogradov] wanted to see me urgently. Our troops had crossed into Sinai and were raising the flag over the Bar-Lev Line. I went out to meet him at General Command Headquarters.

"I was surprised when he told me that Syria was asking for a cease-fire, and that she had requested this from the Soviet Union. I asked him: 'Is this for my own knowledge or for some other purpose?' The Ambassador answered: 'We are telling you this because we have an official request from Syria to do so. And we want you to get in touch with President Asad.'

"I refused point-blank to order a cease-fire. And I asked the Ambassador to convey this to his government. I then cabled President Asad. The next day, October 7, I received a cable from President Asad denying that Syria was asking for a cease-fire.

"About the same time, the Soviet Ambassador asked for another urgent meeting with me. He again claimed that Syria was asking for a cease-fire. My reply to him was a violent one. I told him: 'I am satisfied with President Asad's answer. I take the truth from this answer only.'"

It was, for the time being, the end of Soviet peace efforts. (It was also, not surprisingly, the end of any relationship between Sadat and Ambassador Vinogradov.) But even this clumsy failure was of some reassurance to Kissinger: The Soviets were apparently serious about preserving the peace.

By Monday, however, there were possible grounds for concern. Would the apparent initial successes of the Arabs tempt the Soviets to seek advantage by meddling in the war? True, the Moscow newspapers were reporting the fighting in sober terms. The Moscow rent-a-crowds—a sensitive barometer of Kremlin "public" sentiment—were, to be sure, besieging the U. S. Embassy; but they were still protesting the iniquities of Allende's overthrow in Chile. There were possible clues to a growing split inside the Kremlin, however. In a pointed snub, Soviet Foreign Minister Andrei Gromyko waited until Monday evening to see five Arab ambassadors who had been trying to reach him since Saturday. On the other hand, Brezhnev had now sent telegrams to Algeria, Lebanon, and Jordan, urging that Egypt and Syria "must not remain alone in their struggle against a perfidious enemy." When he read those telegrams, Kissinger was furious—and very worried. But, viewed more coolly, even they might be a hopeful sign: The Soviets are scarcely alone in restoring to bombast on occasion as a cloak for inaction.

The United States had begun military precautions within a few hours of the outbreak of war. The first Saturday evening, the U.S.S. *Independence*—one of the aircraft carriers of the Mediterranean Sixth Fleet—had sailed with minimal fuss from its Greek home port of Piraeus to take up station with its screen of destroyers around the Soviet fleet's patrolling ground between Crete and Cyprus. With nearly eight hundred aircraft on board, the *Independence* alone was a formidable weapon. But the Sixth Fleet's other carrier, the *Franklin D. Roosevelt,* was then brought east from Barcelona; and a third, the *John F. Kennedy,* was finally brought into the Mediterranean from the Atlantic. Among its fifty or so vessels, the Sixth Fleet already deployed a helicopter carrier, the *Guadalcanal,* with nearly two thousand Marines aboard. And this was soon reinforced by another, the *Iwo Jima.*

In its firepower, in its capacity to intervene in the conflict, there was no point during the Yom Kippur War when the U. S. Sixth Fleet was even halfway challenged by the Soviet Mediterranean presence. This remained true even though the Soviets did beef up the sixty or so vessels in their fleet with another thirty craft—including several of their most advanced missile ships— during the war. But to change the course of the fighting—and severely strain détente—the Soviets did not have to intervene directly, merely mount a resupply operation.

Kissinger still had faith in the "structure of peace" he had laboriously been putting together. He pressed on Ambassador Dobrynin the likely damage to their relations should the superpowers become entangled in the war. As he put it later: "We have also urged . . . all the parties in the conduct of their diplomacy now to keep in mind that whatever momentary advantages might be achieved in this or that forum, our principal objective should be to maintain lasting relationships. . . ." Kissinger even took advantage of a speech he was long scheduled to make on Monday, October 8, to a peace conference in Washington, *Pacem in Terris,* to address an almost personal plea to the Soviets. He summarized afterward the ground rules of détente that he had been trying to convey to them: "I pointed out that there are limits beyond which we cannot go. I stated that we will oppose the attempt by any country to achieve a position of pre-dominance, either globally or regionally; that we would resist any attempt to exploit a policy of détente to weaken our alliances; and that we would react if the relaxations of tensions were used as a cover to exacerbate conflicts in international trouble spots." And at *Pacem in Terris,* Kissinger framed his conclusion in un-mistakable language: "Détente cannot survive irresponsibility in any area, including the Middle East. . . ." But Sadat's strategy, of course—the whole thinking behind Operation SPARK—was precisely to involve the superpowers.

To Kissinger, however, Monday—the day of that *Pacem in Terris* speech—was perhaps the most hopeful single day of the war. It was now quite apparent that Israel was not about to win the expected swift victory. It looked as if the Soviets might not be going to intervene. And in Washington, he was successfully stav-ing off Israeli pressure for arms without incurring the wrath of Congress. The situation looked good.

Kissinger told Heikal afterward: "After two days, the battle was still raging fiercely in Sinai. Just as our assessment of your mobilization had proved to be wrong, so our assessment of your combat potential also appeared to be wrong. I asked for the Pentagon's reports on the progress of the fighting and I asked, more than once, for the assessments of the Joint Chiefs of Staff. 'Just what is happening in the Middle East?' I asked. Back came the reply: 'The picture is quite different from our calculations.'" (In fact, the intelligence picture was so confused that, after Monday's WASHAC meeting, Kissinger ordered surveillance of the fighting to be stepped up by all possible means—and since there was no way of getting a satellite on station quickly enough to supplement the copious electronic data which had already been picked up, that meant high-altitude reconnaissance flights. This, as we shall see, was to lead to the first of the U.S. problems with its allies—in this case, Britain.)

But, even though Israel was clearly in for a longer slog than most had predicted, the Israeli ambassador, Dinitz, still seemed fairly relaxed when he saw Kissinger that Monday. "It was the old Israeli *chutzpah,*" one Washington source recalled later. "It wouldn't be over in six days this time, they said, but perhaps in ten or twelve." And, although he raised the question of arms supplies, Dinitz was content with evasions. After the meeting, Dinitz telexed the Israeli defense group in New York: His request for arms had also gotten a "negative," he reported, but Kissinger had added: "There is a chance."

Congress too was proving more pacific than expected. Lobbyist Si Kenen had hoped that the inevitable Senate resolution on the war would explicitly "deplore" the Arab attack. But Scott and the majority leader, Senator Mike Mansfield, were persuaded by the Administration to cool it. Their resolution merely deplored "the outbreak of the tragic hostilities in the Middle East" and advised "that we support the use of the good offices of the United States by the President and the Secretary of State." Still, it did urge withdrawal to the prewar positions. Even so, Jackson and Ribicoff refused to sign it because it was not strong enough. That was Kissinger's doing. As he said to Heikal: "You might notice that we did not stop long at the question of who had begun the fighting."

By Monday, in fact, Kissinger was not unpleased by the course of events. As he recalled afterward: "I said at the time: Circumstances are now suitable for a cease-fire. The Egyptians have proved their military prowess. They have changed the situation in the Middle East: There are now new facts which must be taken into account. The political objective behind Egypt's acceptance of the risk of war has become clear. Further continuation of the fighting would be unjustified. All parties, therefore, should now try to get a cease-fire—and move to political action towards a radical solution to the dispute. So I contacted the Soviets. . . ."

With dramatic suddenness, the situation changed that Monday evening. Reports of the disaster that had overtaken their first counterattack in Sinai—the mauling of Adan's tanks and the cancellation of Sharon's assault—reached the Israeli high command. The bleak conclusion was transmitted to the Washington Embassy. The magnitude of the task facing Israel had suddenly escalated beyond recognition. Gone was the first calm confidence. Israel now knew it could not win—could perhaps not even repulse a determined Egyptian assault on the passes—without supplies from the United States.

Dinitz got the news shortly before he was due to address a dinner of one of the most powerful Jewish groups in the United

States, the Conference of Presidents of Major American Jewish Organizations, at the Shoreham Hotel in Washington. It was a good opportunity for the first application of a little public pressure: "What Israel needs now," Dinitz said in his speech, "is time —and the replacement by the United States of lost equipment." His audience was shocked by the news. Until that moment, Kenen and other Jewish leaders had really believed Israel would mop it up in a few days. "The long period of the cease-fire had led us into complacency," Kenen reflected later. "By now, we had almost begun to think that Israel didn't need more and more arms, that qualitative superiority was enough. Once the war started we thought it would be easy." Dinitz's news had seismic impact.

It is an indication of the uncertainty with which the Jewish lobby viewed Kissinger that, even now, Dinitz and Kenen decreed private rather than public pressure on the Administration. (Even Israeli journalists in Washington had no briefing on the seriousness of the situation until Wednesday.) As the first move in this discreet campaign, Dinitz went to see Kissinger again the next morning, Tuesday, October 9. And this time he would not accept equivocation. Israel needed aircraft, ammunition for its tanks and artillery and, if possible, something to counter the electronics of the SAM-6s. (As Dayan told the Israeli editors a few hours later: "The list of equipment I have seen that we want from the Americans runs into hundreds of millions of dollars.") Dinitz wanted a firm commitment—particularly a promise of new Phantom fighter-bombers. The facts of what happened next can be unraveled, but the motivation must remain speculative. Kissinger told Dinitz that he had already talked through the situation with Nixon. The President had agreed: Israel could have arms; and the requisite instructions had already gone to the Pentagon.

That was almost certainly correct. According to Washington sources, the U. S. Air Force Military Airlift Command was instructed around that time to prepare up to twenty of its biggest transport aircraft for a possible resupply operation. And following another WASHAC meeting that Tuesday afternoon—at which the participants had before them not only the first realistic assessments of Israel's losses in lives and equipment, but also Dinitz's shopping list—the Joint Chiefs of Staff's deputy logistics director, Air Force

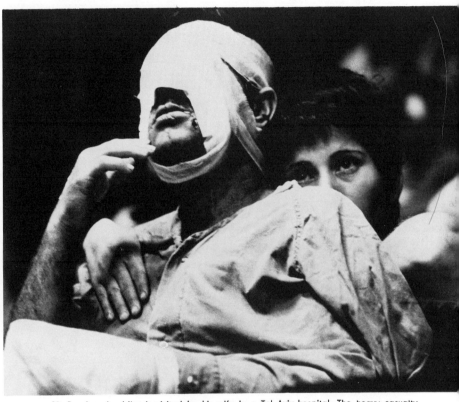

39. Bandaged soldier is visited by his wife in a Tel Aviv hospital. The heavy casualty rate prompted angry questions in Israel.

40 and 41. Captured Syrians and captured Israelis after the Golan fighting. Syria ignored the Geneva conventions, and many Israeli prisoners of war were reported tortured or killed.

42. Kissinger with Morocco's King Hassan in Rabat, first stop on his November peace-making tour of the Middle East.

Major General Maurice Casey, was ordered to begin combing through U.S. inventories at home or in Europe to assemble the supplies required.

But that was not how it looked to the Israelis. On his return from his meeting with Kissinger, a vastly relieved Dinitz sent the military attaché, Major General Mordechai Gur, to the Defense Department to sort out the details. To Gur's horror, he met blank incomprehension. The Pentagon could not just ship arms around the world, he was told. Export licenses were required. And they were the responsibility of the State Department.

Dinitz felt certain that this hassle was temporary. For when he called Kissinger late on Tuesday afternoon to report Gur's problem, Kissinger repeated that the President had authorized whatever supplies were needed. At 7:10 P.M. that evening, the Israeli defense group in New York had the latest telex from Dinitz. Nixon had given the "green light," the ambassador reported. The news came just in time: Some of the less trusting of the New York Jewish leaders had been planning, in the absence of such news, to blow the whole story that evening to the New York *Post*.

Yet, despite this promise, Israel still got no substantial supplies. Certainly, some were shipped. The next morning, Wednesday, October 10, an El Al Boeing 707, its markings taped over, took off from Oceana Naval Air Station, outside Norfolk, Virginia, loaded with bombs and air-to-air missiles. Other flights, even more discreet, took off with American defense technicians, sent to upgrade the electronic antimissile equipment aboard Israel's surviving aircraft.

But until Kissinger had finally to admit that a cease-fire was impossible, no substantial U.S. airlift began. And Kissinger did almost succeed in getting that cease-fire—on terms that amounted to a victory for Egypt. Three things, in the end, defeated him. The Soviet airlift reached proportions that the U. S. Government could not ignore. Sadat rejected the best terms he was ever likely to get. And Washington became increasingly apprehensive that the Israelis might, in desperation, resort to their own small stock of nuclear weapons.

7. The Rejected Victory

There has been much debate about the reasons why, on the morning of Tuesday, October 9, the Soviet Union began its airlift to the Arab combatants. The favored theory seems to be that theological standby, divided counsels within the Kremlin. But the most plausible explanation is also the simplest. The scale and contents of the early Soviet airlift strongly suggest that the Soviet Union wanted precisely the same outcome to the war as Kissinger did: a bruising stalemate after initial Arab success. And in calculating the most effective way to achieve this, the Soviet Union's thinking was a mirror image of Washington's. Kissinger hoped to achieve stalemate by withholding supplies to Israel. The Soviet Union did not think it could achieve stalemate without continuous supplies to the Arabs. But the superpowers' objective appears to have been the same. (And, privately, high Washington officials now agree with this analysis.)

Even the Soviet military assessment seems to have paralleled Israel's own. So long as Israel's forces—and particularly its Air Force—were preoccupied with the Golan battle, then Egypt's bridgehead in Sinai was secure. Israel did not have the resources to risk major engagements on both fronts simultaneously. But the Syrians were losing in Golan. Most urgently, the Israeli pilots were so successfully smashing the SAM-6 batteries that the Syrian armor would fairly soon find itself unprotected against the full might of Israel's air power—as happened for some hours on Tuesday, until the Syrians could bring up more SAMs. And that would settle that. At which point, Israel would turn its attention to Egypt. It followed, therefore, that the longer and more exhausting Israel's struggle for Golan could be made, the safer was Egypt's bridgehead. And the most effective way to increase the cost of Golan for Israel was to upset its grim balance of aircraft lost against SAM batteries destroyed—by supplying new stocks of SAMs.

Obviously, that remains speculation—though it is supported in Washington. All that is certain is that the Soviet airlift to Syria gathered momentum through Wednesday. Giant Antonov-12 freighters landed at the military airfield near the Roman ruins of Palmyra northeast of Damascus. Longer-range Antonov-22s flew in to Cairo. And their cargoes—according to Israeli military sources— were mainly SAM-6s. (Egypt had blazed away at Israeli aircraft with such abandon in the first phases of the war that, even without Israeli strikes, its SAM supplies were also apparently running low.)

What seems to have happened next was that the Soviets found that Syria was still sinking to defeat. So the airlift grew. Fresh aircraft, MiG-21s, were flown in. Fresh tanks were shipped to the Syrian port of Latakia. The Soviet commitment, once started, spiraled out of control. *But little of this happened in the crucial first week of fighting.*

Much of the confusion in the debate about Soviet motives has derived from the fact that both the Israelis and the Defense Department in Washington enormously exaggerated the scale of the Soviet airlift in this first week. Department of Defense briefings talked of more than thirty Antonov flights "in the first wave" of resupply through Tuesday night. The estimates grew to eighty aircraft through the twenty-four hours from mid-Wednesday to mid-Thursday. By Friday morning, the magic figure of one hundred flights into Egypt and Syria a day was being mentioned. Against these assertions, the cautious response of State Department spokesman Robert McCloskey on Wednesday, October 10, that "if this turns out to be a massive airlift it would tend to put a new face on the situation"—with the additional caveat that this could not yet be confirmed—seemed mere vacillation. And when Kissinger later described the Soviet airlift as "limited," he ran into withering scorn from Senator Jackson, among many others.

Inevitably, news of the Soviet airlift dramatically heightened American public agitation for similar help to Israel. Israeli lobbyist Kenen was still advising his cohorts to cool it: "I told them not to harass the government. The help was coming. I sensed it." But throughout the United States, the fund-raising, the rallies, the speeches roared on. In the first five days of the Yom Kippur War, $130 million was raised for Israel in the United States. In New York, the United Jewish Appeal raised $25 million in 48 hours. Not untypical of the rallies, meanwhile, was that in the Chicago Civic Center, at which Mayor Richard Daley enjoined his audience of 5,000: "Go ahead, Israelites. Be sure to remove every Arab from the soil of Israel." (Daley's grasp of either the geography or history of the Middle East was evidently slender.) The pressures mounted on Nixon and Kissinger. Facing the strong probability that—even were the Soviet intervention to cease —the United States would have to mount a massive resupply effort simply to keep Israel in the war, how could Kissinger or his spokesman McCloskey prudently condemn the Soviet airlift? Why should they even tell the truth?

The truth was that the early Soviet resupply effort was on nothing like the scale alleged. Virtually every Soviet aircraft on the airlift had to fly through one of two air traffic control zones: Belgrade or Cyprus. Together, those zones controlled key stages on the Soviet air routes to Syria or Egypt. According to the air traffic control supervisor in Belgrade, Soviet traffic was limited until Friday, October 12, when Soviet aircraft did begin to pass over in "large numbers." Corroboration of this comes from Cyprus, where the air traffic controllers logged *no* abnormal density of Soviet air movement until 3 P.M. on Friday, October 12, when a stream of Soviet pilots began asking for clearance to overfly at twenty-six thousand feet. The pilots claimed they were from Aeroflot, the Soviet civil airline—but they were using military throat microphones. By Friday midnight, the traffic over Cyprus reached a peak: eighteen flights an hour—a total of sixty going over in the first twenty-one hours. Approached about the discrepancy between this evidence and contemporary American accounts, a Department of Defense spokesman—blaming faulty intelligence—acknowledged that the Soviet airlift "was not quite as substantial as we first thought." The revised estimate, he said, was twenty-five to thirty flights a day. (Even that is, by Cyprus estimates, an exaggeration.) In paving the way for an American airlift, the exaggerations were certainly helpful. (When the rival airlifts did get under way in the second week, Belgrade was indeed handling up to one hundred Soviet aircraft a day. But by then it was a race between the superpowers.)

Yet as the superpowers thus edged into open involvement, Kissinger almost succeeded. He brought Israel to the verge of a cease-fire—only to have Sadat reject the offer. Kissinger later gave Heikal a version of what happened: "My proposal was to have a cease-fire in the positions held at that time—that, I think, was October 10. . . . It was not easy to present Israel with a proposal for a cease-fire on the October 10 or October 11 lines. Their opposition to us was furious, because they thought that with the completion of full mobilization they would now be able to change the course of the war. But they acquiesced in the end."

It was not as straightforward as that. Kissinger first broached the question of cease-fire terms with the Israeli ambassador, Dinitz, on the morning of Tuesday, October 9—at the same time as he was reassuring him that supplies would be forthcoming. Dinitz's instructions were still that Israel would only contemplate a cease-fire on prewar positions—an Arab withdrawal, in fact. But as Israel's need for weaponry increased, so did its search for a negotiating position. By Thursday, October 11, according to British diplomatic sources, Israel was suggesting that it might exchange its Syrian gains for its Sinai losses—amounting, again, to a re-establishment of the prewar lines.

But it was also on Thursday, with Golan securely reconquered, that the Israeli Prime Minister for the first time felt free to telephone President Nixon directly, to acknowledge Israel's desperate shortage of materiel, particularly ammunition; for Gur was still hitting obstruction in the Pentagon. Kissinger had sorted out the granting of export licenses. But the Pentagon then in effect said, according to Israeli sources in Washington: "Well, come and get it." The United States would provide supplies, Israel was told, but not an airlift. But Israel, of course, had nothing like the air capacity necessary—though, through Wednesday and Thursday, a couple more El Al Boeings had taken off with fresh supplies.

In response to Mrs. Meir's personal plea, however, Nixon now agreed that the United States would provide not only supplies but also the bare minimum of transport. And, according to the Israelis, a U.S. military transport mainly loaded with ammunition did take off for Israel late on Thursday afternoon, landing at Lod Airport around dawn the next day.

It was clear from what Mrs. Meir said that Israel would shortly be in no position to bargain at all. On Friday morning, Kissinger talked with Israeli Foreign Minister Eban and put the deal plainly. The United States would resupply Israel, he said. But there was no evidence that even fresh supplies would bring the war to a swift conclusion. The longer it went on, the greater grew the risk of Soviet involvement. Israel had won back the territory it regarded as most vital to its security—Golan. Would Israel now agree to a cease-fire in the present positions if the Arabs were also willing? According to U.S. sources, Eban replied that he thought Israel might—but he warned that Mrs. Meir would kick hard. That was all Kissinger needed to know: He was confident that Mrs. Meir's need for arms would overcome her resistance. ("Israel had run out of ammunition," Kissinger said afterward. "Without an airlift, they couldn't have kept going.")

It was then the turn of the Soviet ambassador, Dobrynin. He told Kissinger, after consulting Moscow, that the Soviets thought that international pressure might now persuade Sadat to agree to a "cease-fire *in situ*"—as the crucial phrase in Kissinger's draft described it.

The Kremlin had in fact no reason whatever to think this. That it was nevertheless willing to risk Soviet relations with Sadat by allying with the United States in pressing the plan upon him suggests that, by now, the Soviet Union was quite as uneasy as Washington about the risk of increasing superpower involvement in the conflict. In the event, however, the outstanding consequence of Dobrynin's assurance to Kissinger was a spectacular row between Britain and the United States.

Late that Friday afternoon, Kissinger contacted the British Embassy in Washington and outlined the deal. He had agreed with Dobrynin that Britain would now propose a cease-fire in the United Nations Security Council, making appropriate references to Resolution 242 as the guideline for a long-term settlement, but calling for an immediate cease-fire *in situ*. The United States and the Soviet Union would abstain. The resolution would still, on Kissinger's reckoning, get the nine Security Council votes needed for acceptance. Israel would then accept it. According to the

Soviets, Sadat could then be pressured into falling in line. Would Britain please get on with it.

It was around Friday midnight in London. And the Foreign Office, considering the plan, was puzzled. The Foreign Office was unwilling to jeopardize a good relationship with Sadat—or to put at risk any future peace-making effort—by advocating a cease-fire now, on terms that he would find unacceptable. But the British ambassador, Adams, had consistently reported from Cairo that Sadat, whom he saw frequently through the war, would never agree to a cease-fire except as part of a long-term settlement. Now Kissinger was saying that there was a probability of the opposite. The first thing to do was to check with Sadat.

At 4 A.M. on Saturday, Adams drove once more to Tahra Palace. Sadat was in his pajamas, but wide awake. He had just said goodbye to the Russian ambassador, Vinogradov. The Soviet diplomat had previously been euphoric about the war: "I have had sweet days in Cairo; I have had bitter days. But this is the pinnacle of my time in Egypt." Now, considerably sobered, he had been pressing on Sadat the terms that the Soviet Union had just agreed on with Kissinger. The Soviet argument, echoing Kissinger's, was that Egypt had made its political point: The superpowers would now enforce a long-term settlement. Sadat angrily rejected the proposal as devoid of adequate guarantees. Adams arrived to find Sadat still muttering rude things about Vinogradov. Adams' view of Sadat's position was confirmed in less than a minute. Moreover, Sadat said, Kissinger must already know this. Because two days earlier, on Thursday, October 11, Kissinger had contacted his national security advisor, Hafez Ismail, to ask what terms Egypt would accept—and had been told, most precisely, that only guarantees of a long-term settlement would suffice. Britain, Sadat warned, was being sucked into a super-power "trap." (In a sense, that was of course true: the superpowers were proposing to abstain in the Security Council—leaving the dirty work to Britain—so as not to jeopardize their relations with their respective client states. The U.S.-Soviet hope was still that "international pressure," as evidenced by the Security Council, would somehow do the trick, and relieve them of the necessity of leaning on their allies in the arena.)

A few hours later, the Washington Embassy gave Kissinger

Britain's answer: There was no point in pursuing the plan, because Sadat would not accept it. Kissinger blew up. How dare the British contradict what he had been told by the Soviets? The luckless Washington diplomat relaying the news was treated extremely roughly. "Henry acting the typical German bully-boy," was one disdainful reaction in British Government circles (though, when tempers cooled, the author of that remark was somewhat embarrassed by it).

There was only one thing to do. The Foreign Office sent Adams back to Sadat at 4 P.M. on Saturday. Sadat was apparently amused by the process, but he did not budge: pressure in the form of a Security Council resolution would move him not at all. That evening, Prime Minister Edward Heath called his Foreign Secretary, Sir Alec Douglas-Home, and a couple of senior Foreign Office men to a worried meeting at Heath's country residence, Chequers. The problem now was not merely how to halt the Middle East war but how to smooth what was later described as "this enormous hiccup" in Anglo-American relations. They decided, unhappily, that Britain had no choice but to persist in rejecting Kissinger's plan as unworkable. At 11 P.M., Douglas-Home telephoned Kissinger to tell him.

At this point, sheer pressure of American public opinion would probably have forced Kissinger to begin the massive airlift Israel now so desperately needed. (Israel was down to less than four days' stocks of tank ammunition.) But there was a more deadly reason why the United States Government could not, at this point, risk any other course. Kissinger feared that Israel, facing defeat, might resort to nuclear weapons.

Israel's stock of atomic bombs is, by superpower standards, small. Kissinger has privately said that Washington believes Israel to have three nuclear devices. Israeli sources mention up to six. If the numbers are secret, there is no question where the plutonium in the warheads has come from. In 1957, France gave Israel a twenty-four-megawatt nuclear reactor; its construction, at Dimona in the Negev desert in southern Israel, was completed in 1964. It is now the heart of Israel's nuclear research program.

Israel can separate limited quantities of uranium from the phosphate deposits of the Dead Sea. And the Dimona reactor can convert this into sufficient plutonium to produce one nuclear device per year in the nineteen-twenty-kiloton range—almost exactly equivalent to "Fat Boy," which razed Nagasaki in 1945. If Israel has produced only six bombs—perhaps only three—it is possible that its system for enriching the reactor plutonium to weapons grade is not all that efficient. Or perhaps it reckons that a handful are enough.

The physicist who actually built Israel's bomb is Professor Yuval Ne'eman, now the president of Tel Aviv University. A small man with glasses, Ne'eman looks considerably more the academic than the soldier. Yet he was a soldier from 1948—when he fought through the War of Independence in a French company in the Israeli Army—until 1956. Much of that time, though, Ne'eman was in military intelligence. Immediately after the 1956 war, he was sent to London as military attaché. While he was there, his first task was to perfect his English. Having been born, ironically, in Cairo, Ne'eman's mother tongues are Arabic and French. But he then took a degree in nuclear physics at London University, racing through the course in half the normal time. When he returned to Israel, he went into Tel Aviv University—and built Israel's bomb. (He also computerized Israeli intelligence gathering. During the Yom Kippur War, he was brought back to reorganize military intelligence in the wake of its prewar failures.)

How the Israelis would deliver these weapons is unclear—as are the circumstances under which they would contemplate so terrible an act. Israel does have a rocket, the Jericho, with a three-hundred-mile range—though, like the Egyptian Zafir before it, the Jericho is said to have guidance problems. But while Israel might have miniaturized its nuclear warheads sufficiently to fit the Jericho, the absence of test facilities makes this unlikely. And the Jericho is probably not a reliable enough delivery system. The most likely answer comes from military sources close to the Israelis, who say that the bombs are rather large and unwieldy and that a couple of transport aircraft have been converted to take them.

Perhaps—*in extremis*, facing annihilation at the hands of the Arabs—Israel would do what the United States rejected in 1945 and detonate a bomb over, say, southern Sinai or Egypt's western desert, as a last warning. Or perhaps the first sign would be a black object swinging from a parachute in the blue sky over the heart of Cairo, or Damascus, or Baghdad. . . .

It would be wrong to exaggerate the importance of this risk in spurring Washington to a decision to resupply Israel. Nobody believed Israel was nearly that desperate yet. But it was, certainly, a factor in the equation. On Saturday, October 13, Nixon made the final decision; and next day the American airlift cranked into gear—to the relief of personnel on U.S. air bases who, according to a congressional source, had been driven demented since Tuesday with orders from the Joint Chiefs' logistics staff like: "Get ready to ship such and such, but we don't yet know how. Maybe not in our planes." Even at the last minute, the United States did explore the possibility of mounting a covert resupply operation. But re-equipment on the scale that Israel now needed simply could not be hidden; and U. S. Secretary of Defense James Schlesinger finally convinced his colleagues that open resupply was the only sane policy.

The airlift signaled the decisive break between the policies of the United States and its European allies. No European government could ignore the fact that on Tuesday, the third day of the war, the Kuwait Council of Ministers had announced that they were organizing a meeting of Arab oil producers to discuss the role of oil in the conflict. By the next day, Egyptian and Saudi Arabian oil experts were already discussing ways in which the "oil weapon" might be used. Western Europe obtained over 70 per cent of its oil from the Arabs. Overt support for Israel thus involved a risk most European governments did not think they could afford—and that included even allowing U.S. overflights or landing rights for its airlift. In the end, the United States had to channel its airlift to Israel through the base it leased from Portugal at Lajes in the Azores. For its permission, Portugal too apparently demanded a high price: reportedly, U.S. help in staving off United Nations pressure to force changes in Portugal's African policy. Washington had no choice but to agree. The irony was that, only days before the war, it had been discussing whether to allow its lease on this Azores airfield to lapse.

On Israeli television that Saturday evening, Mrs. Meir did not reveal that Israel had been on the brink of agreeing to a humiliating cease-fire, only to have Sadat reject it. But, in retrospect perhaps shaken by Kissinger's failure, the Prime Minister went out of her way to signal Israel's willingness to talk. Should the Arabs propose any sort of cease-fire, she said, "within a few minutes we would be at the cabinet table and making our decision." She even hinted at the crucial concession Israel would make, indicating obliquely that it would accept a cease-fire with Egypt securely astride the canal. In Cairo, the latest issue of *Al Ahram*—whose editor, Heikal, almost certainly knew of the Kissinger proposal—must finally have disabused her. "The immediate target which Egyptian troops have set for themselves," its military correspondent now wrote, "is to inflict the heaviest losses possible on the Israelis."

So ended the first week of war—and with it Sadat threw away a striking military victory. As Kissinger recalled later: "This first attempt at a cease-fire failed, on Saturday, October 13, for a variety of reasons—including, perhaps, a misassessment of the military situation by some of the participants."

FOUR

ISRAEL'S BIG GAMBLE JUST COMES OFF

1. Armageddon in Sinai

Meeting on Sunday, October 14, the Israeli Cabinet broke off to send congratulations on his eighty-seventh birthday to David Ben-Gurion, the man who led Israel through the War of Independence in 1948–49 (and who was to die soon after this birthday, on December 9). It occurred to more than one of the ministers that the present situation had more in common with that first great crisis of the State of Israel than with the swift and triumphant campaigns of 1956 and 1967. In 1948, too, they had to fight on the Day of Atonement.

The comparison cannot be pushed too far. First, modern Israel is a far more powerful entity than the 650,000 Jews who, in 1948, faced 6 Arab armies without having anything much more to defend themselves with than a United Nations resolution. And the Arab aims had changed. "This will be a war of extermination," promised Azzam Pasha of the Arab League in 1948. It would be seen, he said, "like the Mongolian massacres and the Crusades." Not even the Palestinian guerrillas, let alone Presidents Sadat and Asad, produced anything along those lines during the 1973 war.

The resemblance, however, was that Israel, instead of winning spectacular, and latterly inexpensive, victories against disorganized opponents, was now facing a reasonably cohesive Arab attack—and having to take heavy casualties to repel it. On this second Sunday of the war, the Ministry of Defense announced that 656 Israeli soldiers had been killed so far. (Later, it emerged that this had been an underestimate, because at least 100 more than listed as missing were in fact dead.) The toll was still small compared with the 6,000 or so killed in the War of Independence. But whereas that war had dragged on for more than a year, the 656 admitted dead were the result of only eight days of largely defensive fighting.

It is thus fair to say that, on David Ben-Gurion's birthday, the state he brought into being faced one of the most profound challenges of its brief and stormy history. Yet this was the day on which the balance began to tilt decisively away from the Arab side—at least, in military terms. On the Golan front, it became apparent that the Syrian strength had been irrevocably broken. In Sinai, the Egyptian Army made its supreme effort and was repulsed.

"In the name of Allah the merciful and compassionate"—said Cairo radio on Sunday morning—"at 0600 today our armed forces began developing an offensive eastward according to plan. . . . Our armored and mechanized forces are successfully advancing along the confrontation line." It was this Egyptian dawn attack, preceded by a ninety-minute artillery bombardment, that brought about the decisive test of armored strength in Sinai. As Bar-Lev and Gonen had predicted, Egypt was coming out to fight. As they had also foreseen, this presented the Israeli tank crews with the targets they had been seeking.

The Israelis knew an attack was coming. Since Thursday, Egyptian troops and tanks had been crowding eastward over the pontoons to prepare for the showdown. The best estimate is that during Thursday, Friday, and Saturday, Ismail sent over into Sinai more than five hundred of the seven hundred tanks he had held in reserve. This brought the Egyptian total in Sinai to more than one thousand. At the same time, Israeli tanks were moving west through the Sinai passes, their numbers increasing with the decline of the Syrian threat.

On the afternoon of Saturday, October 13, the Israelis deployed in the area west of the Gidi and Mitla passes could see a huge cloud of dust moving north from Suez along the banks of the canal. The axis of the Egyptian attack, it seemed, would be in the area of the lakes, heading roughly midway between the Khatmia and Gidi passes.

Neither side's claims about the number of tanks that joined battle—and were destroyed—that Sunday can be treated as reliable. But Israel claimed, credibly, that more were engaged than the sixteen hundred British, German, and Italian tanks that fought the Battle of Alamein, two hundred miles on the other side of Cairo, during the same month in 1942.

A veteran of Alamein would have found many familiar features in the Sinai battlefield, quite apart from the similarity of the sandy, slightly undulating terrain. He might have been puzzled by items like the ballistic computers carried in some of the Israeli tanks; but in general he would have found the rules of the game little altered by the passage of thirty-one years. Indeed, he might from time to time have spotted an Israeli crew bringing up a "Super Sherman"—re-engined and regunned, but essentially the same as the Shermans that Montgomery had used at Alamein. Equally, he might have seen among the Egyptian support formations some T-34s of World War II vintage; and he would have been able to trace quite clearly the descent from T-34 through T-55 to T-62. The Israeli Defense Forces' devastating combat advantages arose not from any difference in principle between the weapons on either side, but rather from the detailed improvements made over the years to Western armor—and the skill with which the Israelis took advantage of these.

Because tanks are regarded as the successors to cavalry, armored warfare is often thought to be something like the Charge of the Light Brigade, mixed with a dash of old-style naval battle—fleets of tanks sweeping across the desert, exchanging broadsides with one another. Sometimes it is like that: Janos' tactics on Golan would have been recognized by any of Nelson's frigate captains. The reality is usually less exhilarating. Under battle conditions, tanks grind slowly over the ground, and they rarely if ever fire their guns on the move. Tank fighting is more like a kind of brutal chess match, in which the contestants maneuver to find temporarily static positions of advantage, from which they can deliver sudden and unanswerable blows.

Because they must push engineering possibilities to the limit, tanks are a bizarre mixture of brute power and mechanical waywardness. Simply to build a fast caterpillar tractor is no small trick. Then it must carry a gun of such monstrous power that each recoil hits the tank with a fifty-ton hammer blow, roughly equivalent to its own weight. Add in radios, intercoms, power-operated controls, ventilation systems, and the like, and the possibilities of malfunction are easy to imagine. The M-48 Patton, one of the Israeli mainstays, was found to break down once every thirty-six miles in U. S. Army service. Tanks, therefore, require the cosseting of an automotive society, which confers advantage on a country like Israel.

In battle, one basic proposition dominates tank tactics: No tank can carry enough armor to be safe all of the time. Standard armor-piercing shot, fired at close range, will go through armor more than twice as thick as its own diameter. As the gun of a T-55 fires shot about four inches in diameter, it can punch through eight inches of armor if it gets close enough. The thickest armor on a British-made Centurion—as the Israelis had found for around fifteen years, an unusually tough tank—is just over six inches. It cannot be much more: any tank significantly heavier than the fifty-two tons of a Centurion would be too slow.

This means that any tank that reaches the right position can destroy any other tank—even one theoretically better than itself. Naturally, penetration falls off with distance: At fifteen hundred yards most of the shots from a T-55 will glance off the angles of a Centurion's armor. But the best protection is invisibility rather than distance. An undulation in the ground of around nine feet—scarcely visible to the casual eye—will hide a tank from track to turret hatch.

The chief skill of a tank commander leading a squadron into battle is to use such minor wrinkles in the terrain—the "dead ground"—to reach an attacking position without detection by the enemy. Ideally, he and his squadron can then loom suddenly above the skyline like red Indians in a movie, fire a swiftly destructive volley, and slide back out of sight. Because visibility through even the best of periscopes is strictly limited, commanders must ride as much as possible with their heads in the open. This exposes them to gruesome personal risks not shared by drivers, gunners, and loaders inside the armored shell. Nevertheless, Israeli tank commanders are trained to close their hatches only under heavy artillery bombardment—the risk of splinter wounds is then too pressing to ignore.

The Israelis are helped by the fact that Centurions and M60-A1s —as we illustrate in the pictorial essay, The Tank Battle—are better adapted to this kind of stalking warfare than are Soviet-built tanks. First, they can point their main guns down ten degrees below the horizontal, whereas a T-55 or T-62 gun can be depressed only four degrees. This may seem trivial until one realizes that a tank hiding behind a ridge must point its gun *down* to fire, unless it is to move up and expose most of its hull to return fire. And as The Tank Battle shows, the Western tanks are better adapted to the long, rolling desert terrain in other respects. The Arab T-54/55 commanders had to estimate range by their own visual judgment— "Eyeball Mark I," it is sometimes called. The Patton and M-60 crews had accurate, if delicate, optical-prism range-finding systems that allowed them to zero in on a distant target in a matter of seconds; while the Centurion gunners could use the tracer bullets of a range-finding machine gun to avoid the slow process of correcting successive shots from the main gun by trial and error. This Israeli advantage at long range was heightened by their tanks' armaments. The Arab T-54s and T-55s had only ordinary armor-piercing shot, which gives limited penetration at long range. But almost all the Israeli tanks were equipped with more sophisticated APDS and HEAT ammunition (see The Tank Battle), which remains lethal at greater distances. Only the latest Russian T-62 tanks could match the Israeli armaments; and these were in relatively short supply, despite Soviet deliveries before the war.

In short, while Israel had precisely the tanks needed for its desperate defense of Golan, Soviet armor is better suited to the massed charge and the close-packed melee. And it was just such an attack that the Egyptians launched on Sunday morning. The military arithmetic was now heavily against them, but they had to make it.

The main thrust was made just to the north of Gidi Pass. Before the first wave of tanks went forward, an artillery barrage and several air strikes were directed onto the Israeli positions. An Israeli reconnaissance pilot recalled: "There were four MiGs below us flying very low and firing rockets. Then four Mirages arrived, and we were very happy until we realized that the Mirages were also Egyptian and were attacking our tanks too." Finally, said the pilot, Israeli Phantoms arrived and chased off the Mirages. (Egypt has no Mirages: These were on loan from Libya.)

Attacking at dawn, the Egyptians were coming out of the dark, while the rising light in the east could be expected to produce crisp outlines when Israeli tanks lifted above the skyline. It is not difficult to visualize the drama and horror of the scene: The canopy of dust rising slowly as hundreds of tanks lurched and swayed over the sand, sometimes dashing ahead at twenty miles an hour, sometimes slowed to a crawl by patches of soft going; the clattering of steel tracks and the massed roar of six-hundred-horsepower engines rising and falling as sweating drivers wrestled with gears and clutches; the occasional bark of a gun as a lead tank tried a snap shot at a fleeting Israeli silhouette (but with only thirty or forty rounds of ammunition on board, wise crews would conserve their stock for worthwhile targets). And amid the din of engines and tracks, over and over again, the harsh clank of tungsten bolts striking through armor, or the wicked crack of HEAT shells going off. Sometimes crewmen would leap from a stricken tank. More often, the impact would be followed by the fierce orange flames of an ammunition fire, with a trail of oil smoke rising to mingle with the dust. "Within ten minutes we had lit twenty bonfires," one of the Israeli commanders in Sinai said afterward.

The first wave, he said, "advanced through a wadi and climbed up onto a plateau to our south"—probably Jebel Shaifa, roughly halfway between Gidi Pass and Little Bitter Lake. "Our forces met them on the plateau, and there was a fierce battle. Within an hour most of the enemy tanks had been wiped out.

"After this it was quiet for a while. Then the Egyptians began shelling us, then it was quiet again, and then the second wave of tanks attacked. There were 145 tanks, and when they came into range I brought up the whole of my forces and we hit them with everything we had." The Egyptians tried to bring up mobile artillery pieces to support their armor. "After we had finished off the tanks, we began hitting their artillery."

The battle, he said, was "two-sided, and very fierce." Several times, the impetus of the Egyptian advance brought them up to very close range, and many Israeli tanks also became "bonfires."

The Israelis claim to have destroyed 250 Egyptian tanks that day, many of them in the first hour or two of battle. At 7 A.M. the Israeli military spokesman was already claiming that the attack had been "checked."

Throughout at least the first half of the war, Israeli communiqués were commonly less accurate than the Egyptians'—and not nearly so reliable as their own had been in the Six-Day War. ("They've learned how to fight from us," went a joke in the

Jerusalem *Post*, "and we've learned how to handle information from them.") But the main claim was clearly something more than mere battlefield rhetoric. Just after 6 P.M. that day, the Voice of the Arabs, broadcasting from Cairo, said with truly remarkable frankness that during the fighting "100 of our tanks were hit." The statement, attributed to Communiqué No. 38 from the Egyptian High Command, was dropped when the broadcast was repeated an hour later. But the fact that it was made at all may be taken as confirmation of terrible Egyptian losses.

Splitting the gap between the Israeli claim and the Arab admission suggests that not less than 175 Egyptian tanks were destroyed. There are 4 men in a tank crew: On the Israeli rule of thumb that the whole crew is lost every other time a tank is hit, about 350 Egyptian soldiers must have died in their tanks, or on the sand beside them, during the day. A fair estimate would be that the Egyptians lost about a quarter of the tanks they committed to action—a devastating proportion. (One element in that Israeli success may also be deduced from Cairo's Communiqué No. 38, which added: "Our Air Force has carried out concentrated bombings of antitank rocket positions, which had hampered the advance of our tanks all along the front. . . ." The Israelis did have the French SS-11 missiles. And, according to Shazli, they also now had the U. S. TOW—though Washington sources deny that supplies had been air-freighted by then.)

The Egyptian commanders, Ismail and Shazli, knew the odds against the attack. In armored warfare, as in any other form, there is a basic rule that in the absence of surprise, tactical advantage lies with the defense. Heavy numerical superiority is required to make up for this: It is usually said that an attacking force requires over-all superiority of not less than three to one. And within this it is necessary to produce, by skillful maneuvering, local superiorities of five to one at any point where a major breakthrough is required. By the time they attacked, the Egyptians' superiority was probably not much more than two to one, even in raw numbers. Given the technical inferiority of their tanks, they had—effectively—little or no superiority at all.

Yet some sort of attack had in any event to be launched. The Egyptian bridgehead, barely nine or ten miles deep instead of the planned twenty, was simply too shallow to be defensible. Tanks, even in defense, must have room to move if they are to be effective: Armor plate alone is never enough. "To stand still," in the words of British military historian Kenneth Macksey, "is to invite destruction." While the Egyptians were pinned down, the Israelis, still holding most of the best terrain between the ridge and the Suez Canal, had plenty of elbow room—either to give ground in defense, or to concentrate for a counterattack. Besides, the reduction of activity on the Syrian front would enable the Israelis to transfer more and more tanks to Sinai. Assuming the eventual immobilization of the Syrian Army and the legendary efficiency of Israeli tank-repair shops, the Egyptians could expect to find themselves faced with a tank force one thousand or more strong within a few more days.

That, at least, had been the main plank of Shazli's argument for a fresh Egyptian initiative. Ismail did not accept it; he would have preferred, he said, "going back to the bridgeheads to proceed with their consolidation, to render them a stubborn rock over which the enemy's counterattacks could be smashed." But now he had no choice: "We were forced to launch a wide offensive before the suitable moment. Our object in doing so was to relieve the pressure on Syria."

Even given this imperative, however, Ismail could have proceeded differently. His long-contemplated second phase of Operation BADR did envisage an attack toward the passes along almost precisely the axis of Sunday's assault. But that plan called for another "creeping, crawling" advance with missile infantry, tanks, and SAM batteries slithering forward in careful sequence. The Israelis by now had enough artillery up at the passes to have made even that an expensive operation. Yet it would surely have been harder to stop than the conventional assault Egypt in fact mounted. What the Israelis did—what Ismail allowed them to do—was to draw the Arab tanks out from the protection of the infantry missiles, out from under the SAM umbrella.

The Egyptians did try to bring missile infantry forward with the armor that Sunday. Personnel carriers and trucks were following up close behind the tanks. The attempt failed almost completely. It is one thing for well-dug-in infantry to resist tanks from carefully chosen positions—or to creep over the desert in coordinated fashion. To face well-handled tanks in a fluid battle is something altogether different. Many of the "bonfires" now studded across the desert were personnel carriers and rocket-launching vehicles as well as tanks. Israeli tank crews, accustomed to firing live ammunition in practice battles, are adept at juggling their repertoire of weapons: armor-piercing shot to smash tanks, high-explosive shells to stop personnel carriers, bursts of machine-gun fire to cut down the infantry. If the Egyptian infantry suffered comparably to the armor—which seems likely—the total number of Egyptian dead may have been more than six hundred.

Yet, analyzing the progress of the battle, the Israeli commanders were unsatisfied. A long series of spectacular victories, plus total faith in the superiority of Israeli expertise, had produced in the years before the war a kind of contempt among many Israelis for the canny, counterpunching style of warfare. Sharon's claim that Israel was a "military superpower" was an absurd statement from an officer in an army that could only be fully mobilized by bringing the economy behind it to a virtual halt. But it typified the spirit that led even experienced officers to disregard banalities like guarding flanks and securing communications. To care about such matters was almost akin to cowardice, as when, in Nelson's time, the Royal Navy was so certain of its individual superiority over the French that "for a British Captain to attempt maneuvering for position, even in the most approved and scientific way, would have been at grave risque to his Character. . . ."

That spirit got its comeuppance in the War of 1812, when the British encountered opponents not to be disregarded. And if Sharon had been given his head by the Israeli command, something very similar might have happened to the Israeli forces in the Yom Kippur War. As it was, by the afternoon of October 14, the new and hotly disputed Israeli tactic of caution had finally made possible a repulsing of the long-awaited Egyptian attack so complete that many of the shattered Egyptian units faced difficulty even finding their way back to the bridgehead.

But the Egyptian attack could—and should, the Israeli Sinai command thought—have been destroyed utterly. In many cases, the Israeli tank crews had absorbed so exaggerated an impression of the improvement in Egyptian fighting skill that they had not let the enemy tanks get close enough before firing. This was, of course, not true everywhere: There had been savage close-range combat—as the commander we have quoted described. But the Israelis were not satisfied with merely mauling the Egyptians— they wanted to destroy them, to repeat at last the rout of 1967. And too many Egyptian tanks were getting away. In the evening, an Israeli tank force was sent to cut off the retreat from the Gidi Pass area.

Now was the time for the skill in stalking and navigation— based on their carefully surveyed "going maps" of the Sinai terrain. "We had to follow a very difficult, roundabout route to get into position," the force commander said afterward. "As soon as we arrived, we got into formation and began kindling the bonfires. The battle lasted until three in the morning. We lit about fifty-five bonfires—half of them tanks, the rest artillery pieces and personnel carriers. We didn't suffer one loss. It was a fine battle. That is the way to sum it up: a fine battle." For the Egyptians, the ambush transformed a defeat into the rout that the Israelis desired. It was the turning point for the Egyptian campaign in Sinai, the moment when defeat in some form became inevitable.

In achieving so great a victory, Israel too suffered casualties. In the battle communiqué afterward, only one had a name: Major General Avraham "Albert" Mendler, commander of the armored forces and the front-line sector in Sinai. Mendler was hardly an average Israeli; yet his life had for many of his colleagues a special quality, reflecting as it did not only his country's embattled existence but also the terrible events that gave it birth. Mendler was the only leading Israeli general who had been a victim of Nazi persecution.

He was born Albert Mendler at Linz in Austria in 1929—and to his friends he remained Albert for the rest of his life. Had it not been for Hitler, Albert Mendler would probably have lived on in the ghettos of Europe. But after the outbreak of World War II, the family fled—their passage organized by the Betar movement, which survives in Israel today as part of the opposition Herut (Freedom) party. Betar took Albert and his mother and brother down the Danube, one of the last shiploads of Austrian Jews to escape the gas chambers. In the Aegean their ship was intercepted by a British destroyer, which then accompanied them all the way to Haifa—where, officially illegal immigrants, they were put in a detention camp. Albert Mendler was eleven years old.

He was a good fighter. At sixteen, by now renamed Avraham, he was a commander of the youth wing of the Haganah, the fore-runner to Israel's Army. By nineteen, company commander in the elite Jeep corps known as "Samson's Foxes" in the War of Inde-pendence, Mendler was wounded a few days before the cease-fire. Then he left the Army; but civilian life did not suit him and, after a few months, he re-enlisted.

Like Elazar, Mendler went into armor—to become one of Israel's most noted tacticians: the "Iron Man," he was called. In 1967 he led Israel's tanks in the capture of the Golan Heights, personally taking Kuneitra.

Albert Mendler's last appointment before retirement was to the Sinai armored forces. He enjoyed it. He was an enthusiastic naturalist and something of an amateur archaeologist: He spent his spare hours studying the flamingos on the Bitter Lakes or pot-tering among the ruins of the Via Maris, the Roman coast road over Sinai.

Barely a week before war broke out, Mendler remarked to a friend that this last assignment had been the most satisfying of his career; he was ready, he said, to retire with a sense of accomplish-ment. But, as he warned his fellow officers at the lunch in his honor in Sinai on the Thursday before war, he did not in fact expect to be retiring.

Mendler had prophesied war; after a week of it, on Sunday, October 14, he as correctly prophesied its climax. His last order of the day began: "Before this day is out the full might of our armor, Air Force, and artillery will be brought to bear on the enemy and he will be utterly routed. . . ." Sometime during that victory, a shell hit Mendler's halftrack. Luck finally ran out for the boy who had come down the Danube a lifetime, a nation, ago.

2. The Economics of Caution

Moshe Dayan was in Sinai on Sunday afternoon, and was therefore among the first to know that the war was entering a decisive new phase, that Israel might soon face the dilemmas of victory. He spoke publicly twice during the day: first aboard a helicopter at the front; second on the "Mabat" television current affairs program. Because Dayan's own character is poised between extremes —between decisiveness and vacillation, between frankness and circumlocution—his words commonly shed more light than anyone else's on the confusions of Israeli policy-making. The need this time, said Dayan above the clatter of the helicopter, was not to conquer land but to smash the Arab armies: "Should they sign a cease-fire today, their forces will remain, and they will violate the cease-fire as they did in the past. . . . The aim is to hit and deal blows—the word 'destroy' is not so nice—and to defeat them completely. Then it will be possible to carry out a plan. Before doing this the rest is simply dreams."

But what plan could be carried out? Dayan did not think that even a crushing Israeli victory would lead to peace: ". . . there is no guarantee, and the proof is that we are now in the third war. [By some counts, it was the fourth war; but many Israelis do not include 1956 as "their war"; others, including Golda Meir, counted it No. 5—including the 1969–70 War of Attrition.] This is a basic situation of the State of Israel, which the Arabs do not want to accept. And every now and then they attack it and the Arabs must be killed. There is no limit to this matter. . . ."

Seemingly, Dayan recoiled from this bleak prospect, because he went on to urge: "We must do something positive, not negative. . . . We must build up a state and search for [*indistinct*] . . . and establish the state on a mighty military force and good borders, until one day there won't be a guarantee but there will be neighborly relations and acceptance. . . .

"There is no miracle solution. . . . If there is such a solution I don't know what it is. . . . I have heard and read that perhaps we should take southern Syria and eastern Egypt and the north of I don't know what, etc. But when we have finished, would it be better and easier, and would it solve the problems?"

On the "Mabat" program, he was pressed on the beginning of the war. Had Israel been caught unaware? Should there have been earlier mobilization? Should Israel have struck first? An Arab attack had been possible any time since 1971, Dayan said. In order to be wholly safe "one has to mobilize the entire reserve force, as at present; and as from the end of 1971—we are now nearing the end of 1973—to sit opposite them, so as not to find ourselves in a disadvantageous position. Or, to begin the war. These two options are very, very difficult for us. We desire to live a normal life. . . . They are very difficult, in view of our image in the world. . . .

"The Jewish adage, 'If someone comes to kill thee, hasten thou and kill him' could be simply adapted to our situation. The Arabs want to kill us. Therefore we have to hasten and kill them, especially when they mobilize their forces and make declarations about it. I do not think we have erred by not doing so in the years between 1971 and 1973. Also, with regard to the future, I do not think it would be good if we take the inference of this fateful hour: that whenever we see the Arabs desire war and are getting into a position for it, we should begin a war against them. We would never achieve anything."

Had Israel launched the war itself, Dayan conceded, casualties might have been lower. But: "After all, we want to reach some sort of settlement [with the Arabs]. Had we launched a war a year, half a year, or two years ago, would this have brought us closer to a settlement? I do not think it would."

Dayan's words, tentative and at times almost self-contradictory, give a vivid impression of the problems facing the Israeli leadership with victory in prospect. Israel could go on imposing military solutions—each time at higher and higher cost. But could that lead to anything but a state of permanent warfare and economic ruin? Dayan's reputation outside Israel is that of a "hawk," and an advocate of military solutions. And particular elements of his policy, such as the sowing of Jewish settlements in the occupied territories, can indeed be seen only in hard-line terms.

But before the "Mabat" interview, Dayan made a brief and moving statement on the casualty figures for the first week of war: ". . . we are in the heat of battle, and we cannot express publicly our deep sorrow for the fallen ones. . . . Today, we can only say to the families how much we share their mourning. . . . We should know that we are a nation which is shaped by the fallen ones and the fighters, and we pave our way with the force of the past and the future, with the strength of our sons who build, fight, and fall. . . ." Dayan may be a hawk, but few Israelis have a deeper understanding of the cost, in money and lives and social distortion, of the unremitting military effort to which Israel is committed if his bleak view of the impossibility of peace should prove to be right.

By Monday, October 15—the tenth day of the war—victory seemed closer on the Golan front too. Israeli communiqués depicted Monday as a period of inaction. In fact, the Israelis achieved their farthest advance into Syria. That evening, Rafael Eytan's tanks rolled into Saasa, just twenty miles from the outskirts of Damascus. The best-publicized shooting of the day, however, occurred inside the city of Damascus, which that evening reverberated with small-arms fire for more than an hour. Western diplomats in the city thought it signaled an assault by Israeli paratroopers. Eventually, the police chief revealed that it was only a section of the Damascus garrison demonstrating their approval of a speech by President Asad. (Relieved, the staff of the British Embassy sent a glass of beer down to their doorman, who was happily potting away with his rifle.)

From the text alone, it is not immediately clear why Asad's words should have rated such an exuberantly Texan endorsement. There was a fair amount of rhetoric about the "glorious days of ferocious battles" that the war had witnessed. "With chaste blood," Asad told the Syrian Army, "you have charted on the map of Arab struggle a road which will never change after today. . . ." Much of the speech was devoted to celebrating a new compact of Arab unity, "the pan-Arabism of battle."

Yet amid all the rhetoric, the objectives nominated for this new pan-Arabism remained limited. Asad claimed the "liberation" of Mount Hermon, Kuneitra, Rafid, and several other Golan towns and villages—but only ones on Syrian territory lost in 1967. (As a matter of fact, all but Hermon had been deliberated by the time he spoke.) The Arab aim, he said, was one of "forcing the occupation forces to withdraw before them," and the nearest he came to speaking in terms of destroying Israel—and that not very close—was a claim to have inflicted "losses which deeply shook the Zionist entity."

Asad did speak of a determination to "liberate the whole land"; and this was cited in Israel as evidence that the Arabs were still talking in terms of overrunning Israel proper. The interpretation was invalid. Asad used the phrase in acknowledging, somewhat tortuously, that the Syrian Army had suffered considerable reverses: "With the quick supplies he received and which were added to the calculated reserve force, the enemy heavily concentrated on one sector of our front and began to exert pressures with the larger part of his forces . . . and was able to achieve a limited penetration of our lines." Asad was trying to suggest that the Syrian losses had been confined to a few positions. "Our forces," he went on, "continue to pursue the enemy and strike at him and will continue to strike at the enemy forces until we regain our positions in the occupied land and continue then until we liberate the whole land." So, in context, "whole land" clearly meant the whole of the occupied territory, not the whole of Palestine.

That a speech of such restricted ambitions and such ambiguous news should have evoked such joy may perhaps be ascribed, in part, to the psychological aftermath of the Six-Day War. (The crowds seem also to have believed that Asad had been claiming that the Army had again pushed the Israelis out of Kuneitra.) The facts were that the Syrian Army had committed the bulk of its resources to gaining objectives strikingly less dramatic than those most Syrians had grown up with. This enormous military venture had been thrown back with heavy losses. By any normal military standards, it was a shattering defeat. But, compared to the disaster of 1967, it seemed to Damascus like a triumph. In Asad's words, the fighting had "restored self-confidence to the Arab individual after dressing his wounded dignity." And for that purpose, it was not necessary to prophesy the destruction of Israel.

The world in general, and Israelis in particular, tend to perceive the leaders of the Arab world as fanatical dervishes—a perception, it must be said, that has a good deal of recent history to support it. Yet the image of irrational demagogues, intoxicated with their own rhetoric, does not sort well with the actions of Sadat and Asad in October 1973. Of course, they made errors and blunders. But precisely by trying to keep within the bounds of the practical, they made more impact upon the balance of power in the Middle East than anything achieved in the years of Nasser's windy prophecies.

Asad's speech was to be followed the next day—Tuesday, October 16—by a notably more moderate and immensely more significant statement of war aims by his senior partner in the Arab alliance, Anwar el Sadat. The Egyptian President declared with explicit deliberation that, for the Arabs, this was a war of limited objectives. He also implied that its declaration had been an act of rational calculation. That itself was hopeful: Men capable of rational calculation are also capable of appreciating the stupendous sacrifices that would be required to achieve the total destruction of the State of Israel. The corollary to this is that men who attack without calculating the odds are not particularly likely to endanger what Asad called the "Zionist entity."

Discussion of fit Israeli and American policies toward the Arabs is so dependent upon an assessment of Arab aims that it is worth, first, injecting some facts into the debate—starting with an outline of the burdens placed upon both sides by "no peace, no war." Middle Eastern military budgets now stand at levels not equaled anywhere in the world except Vietnam. For the major contestants—none of them countries with money to spare—arms expenditure even before the Yom Kippur War was beginning to consume nearly a quarter of the national wealth. The need to re-equip after the war with new and still more costly weapons would increase the burden still further.

This burden falls most heavily on Egypt, the military center of gravity of the Arab world. Egypt's armed forces (298,000) are almost as large as those of Syria, Jordan, and Iraq put together (306,650). And Iraq, for all its fervent anti-Zionism, can never make a total commitment to war against Israel—not merely because of the intermittent external danger it faces from its heavily armed and ambitious neighbor, Iran, but also because of the persistent internal threats to its stability from the Kurds and from dissident political opposition elements. No Iraqi president can send the Army too far from home. This is replicated elsewhere. Broadly speaking, it is true that there are one hundred million Arabs whose nationalist emotions are directed against Israel. But most of their armies are simply too far away to do anything about it.

Syria and Jordan, whose borders most intimately march with Israel's, are small countries. Syria's population is just under seven million, Jordan's just over two million. No serious Arab campaign, whatever the objective, can be mounted against Israel without the support of Egypt and its thirty-six million people.

Egypt is not a rich country, though it falls into the upper bracket of the developing world. Together with hordes of rural and urban poor, it has a considerable educated class, capable of dealing reasonably well with the technical requirements of modern war. But the task of maintaining the strength required for confrontation with Israel has grown steadily more onerous upon Egypt.

In 1969, Egypt's military budget was equal to 13 per cent of its Gross National Product (GNP). By 1973, it had risen to 25 per cent. This was almost certainly the highest proportion in the world. South Vietnam's military expenditure reached 17 per cent of GNP in 1972, and North Vietnam's unpublished figures are probably comparable. But the closest rival is—as might be expected —Israel, which in 1972 had a military budget equivalent to 20 per cent of GNP. (By comparison, the Soviet Union and the United States run military budgets around 7 or 8 per cent of GNP, declining slowly in recent years. Most other countries are in the 2 to 5 per cent range, with Britain on the high side at 4.6 per cent.)

In an advanced economy, much of the defense budget can be spent at home. This is true of Israel to some extent: The Israelis even have a useful export trade in arms: mainly Uzi submachine guns and Gabriel missiles. But in Egypt's case, nearly all the basic equipment has to be imported. And, contrary to one widespread impression, the Soviet Union does not supply arms to Arab countries for nothing. On the contrary, the Soviets insist on payment in hard currency, although long-term credits are available. The result is that Egypt's major exports, such as the cotton crop, are mortgaged for many years into the future. (And the Soviet Union got cash on the barrelhead for the arms supplied during the Yom Kippur War: That was where King Faisal's handout went.)

A widely held belief is that the Arab oil-producing states foot most or all of this bill for Egypt. Again, not so: Apart from the unique prewar gifts from Saudi Arabia and Qatar, Kuwait, Saudi Arabia, and Libya had previously given only about two hundred million dollars a year, which covered less than an eighth of Egypt's costs. The wealthiest of the Arab states have deeply conservative rulers, and there is a limit to how much these men will give to subsidize the import of Soviet arms—and therefore of Communist influence—into the Arab world.

There are certain fringe benefits for Egypt. The Army acts as a kind of adult education organization, and conscription soaks up considerable rural unemployment. But at the higher technological levels, the armed services make barely tolerable inroads into Egypt's reserves of skilled manpower; and the steadily rising costs of weaponry make it impossible to finance urgently needed social reforms. In the Nile Delta, batteries of ultrasophisticated missiles for years stood guard around cities in which more than half of the houses were without electricity or piped water. In many Egyptian schools, the children sit two to a chair—or take it in turns to attend in half-day shifts.

By making such harrowing social and economic sacrifice, Egypt is able to support a military force that can undertake limited operations against Israel with a reasonable prospect of success. But the cost of setting out to fight a war of total victory—aimed at the annihilation of the Jewish state—would be beyond sensible computation. Certainly, any major increase in military spending would preclude even the semblance of normal life—let alone social reconstruction—for years to come. Such an increase could probably not be imposed at all without the destruction of the Sadat regime and its replacement by a monolithic military dictatorship.

Just as some American strategists used to hope that the burden of the arms race would destroy the fabric of Soviet society, so some Israelis now favor breaking Egypt economically. (That was an objective at least in mind during Israel's air campaign of the 1969–70 War of Attrition.) The likely result, however, would be a more rather than less intransigent opponent. And in any case, the burden on Israel is also close to overwhelming.

It is chiefly because of the need to import weaponry that Israel has accumulated a foreign debt of almost 4 billion dollars—in per capita terms, the biggest in the world. Interest payments on this debt now run at well over $200 million a year. The particular tragedy for Israel is that before the October war, the rise in its balance of payments deficit had at last been halted, and there was a sign of improvement. The cause was a leveling-off in arms imports—but, of course, the need to re-equip after the Yom Kippur War would more than wipe out that improvement. Inevitably, re-equipment would mean further taxation increases in what was already the most highly taxed country in the world.

Of the other countries seriously involved, only Jordan comes close to matching the Egyptian and Israeli spending in per capita terms. But Jordan—with a Gross National Product not much bigger than the turnover of, say, the Colgate-Palmolive Company —about $800 million—is simply too small to make much impact, at a time when a new combat fighter is cheap at $6 million.

The belligerent Syria has much lower military expenditure than Egypt, and this is not only because of its smaller size. Its population, though distinctly wealthier per capita, spends somewhat less per capita on defense.

But the evidence for an inverse relationship between rhetoric and actual military spending comes most impressively from the wealthiest Arab countries—classically Colonel Qaddafi's Libya. Libya's oil gives it a GNP of about $1,600 per head, not strikingly inferior to Israel's. But Libya's military budget is a pacific 2.6 per cent of GNP. When the Yom Kippur War came to an end, Qaddafi gave an angry interview. "The war should have gone on," he said, "for years if need be, until the Arab or the Israeli side finished each other off completely." It was not difficult for Colonel Qaddafi to call for a long war. He is not fighting it.

3. Hussein Has No Choice

By Tuesday, October 16, however, two more countries had joined the fray. At dawn that morning, in a supposedly combined assault, Jordanian and Iraqi troops attacked the flank of the Israeli advance into Syria. The disaster that promptly overtook them demonstrated a reason for Israeli confidence much simpler than calculations of economic power. However unified immediate Arab political objectives might be, basic military coordination was harder to achieve. Still, the fact that Jordan had entered the war at all was an indication that the longer the fighting continued, the wider it must spread. For Hussein had come into action only with the greatest reluctance. In the end, he simply had no choice.

Shortly before 2:30 P.M. on October 6, an aide had sprinted down the gravel path and into King Hussein's private residence at the Basman Palace, stammering the news that war had begun. Hussein was shattered. "They didn't trust me," he said.

The grounds of the Basman Palace sprawl along the summit of one of the steep hills on which Amman is built. Gazing from his window across the valley to the houses jumbled over the hillside opposite, Hussein realized that, once again, the safety of his country—perhaps his own survival—was in the hands of Egypt and Syria. Now Hussein faced precisely the problem that Zeid Rifai had outlined seven months before: how to ensure Jordan simultaneously against victory and defeat.

In retrospect, Hussein should not have been so surprised by the outbreak of war. True, nobody in Jordan seems to have suspected the real purpose of the Egyptian maneuvers. But some of Hussein's senior officers were well informed about Syria's preparations—and a few, at least, suspected the truth. But Hussein, still in the afterglow of the Cairo summit, was so confident of peace that he had taken no precautions. His small air force was concentrated at its headquarters base. His armored divisions were either on leave or down in the far south on desert training. Now, while the aircraft were hastily dispersed and the armor ordered north with all speed, Hussein's first task was clearly to find out what was going on. He telephoned the two Arab presidents.

It was scarcely a satisfactory way of communicating. No Arab leader could forget how, in 1967, the Israelis—or perhaps the United States—had tapped Hussein's conversations with Nasser. Nobody was going to risk that fiasco a second time. Throughout the war, therefore, Hussein was to have severe difficulty in obtaining from his allies up-to-date details on the course of the fighting. Telephone conversations were confined to careful generalities. And the couriers that shuttled back and forth brought information at least twenty-four hours old—and frequently inaccurate. All this added to Hussein's sense of isolation. In 1967, after all, Nasser had deliberately lied to Hussein about the fate of the Egyptian Air Force. This time, Hussein wanted the truth. But how to get it?

Those first phone calls exemplified the problem. To both Sadat and Asad, Hussein repeated the same, quite genuine, expressions of goodwill. In reply, Sadat was brief, Asad more flamboyant. Even then, Asad was keen that Hussein should enter the war. Sadat, generalized though his phrases were, made it clear that he expected Hussein to do no more than had been settled at Cairo: guard his frontier. But Asad was so full of confidence that, as Hussein recalled afterward, "his attitude was that we should make haste to share in the coming victory."

Hussein was not so naïve as to think that this bonhomie could last. At 11:30 P.M. that first evening of war, the Soviet chargé d'affaires in Amman harangued Premier Rifai for forty-five minutes—"rude and abusive" was Rifai's comment later. After 1967, the Soviets had offered Hussein all the arms he needed—an offer Hussein almost accepted, only to be dissuaded (as he had hoped) by a last-minute counteroffer from the United States. Now the Soviet diplomat pointed to the weaponry that Egypt and Syria were deploying, attacked Rifai for not availing himself of the chance to acquire some of his own, and promised immediate Soviet help should Hussein declare war.

For the first few days, however, Hussein was under no pressure from Arab quarters—except, of course, the incorrigible Qaddafi.

On Monday, October 8, Hussein's new Ambassador in Cairo, Abdel Moneim Rifai, flew back to Amman with the first detailed account of Sadat's actions and thinking. To Hussein's relief, Sadat's message reiterated that Jordan should stay out of the war. Any territory that his forces succeeded in liberating in Sinai, Sadat wrote, would not be worth the loss of territory on the east bank of the Jordan.

But just as Washington and the rest of the world were adjusting to the fact that this was not going to be a short war, so Hussein realized that, as Premier Rifai later put it, "we will have to do more." Hussein talked with Asad daily, and it did not escape him that, while Asad kept assuring him that Syrian forces would be on the river Jordan "any minute," Asad's continuing exhortations to join the battle were steadily less ebullient and more pressing.

So long as Sadat agreed that Jordan should stay out, Hussein could stave off Asad. "It was clear from the first that the over-all command was situated in Cairo," Hussein told a visitor. All that changed on Tuesday, October 9, however. That day, Sadat telephoned Hussein and asked anxiously: "When are you going to launch your attack?" Hussein, horrified, asked what attack. Sadat said merely: "The one we agreed on in Cairo." On the open line no more could be said, and Hussein rang off in bewilderment. "What are they referring to?" he asked a confidant a few hours later.

Then it dawned on Hussein what Sadat meant. At the Cairo summit, Hussein had outlined that "contingency idea": the vague plan for a thrust by Jordanian troops over the Jordan toward Beit Shean, just south of Lake Tiberias. The military thinking behind the plan, insofar as it was clear at all, was twofold. A Jordanian presence so far north would severely inhibit Israel's resupply effort on Golan. And the Jordanian armor could then swing south to recapture the occupied West Bank—or at least its most populous part around Nablus. The choice of route for the assault was dictated by geography. There are only three main bridges over the Jordan, and the northernmost, the Sheikh Hussein Bridge—from which the road leads up to Beit Shean—is the only one where the surrounding terrain permits deployment of armor.

But the very idea of the assault was now madness. The Syrians were in no position to help; and Dayan was dropping heavy hints that Israeli retaliation might include air strikes upon Amman. "Jordan has had its Black September," he said. "King Hussein should beware that he does not bring upon his people a Black October." But, disastrously, Sadat obviously now saw that Cairo discussion as a firm commitment by Hussein.

Next day, Wednesday, October 10, Ambassador Abdel Moneim Rifai was dispatched back to Cairo with the king's personal military advisor, General Amer Khammesh, a former Chief of Staff. Khammesh told the Egyptians bluntly that such intervention by the Jordanians would be suicidal. Sadat relented; Khammesh returned with a compromise. "I had an agreement with President Sadat," Hussein said afterward, "that Jordan would enter the war and mount an offensive across the river Jordan once the Syrians had completely liberated the Golan Heights and the Egyptians had overrun the major desert passes that control Sinai."

Superficially, those impossible conditions let Hussein off the hook. In fact, it was clear that Jordan had to do something. Despairingly, Hussein did even consider a frontal assault across the river Jordan—over the Allenby Bridge and straight up the road to Jerusalem. But the key roads on both sides of the river are narrow defiles in the rock. A handful of Israeli tanks could wreak havoc among an advancing column (just as the two divisions of Jordanian infantry dug into prepared positions on their side of the bank would have taken a high toll of any Israeli advance). And Jordan's Air Force—a few Hawker Hunters—was no match for Israel's terrifying air power. (The Jordanians could not handle a batch of F-104 Starfighters which the United States had supplied; and a consignment of simpler F-5s which had then been promised had not yet entered Jordanian service.) The assessment of Hussein's Chief of Staff, General Zeid bin Shaker, was that the Jordanian armor might get as far as the hills overlooking the Holy City and inflict a lot of damage on the Israelis in the process. But then, without air cover, they would be wiped out in a bloody rerun of 1967.

"If we attacked, it was suicidal, possibly bringing the destruction of the country," one of Hussein's closest advisors said afterward. "But if we stayed out, we would certainly be set up as scapegoats for an Arab defeat. That meant slow death politically. It was suicide either way." For nobody in Amman doubted that the Arabs did face defeat. The United States embassy had seen to that.

Kissinger's policy was to keep Jordan out of the war at all costs. Since Jordan gets more U.S. aid per head of population than any country in the world (fifty million dollars a year, plus military aid), Kissinger had considerable sway. Equally, of course, Israel was reluctant to precipitate conflict with the most pro-Western of its Arab neighbors. So the Jordan Valley remained an eerie haven of peace: the Jordanian farmers bringing their produce over to sell on the West Bank; the local bus service plying its usual erratic timetable across the Allenby Bridge each day; while the "blackout" imposed in Amman was so farcical that the foreign diplomatic community soon realized that they were the only people observing it.

In Kissinger's view, the best way to keep Hussein out of the war was to ensure that he knew exactly what was happening on the battlefield. Common sense would do the rest. So Dean Berger, the U. S. Ambassador in Amman, fed Hussein's staff with intelligence reports. And by Wednesday, of course—when Kissinger, realizing the growing pressure upon Hussein, made his strongest representations to the king—those reports showed just how badly Asad's assault upon Golan had collapsed.

It was precisely this information that pushed Hussein into war. And the fact that the British saw this faster than the United States did was one of the unspoken factors behind the rapid cooling of relations between Washington and London. Because while the United States was pressuring Hussein to stay out of the fight, the advice of the British Foreign Office was precisely the opposite.

This British perception of Hussein's best interests in part reflected the fact that the Foreign Office has always—and not without controversy at times—tended to see British interests in the Middle East as lying with the Arab world, the suppliers of oil, rather than with Israel, where U.S. influence is anyway so overwhelming as to make that of other powers irrelevant. And of all countries in the Middle East, Jordan has the closest relationship with Britain. (Britain works to keep it that way. The Ambassador in Amman, Hugh Balfour-Paul, is one of the most experienced Arabists in the British diplomatic service.) It was inevitable, too, that while the arms that Washington supplied entitled the United States to a respectful hearing, Hussein and his advisors talked more openly through the war with the power less intimately bound to Israel and more clearly concerned that his regime survive. And the British advice, chiming with Premier Rifai's, was that Hussein should attack—but in some fashion that minimized the cost of failure. The Wednesday news from Golan did not leave him long to decide.

Israel's first probing attacks across the Golan cease-fire line on the morning of Thursday, October 11, provided Hussein with the solution. That afternoon, his decision was made: to send armor into Syria to repel the Israeli advance upon Damascus. Israel could scarcely take offense at this limited Jordanian role. More ingeniously, the best way to still the mounting clamor for Hussein to attack across the river Jordan was to send the necessary forces out of the country. At 5 P.M. on Thursday, Brigadier Haled Hajhouj Majali, commander of Hussein's crack 40th Armored Brigade, was ordered to move his brigade north to reinforce the Syrian Army.

It remained a well-kept secret. Diplomatically, that was embarrassing. Britain knew of the decision within hours (if not before it was taken). But the United States remained so sure that its advice had been heeded that even thirty-six hours later—on the morning of Saturday, October 13—local correspondents were still being advised that there was "no chance" of Hussein entering the war. That Saturday lunchtime, Hussein announced his decision to send his best troops "in defense," as he carefully noted, "of our entire sacred holy soil." By then, in fact, Brigadier Hajhouj had already spent a day coordinating plans with the Syrians.

Brigadier Haled Hajhouj Majali was a slight figure with a wizened face and a wry expression, deriving perhaps from the vagaries of his career. For although he had become, at forty-six, commander of Hussein's crack armored unit, in the early 1950s he was actually thrown out of the Army for political reasons—"false," he has always claimed. For five years, he was a schoolmaster. Only in 1957 did he rejoin the Army—taking up his old rank as a by now rather aging second lieutenant. But he went into the armored forces and promotion came rapidly, with training courses in the

United States in 1960 and 1964, and Staff College and then War College in Formosa in 1969 and the start of 1973.

Hajhouj, in other words, was promoted for professionalism. He had also learned caution. Hussein had two armored divisions. One was deployed to back up the infantry on the hills overlooking the river Jordan—the tanks being mainly in the north, in the lee of the Golan Heights. The departure of Hajhouj's brigade to Syria left Hussein with only two brigades of the remaining division. One of those, the 92nd, remained at armored corps headquarters at Mafrak in northern Jordan. That left Hussein with only one brigade of armor to guard his capital. Unlike Egyptian and Syrian commanders, therefore, Hajhouj was as anxious as any Israeli to keep his losses down. He knew what his tanks meant to Jordan.

The political directions reflected this concern. Having decided to help Syria, Hussein spent all Friday, October 12, arguing with the Syrians' plans for his forces. The first scheme advanced by the Syrian Chief of Staff, Shakkour, was to send the Jordanians to the north, to reconstruct the shattered front along the lower slopes of the Hermon range. Hussein turned this down. He had no intention of having his forces cut off from his own territory. Besides, the problems of supply and spares would be insuperable, he argued. Next, Shakkour suggested that the brigade be split up, each battalion reinforcing different Syrian units. That too was turned down. Then Asad even suggested that the Jordanians might come to guard his capital, while the Syrian forces around Damascus went to the front. Hussein said that the Jordanians were determined to see action (or what was the political point in committing them?).

Asad by now needed help on any terms. Hussein had his way. At 9 P.M. on the evening of Saturday, October 13, Hussein went personally to armored headquarters to give Hajhouj the order to move into Syria. By 5 A.M. next morning, Sunday, the brigade was over the border—its three battalions more or less around Dera'a, astride the main road north to Damascus. It was the beginning of a week of disaster.

As the commander of the Israeli advance into Syria, Rafael Eytan, observed afterward: "The Arab 'Foreign Legion' just did not work." The Iraqis were the first to demonstrate this. Like Jordan, Iraq had learned of the outbreak of war only from the early radio bulletins. But after a hurried trip to Damascus by the Iraqi Foreign Minister on Monday, October 8, squadrons of Iraqi MIGs began operating over Golan. At least half a dozen were promptly shot down by Syrian SAM-6s because their IFF gear (Identification Friend or Foe) could not cope with the rapid switches in the SAMs' radar wavelengths. The Iraqi armored forces fared even worse.

How many troops the Iraqis sent into Syria—and when—is disputed. Sources in Damascus recounted afterward how the Iraqi 3rd Armored Division had arrived on Monday, October 15, at Syrian Army headquarters at Katana—just down the road toward Golan from Damascus—to be ordered by the Syrian Chief of Staff, Shakkour, simply: "Fight." But according to Hajhouj, the Jordanian commander, it was on the evening of Sunday, October 14 that—after a day of utter confusion—he was told by Shakkour that he would now take orders from the Iraqi brigadier commanding two Iraqi brigades, one armored and one mechanized infantry, already in the battle. When Hajhouj met the Iraqi officer at breakfast next day, he was not impressed. The Iraqis had by then, he says, been in action for two or three days—using their tanks more as artillery pieces than as mobile weapons, and suffering losses accordingly. Iraqi morale was low. But it was with the Iraqis that Hajhouj was now ordered to mount a combined attack.

The minutiae of the ensuing battle are of interest only to military historians. But the Jordanian tank crews are the best trained in the Arab world—though the need to conserve expensive ammunition has not helped their firing practice in recent years. Potentially, the Jordanians posed the gravest threat that the Israelis on Golan faced at this point in the battle. It is worth outlining why, in fact, their intervention proved so fruitless.

The plan was sensible. The Israeli advance up the road from Kuneitra to Saasa was narrow—a tongue no more than a few miles wide. The Israelis were thus vulnerable to a determined thrust from the south, spearing up to cut the main road and isolate the forward Israeli units. That was the task of the Jordanians in a dawn attack on Tuesday, October 16.

Broadly, the Arab forces arrayed south of the advancing Israelis were as follows (see map, page 240): two Syrian brigades hard up against the old cease-fire line, preventing an Israeli attack due east from Naffak; then the Jordanian brigade around El Harra; then the Iraqis' two brigades east of that. But on the evening of Monday, October 15, as Hajhouj sat with the Iraqi commander making final preparations for the assault next day, the Israelis suddenly attacked the Iraqi positions, drove them southeast until the Iraqis had to regroup around Sanamein, on the road north to Damascus—and they almost captured Hajhouj. His car only just made it southward ahead of the lead Israeli tanks.

Hajhouj told the Syrians that, with the Iraqis now so out of position, the attack was hopeless. Unless the Iraqis could advance abreast of his forces, Hajhouj said, the Israelis could simply take *his* advancing tanks from the right flank—a favorite Israeli maneuver. He was told to carry on. The result was predictable.

At 6 A.M. on Tuesday, the Syrian Air Force began to soften up the Israeli positions on the conical hills that were Hajhouj's initial objectives just north of El Harra. But the Israelis were safely inside the massive pillboxes that the Syrians themselves had constructed. To make any impression, Hajhouj had asked for thirty minutes of aerial bombardment. He got ten minutes.

At 6:30 A.M., the artillery—three Jordanian batteries and about sixteen Syrian—opened up. Under cover of this, the assault was now supposed to start. Hajhouj discovered that the Iraqis had made no preparations to move at all. He postponed the attack for an hour. By 7:30 A.M., the Israeli artillery's response was becoming too effective for comfort, anyway. Two Jordanian armored battalions—fifty-six Centurions, with the third battalion of another twenty-eight held in reserve—rolled forward.

One of the Iraqi battalions did not attack at all. The other moved up only at 10 A.M. The result was inevitable. Free of all pressure from the Iraqis, the Israelis promptly ambushed the right-hand of Hajhouj's two advancing battalions. Ten of its tanks were hit almost at once with SS-11 antitank missiles (and perhaps with TOW). With the battalion commander terribly burned, his number two tried to rally the remaining tanks, but it was no use.

The left-hand battalion did press on and by noon was in position to take its first objective, an Israeli-held hill, from the rear. But it too was about to be ambushed. Hajhouj ordered a retreat and then, barely able to control his anger, went to have it out with the Iraqi commander—only to be greeted as if, together, they had won a great victory. The Israelis, of course, viewed the shambles with grim humor. "Now," one of the Israeli officers said, "they are letting us pick them off one by one." Still, Hussein's honor had been saved.

4. Rival Views of Reality

Had the war been merely a matter of such tactical victories then, Israel could have relaxed. But this was an altogether more serious struggle—as President Sadat proceeded to spell out. That Tuesday an open car drove through the midday Cairo crowds, carrying this man who bore the responsibility for the Arab war. For a man who rations his public appearances, the open car was an unusual touch of flamboyance. But Sadat must have known that by the eleventh day of war, a gesture was required to assuage the emotions of the Cairo crowd.

Sadat was on his way to address a combined meeting of the People's Assembly and the Arab Socialist Union—the most critical speech of his life so far. He preserved, as usual, the appearance of impassivity, making little response, apart from an occasional slightly stiff-backed wave, to the boiling enthusiasm of the crowds. Sadat, now fifty-four, had been a lifelong friend of Gamal Abdel Nasser. Yet it would be hard to imagine two more dissimilar personalities. Where Nasser was physically overwhelming and theatrical, Sadat is slightly built and withdrawn. His forehead bears the *sabiba* dent—acquired by regular contact with a prayer mat and marking him as a devout Muslim. Despite that—and the fact that he was fortunate to survive a reckless youth as an agitator against British rule in Egypt—Sadat's present-day style has marked Anglo-Saxon overtones. During the conflict, he wore only military uniform, but his normal clothes are the casual khaki shirt and breeches of the off-duty officer, with an old pipe gripped in his teeth. Diplomats, groping for an account of his personality in Western terms, have sometimes compared him to Clement Attlee, leader of Britain's first postwar Labour government. New Yorkers, contemplating Abe Beame taking over as mayor from John Lindsay, must have known how Egyptians comparing Sadat and Nasser felt. But Sadat was singularly tough. Western ambassadors who saw him during the war found him unmoved even when news from the battlefield was dramatically bad. "We can lose three tanks for every one Israel loses," he told one such visitor. "But they will reach bottom before we do."

Nobody, quite certainly, was more aware than Sadat of the importance of the speech he now had to make, or of the fact that the war aims contained in it might decide the future of the Middle East for generations to come. "I do not think you expect me to stand before you," he told the Assembly in his flat, slightly pedantic manner, "in order that we may boast together about what we have realized in eleven days. . . ." Nonetheless, he claimed that the Egyptian armed forces had performed "a miracle by any military standard" in crossing the canal. And if that was putting it a little high, he was certainly justified in claiming that the Egyptian Army had been regenerated.

"I would like to say briefly that this nation can now feel safe and secure after the period of fear. It is now armed with a shield and sword. . . ." Then: "We are fighting for the sake of peace—the only peace which is worthy of the name, that is, peace based on justice. . . . It was David Ben-Gurion who laid down for Israel the theory of imposing peace. . . . I really do not know what David Ben-Gurion would have thought had he been in command in Israel today. Would he have been able to understand the nature of history, or would he have remained in a position contrary to history, as we see Israel's leadership doing today?

"Peace cannot be imposed, and the *fait accompli* peace cannot stand or last. . . . Today, we would like to ask Israel's leaders: Where is the theory of Israeli security which they attempted to apply sometimes by violence and other times by brute power for twenty-five years?"

Reading from a prepared text, Sadat moved to the vital business of his speech: the statement of war aims. In mild terms, he upbraided the United States for "setting up a naval and air bridge by means of which it is pouring into Israel new tanks, airplanes, guns, rockets, and electronic equipment. . . ." He had thought of sending a letter to President Nixon, Sadat said, adding drily:

"I hesitated for fear it might be misinterpreted. Instead I have decided to address to him an open message from here. . . .

"First: We have fought and we shall go on fighting to liberate our land which was seized by Israeli occupation in 1967, and to find the means toward the restoration and respect of the legitimate rights of the Palestinian people. In this respect, we accept our commitment to the decisions of the United Nations, the General Assembly and the Security Council.

"Second: We are prepared to accept a cease-fire on condition that the Israeli forces withdraw forthwith from all occupied territories to the pre-June 5, 1967, lines, under international supervision.

"Third: We are ready, once the withdrawal from all these territories has been carried out, to attend an international peace conference at the United Nations. I shall try to persuade my colleagues, the Arab leaders who are directly responsible for leading the conflict with our enemy. I will also do my best to convince the representatives of the Palestinian people to participate with us, and with the whole international community, in laying down rules and measures for peace in the area based on the respect of the legitimate rights of all the people in the area.

"Fourth: We are willing, at this hour and at this very moment, to start clearing the Suez Canal and opening it to international navigation so as to contribute, once again, to world welfare and prosperity. I have in fact given the order to the head of the Suez Canal Authority to start this task immediately after the liberation of the eastern bank. . . .

"Fifth: Throughout all this we are not prepared to accept ambiguous promises or flexible expressions which lend themselves to various interpretations, draining our time needlessly and returning our cause to the stalemate. . . ."

It was not a particularly accommodating speech. Sadat had apparently abandoned the idea of Israeli withdrawal from Sinai by stages—and Golan and the West Bank of the Jordan now appeared nonnegotiable too. But for a military leader, speaking in wartime, it was certainly not violent. Nor were Sadat's remarks about the Israeli "theory of security" very different from those Dayan had advanced. Sadat spoke only of satisfying the "legitimate rights" of the Palestinians: a phrase that could cover many solutions to the Palestinian problem, and certainly something a long way short of the standard guerrilla demand for the replacement of Israel by a new Arab State of Palestine (with, so they claimed, guaranteed rights for Christians and Jews). Indeed, Sadat had chosen his words in such a way that he could clearly withdraw support from any Palestinian group making unreasonable demands.

Sadat's whole speech was that of a man prepared to come to terms with the existence of Israel. He even said: "I would like to add, so they may hear in Israel, that we are not upholders of extermination as they allege. . . ." But Mrs. Meir, speaking just a few hours later to the Knesset, took the view that this show of moderation by Sadat was mere camouflage.

"There is no doubt in our minds," the Israeli Prime Minister told *her* people, "that war was launched once more against the very existence of the Jewish state: Our survival . . . is in the balance. The armies of Egypt and Syria, with the help of other Arab states . . . went to war with the aim of reaching the lines of June 4, 1967, on their way to achieving their main purpose—the conquest and destruction of Israel.

"The Arab leaders profess that their objective is confined to reaching the lines of 4 June 1967. *But we know that it is really the total subjugation of Israel* [our italics]. It needs no fertility of imagination to realize what would have been the nightmarish situation of Israel had we stood on the lines of 4 June 1967. . . ."

In saying this, Mrs. Meir was expressing one of the most important of all Israeli responses to the war: It proved Israel had been right to hold onto the land gained in 1967. Had the Israelis bargained it away, the Arabs would have had them at their mercy. The opportunity to demonstrate this had been one component in Mrs. Meir's rejection of a preemptive strike. And the argument carries such emotional appeal inside Israel that it is almost impossible to refute it. Even to criticize it from outside invites the allegation of callousness toward the proper fears of a beleaguered people, or the claim that one is being brave about other people's dangers. Still, it does no service to Israel to refrain from pointing out that the argument, for all its gut appeal, misses the point. The aim of bargaining away territory would have been precisely to prevent war from breaking out. Many Israelis, of course, will argue that the war would have happened anyway. Perhaps that is right. But if Israel's "theory of security" is that war with the Arabs is always inevitable, that leads straight back to Dayan's nightmare.

Mrs. Meir devoted much of her speech to attacking the Soviet Union for supplying arms to the Arabs—in terms similar to those Sadat had used against the United States. More bitterly, she denounced the embargoes on Middle Eastern arms exports announced by Britain and France—theoretically "even-handed," but undoubtedly of more help to the Arabs than to Israel. "What lover of peace," she asked, "but must view with trepidation the cynicism and partiality displayed in international politics, the selfish and unethical policy followed by enlightened states towards a small country beleaguered and under assault?" She was flintily precise about Israel's war aims: "The time for a cease-fire will be when the enemy's strength is broken. I am certain that when we have brought our enemies to the verge of collapse, representatives of various states will not be slow in 'volunteering' to try and save our assailants. . . . Anyhow, now as in previous wars, the cease-fire depends first and foremost on the strength of the IDF."

Nobody with the smallest sympathy for the history of the Jewish people could have been left unmoved by Mrs. Meir's speech. "The IDF," she said, "is a people's army in the finest and truest sense. The devoted and anxious household of Israel is indivisibly linked to the IDF as a whole as well as to its dearest men and women on active service. . . ." Even so, in terms of policy, it was contradictory. "We have never held war to be a means of solving dilemmas in our region. . . ." Yet: "The repelling of the enemy and the crushing of his strength are the only conditions for safeguarding our future." And: "The Egyptians and Syrians have seemingly not yet been beaten enough to evince willingness for a cease-fire."

The most important line in her speech, however—the one that brought the most emotional response from the members of the

Knesset—was her brief announcement that the Israeli Army was already on its way to a military resolution of the issue with Egypt. "An IDF task force," said Mrs. Meir, "is operating on the western bank of the Suez Canal." It was the world's first news of Arik Sharon's bridgehead.

5. Sharon's Crossing Goes Wrong

When President Sadat achieved his aim and saw the war at last bring the two superpowers to confrontation, he reflected upon the irony that an Israeli action finally sparked it. That action arose from the confused progress and uncertain outcome of Israel's crossing of the canal. And that, in turn, owed much to the wide discrepancies in temperament and training between, on the one hand, Shmuel Gonen and Haim Bar-Lev, and on the other hand, Major General "Arik" Sharon.

Not many Israeli generals go in nowadays for touches like attaching a professor of ancient Hebrew to their staff. Sharon, who took his degree in oriental history, did just that. He is an almost implausible mixture of intellectual brilliance and physical *machismo*. What he is not is an expert in mechanized warfare. Sharon acquired his first military reputation as a brave and ruthless border raider; diligent training in Israel and at the British Staff College at Camberley then turned him into a hard-fighting infantryman. He has some record of success in political maneuver, which many professional soldiers find strange and confusing. He has no comparable record in the equally confusing business of large-scale mobile warfare.

In spite of the Patton legend, success in this branch of combat is not automatically correlated with flamboyance, incaution, or even personal ferocity. Some of its most effective practitioners have been studious technicians like Von Runstedt or cool administrators like Richard O'Connor. Success in a war of movement depends chiefly on an ability, while under emotional pressure, to juggle considerations such as the speed of tanks over various terrains, the availability of fuel, or the likelihood of a rendezvous coming off.

Sharon's records, by contrast, is one of straightforward lust for battle. He first became known as founder and commander of "Unit 101," making raids across the Jordanian border in response to Arab terrorist attacks. In 1953 Unit 101 acquired international notoriety when, in response to an Arab raid that killed an Israeli woman and her child, Sharon and his men blew up a Jordanian village, killing sixty-nine Jordanians in the process, half of them women and children. Sharon said Unit 101 had not known there were people hiding in the houses when they were blown up.

Dayan valued Sharon because in the fifties Dayan was trying to create an officer corps whose philosophy would be to take any objective "by frontal attack . . . paying for it with lives" (*Moshe Dayan* by Shabtai Teveth, 1972). Dayan's aim was to exorcise "Jewish cleverness" from the Israeli Army. Apart from being an act of intellectual self-mutilation, it seems an impractical outlook to imprint on a people whose opponents have many more lives to spend. Perhaps, in the context of Dayan's subtle and contradictory character, this was never more than a dialectical exercise designed to counter the defensive spirit engendered in the War of Independence. But Sharon, at least, adopted the dictum quite literally.

During the 1956 Suez campaign, he was dropped with a parachute brigade to harass Egyptian movements near the Mitla Pass. He was specifically ordered not to attack the heavily defended pass itself, because this was superfluous to the plan Dayan had devised. Obtaining permission for a "patrol," Sharon sent a large detachment straight up the pass into an Egyptian ambush. He then had to commit the rest of his brigade to extricate the trapped force, and after losing 38 killed and 120 wounded—more than in all the other "breakthrough battles" of the campaign—Sharon took the pass, killing some 200 Egyptians. It was magnificent, but it was not clever; and it cemented Sharon's reputation for indiscipline. Had it not been for the friendship 30-year-old Colonel Sharon had already established with David Ben-Gurion, he might have been severely punished.

Sharon's role in the 1967 campaign further revealed his mixture of military skills and weaknesses. Sharon commanded the *ugda* (task force) that was to break through into Sinai along the central route toward the Khatmia Pass (see map, page 70). It was first necessary to capture the road junction at Abu Ageila, but this turned out to be much more strongly defended than Sharon's field intelligence had suggested. A swift "regardless of cost" attack failed, and Sharon then had to reduce the Egyptian defenses with a complex assault, in which he coordinated forces converging on the Egyptians from several directions at once. It was conducted with great skill and determination—and some finely calculated timing. But Sharon's adventurism asserted itself in the daunting risks he took, leaving his forces unprepared for a possible Egyptian counterattack in the course of the battle. (Luckily for Sharon, it did not come.) And the victory left Sharon's *ugda* weary, with much of its potential mobility expended. When Sharon was then given the task of catching an armored formation under General Shazli, which had been stationed at Kuntilla and was virtually cut off, the last of the Shazli force managed to slip away behind the Sharon *ugda* after nightfall. One historian of the campaign concluded that Sharon was "more expert at positional battles than mobile desert warfare."

Sharon nonetheless sees himself as a custodian of the grand tradition in the Israeli Army. Bored by planning and logistics, he professes a large contempt for those like Bar-Lev or Adan, who excel in such matters. This contempt is expressed at a personal level: Sharon, whose own larger-than-life personality resembles that of a Texas rancher, genuinely thinks it improper that the Israeli Army should be led by respectable suburbanites with degrees in economics.

Granted his aptitude for a hard-fought positional battle, Sharon was probably a good choice in theory for the task of seizing and securing an Israeli bridgehead across the canal. In the event, his complicated maneuvers got hopelessly behind schedule—and when that happened, Sharon ceased to be the carefully trained infantryman, and reverted to type.

Sharon had picked out a spot for a canal crossing well before the war, when he was running the Sinai command. Between Lake Timsah and the Great Bitter Lake, the north-to-south canal road runs a mile or two east of the bank. But just above the entrance to the Great Lake, two side roads branch off to the west within a thousand yards of each other and come together at the bank of the canal. At this point—the canalside apex of the triangle of roads, roughly thirteen miles south of Ismailia—Sharon had the massive sand ramparts of the canalbank thinned down, and he marked out the weakened section with red bricks. Nearby, he and a vehicle park laid out—one hundred yards by four hundred yards —protected by high sand walls.

Late on the evening of Sunday, October 14—when Bar-Lev and Gonen were satisfied with the destruction wrought that day among the Egyptian tanks—Sharon was at last given permission to launch his drive across the canal. The attack was code-named Operation Gazelle.

Israel's resources were limited. Sharon had at his disposal in the central sector roughly a division of tanks, though the Israeli Army does not use the term: three armored brigades, originally of ninety to one hundred tanks each, but depleted by a week's fighting. He also had a brigade of infantry, including paratroops; and a special force of engineers with earth-moving equipment, self-propelled barges, and bridging equipment, plus such exotic additions as tanks with "camera booms" to hoist spotters twenty feet above the battlefield.

Facing Sharon were the Egyptians' 21st Armored Division and the 16th Infantry Division. They were the core of Egypt's Second Army, commanded from Ismailia by Major General Saad Maamun. Although battered by Sunday's defeat, both divisions were still formidable opponents. Sharon's forces had destroyed on Sunday about a hundred of the 21st Division's tanks; but that left two hundred intact. The men of the 16th Infantry Division, complete with missiles, were securely astride the roads to the canal from Sharon's position near Tasa (see map, page 331). And Tasa lay eighteen miles northeast of Sharon's chosen crossing point. Somehow, the roads had to be cleared of their Egyptian defenders.

"The problem," said Sharon, "was how to reach the water and establish the bridgehead in the same night. We had to do it before daylight, because if we lost surprise no doubt we would have found quite a number of tanks waiting for us on the other side." Sharon's solution was, by his own account, "complicated." But, he said, "it worked." It didn't.

At dawn on Monday Sharon began to brief his officers. The engineer in charge said that, with only ten bulldozers allotted to him, he would not be able to breach the ramparts of the canal in time to have the bridgehead established at first light. "I told him to look for the red bricks," Sharon recalled. "And when the time came he found them in the dark and he did it." On Monday afternoon, Bar-Lev gave Sharon final clearance for the attack. At 5 P.M., as dusk began to gather, Sharon's forces began to move.

The essence of Sharon's plan was to use one of his armored brigades to divert the Egyptians' attention, while another brigade won control of the road leading southwest from Tasa to the Great Lake. This road (see map, page 332) linked up with the main canalbank route only a few thousand yards short of the southernmost of the two side roads leading to Sharon's crossing point itself. The area of the road junctions was known as the Chinese Farm, because some time before the Six-Day War Japanese agricultural experts had conducted irrigation experiments there—the Israeli soldiers who overran the farm assumed the documents they found were in Chinese. Once Sharon was in control of the roads to, and the junctions around, the Chinese Farm, he would be able to send his engineers, motorized barges, and paratroops through to secure a crossing—while his third and last tank brigade would stave off counterattacks by the Egyptians around the Chinese Farm itself.

It was *not* Sharon's job to take his forces over the canal in any strength. He was ordered only to establish a bridgehead on the west bank. His force of paratroopers were all picked veterans; their orders were to cross the canal once Sharon's tanks had broken through and then to hold about two miles of the west bank at all costs. To support them, Sharon was given barges on which to ferry a handful of tanks across.

Sharon's main task, however, was to establish and maintain a safe corridor to the east bank—especially the road from Tasa and the side roads from the Chinese Farm to the water's edge. The actual crossing force was already assembling under Major General "Bren" Adan on the foothills in front of the Gidi Pass. Adan's men—three brigades of tanks and other brigades of paratroopers in halftracks—were then to sweep down to the canal and cross it to relieve any surviving paratroopers and expand the bridgehead, as soon as Sharon could hold open the corridor in Sinai against the inevitable Egyptian counterattacks. But the crucial factor was that Adan's tanks could not cross in any strength until Sharon's engineers had pushed a bridge across the canal—which Sharon had then to defend.

The whole operation went disastrously wrong—starting with Sharon's timetable. It would be an understatement to call his schedule a bold one. Sharon's first paratroopers were supposed to be crossing the canal in rubber boats by 11 P.M. That meant that the vital sections of the tank force had just about five hours in which to cover a complex twenty-mile route behind enemy lines, fight a night battle, bring up the engineers, and then lead them and the paratroopers through to the crossing point. Large parts of the route were through trackless dunes—and tanks, traveling off the road at night, can rarely average more than five miles an hour.

At 5 P.M. one of Sharon's armored brigades, positioned north of the Tasa-to-Great Lake road, launched an attack due west toward Ismailia. This was the diversion: a hard-fought one, which gradually drew the main weight of the 21st Armored Division north toward the axis of the Tasa-to-Ismailia road. "Right through the night," said an Israeli survivor of the battle, "we advanced slowly, slowly, against fierce resistance."

One hour later, in rapidly deepening twilight, Sharon's second armored brigade swung off the road in a southward curve. Under cover of darkness, the tanks headed southwest and, with no interference from the Egyptians, drove through sand ridges and dunes toward the Great Bitter Lake. Here, they were heading through the "gap" between Maamun's Second Army and the Egyptian Third Army to the south. Israeli field intelligence, maintaining its usual high efficiency, had indentified the traditional weak spot that occurs in areas of overlapping command. That, together with the tactical skill of the Israeli tank commanders, largely explains the lack of opposition as they drove southwest. Reaching the road by the lake shore, the column of Israeli tanks turned to race north, with the water securing its left flank.

The column was from the battered 14th Armored Brigade, survivors of the initial Egyptian assault on Y-Day. Leading them was Colonel Amnon Reshef; he had particularly requested that his men be allowed to spearhead this Israeli fight back. "We turned north along the canal road, tank by tank," Reshef said later. "There were swamps on one side and irrigation ditches on the other. We took the Egyptians completely by surprise until they woke up and began shooting at the tail of the column from only forty yards' range." At this point, Reshef's tanks were only a few thousand yards past the more northerly of the two crucial canal side roads. (For simplicity, we propose to follow the Israeli military terms and call the northerly turnoff the T junction and the southerly side road the Y junction. The map, page 333, shows the ground.) As Reshef's tanks ran into heavy Egyptian fire, they deployed hastily off the road and began the bitter tank battle that—with occasional pauses—was to last through most of the next two days.

Reshef's job was to hold off the Egyptians as far to the north as possible past the two side roads to the canal. As his tank crews now grimly set about this, Sharon's next task was to open the main road coming down to the crossing point from Tasa. This was blocked by the Egyptians of the 16th Infantry Division, but Sharon had a plan to clear them. He detached a battalion of tanks from Reshef's brigade and sent them up the road back toward Tasa to take the Egyptian forces in the rear.

But the intensity of the Egyptian response disrupted the plan. Reshef's men could not fully secure the perimeter north of the vital roads to the water's edge. And by this time the operation was running well behind schedule. The men who should have been paddling across the canal were still in Tasa. Not until midnight could the eastbound task force, taking the Egyptians on the Tasa road from behind, break through successfully. Only then could they link up with the paratroopers, mounted on halftrack personnel carriers. Reversing direction, the tanks now led the halftracks back toward the canal, with the engineers and their equipment coming behind. Swinging north up the canalside road, they then veered west at the Y junction to reach the water's edge. Around 1 A.M. Sharon himself, with a command group of about two hundred men, had already paddled across the hundred-yard width of the canal and clambered up the western bank. Israel was in Africa.

On the west bank—to begin with, at least—they found themselves without opposition, looking out over a moonlit landscape, lightly wooded. The trouble was all behind them in Sinai. Two miles back from the eastern bank, around the Chinese Farm road junctions, the night was lit by gun flashes, rocket trails, and streams of tracer. Some of the paratroopers had been left behind to secure the Y junction in readiness for the heavy equipment to come through. But a force of Egyptian infantry had managed to infiltrate to within one hundred yards to the north. They had rocket launchers and wire-guided missiles. So the northerly T junction was now impassable, and even the spur road from the southerly Y junction was under attack from time to time.

Maps 9, 10, and 11 Sharon's crossing: the Chinese Farm battle
For "Operation Gazelle," General "Arik" Sharon's plan for crossing the Suez Canal, the essentials were speed and surprise. Sharon aimed within the first night to reach the canal through the gap between the Egyptian Second and Third armies discovered by Israeli intelligence, and to bridge the canal by dawn. Starting at dusk on October 15, one of his three armored brigades launched a diversionary attack to the west, while another swung southwest toward the Great Bitter Lake. From the lake shore, it raced north to the crossing point.

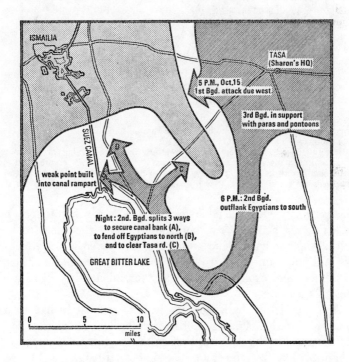

ISMAILIA

TASA (Sharon's HQ)

5 P.M., Oct.15: 1st Bgd. attack due west

3rd Bgd. in support with paras and pontoons

SUEZ CANAL

weak point built into canal rampart

6 P.M.: 2nd Bgd. outflank Egyptians to south

Night: 2nd. Bgd. splits 3 ways to secure canal bank (A), to fend off Egyptians to north (B), and to clear Tasa rd. (C)

GREAT BITTER LAKE

0   5   10
miles

As it did so, the brigade split into three: One group headed for the canal, another to the east to link up with the third brigade, and a third went north to establish a secure perimeter. By midnight, the linkup had been achieved with the third

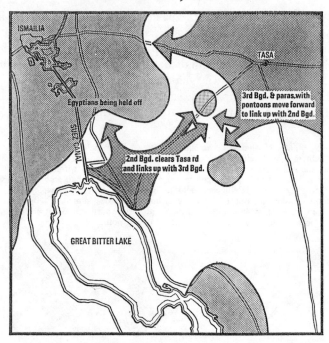

ISMAILIA

TASA

Egyptians being held off

3rd Bgd. & paras,with pontoons move forward to link up with 2nd Bgd.

SUEZ CANAL

2nd Bgd. clears Tasa rd and links up with 3rd Bgd.

GREAT BITTER LAKE

brigade's paratroopers, and an hour later Sharon himself was over the canal, with about two hundred men.

But the crucial objectives were not achieved: By dawn, the bridge was not established, and even the roads leading to the crossing point were not secure. And the northbound group had run into heavy Egyptian fire after a few kilometers: It was now deployed for a battle that was to last most of the next two days. On the

Meanwhile, a considerable tank action was being fought by Reshef's men another few thousand yards up the canal to the north. Another battle—the advance of the diversionary attack—was still going on some ten miles to the northeast. And minor skirmishes were exploding here and there along the entire road back to Tasa.

Through all this, bulldozers, excavators, and barges had to be conveyed for the building of the vital bridge. As Sharon said, traffic control in the dark was the key to everything. "If important equipment like the rafts [they were motorized barges] had missed the Y junction, and gone on to the T junction, the operation would have been over right then," he said (because the Egyptian

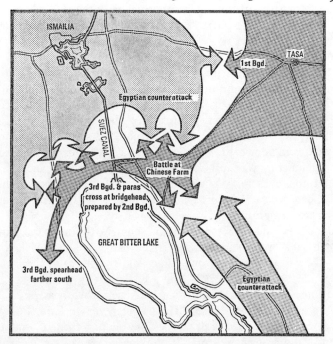

night of October 16, a coordinated Egyptian attack launched what became the Battle of the Chinese Farm. A few hours earlier, and with strong air support, this move would probably have liquidated the Israeli crossing force. As it was, it came close to cutting it off, but the Israelis just held onto the approach to their bridgehead. It was only when fresh Israeli tanks under "Bren" Adan crossed the canal that the bridgehead was properly secured behind the Third Army.

missile infantry would have destroyed the gear). As it was, the assault was running desperately late. The paratroop force was supposed to have been established on the west bank by 11 P.M. It did not get there until 3 A.M., four hours behind schedule. At dawn, the barge units had not even reached the crossing point: So far from there being a bridge thrown across the canal by dawn, even the ferrying operation had not begun. One of the officers in Sharon's command group looked out of the Egyptian bunker in which he had established himself, and surveyed the empty water. "Where is the bridge?" he asked. "No bridge," said the man next to him.

Sharon reacted with characteristic insouciance to the fact that he and a small party of infantry were now isolated at dawn on the wrong side of the canal. "Fellows," he said, "don't worry about a thing. The secretary of the Likud party is here with you."

With first light, the Egyptian Second Army's artillery zeroed in on the road junctions, making it a nerve-testing journey for the men who had to bring through the barges—cumbrous, rectangular steel floats, carried on flatbed trucks. The navigator of the lead barge, a Sergeant Zvi from Netania, described his unit's "baptism by fire": "There was a tank battle on both sides of the road, and we were going down the middle. It was a battle for the junction and the junction was in their sights and they hit every vehicle that went through there. We were a slow convoy, very easy to hit. . . . There were a few hits . . . a few holes. With dawn, we got to the crossing area."

On either side of the new-cut breaches in the ramparts, anti-aircraft guns were being set up as the barges splashed weightily into the still water. With one barge, said the sergeant, there was "a problem"—presumably, it had been holed by shellfire at the road junction. But at the crossing area itself, there was no shell-fire, nor any other resistance. "The barges began to ferry the first force, which positioned itself on the other shore, a force of armored infantry and an armored force." Working in life jackets, half-submerged in water, the engineers lashed tanks, one at a time, on to barges, and sent them chugging slowly across.

Not far from the western bridgehead was the wreckage of four Egyptian tanks. They had turned up at some point in the dark hours—possibly investigating, but equally possibly bound on some routine military excursion—and the paratroopers had knocked them out with missiles. But to the Israelis' amazement as the sun gathered strength, there was no further interference from the Egyptian Army. By 9 A.M., thirty tanks and about two thousand men had crossed the canal. On the western bank, the sergeant from Netania found that "there was a very pleasant atmosphere. Blue skies, very quiet, like on training. We still hadn't been ranged in on from the ground. . . . It was a peaceful atmosphere, really pastoral."

A few miles back from the crossing point, however, on the eastern bank, there was nothing pastoral about the scene. Reshef's 14th Brigade, now joined by the last of Sharon's three tank brigades, was still engaged in savage fighting all along the northern perimeter of the corridor leading back to Tasa. Aharon Bar, a tank driver who had been in action throughout that night, later told how the war ended for him: "In the morning, fog covered the area. As it dispersed, we found that we were facing huge masses of missile-carrying infantry. . . . We got into a hollow, behind a crest. From time to time we tried to get out, but the missile fire against us was too heavy. Then we got an order to attack."

The whole crew agreed that it was "suicidal," but they went forward over the crest. After a few minutes, Bar felt "something I had never felt before in my life. I didn't understand what was happening to me, but I knew it was something very serious. . . . The tank was full of gas. . . ." A missile had hit the tank low down, and the explosive jet of hot gas from its armor-piercing warhead had taken one of his legs off below the knee. "I opened the driver's hatch and got out: Only then did I realize there was an empty space below my left knee. I stood on one foot, holding onto the tank." Under small-arms and artillery fire, the crew abandoned the wrecked tank and dragged Bar painfully out of the battle zone.

On the west bank, meanwhile, it remained peaceful and sunny —"just like Acapulco," one of Sharon's officers said later. But Sharon himself should not have been on the west bank at all. His job had been to establish a corridor to the east bank for Adan's main crossing force. And on any orthodox military measurement, Sharon's attempt to establish that had been a disaster. Starting with a division, Sharon had managed after sixteen hours of frantic activity to get a force of rather less than battalion of infantry across the canal, plus a little armored support. There was no bridge, and because of shell damage done to the bridge sections on the way through, there was now no chance of establishing one within the next twelve hours. Considering the amount of shooting that had been going on in the whole Tasa-to-Bitter Lake-to-Ismailia triangle since the previous evening, the Israelis had no right even to hope that they still had the advantage of surprise. And, according to Israeli estimates, Sharon had already lost one hundred dead and three hundred wounded.

Sharon himself had predicted that if the Israelis lost surprise, they could expect to find "quite a number of tanks" coming in to attack them. Had an Egyptian force in any kind of strength turned up to challenge his bridgehead on Tuesday, there would have been nothing whatever the Israelis could have done about it. To get a division-strength force of their own across the water by barge ferry would have required about a thousand trips.

The Israeli high command had launched the crossing venture knowing that they faced a complex set of options with only limited resources. They needed to win some major prize before the imposition of a cease-fire, which could not be many days away now. The risk they faced was that one incautious move could cost them several high-class armored brigades—a loss that simply could not be permitted to occur.

6. The Battle of the Chinese Farm

What happened next was the result of remarkable ineptitude on the part of the Egyptian Army—and behavior on Sharon's part that his admirers regarded as a manifestation of genius, and his enemies as a descent into military dementia. "He was very sophisticated," said one of Sharon's officers. "He said: 'To hell with the bridgehead, the important thing is to get behind the Egyptian lines.'"

Sharon, naturally enough, recounts the incident in somewhat blander terms: "I called headquarters and told them that we could move forward, that we were at a turning point. But headquarters did not feel that the bridgehead was secure." Indeed, headquarters did not. When Gonen and Bar-Lev heard that Sharon's plan was simply to abandon the western crossing site and make off into the Egyptian rear areas, they emphatically did not think it was a "sophisticated" response. Gonen told Sharon to dig in around the bridgehead and hold it until a new attempt at bridging could be made by Adan's forces, now hastily advancing. It was the correct move, according to the book—indeed, anything else would leave the engineers virtually unprotected on the east bank. Sharon replied that to dig in on the west bank would merely make his little force so conspicuous that even the Egyptians would realize what an easy target was being offered. These were not viewpoints that could be reconciled: The conversation ended on an abusive note.

"Gonen," Sharon shouted into the radio, "if you had any balls, I'd tell you to cut them off and eat them." With that, he hung up, started splitting his tiny force into raiding parties, and sent them out to search for SAM sites, fuel dumps, and anything else that seemed worth attacking. Slightly awed, one of Sharon's staff said that the Army might well respond by kicking Arik out.

"So?" said the unrepentant Sharon, "I'd join up under another name."

Leaving only a token force at the crossing point, the raiders fanned out through olive groves and patches of scruffy pine. The larger parties were led by a couple of tanks apiece, with halftracks following. But, in keeping with the piratical nature of the enterprise, anyone who could make a case for striking out on his own was more than welcome to do so. Two officers, for example, began by hijacking an Egyptian armored car. Meeting a convoy, they waited for it to pass them, then shot it up from behind and made off. Finding a fuel dump by the road, they drove in and threw some grenades around to fire it. When the armored car ran low on fuel, they hijacked a Jeep for the return journey. Inevitably, much of the damage inflicted was relatively trivial. But the raiders enjoyed themselves and perhaps rattled several Egyptian units in Sinai by firing occasional shots into their rear from the west bank and then hoisting the Israeli flag conspicuously on the canal ramparts. As Sharon observed, nothing so demoralizes an army as finding its enemy behind it. They also destroyed around twenty tanks. And crucially, by midday, according to Sharon, four SAM missile complexes had been knocked out. A cone of sky had opened over Egypt in which Israeli aircraft could now operate without inhibition.

Meanwhile, why was there no coordinated effort to cut the Israelis off or to destroy them on the west bank? What was going on inside the Egyptian command center? What was being registered on those illuminated glass maps supposedly showing all details of the ever-changing front?

General Ismail had gone into his command center to take charge of operations on October 2, four days before the war began. And Tuesday, October 16, was the first day on which he came out onto the street again—to go to the People's Assembly with President Sadat. According to Ismail's own account, he knew nothing about the Israeli crossing when he set out to drive to the Assembly. That was at about midday—by which time the Israelis had been on the west bank for about eleven hours.

When Sadat failed to mention the invasion in his speech, the Israeli political and military command assumed that this was deliberate. (The Israeli military had pleaded with Mrs. Meir not to mention the bridgehead either; but she needed a political boost.) According to Israeli spokesmen, however, Sadat's silence showed the existence of a "political dilemma" inside Egypt. Complex speculations were mounted about the various degrees of face the Egyptians might lose according to which troops they used to try to destroy Sharon's force.

Understandably, it did not occur to the Israelis that perhaps Sadat and Ismail just did not know what was happening. Yet Ismail's version is that the first he knew of the invasion was "information . . . which I found waiting for me after my return from the People's Assembly session." This, he said, referred to "the infiltration of a small number of amphibian tanks." The message added that in the estimation of the local command "it was possible to destroy them quickly," and a "storm battalion" had been moved to face them.

Not only had Sharon's men been operating on the western bank since 1 A.M.; since Monday evening, there had been continuous Israeli activity in the Ismailia sector of the Sinai front. On the eastern bank, the Israelis had suddenly pushed their front forward ten miles, and in the process gained control of the important Tasa-to-Great Lake road. Egyptian and Israeli tank and infantry units had been battling in and around the Chinese Farm road junctions since 10 or 11 P.M. on Monday night. On the west, immediately opposite the Chinese Farm, at least four Egyptian tanks had been put out of action sometime between 1 A.M. and dawn. Most significant of all, four SAM sites in the area had ceased to function. It should have been obvious that, however small a party was actually across the canal, something a good deal larger was brewing up. Yet nobody formed this into a coherent picture, either in General Maamun's headquarters at Ismailia, nor in the war room run by Ismail and Shazli. And, to the south, it seems that the Third Army, under Major General Abdel-Moneim Mwassil, did not know that anything unusual was happening at all. Military sources in Cairo later claimed that Sharon had landed on a strip of bank held—more as a political gesture than in expectation of fighting—by Palestinian troops, men of the Ain Jalloud Brigade of the Palestine Liberation Army. The Egyptian regulars had some contempt for this ragtag-and-bobtail force. When the Palestinians by the canal radioed to divisional headquarters and, almost incoherent with excitement, reported the crossing, the Egyptians simply assumed the Palestinians were exaggerating as usual. (But Shazli says this is "not quite correct.")

Just as its own canal crossing had shown the virtues of the Egyptian Army, so its response to the Israeli crossing on October 15–16 cruelly exposed the faults. The Egyptian military machine does best in set pieces: working out and carrying through large and elaborate plans. It has competent administrators, and a sufficient number of men who can handle tanks, guns, and rocket launchers with courage and tactical skill. But in mobile warfare, the most vital of all commodities is information. "Speed of reaction in command decides the battle," Rommel had written in *The Rules of Desert Warfare*. Therefore, he said, "results of reconnaissance must reach the commander in the shortest possible time," and "commanders of motorized forces should be as near as possible to their troops." On both counts, the Egyptian Army failed in this war, as in previous ones.

There was still no equivalent to the incessant Israeli patrol and reconnaissance activity. Field intelligence—mapping enemy dispositions by analysis of radio intercepts, noting the unit affiliations of prisoners, and the like—remained an underdeveloped art. At the most basic level, the Egyptians simply did not tell each other what they were doing. Radios and field telephones were rarely used. Junior commanders simply fought the Israelis as and when the Israelis presented themselves, and gave no priority at all to making combat reports. Even divisional commanders—men equivalent to Sharon—had little or no independence of action. In effect, there were no command centers closer to the fighting than Ismail's war room. An Egyptian officer, asked after the war who had been the over-all *field* commander, said simply: "Ismail" —sitting underground in front of his multicolored maps. "I was half an hour from the Mitla Pass," an Egyptian tank officer told Drew Middleton of the New York *Times*, "just half an hour." Asked why he had not advanced to take the pass, the officer shrugged: "Ask them in Cairo," he said.

The paradox is that ordinary Egyptians are scarcely uncommunicative at the personal level. Lack of military communication stems from the fact that the Army, like most other Egyptian institutions, remains a hierarchical bureaucracy, in which promo-

tion—under Nasser's rule—depended upon seniority and orthodoxy, rather than upon individual claim to merit. Communication
within the system in peacetime follows elaborate formalistic procedures—involving, usually, large amounts of paperwork. Rather
than being modified by the strains of war, this attitude simply goes
into suspension. The result is total stultification of the initiative
of junior officers—precisely the cadre on whose wits mobile warfare depends. It is a question of the first importance for Israel
whether this will remain so, now that the upper levels of the
Egyptian Army are beginning to be penetrated by younger officers
promoted on merit. But it was still the case for the eighteen or so
crucial hours of October 16, while the Israeli crossing of the canal
was in its most vulnerable stage.

Ultimately, Sharon's bridgehead was saved by a single fact: To
mount an operation involving both the Egyptian Second Army
and the Third Army, it was necessary to circulate orders bearing
signatures from four different staff officers. Not until after dark on
Tuesday, October 16, did the Egyptians mount a coordinated
attack on the eastern approaches to the crossing point.

Late as it was, it nearly succeeded. The Second Army came
down from the north in full weight, and the Third Army came up
from the south. Their aim was to relieve and reinforce the Egyptian infantry holding out around the Chinese Farm Israeli enclave.
If that had been achieved, it would have been the end of the
Israeli plans—and of Sharon—because a serious volume of fire
from the farm area would make the crossing point untenable.

"Bren" Adan's division—the nominal crossing force—had now
fought its way down to the Chinese Farm, re-establishing its own
corridor as it came. It was Adan's forces and the gallant remnants
of Reshef's 14th Brigade who now fought the Battle of the Chinese Farm. Sharon, meanwhile, remained untouched on the west
bank—giving rise to Bar-Lev's acid comment: "It may be less
glamorous to fight for the holding of a bridgehead than to drive
your tanks into Africa. Nevertheless, the holding of a bridgehead
may be the crucial move in a battle." (To which Sharon has replied that the choice of Adan rather than himself to "invade"
Africa was politically motivated.)

All Tuesday night, a savage tank-to-tank conflict raged around
the Chinese Farm. Darkness cut down the value of the Egyptian

infantrymen's antitank missiles. But because ranges close in at night, it also cut down the Israeli tank crews' advantage in long-range gunnery. It was a complicated battle, in which the out-numbered Israeli tanks were under fire from two and sometimes three directions at the same time. But the engineers at the canal-side had no difficulty in appreciating its practical significance. "They closed off the road behind us," said a sergeant-navigator simply.

The Israeli engineers had stopped ferrying as darkness fell on Tuesday evening. But they still had not had time to put a bridge together. At dawn on Wednesday, while the tank battle raged on, they began ferrying again. Almost at once, Egyptian artillery in-tervened. "I was on the barge when we got to the bank on the other side," recalled a veteran of the battle. "We were taking two halftracks and a Jeep. The moment they got off, exactly, the shelling started. The first shell fell some twenty meters away in the water. The next shell fell beside the barge on the shore. . . ."

Sergeant Zvi from Netania found that Tuesday's "pastoral" at-mosphere was replaced on Wednesday by "a murderous pace." The Egyptians, he said, "had both shores ranged in. The moment a barge set out from one shore there'd be a terrifying barrage on it. When it got to the other bank they'd shell it again." Now men were being killed and wounded in considerable numbers. "I haven't seen the wounded of other countries," said the sergeant, "but I saw our injured. I saw wounded who refused to let people help them, walking with their infusion flasks [of blood or saline solution] in their hand to the collection station. . . . You see amputees; you see them writhing with pain, but they don't make a sound."

Soon the banks were littered with dead fish, killed by the shock waves of exploding shells. The barrage began to sink Israel's barges. "Two miracles occurred," recalled an Israeli lieutenant. "Our company commander got his foot caught in a crack in the barge [when it sank]. I think he was the only person to go down to the bottom of the canal and come up with nothing worse than a fractured foot. He went wild down there in the water—and that freed his foot. The other case: One of our navigators didn't know how to swim. . . . He began sinking [with the barge]. At that moment, a life belt floated out of the crew cabin and got hooked around him from below and brought him to the surface. . . ."

Desperate to cut off the bridgehead, Egyptian Chief of Staff Shazli took personal command on Tuesday evening of the assault on the Chinese Farm. He organized a scratch division from the remnants of the 21st, together with two armored battalions hurriedly brought north from Third Army formations at the southern end of the canal. And the force did push up as far as the southerly Y junction. But Shazli and his commanders were simply no match for Adan's gunners. The formation was torn to pieces; and Shazli himself later returned to Cairo in disgrace. He was not, after all, invincible.

Thus, slowly and bloodily, the Egyptian resistance at the Chinese Farm was reduced. More than one hundred Egyptian tanks were destroyed. And the fire at the crossing point began to slacken enough for the Israeli engineers to get the pontoons in position for their much-delayed bridge. Even so, artillery fire and occasional air strikes made it a dangerous and nerve-testing job. "We were under fire the whole time, very serious fire," recalled the officer who commanded the bridging teams. "Our boys were . . . a target for all the guns and planes in the neighborhood. . . . Everybody here lost a friend."

"When a plane comes down on you," said a soldier, "it's something frightening. Everybody who isn't shooting back at him dives for the ground with his head in the earth. But when our Mirages came in, they were shooting down MiGs one after the other. People . . . stood on the embankment, clapping like at a football match." Such air cover was possible because Sharon's raiders had now torn a hole fifteen miles wide in the SAM umbrella.

That, perhaps, was the best argument in favor of his defiance of Gonen. The Israeli pilots seized brilliantly the chances offered by the air space Sharon's raiding parties had cleared. A standard technique swiftly developed. The Israeli ground-attack aircraft would approach very low over Sinai, swoop up to gain height in the cone of air space now cleared of SAMs, then dive to put down a curtain of rocket and cannon fire for the Israeli forces around the perimeter of the bridgehead and the corridor to it. For the first time, Israeli tank commanders could call down air strikes to clear positions ahead of them. And as the Egyptians on the west bank faced once more the classic Israeli combination of armor and air strikes, they were once again unable to cope. Slowly, the Egyptians retreated and the bridgehead expanded.

Nonetheless, the fact was that a plan that had originally failed dramatically was essentially being bailed out by the fighting qualities of the Israeli rank and file. Around the middle of Wednesday, thirty hours behind schedule, the bridge was in place and the first of Adan's three tank brigades began to roll across, followed by two brigades of mechanized infantry.

Surprise, of course, had been totally lost, and for the rest of the week the bridge and its whole environment remained a perilous place. But the Egyptian attacks were distinguished more for their stubbornness than their coordination: Confusion in the Egyptian command continued to work powerfully for the Israelis. After Tuesday night's battle, the Egyptian chief military spokesman, Major General Izz ad-Din Mukhtar announced confidently that the Israeli force on the west bank had been cut off. This, it appears, was based on a claim from General Maamun in Ismailia that the Chinese Farm attack had achieved all its aims. But Shazli must have known the truth; by this stage, anyway, according to Sharon—whose men were listening in—the Egyptian communication system was "perverted by lies."

On Wednesday night, the Second Army's unhappy commander, Maamun, attempted an attack against the growing force established on the west bank, and was badly beaten. Now Ismail bitterly regretted having committed virtually all of Egypt's frontline armor to Sinai. When a Western diplomat asked one of Ismail's officers why Egypt did not move up its reserves against Sharon and Adan, the officer, near hysteria, replied: "Reserves, what reserves?" The survivors of the five hundred tanks Ismail had sent to the east bank could have been withdrawn once more. But Sadat vacillated for thirty-six hours before agreeing to that humiliation. And then, on War Minister Ismail's admission, "information was interrupted due to changes of responsibilities which we had made in some commands in the emergent circumstances." A few days later, it became known that General Maamun had suffered a heart attack and been replaced by Major General Abdul Moneim Khalil. Maamun was said to have been in poor health for some time and to have had a history of heart attacks.

At the same time, Shazli was dismissed as Egyptian Chief of Staff. After the war, with characteristic frankness, Sadat recounted what had happened. "When the Israeli forces made their counterthrust on October 16, I ordered General Shazli to go personally to Ismailia within ninety minutes to hold the Israelis within the limits we had already defined around the lake.

"I do not want to go into the details of the events that occurred during the next three days. But on Friday, October 19, the War Minister, General Ahmed Ismail, called me after midnight. I went to the command headquarters to find General Shazli collapsed. He was saying that the war was over, a disaster had struck, and that we had to withdraw entirely from Sinai. . . .

"I was afraid that Shazli's despair might demoralize other commanders in the operations room—which was Israel's main purpose of the operation. So I relieved General Shazli and appointed Lieutenant General Abdel Ghani el Gamasy in his place."

Sadat forgave Shazli his lapse, though. "The man had crossed the canal and stormed the Bar-Lev Line . . . This was Shazli's achievement. And the collapse he suffered later was only human."

Established at last on the west bank of the canal, what should Adan and Sharon now do? An apparently glamorous option would have been to drive deeper into Egypt, heading southwest until Cairo could be put under threat from artillery. To do so would have brought deep satisfaction to a great many ordinary Israelis, seeking emotional release after the first anxious days of Arab success. But in military terms, it would have been an insane gamble: a fifty-mile advance between two Egyptian armies, which had been battered but certainly not destroyed.

There were physical difficulties about going north up the canal, because of the "agricultural barrier" west of Ismailia: that is, the Ismailia Canal and the irrigation works built around it. To make a way through this, and cut off the northerly Second Army in Sinai from its base in Egypt, would be a long and costly job. It would require a northward advance of some forty miles, after which the whole right flank of that advance would have to be turned into a front capable of resisting a breakout attempt by the Second Army.

The best option was to wheel south and cut off the Third Army. The route lay over firm, open sand where the Israeli columns could make maximum speed. And better still, for some twenty miles the Israelis would have their left flank protected by the Bitter lakes—a barrier that neither side could cross in strength. Once in position to the south, the Israelis would only need to control a front of some fifteen miles between Shallufa and Suez in order to have the Third Army trapped.

Given the slenderness of Israel's resources, the southern thrust was clearly the correct move. But, clumsily aimed though they were, the Egyptian blows had slowed the Israelis. The chief responsibility for delay, however, lay within the Israeli Army itself. Sharon, of course, blames it on a failure of nerve in the higher command: a swifter backup on Tuesday, he says, would have made the vital difference. "We moved too late," he said. "They just didn't have the right picture at headquarters." Arguably, Sharon's bold response to the situation on Tuesday morning was tactically correct. All the same, it was his failure to get the bridge across on schedule that lost the vital twenty-four hours. By the time Bren Adan's tanks began to pick up speed for the long run south to Shallufa and Suez, time was running strongly against the Israeli Army and its hopes of total victory.

7. Enter the Oil Weapon

Israel was running out of time for two reasons. The superpowers were growing anxious over their involvement. And the world at large could not afford the war. In the second week of fighting, the "oil weapon" began to bear against Israel—indirectly, but with considerable effect. It could only be indirect, because Israel itself has no need of Arab oil—at any rate not while the Abu Rodeis oil wells on the west coast of Sinai remain in Israeli hands and the Shah of Iran is friendly. It was doubly indirect because the United States, Israel's one indispensable supporter, is of all major industrialized countries the least vulnerable to a Middle East oil embargo. Many of the countries that could be most seriously damaged by an embargo were already well disposed toward the Arabs before the war began—at least, insofar as the Arab aim was recovery of occupied territories rather than obliteration of the State of Israel. The theory, of course, was that pressure on Western countries in general would bring pressure upon the United States, and the United States would in turn bring pressure upon Israel to accept a cease-fire on terms favorable to the Arab cause.

It was the same method as the one used by the old woman in the nursery rhyme who made the water quench the fire, to make the fire burn the stick, to make the stick beat the dog, to make the dog bite the pig, because the pig would not go and she wanted to get home to supper. The trouble was that applying the method to international politics turned out to be a tricky and unpredictable business. Still, the United States could hardly claim it had not been warned.

Since the closing phases of World War II, U.S. policy in the Middle East had been founded upon two assumptions. The first was that the nations of the Middle East fell into two categories:

those with oil and those without. The second was that those Arab rulers with oil were, in the last analysis, more anti-Communist than they were anti-Zionist. Provided it was willing to prop up these oil sheiks, therefore—and so long as the struggle against Israel was Soviet-backed—the United States could also prop up Israel with impunity. For a generation, that policy worked. By the early 1970s, however, it was clear that this juggling act could not be sustained much longer. The Yom Kippur War did no more than hasten its collapse, though in dramatic fashion. That the United States at large—virtually all, bar a few policy makers in Washington and a handful of the more realistic oil company executives—was extraordinarily slow to foresee the consequences of this was due principally to a misassessment of the degree to which the United States controlled its own energy resources, rather than to any delusions about the Middle East.

The United States entered the Middle East in major fashion in 1928; obtained what was to become the Aramco (Arabian American Oil Company) concession in Saudi Arabia in 1933— by an order of magnitude, the most profitable single deal in modern history—and, ever since, had been conscious of the vital necessity of ensuring the availability of this oil to the Western Hemisphere. From 1943 onward, one of the main thrusts of President Roosevelt's foreign policy—particularly *vis-à-vis* the British Empire—had been to increase American influence in the Middle East. Indeed, he was under pressure from both the Joint Chiefs of Staff and his Secretary of the Interior, Harold Ickes, to go farther than he did to safeguard supplies from the area. And through the twenty-five years that followed, the United States successfully beat off all challenges to its hegemony over the richest oil reserves in the world—most notably by the overthrow, in a CIA-directed coup, of the attempt to nationalize Iranian oil in 1953. All this time, the oil companies—corporated empires so vast as to be virtually impregnable to pressure from the peoples from whose lands they were extracting this wealth—kept the price of oil steady at somewhat below two dollars a barrel. The importance that this cheap energy had for the economic growth of the West is incalculable.

While thus acknowledging the global strategic importance of the Middle East, however, the United States drew no political conclusions affecting its policies toward Israel. In the first place, the oil states showed no inclination to wield their oil reserves as a weapon of international power politics. And, even if they did, the United States was invulnerable to such pressure: It did not need Arab oil. Or so everyone thought.

True, as far back as 1950, a lonely handful had been drawing graphs of expected U.S. energy demand vs. expected supply and reaching worrying conclusions. By 1952, a presidential commission on American raw materials policy noted the "extraordinarily rapid rate at which we are utilizing our materials and energy resources." By 1966, one of the major oil companies, Atlantic Richfield, said bluntly in its annual report: "The nation faces the prospect of an energy gap."

But the graphs of doom had always been confounded. More oil had always been found, either inside the Americas or at least in parts of the world not controlled by potentially hostile Arabs. It seemed the natural order of things that this should continue. Certainly, the U. S. Government and U.S. industry behaved as if it would. Coal deposits, for example, constitute almost 90 per cent of the United States' total indigenous energy reserves; yet coal use—and the coal industry—declined steadily, until three quarters of U.S. energy needs were met by oil and its products. And what prodigiously growing needs they were. In the decade to 1973, the standard American car actually increased in bulk by more than a third of a ton—and gasoline consumption went up accordingly. The most significant social movement in America, the flight to the suburbs, was postulated on, utterly depended on, an indefinite future of cheap gasoline. Almost without thought, American consumer goods, too, were ever greedier in energy consumption. Color television sets require voltages more than a third above those for black-and-white sets. Frost-free refrigerators use 40 per cent more electricity than the ordinary kind. Trivial examples, except that they were replicated across the American economy.

By the early 1970s, the United States, with just 6 per cent of the world's population, accounted for 30 per cent of the world's energy consumption. It was calculated that, if the rest of the world consumed energy at the American rate, global resources would be exhausted by 2010. The fine calculation was almost certainly too pessimistic; the trend was still unmistakable.

The United States' own energy resources—at least of oil and natural gas—were certainly being exhausted. In 1970, output peaked from domestic U.S. oil wells. Output of domestic natural gas also peaked in 1970, and even declined in 1973—though politics partly accounted for that. A 1954 U. S. Supreme Court decision had ratified the U. S. Government's powers to control natural-gas prices; and, in obeisance to the cheap energy policy, successive administrations had priced gas so low that users wasted it while exploration waned.

Oil policy evidenced similar governmental confusion. A foreign tax offset system, in operation since 1950—U.S. oil companies could offset against domestic tax liability all oil royalty payments made to the producing countries—not only made foreign operations more profitable than domestic drilling, but also ensured that higher world oil prices meant higher after-tax profits. U.S. refinery construction was at a standstill: To keep pace with domestic demand for oil products, principally gasoline and heating oil, the United States needs to bring one major new refinery on stream each year. By 1973, no such refinery had been built for four years. The growing ecological lobby—appalled (to foreign eyes, rightly) by the devastation that corruption, poor to nonexistent planning, and the unheeding pursuit of wealth had wrought across the United States—had taken the argument to the other extreme and effectively blocked the construction of a new refinery at any of the suitable deep-water sites on the eastern seaboard. (U.S. refinery capacity actually declined slightly in 1972). The lobby had also blocked for three years the construction of the pipeline to bring oil down from Alaska's North Slope to the U.S. market.

Even in the short term, in other words, U.S. energy policy seemed almost calculated to increase U.S. dependence upon foreign sources. But while reform of the more blatant idiocies would restore an illusion of independence, in the medium to long term there was little that the United States could do—as a few statistics swiftly indicate. As late as spring 1970, the best U. S. Government and industry estimates put U.S. demand for oil in 1980 at no more than 18.5 million barrels a day (mbd; a barrel is 42 U.S gallons). Of this, it was reckoned that only 5 mbd would have to be imported. And it was considered dangerous if more than one tenth of those imports were to come from the Eastern Hemisphere

—basically, the Persian Gulf. Indeed, the preferred policy was that not more than one twentieth of the United States' oil imports should come from there.

The forecasts were hopelessly blithe. Between 1969 and 1972, U.S. oil imports increased by 52 per cent; its imports from the Middle East rose by 83 per cent. By 1973, U.S. domestic consumption was already just above 17 mbd and rising inexorably. To meet this demand, imports were already well over 6 mbd—and of these, a fifth was from the dreaded Eastern Hemisphere. At the end of 1970, in fact—within a year of the formulation of the forecasts and recommendations above—the U. S. State Department's oil experts had reworked the arithmetic to give a dauntingly different picture. Their forecasts were that the United States would by 1980 be importing 24 mbd (almost five times the previous estimate) and that two thirds of this would come from the wells of the Eastern Hemisphere. Even with maximum diversification of sources within the Eastern Hemisphere, it still looked as if the United States would by 1980 need to take at least 8 mbd and perhaps 11 mbd from the Middle East.

There was nowhere else to go. Known available Free World oil reserves—that is, excluding those of the Soviet Union and China—total about 500 billion barrels. At least 300 billion barrels of this lie beneath the Arab lands of the Middle East or North Africa, the overwhelming proportion of it around the Persian Gulf. And while the known global reserves will certainly increase, the chances are that the known Middle East reserves will increase as fast as, or even faster than, those anywhere else. (The vaunted Alaskan fields, for example, are *in total* equal to no more than a couple of years' *increment* in proven Middle East reserves.) Moreover, even within the Persian Gulf, the oil is unevenly distributed. Abu Dhabi is known to be lying on top of 22 billion barrels; the Shah of Iran is the fortunate custodian of 55 billion barrels; Kuwait has 78 billion. Saudi Arabia, by contrast, has known reserves of 157 billion barrels.

Saudi Arabia thus has nearly a quarter of the non-Communist world's oil supplies—and some Aramco experts reckon that the true Saudi reserves are 3 times that. To satisfy Western needs, Saudi extraction of these reserves was scheduled to increase from the 1970 level of 8 mbd to more than 20 mbd by 1980. But it was by no means clear why it was in Saudi Arabia's interest to do this. Its income was already so great that in 1972 it was able to spend only 30 per cent of its budget, the rest joining reserves that by 1973 stood at $3.2 billion. By 1980, should the Saudis agree to increase production to slake the West's demand, its 5 million people would be earning, even at constant oil prices, $100 million a day. In other words, even in peace, the Saudis might be tempted to cut back production, because such a move would so clearly be in the country's interests. The Arabs might not be able to drink oil—as the optimists in the West never failed to point out—but they could not eat dollars either. And in the 1970s they had been watching their currency reserves eaten away by inflation and devaluation.

By the spring of 1973, in fact, it did seem as if the United States could within a decade continue its policy of friendship and arms for Israel only at the greatest risk of disaster—because the man sitting on more oil than anyone else in the world, His Majesty Malik Faisal bin Abdul Aziz al-Saud, monarch of Saudi Arabia, was no longer likely to turn a blind eye. And with every day that passed, his power literally to cripple the United States and the West would increase.

Few men in history had enjoyed so remarkable an elevation to global power as King Faisal of Saudi Arabia. Born into total obscurity sixty-eight years ago, the third son of a then-unknown desert sheik, he suddenly appeared now as possible master of the world's destiny. By any reckoning, it was an astonishing transformation. When Faisal was born, neither Arab oil extraction nor the Saudi kingdom—nor, for that matter, Israel—existed; and Arabia itself was a land of such isolation and austerity that only three Europeans were known to have penetrated its interior in the whole of the previous century. Three years before Faisal's birth, his father, Abdul Aziz ibn Saud, had stormed the mud walls of the little town of Riyadh, put the defenders to the sword—in the name of Allah—and proclaimed the resurgence of his clan as the lords of central Arabia.

Faisal was over twenty before the state that his father created began to be recognized by the world at large. He was over forty before Saudi Arabia enjoyed its first modest windfall of oil revenues from Aramco; and he was nearly sixty when, in 1964, the pressure of events and his own peculiar qualities made him King, in place of his spendthrift brother, Saud.

Faisal's character was forged, therefore, in circumstances utterly remote from those in which he now found himself; yet it was this character that made his potential hold over the West so worrying.

A devout and ascetic Muslim in the desert tradition, Faisal learned to live and rule in poverty, as the laws of Islam and the tribe commanded, through a combination of universal faith and personal autocracy. As his father's Foreign Minister, however, traveling the world as a young man, he saw enough of other ways to realize their strength and his country's need to accommodate them. And he eventually became King because he seemed better fitted than others of his family to marry old ways and new.

His faith, meanwhile, made him at once anti-Zionist and anti-Communist—so much so, indeed, that at times he hardly seemed to distinguish between the two. As King of Saudi Arabia, he was also keeper of Islam's holiest places: Mecca and Medina. And as host to the annual worldwide pilgrimage to those shrines, he was bound to feel a special obligation to protect Muslim Arab rights in Palestine. Equally, as a true believer, and a traditional monarch as well, he abhorred the godlessness of communism and the political threats it encouraged in other secular revolutionary movements. These ingrained attitudes filled Faisal for many years with paralyzing inhibitions. At home he wanted Aramco's money to consolidate his rule and develop the country. Yet he would not permit this new prosperity to undermine the foundations of Islam on which he set such store. So he crawled toward the future more slowly than many thought wise, and clung to American friendship when other Arabs rejected it. And while he supported the Arab cause against Israel, his fear of communism, atheism, and revolution made him the scourge of more "progressive" Arab regimes, drove him to oppose the Soviet Union even after Moscow had become the chief sponsor of the Arabs, and forced him, once more, into the arms of Israel's friend and armorer, the United States. (His consequent reputation as an "arch reactionary" and "American stooge" helped fuel more than one attempt upon his throne.)

Ironically, it was Israel that first loosened some of Faisal's bonds. By its swift and humiliating victory over Nasser in 1967, Israel destroyed the Egyptian President's ability to seriously threaten Faisal's position. The Egyptian Army was withdrawn from Yemen, where it had been supporting a republican-revolutionary movement for the previous five years. Faisal in exchange joined Kuwait and Libya in underwriting Egypt's economy and renewed war effort. Simultaneously, Israel's annexation of the Old City of Jerusalem—third in holiness only to Mecca and Medina in Muslim eyes—deepened Faisal's anti-Zionist resolve into an obsessive determination to secure a "just settlement," above all, the restoration of Arab rights in Old Jerusalem. Instead of the archreactionary and American stooge, Faisal now became the indispensable and respected paymaster of the new Arab struggle. Then, at a personal level, Faisal's relationship with the devout, somewhat conservative, Sadat was a good deal closer than his ties had been with Nasser.

Meanwhile, the use of oil in this struggle was pressed upon Faisal by events elsewhere in the Arab world. In September 1969, white-bearded old King Idris of Libya was overthrown by a colonel in his Army, Muammar Qaddafi. The new President rapidly demonstrated that an Arab leader could be fanatically anti-Communist, as ardently anti-Zionist—and wield the power of oil to singular effect. It was Qaddafi who, in the spring of 1970, moved to cut back Libyan oil production in the name of conservation. It was Qaddafi who at the same time demanded of the oil companies the first major increase in oil prices in two decades. And it was Qaddafi who, by the spring of 1971, had perfected his "salami tactics" of picking on the most vulnerable of the oil companies operating in Libya to such effect that oil company solidarity—hitherto impregnable—was finally smashed. And as, one by one, the companies settled, it was Qaddafi who, to spur them on, threatened to cut off supplies.

Qaddafi's tactics electrified the other oil-producing countries—not merely because the tactics demonstrated how to get more cash, but because they showed up the rulers of those countries as pusillanimous in their demands to date. On their mettle, the Gulf producers promptly pushed through a rival price increase in February 1971. Libya at once embarked upon another round. Up the spiral went. To Washington, however, the ominous nature of these developments was not confined to the problem they posed of how the rest of the world could pay what would clearly soon be monstrous oil import bills. The process had finally demonstrated to the eleven members of the Organization of Petroleum Exporting Countries (OPEC) that against a determined and united assault, the West was powerless. Since OPEC's member states—seven of them Arab—controlled among them 90 per cent of the Free World's known oil reserves, this was scarcely surprising. The surprise was that it had taken so long to translate potential into actual power.

Libya, at least, was now determined to use this power against Israel and its most powerful backer. Qaddafi's Prime Minister, Abdel Jalloud, made the threat explicit in the autumn of 1973. Referring contemptuously to "Nixon and his gang," Jalloud said: "We don't want Japan, Europe, or America to suffer a cold winter. But neither do we want our oil or its profits to go to the United States, where they are transformed into destructive weapons again us." It seemed improbable that the other Arab producers would not follow suit. As one American expert, James Akins—State Department energy policy director now turned ambassador to Saudi Arabia—said: "This time the wolf is here."

It was almost certain that the one oil producer with the power to hurt the United States, King Faisal, would join a concerted Arab campaign. He had been warning American officials for two years, in private, that the United States must alter its stand on Israel. To Ambassador Akins, Faisal pointed out that after World War II, the Arab countries had looked to the United States as the land of freedom: "You have lost all of this," he said. "One country after another has gone. Libya and Iraq were pro-Western monarchies. Now Qaddafi is anti-West and the Communists are penetrating into the Arab world." The reason, Faisal said, was the United States' one-sided backing of Israel.

In the spring of 1973, Faisal even gave an interview to U.S. television, in itself an unusual event, to convince the United States of his seriousness. His message was blunt: "We do not wish to place any restrictions on our oil exports to the United States, but America's complete support of Zionism against the Arabs makes it extremely difficult for us to continue to supply U.S. petroleum needs and even to maintain friendly relations with America."

Faisal's leverage was immeasurably strengthened by the United States' predicted need for not merely the maintenance of Arab oil supplies but also their vast increase by 1980. In the long run, Faisal did not have to impose anything as dramatic as an oil embargo. All he need do was to hold Saudi production steady. As Faisal's oil minister, Ahmed Yamani, explained in Washington in the spring of 1973: "What we should do [in our own interests to conserve our reserves] is to produce exactly what we need to finance internal development. If you want me to produce more, I will only hurt myself. If you are not ready to help me, why should I hurt myself to help you?" Yamani, as a State Department official observed, was playing for "real marbles." Nor could it be held, so far as the State Department could see, that Faisal was being unreasonable. "What Faisal is asking for is a little balance in U.S. policy," one official said at the beginning of September. "He used to feel he had a lot of friends in Washington. But now all he reads in the papers is about additional U.S. economic and military aid to Israel."

That, in general, had been the background to the gloomy study of the United States' Middle East policy options that Kissinger's National Security Council staff prepared through January 1973. It was also the thinking behind that intelligence assessment produced in May by the State Department's Intelligence and Research Bureau, forecasting that if war did break out in the Middle East—a "45 per cent chance"—then disruption of Arab oil supplies was to be expected.

But U.S. energy policy, too, was paralyzed by Watergate. That INR assessment was incorporated into a National Intelligence Estimate, a formal study embodying the views of the whole intelligence community, which was sent to the White House. Nothing happened. Though Nixon had previously shown himself very conscious of the United States' energy problems, yet, from the end of March 1972, when Watergate burst, until the end of June 1973 —when the President belatedly appointed one John Love as "energy czar"—no steps to avert the impending disaster were taken. And Love was powerless: In five months in office, he saw Nixon alone only four or five times. And John Ehrlichman—who, as Nixon's chief advisor on domestic affairs, was Love's conduit to the President—later acknowledged: "Love didn't have the levers available to him."

Only on September 9–10, 1973, did Nixon at last call a full-scale White House conference to review the United States' energy position. The predictable conclusion was that a crash program to re-establish U.S. independence of resources was required. The United States ran the risk, Nixon afterward acknowledged, of being "at the mercy of the producers of oil in the Middle East." His plan, he said, aimed at energy self-sufficiency within three to five years—though the sum of measures he proposed seemed unlikely to achieve that. Unwisely, however, Nixon then tried to bluster. Should the Arabs endeavor to exert pressure, he warned, the oil-consuming countries might themselves take joint action in retaliation. It was an empty threat, at least two years too late to be feasible—as, just a month later, the Arabs proceeded to demonstrate.

When the Yom Kippur War began, the Arab producers were in a position to wield the oil weapon almost at once—for the oil ministers of OPEC had just begun to bargain a massive price increase at a series of meetings with the oil companies in Vienna. But although the OPEC demands stiffened somewhat after fighting began, the Saudi oil minister, Yamani—heading the OPEC delegation—stressed that they were there to "talk oil, not war." And actions in the Middle East appeared to indicate some disunity among the Arabs, certainly an unwillingness to go too far, too fast in unsheathing the oil weapon. At the outbreak of war, for example, Iraq promptly nationalized the minority U.S. interest in the Basrah Petroleum operations in southern Iraq, but gave informal assurances that the two U.S. companies involved, Exxon and Mobil, could have continued access to the oil, though only at market prices. To the same two companies, Egypt actually offered to clear the way for a special plane to bring their negotiators to Cairo to sign up Mediterranean offshore rights earmarked for them earlier in the year. (Egypt also pressed on with the finalizing of a massive Suez pipeline deal with a firm of U.S. engineers.) In Saudi Arabia, meanwhile, the worst indicated to Exxon, one of the four U.S. companies in Aramco, was that Faisal was thinking of cutting Saudi production from 8.5 million barrels a day to 7 mbd unless the United States changed its Middle East policy—a serious enough threat, but scarcely all-out economic warfare.

It was, in fact, pressure from Kuwait—not hitherto noted as one of the most active participants in the struggle against Israel—that finally propelled the Arabs down the road to economic confrontation. On Tuesday, October 9, the Kuwaiti Council of Ministers—under heavy pressure from their own Assembly—announced that they were organizing a meeting of Arab producers to discuss the role of oil in the conflict. The Persian Gulf "chapter" of OPEC was already scheduled to meet in Kuwait on Wednesday, October 17. In spite of the presence of the non-Arab Iranians, this would be clearly a suitable time for the Arabs to produce their manifesto. The day after the Kuwait *démarche,* Saudi and Egyptian oil experts began preliminary talks on the form in which the oil weapon might be used.

Still, Faisal tried to avert a clash. In a final effort to persuade his old allies, Faisal sent his Foreign Minister and close friend Omar Saqqaf to Washington on Thursday, October 11. Saqqaf carried with him an urgent note from Faisal to Nixon, requesting clarification of the United States' position and a warning that oil cuts would follow if it had not changed. Kissinger met Saqqaf the next day, Friday, October 12, and tried to reassure him. But by now, Kissinger's last hopes of winning a swift cease-fire were fading before Sadat's refusal to budge. A major resupply effort to Israel looked inevitable. The Americans suddenly realized that the Saudis were about to impose the threat Faisal had warned of for the previous two years. So there could be no misunderstanding, the Kuwaiti ambassador in Washington, Salem al-Sabah, spelled out the threat publicly: "We intend to withold oil from any nation which supports the Israeli aggression."

The crucial oil meeting was held in Riyadh on Monday, October 15, two days before the producers were due to gather in Kuwait. At just about the time that Sharon and his officers were getting ready to cross the Suez Canal, an Egyptian delegation arrived in the Saudi capital for talks with Yamani, Faisal's oil minister. The purpose of the meeting was to ensure that Egypt, the major Arab political power, and Saudi Arabia, the biggest oil producer, would turn up in Kuwait preaching the same line. There had, in fact, been months of discussion between Egypt and the Saudis on the possible uses of the oil weapon. The first joint study groups seem to have begun work on the topic around January 1973 after a flurry of contacts between Faisal and Sadat. But not all differences had apparently been resolved.

Now the Egyptians, led by Oil Minister Hilal, wanted to go farther than the Saudis would agree. But both sides were prepared to be fairly moderate—or, at any rate, moderate by the standards of what actually began to happen a few days and weeks later. But then, Sheik Ahmed Zaki Yamani is not, by any possible account, one of the world's radicals. He studied law at New York University and Harvard, and at thirty-two he was serving on the board of Aramco. Although twenty years younger than King Faisal—Yamani was forty-three—he is just as much a Moslem conservative: his relationship with the King is said to be one of "father and son." It was largely at Yamani's insistence that the Saudi-Egyptian talks ended with an agreement merely to go for 5 per cent monthly cutbacks in oil production, plus a program of selective embargoes. It was a cautious policy and one that allowed considerable flexibility for negotiation between individual countries.

Nothing was to be said about this plan until after the meeting in Kuwait. Unfortunately, there was already a certain amount of confusion in the air when the Arab oil delegations went into session at the Kuwait Sheraton around 11 A.M. on Wednesday, October 17. And by nightfall, it was almost total; for during the small hours of Wednesday, the Gulf members of OPEC (five Arab states plus Iran) had already announced through their Iranian chairman that they were demanding a 70 per cent rise in the posted price for crude oil. (This was in response to the companies' request for an adjournment of the Vienna meetings.) Throughout the day, the distinction between this continuing attempt of *all* oil-producing countries to get more money for their oil, and the immediate attempt of the *Arab* oil producers to affect the outcome of the Yom Kippur War became steadily more blurred. So did the distinction between the Organization of Petroleum Exporting Countries (OPEC) and the Organization of Arab Petroleum Exporting Countries (OAPEC). Several reporters stated that the OAPEC production cuts had been announced through the Iranian chairman of the Gulf OPEC. The Iranians, of course, far from cutting off any Western oil supplies, are major suppliers to

Israel; and the entire Iranian delegation tactfully left town as soon as their business with price negotiations was over.

Nor did the crucial communiqué make things altogether clear when it was finally produced around 9:30 P.M. There was only one copy of it, hastily handwritten in Arabic. Some essential phrases were lightly crossed out and others penciled in. When the two flimsy sheets of lined writing paper were grabbed from the OAPEC spokesman, they were put through the hotel copying machine for distribution to those journalists who could read Arabic. But the alterations did not show up well on the copying paper. Thus many reporters failed to notice that at the last moment the OAPEC members had softened the basis on which they would be prepared to resume full oil deliveries—substituting the vaguer term "United Nations Resolutions" for a specific mention of Resolution 242.

That was not the only important provision that did not show up clearly. An arrow pointed to the inclusion of the phrase "and the legitimate rights of the Palestinian people must be restored." This had been added only after members of the Kuwait Palestine Liberation Organization heard that the draft being discussed did not mention them, and descended on the Sheraton by taxi to complain to the oil ministers. Even so, the point was mostly missed; and none of the oil ministers was prepared to stay behind and help with the interpretation of the communiqué. Indeed, Sheik Yamani, its chief architect, was en route back to Riyadh in his private jet even before the document was issued.

But however it was reported, the document's moderation was a victory for the Saudis. The Arab radicals wanted to go much farther. Iraqi Oil Minister Sadoon Hammadi had demanded "total nationalization of all American oil interests; withdrawal of all funds invested by Arab States in the United States . . . breaking of diplomatic relations between all Arab oil producers and the United States" Libya's Izz al-Din al-Mabruk, a London-trained lawyer, once one of King Idris' civil servants but now Qaddafi's nationalization expert, wanted expropriation extended to all foreign-owned oil companies, not just American ones. Belaid Abdessalam of Algeria, who had run economic affairs for the FLN during the Algerian War, held that a 5 per cent cutback would not hit Europe hard enough.

There was no stopping the combination of Saudi oil power and Egyptian political clout, however. The communiqué, once the text was established, emerged as brief and cautiously worded. It asserted that the Arabs were under no obligation to accommodate the world by pumping out their finite reserves of oil at a pace dictated by others. Then came the immediate diplomatic point: "The international community is under an obligation to implement UN resolutions and to prevent the aggressor from reaping the fruits of his aggression." More bluntly, the industrial nations were expected to force Israel to withdraw. As one of the delegates at the Sheraton said, "This time, neutrality is not enough. Countries must be positively for us. Those who are not for us are against us." Those words were to be translated within a few days into concrete moves against Holland and Japan.

The document went on to say explicitly that the members of the "international community"—which really meant Western Europe and Japan—must not only bring their own pressure to bear on Israel over the question of the occupied territories, they must also persuade the Americans to do likewise. Only then would the oil flow freely again. After this threat of the stick, a carrot was offered—one that was immediately to be munched by Britain, France, and Spain: "Any friendly state which has extended or shall extend effective material assistance to the Arabs" would get as much oil as before the cutback. And this exceptional treatment would be extended to "any state which takes important measures against Israel."

The statement ended with a conciliatory appeal for support, addressed to the American people. That was a Saudi addition to the communiqué, for most of the other producers had already indicated that they intended to boycott the United States completely within a few days. But the Saudis still hoped, despite the fact that the United States was now airlifting arms to Israel, to win some kind of concession from their American friends. Sadoon Hammadi of Iraq, in fact, regarded the communiqué as so feeble that he refused to sign it.

Alone among the Arab oil producers, King Faisal wanted to give the Americans time. Privately, he had assured James Akins, U.S. ambassador in Riyadh, that he would in any event not embargo Saudi shipments to the United States until the end of

November. America could have six weeks grace to end the war by one means or another.

While the oil ministers were meeting in Kuwait, in fact, the Saudi foreign minister, Omar Saqqaf, was still in Washington talking to President Nixon. The talks, which also included the foreign ministers of Kuwait, Algeria, and Morocco, appeared to be remarkably cordial. When they were over, Saqqaf described Nixon as "the man who had put an end to the Vietnam War" and as a figure who might well play an important role in a settlement for the Middle East. Nixon himself said that there would be a settlement, which would be "peaceful, just, and honorable." Saqqaf, as the United States must or should have known, is so close to Faisal that the King would expect the minister to be treated as an extension of himself. On the basis of Nixon's assurances, therefore, the Saudis felt that the Americans, if not on the point of changing their policy, were at least not going to exacerbate the situation.

Then came the bombshell. On Thursday, October 18, the day after he had talked with Saqqaf, President Nixon asked Congress to provide $2.2 billion for "emergency military aid" to Israel. From the American viewpoint, this was little more than the routine financial arrangement necessary to cover the military aid that was already being sent to Israel, the dispatch of which had been announced before Saqqaf met the President. Faisal, however, saw it as a personal betrayal. (And his fury was only increased when the United States presented him with an *aide-mémoire* of Nixon's assurances to Saqqaf that the Saudis regarded as a totally distorted account: "That filthy document," Faisal privately called it.)

On Friday, October 19, the Saudi Royal Cabinet went into a lengthy emergency session. The next day, October 20, it was announced that all oil exports to the United States were being suspended forthwith and "at the instructions of King Faisal . . . a *Jihad* [Holy War] is called. As *Jihad* is the duty of all Moslems, every citizen in this country is called on to back the freedom fight." The Royal Court said that the abrupt change in policy was due to "increasing American military aid to Israel."

The significance of the statement was not confined to the loss of the United States' 638,500 barrels of Saudi oil a day—although no other Middle Eastern contribution really matters to the United States. Far more important was the fact that, as a Beirut oil consultant put it, "If Saudi Arabia moves to B, then every other oil producer must move at least that far, if not to C." The most conservative power in the Middle East had at last moved to a starkly anti-Western position.

Faisal did not see it in those terms. He was acting in accord with that old Arab proverb, "The enemy of my enemy is my friend: the friend of my enemy is my enemy." In the last resort, Israel was the enemy that counted for him—as it was for all the Arab leaders. And if the United States or any other nation wished to be Israel's friend in war, it would have to be Faisal's enemy. It was, in short, the law of the desert that prevailed—as, in Faisal's life, it nearly always had done. For however astonishing his elevation from the role of unknown Arabian princeling to that of a ruler with worldwide power, it was not Faisal but the world around him that had changed. By his own lights he remained as faithful as ever to the beliefs of his own harsh land—and if that meant his personal loyalties could run deep, it also meant that his hostility, once aroused, would indeed be implacable. The game was becoming dangerous for the backers and spectators as well as the players. The necessity for both superpowers to bring it to a halt was becoming too powerful to be denied.

FIVE

THE SUPERPOWERS
CALL IT QUITS

1. Kosygin Has to Hurry

The Soviet Union had become convinced of the need for a cease-fire after a very few days of fighting. Indeed, this conviction was so powerful that it had caused the Soviet Union to imagine, or at least hope, that President Sadat was ready to talk peace before that was in fact the case—a misjudgment that, as described earlier, led to considerable loss of sleep by President Sadat and Sir Philip Adams, the British ambassador in Cairo; and, rather more significantly, opened a rift between the British Government and Henry Kissinger that would take months to close.

Basically, the Soviet desire for peace was no more than a view that the Egyptians should quit while they were ahead. This sprang, no doubt, from a profound pessimism about the ability of the Egyptian Army to deal with a powerful Israeli counterattack. The Soviets feared, correctly, that the longer the war went on the more likely it became that the Egyptians would suffer major military reverses, which would lead in turn to incalculable prospects of escalation. By Tuesday, October 16, the Soviet Union was ready to apply pressure on its own "client," Egypt. To judge from the evidence available, what happened between the two super-powers over the days that followed was not so much a detailed bargaining over diplomatic points as a simple process in which American anxiety grew rapidly to match that of the Soviet Union —producing, by the weekend, a situation in which their joint approach to the Security Council was not merely possible but inevitable. The superpowers decided, in effect, to call it quits. As both of them speedily discovered, the problem was then to persuade their respective clients to see it that way.

The Danes were, to their surprise, the first witnesses of the Soviet Union's mounting concern over the Middle East. By long-standing invitation, the Danish Premier, Anker Jorgensen, was in

Moscow as the second week of war got under way. It was thus to Jorgensen that Soviet party leader Leonid Brezhnev said earnestly: "Détente and better relations between the two social systems is still the cornerstone of Soviet foreign policy." And it was Jorgensen's appointment with Prime Minister Alexei Kosygin that was canceled at the last moment on Tuesday, October 16. Kosygin, the Kremlin said apologetically, had gone on an "urgent mission." He had flown in secret to Cairo.

Why Kosygin set off in such a hurry is unclear. True, it was midday Tuesday Moscow time when news of Sharon's crossing began to seep through the Egyptian military machine. Perhaps the Soviet mission in Cairo picked that up. But why should the Soviet Union have been perturbed by what the Egyptians were at that stage calling a "minor infiltration?"

There is a further possibility: Had Moscow learned of Egypt's growing military plight from its own satellite surveillance? The Soviet Union's Cosmos satellites shared the disadvantage of the Agena D that the United States had on station: Their pictures could only be recovered when the satellite landed. But the Soviet Union surmounted this problem during the war by putting up a leap-frogging series of six satellites, bringing each down after six days. And the third of that series, Cosmos 598—launched from the Archangel pads on October 10—was recovered on October 15. By the next day, therefore, the Kremlin was in a position at least to work out from those pictures the extent of the disaster that had overtaken Egyptian armor in Sinai on Sunday, October 14. Support for this hypothesis is the fact that several days later, officials in the Kremlin remarked that the Egyptians had tried to "mislead" Kosygin and his party about the true state of military affairs. "There had been a Stalingrad in Sinai and they would not admit it," the Soviets said.

Certainly, Kosygin wasted no time. He arrived in Cairo at 5 P.M. on Tuesday. And, starting that evening and going through to the night of Thursday, October 18, he had five sessions with Sadat. They were all shrouded in deep secrecy, and Sadat has declined to speak of them since. But there is one source that suggests the settlement Kosygin was trying to achieve—may even have gotten—before Adan disrupted matters.

The Egyptian position was that there would be no cease-fire

until the Israelis agreed to withdraw to the pre-1967 lines. It was a fine, bold negotiating position. But it was based on what Henry Kissinger was so delicately to call "a misassessment of the military situation."

Also in Cairo while Sadat and Kosygin met was Milos Minic, the Foreign Minister of Yugoslavia. Yugoslavia has traditionally close links with Egypt, dating back twenty years to the time when Tito, Nasser, and Jawaharlal Nehru developed the principle of nonalignment. And an immediately practical reason for Minic's presence was that the idea had been canvassed at the United Nations—seemingly by Egypt—that the Yugoslavs and possibly the Indians should provide a large part of any peace-keeping force that might be required for the Middle East. It is likely, therefore, that the Cairo correspondent of the official Yugoslav news agency Tanjug knew what he was talking about when, on Friday morning, he reported the results of Kosygin's trip. According to Tanjug, Kosygin had obtained Egyptian agreement to a four-point plan that would stop the fighting—but at the price of bringing the superpowers very directly into the arena.

The first of the four points modified the precondition on which Egypt would be prepared to stop fighting. Instead of total Israeli withdrawal to the pre-1967 borders, it became withdrawal to those borders "with minor corrections." It was scarcely a large concession —but then, nor could anyone say that the cease-fire lines that Egypt had to accept three days later were really "minor corrections." Still, in the context of Sadat's confident speech to the People's Assembly on Tuesday, as Kosygin flew in, this represented movement of a kind.

At all events, Kosygin was sufficiently confident that in Washington, on the morning of Thursday, October 18, the Soviet ambassador, Dobrynin once again went to see Kissinger. On the basis of fresh instructions that had emanated from Cairo—given the time lag, they must have been sent after Kosygin's two meetings with Sadat the day before—Dobrynin pressed once more for U.S. help in arranging a cease-fire on the basis of an Israeli agreement to withdraw to more or less the pre-1967 lines. But whereas all previous Soviet proposals during the conflict had envisaged as part of the long-term settlement an *immediate* Israeli withdrawal from the occupied territories, now Dobrynin talked of a withdrawal in stages. Kissinger simply turned down the idea. He had nothing against it in principle. He merely told Dobrynin that, with the war now going their way, the Israelis were very unlikely to accept it. As Dayan had just said: "Every day that passes is to Israel's benefit." Sadat had missed his chance. Dobrynin telexed Kissinger's reply directly to the Soviet Embassy in Cairo.

By the time it reached Kosygin, the Soviet premier had learned the magnitude of Egypt's mess on the west bank. (Western diplomats in Cairo say that Sadat confessed to him that Thursday morning. But Kosygin probably had his own suspicions by then. He had telephoned the Kremlin several times during his visit.) Kosygin, appalled by the news, seems to have done the only thing he could. He appears to have told Sadat to hang on militarily at all costs while the Soviet Union tried to get the best cease-fire deal now possible. Then, having briefed Brezhnev in Moscow about the situation—leaving him to talk to the United States—Kosygin took off for Damascus and Baghdad, presumably to see what sort of terms he could now pressure Syria and Iraq into accepting.

As Moscow prepared to take action, the Soviets genuinely seem to have thought that some deal along the lines that Tanjug had outlined was still possible, given U.S. help. The problem was the price that, according to Tanjug, Kosygin had been forced to pay to win Sadat's concession on ultimate borders; for the remaining three points of the neat package Kosygin and Sadat had agreed on, before the disaster on the west bank, apparently said that the borders of the conflicting states would be guaranteed by the two superpowers and by the Security Council; that there should be international forces to police the cease-fire; and that the Soviet Union and the United States would safeguard the borders "by virtue of their physical presence, separately or in concert with other parties." It was, presumably, the best Kosygin could do; but, if so, it was an ominous indication of the Soviet anxiety to end the conflict by any means. Just one week later the very question of the introduction of a superpower military presence in the Middle East was to precipitate a quasinuclear confrontation between the United States and the Soviet Union. And even as Kosygin flew out of Cairo, a flight of Soviet Antonovs was bringing in three hundred Soviet military personnel—to reconstruct, if possi-

Two features characterized the war: massive conventional tank battles, **the biggest since World War II**; and the use of missiles, the first time they have played a dominant part in a major conflict. There is no doubt that in tank-to-tank confrontations, the Israelis more than held their own, despite being outnumbered, and the next few pages analyze why. Yet, for a long time, Israel's traditional virtuosity with armor and air support was severely limited by the Arab missile arsenal, described in the second pictorial essay.

THE TANK BATTLE: The numerical balance as the fighting began

According to estimates published shortly before the war, the Egyptians began with 1,650 Soviet T-54 and T-55 tanks (the two differ only in small details) designed in the midfifties, plus about 100 of the main modern Soviet battle tank, the T-62. The Syrians had about 1,100 T-54/55s and an unknown number of T-62s, perhaps another 400. (Between them they also had some 300 World War II-vintage T-34s, though these seem mostly to have been dug into static posi-

tions as supplementary artillery.) As the war progressed, Iraq committed up to 250 of its T-54/55s, and Jordan about 100 British-made Centurions. So the total effective Arab commitments was well over 3,000 tanks.

The Israelis had about 1,700 tanks at the start of the war, about half of them Centurions and the remainder mostly American Patton M-48s (fifties vintage, but mostly later models with 105mm guns), with some up-to-date M-60s. They also used in a battle-tank role about 150 Super Shermans (a World War II American veteran that the Israelis themselves had upgraded by adding a large 105mm French gun) and some remodeled Soviet T-54/55s that they had captured from the Egyptians in the Six-Day War and equipped with British-made 105mm guns.

These figures, based on estimates by the London-based Institute of Strategic studies, dated September 1973 and updated by U.S. Pentagon estimates, do not include tanks delivered from the United States and the Soviet Union during the war. These deliveries are believed to have further increased the numerical balance in favor of the Arab countries, particularly Syria. But how effective the additional arms shipments were depended to some extent on the availability of highly trained crews and maintenance teams, which were in short supply on both sides, but particularly so in the Arab armies.

The Arabs' numerical advantage must also be weighed—as we shall see on the following pages—by examining the relative effectiveness of the tanks' armaments and exploring how well the different types of tanks are adapted to fighting in hot desert terrain. The totals here show the crude odds that Israel faced, even excluding the Arabs' aged T-34s, and the entry, late in the war, of the Iraqi and Jordanian contingents.

ISRAELI

American Sherman
(M4A3E8)
with French 105mm gun
Total: 150

ARAB

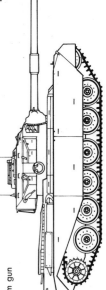

British Centurion
with standard 105mm gun
Total: 850

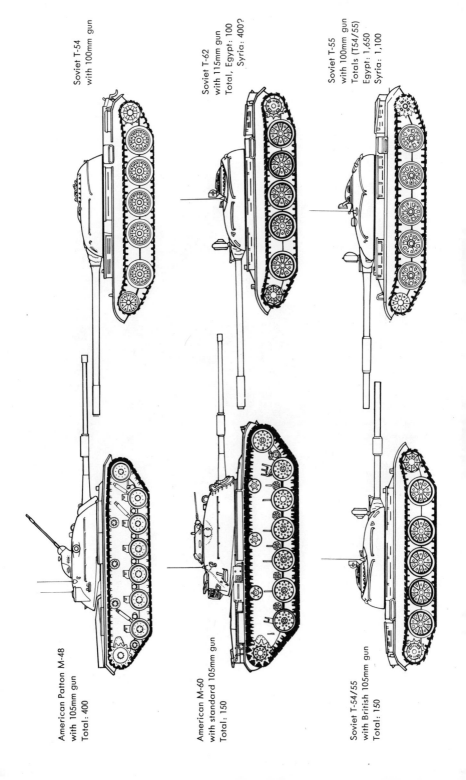

Soviet T-54
with 100mm gun

Soviet T-62
with 115mm gun
Total, Egypt: 100
Syria: 400?

Soviet T-55
with 100mm gun
Totals (T54/55)
Egypt: 1,650
Syria: 1,100

American Patton M-48
with 105mm gun
Total: 400

American M-60
with standard 105mm gun
Total: 150

Soviet T-54/55
with British 105mm gun
Total: 150

THE TANK BATTLE: The ammunition

Loading up a Centurion tank in Golan. The ammunition is 105mm APDS (armor-piercing discarding-sabot). The pointed tip of its thin penetrating bolt of hard heavy metal is clearly visible.

First published picture of the latest Soviet 115mm ammunition inside a captured Syrian T-62. The long thin rounds are APFSDS (see next diagram), which fly and penetrate like a massive arrow.

During a brief pause from battle near the Golan front: A crew member of an Israeli M-48 sits on his tank holding a 105mm HEAT (high-explosive antitank) shell, as used in NATO tanks.

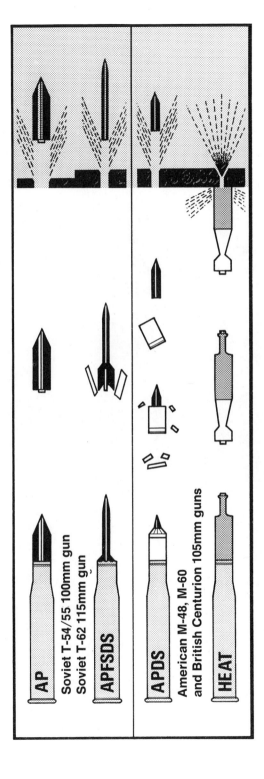

AP

Soviet T-54/55 100mm gun
Soviet T-62 115mm gun

APFSDS

APDS

American M-48, M-60
and British Centurion 105mm guns

HEAT

The diagram shows how different types of ammunition work. The vast majority of Arab tanks (Soviet T-54/55s) have only simple AP (armor-piercing) ammunition —a solid, full-caliber shot of steel. Because there is no way of concentrating its energy, the penetration through armor plate is only half that of other types. However, the few modern Soviet T-62s used by the Arabs did have the more sophisticated APFSDS (armor-piercing fin-stabilized discarding-sabot) ammunition. As this leaves the smooth 115mm barrel, the "sabot" (a sort of lightweight packing) is stripped off by air resistance to reveal a long, thin "arrow" of hard, heavy metal. Almost all of the energy from the gun is thus concentrated into a smaller diameter, greatly increasing penetration. APDS (armor-piercing discarding-sabot) used by the Israelis works on a similar principle. Stability in flight, however, depends on the spin imparted by the gun's rifled barrel, rather than on fins, so the central bolt cannot be quite so thin. At long range there is little to choose between the two kinds of stabilization, since the drag from fins slows down the Soviet shot.

The Israelis' American tanks also use HEAT (high-explosive antitank) shells, which employ a quite different idea. The shells are hollow and contain high explosive. When this detonates at first contact with the target, it "implodes" onto a cone of copper inside the shell. The cone is shaped in such a way that it turns into a thin jet of molten copper, moving at huge velocity, which literally hoses its way through the armor plate. HEAT charges which do not depend upon velocity of impact are thus also used in slow-moving antitank missiles.

THE TANK BATTLE: Which tanks were best suited to the desert terrain?

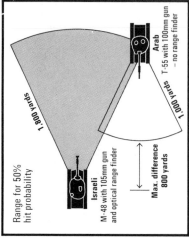

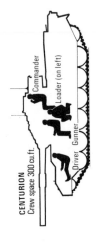

Israeli
M-48 with 105mm gun and optical range finder

Arab
T-55 with 100mm gun – no range finder

Range for 50% hit probability

1,800 yards

1,000 yards

Max. difference 800 yards

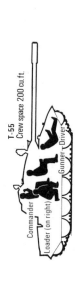

T-55
Crew space 200 cu.ft.

Commander

Loader (on right)

Gunner

Driver

CENTURION
Crew space 300 cu.ft.

Commander

Loader (on left)

Gunner

Driver

From the first foothills of the mountain passes, a panorama of the classic desert terrain of the big Sinai armored battles (the smoke rising on the horizon is from the barrage on the canal). Fighting on these rolling sand dunes requires tanks with special characteristics, illustrated on this and following pages. There is no

doubt that the British and American tanks—bred partly from the experience of the North African campaigns in World War II—are better adapted to desert fighting than Soviet tanks, conceived for the different vistas, climate, and types of cover found in Europe.

Range (see right) is crucially important in desert fighting. Apart from the characteristics of their different types of ammunition, the Soviet tanks rely purely on visual judgment for range-finding. The American tanks, by contrast, have a sophisticated device of optical prisms for estimating range, while the British Centurions have a neat and simple system of zeroing in with tracer bullets from a range-finding machine gun before the big round is fired (the system thus corrects for side winds). The net result is a gain of up to half a mile at long range, for comparable accuracy.

Desert heat is another factor. Soviet tanks tend to overheat in the desert, and are often used with their engine louvers vulnerably open. But the main effect is the subjective one on the crew, who are cramped into a smaller, hotter space in Soviet tanks (see scale drawing at right). The consequent fatigue can critically affect firing accuracy and other technical functions.

THE TANK BATTLE: The tactics of fighting in the desert

American M-48

8' 7"

Soviet T-55

7' 11"

British Centurion

8' 7"

In a fold in the Sinai sand dunes: an Israeli Super Sherman in "hull down" position.

Soviet tanks, built for the plains of Europe, are designed with low, rounded profiles to present the minimum target to enemy guns. The scale drawings show the contrast in height between the T-54/55 and the larger Western tanks. This Soviet geometry involves a crucial disadvantage, particularly in desert terrain.

Because of its low turret, the Soviet gun can depress only four degrees, compared with ten degrees by its Western counterparts. The diagrams show the result. Tank commanders like to keep "hull down" as long as possible (i.e., with the tank hull out of enemy view). As can be seen, a Soviet tank with its limited gun depression becomes much more exposed when it moves up a sand dune to firing position.

Such considerations gave the Israelis a marked advantage in tank-to-tank confrontations. But the Arabs nearly tilted the tank battle—and the air battle —the other way with their Soviet missiles. The antitank weapons are illustrated in a pictorial essay on the missile war.

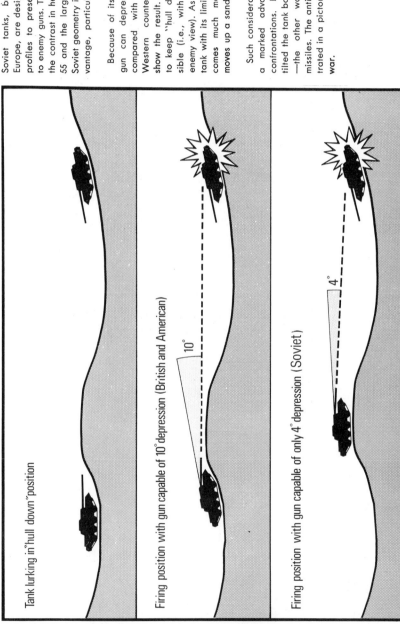

Tank lurking in "hull down" position

Firing position with gun capable of 10° depression (British and American)

Firing position with gun capable of only 4° depression (Soviet)

THE MISSILE WAR: The Arabs' arsenal of Soviet surface-to-air missiles

A SAM-3 missile (NATO code name, Goa) captured intact on its transporting vehicle during the final thrust west of the Bitter lakes (before firing, it is removed from the truck and operated from a fixed launching site).

SAM-3 is twenty-two feet long, has a slant range of seventeen miles, and can be used against low-flying aircraft. It is controlled from the ground by a radar system that tracks both missile and target and calculates the missile's path.

Propulsion is in two stages. The rear section, with its large, rectangular stabilization fins, is a solid-fuel booster rocket. This separates after launch, leaving the missile to fly on liquid fuel, its direction controlled by the forward "canard" fins and by the small rear fins just behind the V-shaped main wings.

For the Arabs, the main disadvantages of the SAM-3 and SAM-2 (following) were their relative immobility and the fact that most of their electronic secrets had been cracked by the Americans in Vietnam, making countermeasures possible.

Above is a SAM-2 launching site overrun by the Israeli attack north of Suez city. SAM-2 (NATO code name, Guideline) is used mainly against high-flying aircraft (up to 50,000 feet). Its propulsion and control are similar to those of the SAM-3, but it is readily distinguishable by its greater length (35 feet, 6 inches) and by the tapered stabilization fins on its solid-fuel booster stage.

Like SAM-3 it has ground-command radar guidance, making it easier to devise electronic countermeasures to protect overflying aircraft.

SAM-6 (left), used in combat for the first time, was the missile that gave the Israeli pilots most trouble. It is mounted on a mobile launcher, with an accompanying radar vehicle, making fixed sites unnecessary. Its length has been kept to only nineteen feet by the ingenious device of using the casing of its solid fuel-booster rocket to act as the combustion chamber for its ramjet second stage. Its guidance system (see next diagram) is more difficult to counter than that of SAM-2 and SAM-3.

THE MISSILE WAR: SAM-6 in operation, and how it extended the missile screen

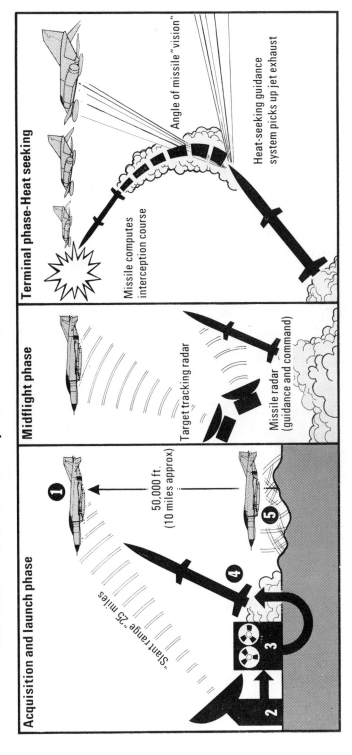

Acquisition and launch phase

❶

50,000 ft. (10 miles approx)

"Slant range" 25 miles

❹

❸

2

❺

Midflight phase

Target tracking radar

Missile radar (guidance and command)

Terminal phase–Heat seeking

Angle of missile "vision"

Heat-seeking guidance system picks up jet exhaust

Missile computes interception course

Above is a schematic diagram of the two-phase guidance system of SAM-6. The aircraft (1) is detected by the targeting radar (2) with its associated computer (3), which calculates the launching instructions for the missile (4). Another ground radar tracks the missile in midflight and guides it toward target. In the terminal phase, the missile takes over the guidance itself, using a heat-seeking device that directs it toward the infrared radiation from the plane's jet exhaust. SAM-6 is also used against low-flying aircraft (5), though its range is then reduced to 15 miles and acquisition is more difficult because of radar "clutter" from the ground.

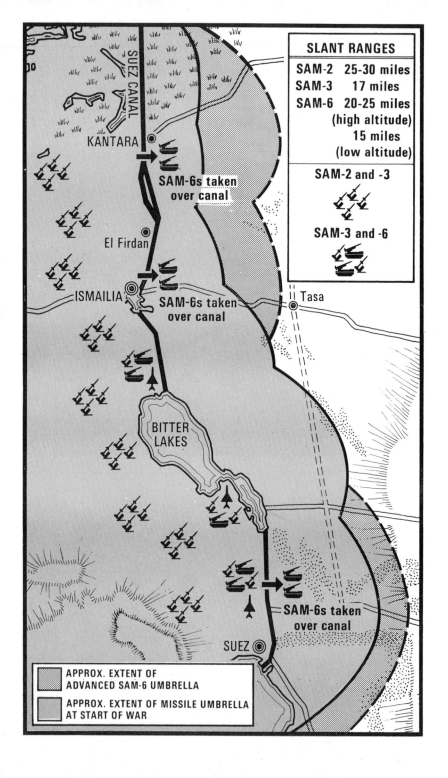

SLANT RANGES

SAM-2 25-30 miles
SAM-3 17 miles
SAM-6 20-25 miles
(high altitude)
15 miles
(low altitude)

SAM-2 and -3

SAM-3 and -6

SUEZ CANAL

KANTARA

SAM-6s taken
over canal

El Firdan

ISMAILIA

SAM-6s taken
over canal

Tasa

BITTER
LAKES

SAM-6s taken
over canal

SUEZ

APPROX. EXTENT OF
ADVANCED SAM-6 UMBRELLA

APPROX. EXTENT OF MISSILE UMBRELLA
AT START OF WAR

THE MISSILE WAR: The countermeasures tried by Israeli pilots . . .

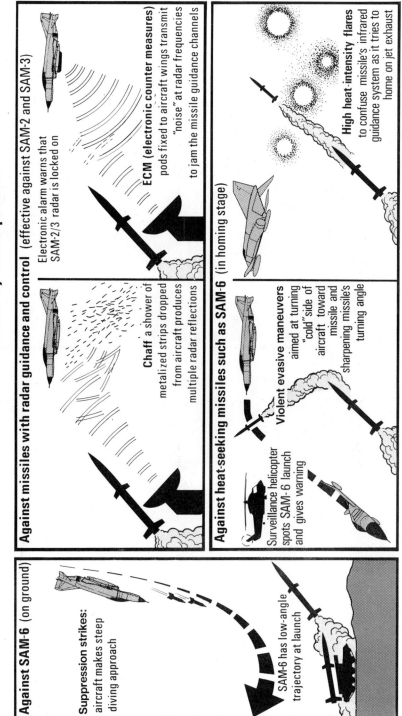

Against SAM-6 (on ground)

Suppression strikes: aircraft makes steep diving approach

SAM-6 has low-angle trajectory at launch

Against missiles with radar guidance and control (effective against SAM-2 and SAM-3)

Electronic alarm warns that SAM-2/3 radar is locked on

ECM (electronic counter measures) pods fixed to aircraft wings transmit "noise" at radar frequencies to jam the missile guidance channels

Chaff a shower of metalized strips dropped from aircraft produces multiple radar reflections

Against heat-seeking missiles such as SAM-6 (in homing stage)

Surveillance helicopter spots SAM-6 launch and gives warning

Violent evasive maneuvers aimed at turning "cold" side of aircraft toward missile and sharpening missile's turning angle

High heat-intensity flares to confuse missile's infrared guidance system as it tries to home on jet exhaust

... and Arab countercountermeasures

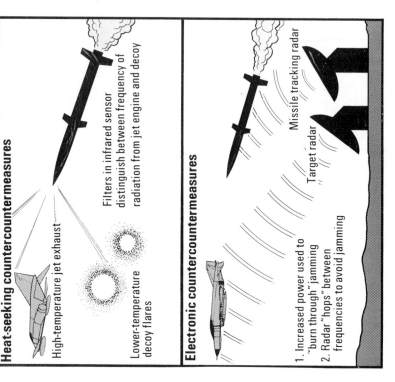

Heat-seeking countercountermeasures

High-temperature jet exhaust

Filters in infrared sensor distinguish between frequency of radiation from jet engine and decoy

Lower-temperature decoy flares

Electronic countercountermeasures

Missile tracking radar

Target radar

1. Increased power used to "burn through" jamming
2. Radar "hops" between frequencies to avoid jamming

Most of the electronic secrets of SAM-2 and SAM-3 were known before the war. In Vietnam, the Americans had developed ECMs (electronic countermeasures) consisting of a cockpit alarm (nicknamed "Samsong") to warn when missile radar is locked on, and underwing pods that transmit rival signals to jam the radar guidance. Both these were of little effect against the new SAM-6, even in its midflight radar-guided phase, because its guidance frequencies were unknown (the problem was complicated because SAM-6 uses at least four different frequency bands). The Israelis were reduced to using the World War II device of dropping showers of "chaff" to blur radar acquisition—although for maximum effect even this method requires knowledge of the frequencies, since the length of the pieces of chaff should ideally be a multiple of the radar wavelength.

In SAM-6's heat-seeking homing phase, no such electronic response was possible. There were Israeli attempts to confuse infrared sensing by dropping decoy flares. Otherwise all that could be done was to fly violent evasive tactics. One high-g maneuver, which pilots have labeled the "split-S," involves two aircraft. The lead plane dives sharply into and across the missile's approach, as in the diagram, while the following plane dives across the first plane's vapor trail. It sometimes worked: But very often the dive took the planes into the range of the Arabs' highly efficient Soviet ZSU-23 radar-controlled antiaircraft guns, where they got chewed up by flak. There were many attempts at direct suppression strikes against the mobile SAM-6 launchers (see diagram), though these were obviously highly risky.

There is some evidence that toward the end of the war, the Soviet technicians were producing a new generation of countercountermeasures (see diagram right). The use of decoy flares was fairly easily nullified by fitting filters to distinguish between the flares and the jet engines. And although satellite surveillance may have produced some knowledge of SAM-6's operating frequencies, there was the possibility of using increased radar power and switching from frequency to frequency to confuse jamming devices.

THE MISSILE WAR: The infantry missiles that tilted the tank battles

Sagger, the Soviet wire-guided "suit-case missile" that greatly embarrassed Israeli tanks. It can be carried by a single infantryman in a case that converts into a launching platform. On firing (left) the missile flies like a fast model aircraft paying out fine electrical wires behind, attached to the joystick guidance assembly (above right). It has a bright tail light for identification, which the operator tracks visually onto target with his joystick. Its armor-piercing charge works on the HEAT principle. As well as its infantry use, Sagger can also be fired from a special armored vehicle. The one in the picture (below left) was captured intact by the Israelis.

Approx ¼ mile to "gather" missile on line of target

Joystick with simple sight

Bright tail light for keeping visual track of missile

Launcher

SAGGER – maximum range 1 mile

Right: The main problem of controlling Sagger is in "gathering" it onto the line of the target after launching it from a remote position. This usually takes a quarter mile. Once on target, nerve rather than skill is needed.

Below: The American "second generation" wire-guided missile, TOW, which the Israelis put into action later in the war. It is more sophisticated than Sagger, with automated gathering and steering, but more cumbersome and expensive. The operator merely has to hold the cross wires of his sight on the target, and the computer does the rest. Because less skill is required, it is likely to be more effective in the heat of battle. Wire-guided missiles typically take ten seconds to reach target, which can seem a long time when the operator is exposed to fire.

Operator simply keeps cross hairs of sight on target. Everything else is done electronically

Loader

Launcher

Telescopic sight plus built-in infrared sensor which keeps track of missile

Folding fins

Wires unwind from back of missile to carry guidance instructions from computer

Computer measures any deviation of missile from target and corrects its flight path

Target

TOW – maximum range 1¾ miles

ble, the rapidly disintegrating Egyptian SAM defenses. Whatever their desires, the superpowers were being sucked still more deeply into the war.

Back in Washington, Kissinger could see not merely this danger; he saw others nearer home. So far, his tactics for ending the conflict had failed; yet in pursuing them for as long as he did, Kissinger had taken risks and made powerful enemies. Some of these were predictable. It can have surprised nobody when a known opponent of détente such as Senator Jackson said: "In recent months, the flow of Soviet arms into Syria reached flood-like proportions, and yet Dr. Kissinger comes before the American people to say that Soviet behavior has been moderate and not irresponsible. I cannot agree. I believe that Soviet behavior in the Middle East has been reckless and irresponsible. . . ." To those who recalled U.S. shipments to Israel, Jackson was doing no more than exhibiting tunnel vision; but he was a powerful senator. When Melvin Laird, formerly Defense Secretary now translated to the White House as a presidential aide, said: "The only manner in which détente can be proven is by deeds, not words, and the Soviet Union had not been performing as if dé-tente were here"—winding up to the conclusion that "a confrontation of sorts" already existed between the Soviet Union and the United States over the war—that was more alarming. Was Laird speaking with Nixon's knowledge? The State Department spokesman, the able Robert McCloskey, might try to soothe matters by assuring an increasingly skeptical capital that the superpowers were in "serious discussions." The fact was that by the evening of Friday, October 19, Kissinger's discussions were getting no-where—and his freedom of maneuver was diminishing.

For days now, the Jewish lobby in Congress had been piling on the pressure. On Monday, October 15, with the airlift under way, Hubert Humphrey, Jackson, and ten other senators began to circulate a rough draft of a Senate resolution commending Nixon for thus supporting a "strong and secure Israel" and resolving that "Israel's *deterrent* [our italics] strength be implemented by continuing to transfer to Israel, by whatever means necessary, Phantom aircraft and other equipment in the quantities needed by Israel to repel the aggressors." A similar resolution was introduced in the House.

It was now, according to the lobbyist Si Kenen, that he began his all-out *public* effort on behalf of Israel. Congress had not needed that much encouragement to put forward those resolutions. But it was important to get public opinion behind them. (Kenen explains that a congressional resolution is useful, first, because it crystallizes congressional opinion, forcing members to take sides; and, second, because of the impact it has upon the public.) Kenen's organization, AIPAC, now began a telephone blitz as part of a concerted campaign to influence Congress. When the resolution was finally introduced in both houses on Thursday, October 18, it had 63 Senate sponsors and 237 in the House. (It ended with 70 and 269 respectively.)

Kissinger was thus looking next day for any opening—even the Kosygin-Sadat proposals that Ambassador Dobrynin presented to him early that Friday evening. As Kissinger recalled later: "We began exploring a new formula for ending the war that evening, although it was still unacceptable to us." Precisely what was unacceptable is disputed: Soviet sources claim that the idea of superpower guarantees was broached then; Kissinger has denied this. The U.S. version is that the package fell short because it gave no indication of the procedure by which direct Arab-Israeli talks would start following the cease-fire, or even *if* they would start—the only sort of deal Israel would be interested in, and a topic that had been engaging the ingenuities of Dobrynin and Kissinger, without success, for some days. On Kissinger's timing, it was midway through Friday evening, however, that the outlook changed dramatically. "While we were still considering that formula," Kissinger said, "Secretary General Brezhnev sent an urgent request to President Nixon that I be sent to Moscow to conduct the negotiations in order to speed an end to hostilities that might be difficult to contain were they to continue." (Kissinger's sequence may be wrong here. Other Washington sources recall that the Moscow invitation arrived on Friday morning, while Kissinger was actually at the White House with Nixon, and that there followed several hours of discussion in Kissinger's office in the State Department—during which one suggestion was that the United States should respond by requesting Soviet Foreign Minister Gromyko to come to Washington instead—before Kissinger decided to accede to Brezhnev's request.)

Kissinger later told Senate majority leader Mike Mansfield that Brezhnev's note—it came through on the "hot line" telex to the White House—had called for discussions "on means to end hostilities in the Middle East" and requested "not that Kissinger come in a matter of days but that he come there in a matter of hours." According to the version later fed to Israeli diplomats in Washington, Brezhnev warned that the Middle East situation was now such that the Soviet Union stood on the brink of decisions "from which there could be no retreat" and invoked the "crisis control" procedures laid down in the U.S.-Soviet accords of 1971–72, under which either side could call for urgent talks.

The White House needed no persuading of what that might imply. But Kissinger had to sit through a dinner that evening given by the head of China's new liaison office in Washington, Huang Chen—a pleasant enough experience normally, but in this case a secret agony of wasted time. He finally cut out at midnight and drove straight to Andrews Air Force Base outside Washington. At 1 A.M. on Saturday morning Kissinger and a team of nineteen officials—including Middle East veteran Joseph Sisco —took off for Moscow.

Thus, having begun as bystanders and escalated to armorers, the Soviet Union and the United States had now accepted a decisive further commitment as arbiters. The only role left for them to play was that of direct combatants. To avert that, the superpowers had now taken over. It was signaled to Israel in unmistakable fashion. Before going to his Chinese meal, Kissinger had telephoned Israeli Foreign Minister Abba Eban, who was busily packing his bags in New York to return at last to Israel. "Someone important is calling me," Kissinger hinted, but—having good cause to know how many telephones are tapped around Washington these days—Kissinger would not go into details. Not until Eban saw a French evening newspaper when his flight touched down at Orly did he learn who that "someone" was. And although Israel's Washington ambassador, Simcha Dinitz, had been told that Kissinger's destination was Moscow, Dinitz knew nothing more. Diplomatically, the Israelis were now reduced to spectators of their own fate. Militarily, of course, the initiative was still theirs. The question indeed was whether a superpower deal could now be struck, pushed through the Security Council, and imposed upon the belligerents before Bren Adan's Centurions could emulate Caesar's and divide the Egyptian Army into three roughly equal parts.

2. Kissinger Patches up a Truce

On Sunday, October 21—the sixteenth day of the war—the Egyptian high command in Cairo held its first press conference since the opening of hostilities. The chief military spokesman, Major General Izz ad-Din Mukhtar, advanced the theory that Egypt had already beaten Israel in the field but now had to contend with the might of the United States; even so, he claimed, Egyptian troops covered the Sinai front from the Mediterranean to Suez. He put total Israeli losses on the Egyptian front at 600 tanks, 400 armored vehicles, 23 naval vessels, 25 helicopters, and 303 aircraft. When a correspondent pointed out that the combined Egyptian and Syrian totals amounted to a claim that Israel's Air Force of just under 500 planes had lost 600 in action, Mukhtar replied smoothly that the apparent discrepancy was explained by the scale of the United States' resupply operation. (In fact, Mukhtar's air loss figures were inflated tenfold: more than 80 of Israel's 115 aircraft and helicopters lost through the war were destroyed over Golan.)

Mukhtar was curtly dismissive of the Israeli bridgehead on the west bank of the canal. He was willing to concede that there were two small pockets of Israelis about ten kilometers into Egypt in the Deversoir area—though both, he said, were hopelessly besieged by thousands of Egyptian troops. (This grudging admission was at least an advance on his first assertion, made the previous Wednesday, that the Israeli task force had been "wiped out.") Mukhtar now admitted the bridgehead as a pinprick in the Egyptian grand strategy, but no more. In response to a questioner, he said that the Egyptian supply arteries, the main Cairo-to-Ismailia road and the Cairo-to-Suez roads to the south, were not threatened.

While these assurances were being given, the northern vanguard of the Israeli forces west of the canal was taking up positions on a line two miles south of the Cairo-to-Ismailia road, bringing it well within range of Israeli artillery. But the bulk of the Israeli forces—and the reinforcements that came surging over the pontoons north of Great Bitter Lake all day—were driving south toward Suez, stopping only briefly to dismantle a few missile sites, the last of those that had provided the Egyptians with their air umbrella for the Third Army's original advance. The comparative freedom of the skies enjoyed by the Israeli Mirages and Phantoms on that day testified to the success of the ground action. Increasingly, the Egyptians found themselves having to commit their own precious MiGs in an effort to halt the Israeli advance.

The Israeli information service, which in victory became more cautious as Arab claims got wilder, claimed that seventeen Egyptian fighters were downed in the day's action. That was almost certainly a deliberate underestimate. When the Israelis crossed the canal, the Egyptian Air Force had to come out and fight. Cairo sources told *Aviation Week* after the war that Egyptian aircraft fought 18 major air battles over the Israeli bridgehead—with Egyptian pilots flying 2,500 sorties in a week as MiG-17 and SU-7 fighter-bombers tried to destroy the buildup of Israeli equipment and the bridge itself. The Israeli claim—also given to *Aviation Week* after the war—was that the Egyptians lost 200 aircraft in those battles, for the loss of 3 Israeli.

In this struggle, the U.S. resupply effort was now crucial, as the Egyptians realized. "We could see the effects of American aid after October 16," Egypt's deputy premier, Mohammed Abdel Hatem, said afterward. "From October 6–16, there was a marked decline in the effectiveness of the Israeli Air Force. They began with 3,000 sorties a day and declined to about 1,500 on October 16 [the day Sharon crossed]. But after October 16, the number of daily sorties increased sharply once more."

New tanks were arriving as well. At first, the giant U.S. C-5A Galaxy transports landed only at Lod Airport; but as the airlift got under way through the week of October 14–20, some Galaxies carrying M-48 and M-60 tanks landed in Sinai itself, at the airstrip at El Arish. This got the tanks to the front a few hours faster; but since Sinai is Egyptian territory, it might have been thought politically tactless.

Egypt was by now scarcely concerned with such niceties. By nightfall on Sunday, October 21, the Israeli bridgehead extended west of the canal to a distance of eighteen miles from the waterway along a front some twenty-five miles long—from just short of the Ismailia-to-Cairo road in the north to Little Bitter Lake in the south. Within this area there remained pockets of determined Egyptian resistance. And the advance guard of the Israeli troops was still some miles short of the Cairo-to-Suez road, the main lifeline of the Egyptian Third Army, which still held to the wedge of territory on the west bank extending from the southern tip of Little Bitter Lake to a point a few miles south of Suez. By any intelligent military assessment, however, the Third Army, numbering some twenty thousand men, and with an estimated two hundred tanks still intact, was highly vulnerable.

Nor did the Egyptians have any immediate means of saving the situation. Turning an army around is a cumbersome business, even with highly competent noncommissioned officers to do the donkey work. The Third Army's rear echelons were finding the task almost beyond them. Meanwhile, Egypt had on the west bank no serious forces at all. When an Israeli column speared southwest from the air base at Fayid—one of five major airfields they overran—in the general direction of Jebel Ajuba, the Egyptian forces sent up to block their path consisted mainly of training detachments from the armored and infantry schools. It was as bad as that.

In Moscow the accelerating Israeli *Blitzkrieg* concentrated minds wonderfully. The implications of the Israelis' success west of the canal were not lost on the U. S. Secretary of State, Henry Kissinger, and the Soviet leader, Leonid Brezhnev. Brezhnev knew, and Kissinger appreciated, that the Soviet Union could not stand idly by while the Egyptian war machine was systematically smashed and the Israeli Army fulfilled David Elazar's graphic promise to "break the bones" of the opposition. Willynilly the two superpowers were being drawn into confrontation. By Sunday a situation existed—with the Egyptian and Israeli armies ranged in fighting order on the *wrong* sides of the canal—in which both sides could claim a victory for domestic consumption. It might obtain for another twenty-four hours, forty-eight at best. Thereafter, given the pace of the Israeli advance, even Cairo's propaganda machine would find it impossible to conceal the military humiliation. Arab pressure on the Soviet Union to even the score would intensify.

The U.S. team did not begin work in Moscow until late Saturday evening. Brezhnev opened the proceedings in a bellicose mood. The Soviet Union, he apparently warned, "would not permit" a repeat of 1967. To prevent it, the Soviet Union might even have to move to what Kissinger later quoted to the Israelis as "a phase of further involvement with incalculable consequences." While he may have been dramatizing the encounter somewhat—Israel should grasp the stakes it was now playing for—Kissinger's account is plausible. But he portrayed himself as having been taken aback by Brezhnev. That is most unlikely. He may initially have been surprised by the intensity of Brezhnev's concern; it is uncertain whether Kissinger knew how bad the military situation was until the Soviets told him. Once that was clear, however, Brezhnev's aggression was comprehensible, even predictable. What else could the Soviets do but put a bold negotiating face on things?

Brezhnev's demands that Saturday evening—basically, a reversion to the old "back to 1967 at once" formula—were worse than unacceptable: They were unrealistic. Kissinger resolved to ignore them. As the meeting broke up on Saturday night, he promised to "take note" of the Soviet proposals. But, after discussions late into the night among the American delegation, Kissinger in fact opened proceedings the next morning, Sunday, by making no reference to Brezhnev's formula and instead tabling his own—which had been drafted on the flight out.

Brezhnev at once dropped his hectoring manner, made no further reference to his own demands, and settled down to a businesslike discussion of the United States proposition. "He could tell the Arabs he had done his best, but now it was time for serious talks," one American participant concluded later. By early Sunday evening, after only ten hours of talks, Kissinger and Brezhnev had reached agreement on a cease-fire package. The terms—summarized in the form that the superpowers now proposed to push through the Security Council—read:

> The Security Council:
> 1. Calls upon the parties to the present fighting to cease all firing and terminate all military activity immediately, no later than twelve hours after the moment of the adoption of this decision in the positions they now occupy.
> 2. Calls upon the parties concerned to start immediately after the cease-fire the implementation of Security Council Resolution 242 in all of its parts.
> 3. Decides that immediately and concurrently with the cease-fire, negotiations will start between the parties concerned under appropriate auspices aimed at establishing a just and durable peace in the Middle East.

It was mercifully brief, but left a lot unexplained. So much was vague, in fact, that the next phase was clearly going to be tricky: selling this package to the combatants. In Cairo President Sadat was being kept abreast of developments by the Soviet ambassador, Vladimir Vinogradov, forcing an uncomfortable intimacy upon two men who now found it difficult to remain on speaking terms. At 9:30 P.M. Sunday, Vinogradov informed the Egyptian leader of the agreement's terms. For Sadat, the prospect of a cease-fire must by then have come as a reprieve; though he knew he would have an uphill task selling the rest of the package both to his own Cabinet and to the other Arab governments, who did not yet appreciate the gravity of the Egyptian Third Army's position.

U.S. treatment of the victorious Israelis was more brutal. Early on Sunday afternoon in Washington—late evening, of course, in Moscow—Ambassador Dinitz was summoned to the White House and presented with the text of the agreement by Nixon's chief assistant, General Alexander Haig. It came as a bombshell. An incredulous Dinitz promptly telephoned its contents to Mrs. Meir in Jerusalem. It was then 9:30 P.M. in Israel—just about the same moment that Sadat was hearing the news from Vinogradov—and Mrs. Meir at once convened a Cabinet meeting. It was, not surprisingly, a heated gathering. But the superpowers were not prepared to delay. While the Israeli Cabinet was considering this proposal to snatch equivocal compromise from the jaws of imminent victory, the rusty machinery of the UN Security Council began to clank into motion. A meeting was convened for 10 P.M. that Sunday evening, New York time—4 A.M. Monday in Israel. Mrs. Meir's Cabinet had just six hours in which to accept the proposal.

The Israelis were furious over both the content of the deal and the manner in which it had been presented to them. Haig had made it clear to Dinitz that not even the wording of the clauses could be changed. That left Israel little choice. As Mrs. Meir said afterward: "When Washington and Moscow agree upon a course of action, there isn't a lot of room for us to maneuver." Nevertheless, the Israelis maneuvered. It is a measure of Israel's failure to grasp how the United States now perceived its most urgent interests in the Middle East that some of the Israeli ministers at that meeting still flatly refused to accept any cease-fire that left Egyptian forces in Sinai. Others, more cunning, pointed out that if Israel had to accept the cease-fire, the least they should do is arm themselves with the most substantial possible bargaining counter. The Israeli command had reckoned that they needed three days to complete the encirclement of the Third Army. Could that be speeded up? And could Israel stave off the cease-fire in the meantime?

It was worth a try. At 2 A.M. Monday morning Israel time (8 P.M. Sunday in Washington) Mrs. Meir telephoned President Nixon—"to test the water," as Israeli ministers later put it. The water proved chilly. Nixon was excessively polite about the "glorious achievements" of the Israeli soldiers. And he pointed out what advantages he could in the agreement. But, according to U.S. and Israeli sources, when Mrs. Meir broached the nub of the matter—a possible delay in implementing the agreement for, say, twenty-four hours—Nixon turned the idea down flat. Mrs. Meir pointed out that the first clause of the resolution could as easily refer to twenty-four hours as to twelve. The extra time, she explained, would give both sides the chance to tidy their positions in preparation for the cease-fire—reducing the risk of nasty shooting incidents between exposed salients, for example. Nixon, not born yesterday, apparently replied that he most earnestly requested Israel to accept the resolution in the form in which it was to be submitted to the Security Council in rather less than two hours. It was, he said, U.S. policy.

Mrs. Meir did win one concession. Kissinger would return from Moscow via Tel Aviv—to be seen publicly consulting with the United States' valued allies, the Israelis. That, at least, would help Mrs. Meir sell the cease-fire domestically. Apart from that, although the Israeli Cabinet talked on for almost two hours after Mrs. Meir's abortive call to Nixon, the ministers could see no choice. At 4 A.M. the meeting broke up. Israel would accept the cease-fire—although in the remaining few hours its troops would make every gain they could.

Israel's decision came at the last possible minute. A few minutes after 10 P.M. Sunday in New York—as Mrs. Meir's ministers wearily made their way home in Israel—the Security Council was called to order by its president, Sir Laurence McIntyre of Australia. He presented to its members a draft of a resolution, No. 338, cosponsored by the United States and the Soviet Union. Its three clauses were those agreed in Moscow. Clause 1 called for a cease-fire *in situ*. Clause 2 made the necessary genuflection toward Resolution 242 as the basis of a long-term settlement. Clause 3 proposed immediate face-to-face talks between the Arabs and Israel.

Of all the Security Council members only China could find much to say against it. Peking's representative, Huang Hua, proclaimed, irrelevantly, that his country could not go along with any resolution that did not "condemn all the acts of aggression by the Israeli Zionists in the strongest terms . . ." and showed his disdain by abstaining from the voting. (Mr. Huang clearly did not grasp that the resolution was Egypt's only hope of staving off the most spectacular Israeli "act of aggression" yet.) The other members more realistically reflected the unanimity of the 2 superpowers and voted unanimously, 14–0, for the proposal after only 2½ hours of debate.

There was, after all, little to say. Sadat would presumably welcome the cease-fire but dislike the price. His strategy had been to continue fighting until he got a cease-fire indissolubly wedded to a long-term settlement. Yet this agreement did nothing—publicly, at any rate—to resolve the fateful ambiguities of Resolution 242; instead, Sadat was now committed to immediate face-to-face talks with Israel: the *de facto* recognition that the Arabs had always seen as a major bargaining counter. But the agreement did offer the prospect of recovering more territory.

For the Israelis, the agreement contained the incentive that it offered the opportunity, long sought, for face-to-face bargaining with their Arab neighbors—though the vague reference to "appropriate auspices" might worry Israel, which has a well-founded fear that one likely auspice, the UN, is heavily biased against it. In the immediate context of the battlefield, however, the Israelis were unquestionably being asked to make the larger concession. Moreover, the only sanction against their pressing home their military advantage was self-restraint—never a very convincing deterrent in time of war. Still, as a British diplomat remarked, "Henry and the Russians did a pretty good cobbling job"—with one flaw.

Between the first clause of Resolution 338—calling for a cease-fire within twelve hours' time—and the subtle incentives held out in Clauses 2 and 3, there was what British Foreign Secretary Sir Alec Douglas-Home later called, with masterly understatement, "a gap." Despite urgent diplomatic representations to the United States by both Britain and France before the UN vote, the agreement contained no proposals for observation or enforcement of the cease-fire. It was an ominous omission.

3. "Metternich," She Said

Israel now used the few hours left before peace to consolidate what gains it could. At 10:53 A.M. on Monday—eight hours before the cease-fire resolution was due to come into effect—Israeli forces successfully completed one of their most costly single actions of the war on the Syrian front. Helicopter-borne paratroopers and infantry of the elite Golani Brigade suffered fifty dead and about two hundred wounded during an assault on the Syrian-held positions on the seven-thousand-foot ridge below the summit of Mount Hermon.

The Syrians had captured the heavily fortified Israeli emplacement on the mountain during the first twenty-four hours of the war, and this was Israel's second attempt to retake it. By losing the position at the outset of the war, the Israelis had lost, as we have seen, a considerable military advantage. The strongpoint overlooked the entire Golan plateau. But the loss of Mount Hermon was much more than a simple military defeat. Nine months before Yom Kippur, the Israeli internal security service, the Shabak, had uncovered a spy and sabotage ring based in the Druze village of Majdal Shams—at the foot of the road that leads up to the mountain fortress. The ring was found to be linked with a network run from Haifa by a local bookseller. It was one of the largest and most sophisticated espionage operations ever uncovered in Israel.

Traumatically, the investigation into the ring revealed that native-born Jews, *sabras*, were involved—for the first time since the establishment of the state. The affair, which ended with the conviction of two Jews and three Arabs as ringleaders, left its mark on the national psyche. During the trials, it was said that top-secret information of a military nature had been passed to the Syrians: It concerned a "secret weapon." At least part of the information, however, concerned that elaborate Israeli fortification on Hermon. Detailed drawings of the entries and exits to the labyrinth of bunkers and connecting corridors, even specifications of the relative strengths of the armor-plated doors and the layouts of surrounding mine fields and booby traps found their way into Syrian hands.

In spite of this, when Syrian paratroopers landed by helicopter on the first Sunday to take the fortress, it contained only a token Israeli fighting force—most of those relaxing off-duty, oblivious to the supposed alert. The Syrians got into the fort by one of the simplest ways—a door that was normally reserved for escape in case of emergency, and could be opened more easily than the others. "Someone should be court-martialed for this," an Israeli military expert later observed.

The Syrians were unable, however, to flush out the entire Israeli garrison. Some literally locked themselves in; others managed to escape and take word down the mountain that, although in military terms the fort had fallen, some troops were still inside. An expedition was launched, by members of the Golani Brigade, to rescue them. It failed, with the loss of thirty dead. Those Israelis still inside, weakening through lack of food and, particularly, water, gave themselves up. The Israelis later reported to the International Red Cross that five were killed as they came out with their hands up. Their bodies were mutilated.

The second attempt to recapture the position was more determined—this was Israel's last chance. It included the use—for the first time on the Israeli side in Golan—of helicopter-borne troops. They were helped by infantry, artillery, armor, and the Air Force. The assault was extended along the ridge into Syria to ensure full command of the strategic position on Hermon. At 2 P.M. on the afternoon of Sunday, October 21, paratroopers were landed behind the Syrian positions farther along the ridge toward Damascus, while a frontal attack was made up the side of the mountain. The Syrians responded immediately with strafing runs by MiGs—nine of which, the Israelis claim, were shot down.

The Golani Brigade began their grueling climb up the side of the boulder-strewn mountain under cover of the early evening dusk on Sunday. They had a rough time. The Syrian commandos on top had had two weeks to select—and strengthen—their sniping positions covering the slopes: They inflicted heavy casualties.

A Golani infantryman recalled: "We climbed in the dark, vertically, with almost no handholds. We climbed for eight hours, feeling all the time someone was spying on us from above. We knew that once we reached the top we were on our own. The armor stayed below near the end of the cable railway. [The Israelis had built a ski run on Hermon over the previous two years.] Aircraft and artillery couldn't operate in case they hit us. On top the Syrians had a warm welcome for us. In every nook and cranny, they had not one but seven snipers. In the first light we suddenly found ourselves at arm's length with them. We actually had fist fights. Everyone was shouting at everyone. Then there was a Syrian air attack."

Another remembered: "The snipers used the classic trick of raising helmets on a stick to draw our fire; they had made positions for themselves around the fort, not in it. Most of them were lying down; they used telescopic sights, and the sun was behind them—right in our eyes. They threw grenades at anything that moved; many of our wounded were from grenade fragments." The fiercest fighting was from 6 A.M. Monday onward. By 11 A.M. the Israeli and Golani flags were fluttering from the radio antennas on top of the fort. Kelvin Brodie, a *Sunday Times* photographer, followed the Golani Brigade up Mount Hermon. His abiding memory was not of the victory he photographed: "The Syrian snipers had piled up low walls of little rocks to lie behind. And as you climbed up the hill after the troops, every one of those walls seemed to have blood on it."

Henry Kissinger arrived in Tel Aviv that same Monday morning, fresh from his diplomatic labors in Moscow. He waved cheerily to the pressmen assembled at Lod Airport and walked deliberately past the microphones optimistically arrayed for an impromptu press conference. The most recent secrets of the Kremlin were for the ears of the Israeli leadership alone.

Israeli agreement to the cease-fire had been, of course, contingent on Egyptian and Syrian acceptance of UN Resolution 338 as well. So far, no official word had come through from Egypt or Syria, however. And within Israel itself, there were already the beginnings of a sour reaction to what many considered a premature cessation of hostilities just as Israel was getting on top. Before the day was over some of this opposition was focused through the right-wing Likud coalition. It rejected the cease-fire and announced that it would oppose it in the Knesset: "Out of a sense of national responsibility we call on the people in this grave hour to strive for cancellation of this deplorable policy of the government. . . ." Even the normally mild-mannered Haim Herzog complained of the "unprecedented haste" with which the Security Council had endorsed the Soviet-American deal. With both popular and military sentiment running against a cease-fire, the Israeli leadership was anxious for reassurance from the U. S. Secretary of State.

Kissinger was in Israel for almost five hours, and spent three and a half of them in a secret meeting place just north of Tel Aviv —in fact, Mrs. Meir's house. He first spoke with Mrs. Meir, alone, for an hour and a half. Kissinger tried to appease her anger over the manner of the cease-fire by pleading that he had tried to telephone her from Moscow with the text of the cease-fire agreement, but that "technical factors" had prevented it. It is fair to speculate that, apart from a Soviet reluctance to countenance any contact with Israel from their soil, an additional "technical factor" may have been Kissinger's reluctance to let the Soviets overhear the problems he would inevitably meet in selling the deal to the Israelis. The agreement, after all, was posited on the assumption that each superpower could, in the last analysis, control its client. Should the Soviets suspect that the United States could not, in fact, control Israel, the risk of unilateral Soviet action to rescue the Egyptians would perceptibly heighten.

Kissinger impressed upon Mrs. Meir that the United States *did* want an immediate cease-fire and did *not* want the destruction of the Egyptian forces. It was a point he reiterated when the meeting broadened to include Deputy Premier Yigal Allon, Defense Minister Moshe Dayan, ex-Ambassador Yizhak Rabin, and Foreign Minister Abba Eban. Kissinger then spent much of the time reassuring them that there was no "secret deal" between the superpowers. The Israelis were not inclined to believe him—and the more advantages Kissinger spelled out in the cease-fire agreement, the more their skepticism grew. He was, for instance, at pains to stress that the Soviets—if not yet the Arabs—had at last agreed to the idea of face-to-face Arab-Israeli talks, rather than negotiations through third parties. Still better, he said, the draft the Soviets had produced did not refer to the "rights of the Palestinians"—a concept the Israelis claim implies the dismemberment of Israel. Instead, it followed UN Resolution 242, which refers to "a just settlement of the refugee problem," thus remaining open to economic and social interpretations rather than political ones. And Resolution 338 did not even clear up the ambiguities of 242 on the question on partial or total Israeli withdrawal. That was still open to bargaining.

That was the point the Israeli ministers could not credit. To them, it was inconceivable that the Soviets had not agreed with Kissinger at least on the guidelines to a final settlement—perhaps on the basis of the abortive Rogers talks back in 1969. And that meant total Israeli withdrawal from Sinai. Kissinger assured them that this was not the case. But his reassurance that no secret deals had been struck outside the ambit of those three typed clauses was vitiated, in Israeli eyes, by his simultaneous reassurance that the Soviets had orally agreed to an exchange of prisoners within seventy-two hours of the cease-fire. What else had been orally agreed? Kissinger tried to explain the Soviet imperative: to prevent a total defeat of Egypt. He repeated once more that this was the U.S. aim too. Militarily, therefore, an immediate cease-fire—on any terms—had been the overriding objective of Moscow.

Certainly, the cease-fire would have to be followed by negotiations toward a permanent settlement. Kissinger accepted Sadat's position on that; but he pointed to the concession—face-to-face talks—that the Soviet Union had made to this end. In those talks, Israel would have to agree to withdraw from at least the great bulk of occupied territory. "It will be necessary for all sides to make substantial concessions," he tactfully said. Nor did he hide the conclusion of the superpowers: that they would have to oversee this bargaining process. That sounded foreboding to the Israelis. And if the fundamental need to leave Sadat with some kind of negotiating base was obvious enough to the winner of the Nobel Peace Prize, Mrs. Meir and her colleagues are of another and starker cast of mind.

Subsequently, it was claimed that Kissinger did not adequately impose his authority on Mrs. Meir. The truth was the reverse:

what followed stemmed from Mrs. Meir's appalled reaction to Kissinger's toughness. Kissinger is a man of nuances who can normally afford to speak softly because the big stick of American power is always implicit. But in the context of American-Israeli relations this implied authority did not exist in Israeli eyes, since it was unthinkable to them that American power could ever be used against them. Despite the fact that their war machine was dependent on American aid, the Israelis' perception of Kissinger's role was thus that he should come as a man asking a favor, not imposing a solution. When Kissinger's predecessor, Rogers, had tried a tougher tack, he had been briskly capsized.

The cease-fire ultimatum had, at a stroke, overturned this Israeli confidence in their position *vis-à-vis* the United States. Mrs. Meir's track record, both in and out of office, suggested a flinty attitude to any idea that might compromise Israel's security. Kissinger's stalling over supplies to Israel in the vital first week had outraged her. Now she was learning—as Sadat had learned a year before—that to the superpowers, détente was, in the last resort, more important than the advancement of their client states' political aims. Precisely as Sadat had concluded, Mrs. Meir now realized that to achieve anything, her country would have to seize the initiative while it could.

When Golda Meir became Prime Minister in March 1969, after the death of Levi Eshkol, there were many who doubted the wisdom of appointing a woman already over seventy, whose health was suspect and who—although she had been Foreign Minister before retiring in 1965—was hardly a national figure. The doubters were rapidly silenced by her firm control of a centrifugal Cabinet and her flair for personal negotiation with world leaders. Her popularity reached a peak of 89.4 per cent in a national opinion poll in 1972 and has fallen little since then. The standard joke about Mrs. Meir being "the strongest man in the Cabinet" had a core of seriousness. She speaks in a low growl, and with her large head and shoulders—all that most people saw of her on the television screen—this gives an impression of natural authority.

Mrs. Meir saw no contradiction in the fact that a woman should head a nation in a constant state of readiness for war. She was as much concerned with security as any man in the military establishment, believing that a strong and independent Israel is the only guarantee of the Jewish people's survival. "When people ask me," she once said, "if I am afraid, because of Israel's need for defense, that the country may become militaristic, I can only answer that I don't want a fine, liberal, anticolonial, antimilitaristic, dead Jewish people."

This remarkable woman was born Golda Mabovitch, daughter of a carpenter in Kiev, in May 1898. The family immigrated to the United States and settled in Milwaukee when Golda was eight years old (she still speaks English with a strong American accent). In 1921, after marrying Morris Myerson, she left with her husband for Palestine. Both her children were born in a kibbutz.

As they grew up, she became steadily more involved in Zionist politics. When the British arrested most of the male Jewish leaders in the 1940s, she became acting head of the Jewish Agency's Political Department in Jerusalem, and was among those who negotiated with the British up to the creation of the State of Israel. Before the state was established, Golda went to Trans-Jordan, disguised as an Arab woman, to meet King Abdullah in a bid to persuade him not to join in the expected attacks by the Arab states on Israel. She became Israel's first envoy to Moscow, and a year later joined the Cabinet as Labor Minister. After her long spell as Foreign Minister (1956–65), she spent four years as secretary to the Labor party before taking over as Prime Minister (acquiring in the process a formidable grasp of the party machine).

Mrs. Meir's style of government was democratic but intensely personal. According to one close student of her method: "She listens carefully to what her colleagues have to say, then presents as a consensus what she had decided beforehand." As likely as not what had been decided beforehand was decided over the coffee cups at her "kitchen Cabinet"—Mrs. Meir's Saturday evening sessions at home for a few senior ministers. (The regulars at those sessions included Yigal Allon; Moshe Dayan; the Minister without Portfolio, Israel Galili; and Pinhas Sapir, the Finance Minister.)

Mrs. Meir and Kissinger had never met before; on her visits to Washington, he had kept out of the way. Now, she and her ministers found the U. S. Secretary of State's presentation too cold-blooded for their taste. Asked after the meeting about her impressions of him, Mrs. Meir replied curtly: "Metternich" (no doubt aware that the young Kissinger had acquired his doctorate with a thesis on that famous wheeler-dealer on behalf of the status quo). After the war, when Mrs. Meir visited the White House, President Nixon remarked on the coincidence of their both having Jewish ministers in charge of foreign affairs. "Yes," was Mrs. Meir's alleged reply, "but mine, I think, speaks better English."

In the light of later events, it is clear that, despite his graphic account of Brezhnev's mood in Moscow, Kissinger did not impress the Soviet determination to achieve an immediate cease-fire strongly enough upon the Israeli "kitchen Cabinet" to outweigh the Israelis' mounting conviction that he would, if necessary, sell them out at the peace talks. At the time, however, Kissinger had every reason to be pleased with his mission. Before the U.S. party left Israel, word came through that Sadat had accepted the truce. In Jordan, King Hussein seemed strongly disposed to acceptance despite an Iraqi rejection and a deafening silence from Damascus. Kissinger knew that the Soviets were working on Asad.

Besides, the Golan front—tricky as it might be—was not where the danger to international peace lay. In the south, where the really explosive situation existed, Kissinger appeared to have secured his objective. In the space of twenty-four hours, he had contrived to bring all the elements together: superpowers, United Nations, and the two main combatants. Kissinger flew out of Israel that Monday afternoon with a reasonable assurance that a cease-fire would take place at 6:52 P.M. local time—two hours after his plane took off and precisely twelve hours after the passage of UN Resolution 338. It seemed the high point of détente. Moreover, as Kissinger and his aides flew home, they reflected on the chastened briefing that they had been given in Tel Aviv on Israel's view of the war. "We thought we left behind us a very sobered Israeli military establishment," one American official remarked later. He was, apparently, wrong.

4. The Battle of the Cease-fire

An hour before the scheduled cease-fire, Major General Shlomo Gazit summarized Israeli achievements in the war at a press briefing in Tel Aviv. The Army, he claimed, was in control of 1,200 square kilometers on the western bank of the canal. In Syria the line had been extended to include 600 square kilometers of territory beyond the 1967 truce line. Since the beginning of the war the Egyptians had lost 240 planes, the Syrians 212. One thousand "enemy" tanks had been taken out on the Egyptian front and another 1,000 on the Syrian front. Gazit claimed that Israeli troops were now straddling the main roads and railway leading from Cairo to Suez in the south. Asked how he would describe the over-all position, Gazit replied: "It is a very big victory which could have been bigger." Over the next forty-eight hours, in what was theoretically a cease-fire situation, that victory did somehow become very much bigger.

The Israeli claim to "control" so much Egyptian territory, including the vital supply route to the Egyptian Third Army, was somewhat exaggerated. While it was true that some Israeli units had reached the main Cairo-to-Suez road at a point about ten miles from Port Suez, these were well in advance of the main Israeli force. Sharon's failure to get that bridge across in time for Adan's tanks had delayed the whole plan to encircle the Third Army by a critical margin. Sharon himself acknowledged the importance of the delay, though naturally blaming his superiors: "We moved too late. We defeated the Egyptians but we didn't finish the war." Chief of Staff Elazar, in his cease-fire order, echoed the disillusion: "We have emerged victorious, though our victory is not yet complete."

Moreover, in the areas of Israeli "control," there were still Egyptian troops in fighting order. No hard-and-fast line existed between the two armies. The task of deciding where the line ran would in all probability ultimately fall to tidy-minded men from the United Nations. In such a complex situation, the Israelis ran the risk of having even their potential stranglehold on the Third Army tidied out of existence. This process might not be long delayed, although the Security Council had, as we have seen, failed in Resolution 338 even to alert the men of the UN Truce Supervisory Organization who had kept watch on Israel's borders since 1967. At the time of the cease-fire there were some forty-two UNTSO men cooling their heels in Cairo, to which they had been evacuated from the Suez Canal area after the war started.

Before anyone could propel them toward the new front lines, the war was on again. Both sides claimed that the other started it. The most extended version of how it happened was provided by Israel at a subsequent UN meeting. Its representative, Yosef Tekoah, claimed that there had been "virtually no time during which the Egyptian forces stopped shooting." Tracing the official Israeli version of events in the hours immediately after the 6:52 P.M. cease-fire deadline (1852 hours on the twenty-four-hour clock), Mr. Tekoah said: "The shooting became particularly violent at 2038 hours when Egyptian forces opened fire on the Israel bridgehead on the west bank of the Suez Canal from the east and from the north. At 2056 hours the Egyptian forces opened fire on the Israeli bridgehead from north of Deversoir. Later, Israeli forces were shelled from bazookas. At 2132 hours there was bazooka shelling. . . . While this was taking place the spokesman of the Israel Defense Forces repeatedly drew attention to these Egyptian attacks. . . . At 0555 hours [on Wednesday morning] the IDF communiqué stated that the Egyptians had opened artillery fire on Israeli forces toward the end of the night of 22–23 October; at 0800 hours that the Egyptians had opened fire on Israeli forces on the west bank of the Suez Canal; and at 0900 hours, that the Egyptian forces were continuing to violate the cease-fire in the southern sector of the Suez Canal.

"Facing this situation, the Israeli defense forces were ordered to continue fighting in this sector of the front. It is clear who accepted the cease-fire and who rejected it, who has observed it and who has violated it."

Allocation of responsibility for renewed fighting was less clear

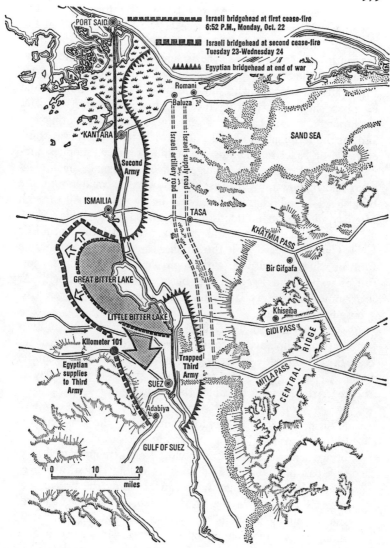

Israeli bridgehead at first cease-fire
6:52 P.M., Monday, Oct. 22

Israeli bridgehead at second cease-fire
Tuesday 23-Wednesday 24

Egyptian bridgehead at end of war

PORT SAID

Romani

Baluza

KANTARA

SAND SEA

Second
Army

Israeli supply road

Israeli artillery road

ISMAILIA

TASA

KHATMIA PASS

Bir Gifgafa

GREAT BITTER LAKE

Khiseiba

LITTLE BITTER LAKE

GIDI PASS

RIDGE

Kilometer 101

Egyptian
supplies
to Third
Army

Trapped
Third
Army

SUEZ

MITLA PASS

CENTRAL

Adabiya

GULF OF SUEZ

0   10   20
miles

Map 12 Israel in Africa: the bridgehead grows

to war correspondents in the area. It was certainly true that the Egyptian soldiers—particularly those of the Second Army in the north, unaware of the magnitude of their comrades' plight to the south—were as furious as the Israelis over the cease-fire. (One brigadier in the Second Army reportedly had to threaten to mortar any of his own troops who did not cease fighting.) So sporadic Egyptian shooting after the truce was predictable. But the UN resolution, after all, called not only for a halt to all firing but also for the termination of "all military activity." There was scant evidence of Israel terminating its buildup of men, supplies, ammunition, and armor in the bulge west of the canal. Israeli engineers had by now thrown three bridges over the canal around the bridgehead—one bridge specifically for heavy vehicles. All through Monday night, the pontoons were jammed with traffic. Many of the Israeli tanks were still emblazoned with the optimistic label "Cairo Express," while the supplies came in every conceivable form of wheeled transport, with hugh Tnuva milk tankers (now full of water) and Egged Tours buses especially prominent. At least some of the Egyptian artillery fire seems to have been a response to this buildup.

As we have implied, Israel had the strongest possible motives —military and diplomatic—to take advantage of any breach of the cease-fire. In the early hours of Tuesday morning, Insight reporter Philip Jacobson joined the convoy to observe the first day of "peace." After his tour, he cabled the following dispatch:

> A little matter of twenty-four hours after the cease-fire was supposed to have begun, I was lying face down on a pontoon bridge across the Suez Canal while Israeli troops blazed away at a pair of Egypt's "Frog" missiles sailing majestically overhead in the dark. I had just begun crossing the bridge back towards Israel when the firing started, strings of bright red tracer, trailing up from both banks. For one heart-stopping moment, we appeared to be the targets: It seemed a good idea to get off the bridge. I was rolling vigorously to one side when the strong right arm of the *Daily Mirror's* Anthony Delano stopped me from dropping into the canal. When we did raise our heads, it became clear that the "Frogs" —big, free-flight rockets packed with 1,000 pounds of high

explosive—were the real targets. You could see their bright orange exhaust quite clearly, followed by streams of tracer fire: When last seen, they were still heading east, presumably aimed at Israeli positions beyond the canal. It was a suitably dramatic finale to what was, even by Middle East standards, a comprehensively flouted cease-fire. Earlier, a mile from the bridgehead on the Egyptian side, we had passed an uneasy hour in a fetid Egyptian slit trench while an artillery battle was fought out. The Egyptian gunners were going for the pontoons which the Israelis had thrown over the canal at the northern end of the Great Bitter Lake. Their shells were falling well short, uncomfortably near us.

A few hours before that, I had enjoyed a grandstand view of what was quite clearly the beginning of a major Israeli armored attack, scores of tanks roaring down a sand road while crewmen secured equipment and checked their guns. We could hear heavy guns firing in the distance, and great plumes of white smoke were rising on the southern horizon. "What's going on?" someone asked our escort officer, a graying colonel with a splash of campaign ribbons on his chest. "Just deploying to new positions, I imagine," he replied. Simultaneously, two Egyptian MiGs passed overhead with Israeli Mirages in hot pursuit. After a perfunctory dogfight, both MiGs spiraled down, bright flashes marking explosions of their bombs and fuel.

What we were watching, it turned out, was the Israelis' attack round the town of Suez, ten miles to our south—the last major action of the war. Perhaps our colonel really didn't know. "You must remember, Philip," he had explained, "that we made it clear we would return blow for blow."

This was the official line, and he served it up with a commendably straight face. But after jolting for hours around Israeli-held territory on the Egyptian side of the canal in an open Army truck, I can only say that it did not look that way to me. From where I stood—occasionally lay—the Israelis appeared to be engaged in what I believe is known as "line straightening" among military men. On this occasion, it involved cutting the main roads from Cairo to Suez and tightening a huge ring around the Egyptian Third Army.

I should have realized we were in for an eventful day when, before we left Tel Aviv, the escort handed out steel helmets and field dressings. The helmets were sand-colored, bowler hat type, vintage Dad's Army; they were painful to wear, and occasioned much rude comment from the Israeli troops. The instructions stamped on my field dressings were in Hebrew and German, neither of which I speak. And the package, I later discovered, could hardly be hacked open even with my newly acquired Japanese version of the famed Swiss Army knife.

An hour out of Tel Aviv, we began passing huge military convoys grinding towards the canal. It all looked, as someone said, like business as usual. The bridgehead was a shambles. There had been heavy fighting around it and the Israeli engineers were still cannibalizing wrecked trucks and half-tracks with blowtorches. On the Egyptian side, we met Haim Topol, Israeli actor, film star, and volunteer driver for the duration. He seems to have been following me around for days, popping up in every trench and dugout: He had acquired a brand-new Uzi submachine gun since our last encounter. All round the bridgehead the ground had been torn and furrowed by shells; smashed bunkers and wrecked gun positions marked the path of the Israeli tank force which had fought its way across the canal five days earlier. We stopped for a moment under some pine trees; glancing up, I saw a helmet caught high in the branches. "Look out for the steps of Moses," a tank driver shouted as we passed, "he came from the other direction, you know."

The smell of death came very quickly. First, a faint whiff of corruption: The Israelis are scrupulous about burying enemy dead, and you could see neat lines of graves with individual markers. Those were the early casualties. Further on, Egyptian corpses had been collected in hastily dug pits, still awaiting proper burial, and the smell became much worse. In the back of the truck, you smelt the corpses before you saw them: The most recent dead, killed the night before, perhaps even that morning, lay sprawled along the road near the charred tanks and lorries.

The flat, hard sand on both sides of the road was crowded

with blackened and twisted vehicles. One convoy of half-tracks had clearly been attacked from the air: The smashed armor lay in almost perfect line at right angles to the road where the panicking drivers had fled. The Egyptians had dug many of their aging T-34 tanks hull down into the sand, for use as fixed artillery: It is tactically sound, but only if you control the air. In half a mile, I counted eighteen tanks, all incinerated in their pits, neatly winkled out by Israel's pilots. The crews never stood a chance.

As the day wore on, our escorts became noticeably more glum. As far as I could see, the whole idea of taking us so deep into Egyptian territory—more than twenty miles from the canal—had been to show us Egyptian violations of the cease-fire. These were in short supply, where we were at least. There was, it is true, a continuous rumble of heavy artillery from the south. "Incoming," announced our escort. "How can you tell from here?" I asked. "Experience."

By late afternoon, we remained sadly unviolated. As we drove towards Suez for a prearranged briefing, there was a flurry of activity among the tank crews lounging by the road. Squadron after squadron started engines and moved south at speed, roaring up behind our truck. The radio Jeep which had been guiding us stopped suddenly and the escort officers gathered round in the swirling dust. They hurried back looking worried. "Sorry, no briefing, arrangements got a bit confused."

It must have been the last straw—a bunch of nosy journalists turning up as the attack on Suez got under way. As we drove back to the bridgehead, escorts muttering to each other in Hebrew, the big guns began firing more heavily behind us.

Then it happened. A mile from the bridgehead, traffic was halted: There was shelling, indubitably Egyptian. The escorts hustled us happily into nearby trenches and we celebrated with soft drinks liberated from a canteen lorry. An American radio reporter started work: "Under fire near the Israeli bridgehead."

By nightfall on Tuesday the Israeli Army had closed the trap on the two surviving divisions—twenty-thousand men and two-hundred tanks—of the Egyptian Third Army. Driving forward on the ground, bombing and strafing from the air, the Israelis pushed well south of the main Suez road to envelop the city. The attack on the town of Suez itself was repulsed after costly hand-to-hand fighting. But advance Israeli units pressed on to the port of Adabiya on the Gulf of Suez, near the oil refineries south of the city. All conceivable supply routes—for ammunition, food, and, above all, drinking water—to the Egyptian forces over the canal were now controlled by Israeli armor and artillery. Provided the Israelis could maintain their positions, the capitulation of the Third Army was only a matter of time. Israel had won its own bargaining counter.

In its summary of the day's fighting, the Jerusalem *Post* quoted "a military source" with the demure observation: "The line may have changed somewhat, and not to our disadvantage." An Israeli infantry sergeant put it a little more bluntly to a correspondent near the front. "If they let us," he said, "we can make them come out of the east bank with their hands up and their tongues out."

5. Washington's Nuclear Alert

Kissinger's reaction to the news of Israel's decisive achievement was immediate and horrified. "My God," he said to an aide, "the Russians will think I double-crossed them." He thought for a moment, then added: "And, in their shoes, who wouldn't?" So began the slow ascent to nuclear confrontation.

Sadat was already in trouble over the cease-fire. He had briefed three envoys to tour Arab capitals and explain why, only a few days after Egypt had declared it would never agree to a truce unless Israel withdrew to its 1967 frontiers, a cease-fire was now an immediate necessity. The initial reception the message got throughout the Arab world was cool.

Syria, too, had finally and reluctantly agreed to a cease-fire—though only after intense Soviet pressure. At this point, it is relevant to the story to spotlight one of the more important *personae* throughout the Syrian drama: the Soviet ambassador, Nuritdin Mykhitdinov. He had arrived in Damascus after an eventful career. His background might have been deduced from his name, a Russianized version of the Arabic Nur-ed-din Mohieddin. Mykhitdinov was in fact born in 1917 to poor peasants near Tashkent in Uzbekistan—one of the southernmost republics of the Soviet Union, the heart of Soviet Central Asia, and historically the closest of all Soviet republics to the Arabs. (Uzbekistan was once ruled by the Arabs; Tashkent had been the site of one of the earliest and greatest Islamic libraries.)

To this tenuous temperamental affinity with the Arabs, Mykhitdinov added considerable political clout. Through the 1940s, he had worked his way up the Uzbek party apparatus, until, in 1952, he became a member of the Moscow-based Soviet central party committee. In December 1957—following the ousting of Molotov, Malenkov, and other members of the Stalin old guard

—Mykhitdinov finally made it to the supreme body, the Soviet Presidium (commonly known as the Politburo). Meanwhile, he retained the job of central committee secretary. Mykhitdinov, only forty, was clearly being groomed for yet higher things.

As swiftly as he had climbed, he fell. In 1962, he was stripped of all posts. The reasons were never explained; but they could well have been connected with the "nationalist deviations" exposed in Uzbekistan around that time. Six years later, in 1968, Mykhitdinov at last surfaced once more—in Damascus.

It had been a long drop; but, ironically, it was to serve Soviet interests well. Mykhitdinov now brought to the task of pressuring the Syrians into a cease-fire considerably more toughness and inside knowledge of the top Soviet hierarchy than most ambassadors could claim. He certainly leaned on Syria. He had a Soviet freighter pull out of Latakia without unloading its military cargo. He ordered the ending of all airlift supplies except small-arms ammunition. He even threatened to send home the Soviet technicians helping the Syrians to repair and redeploy the crucial SAM defenses.

The Syrians did not want a cease-fire for uncomplicatedly bloody reasons. Their Chief of Staff, Shakkour, had amassed enough tanks for a major counterattack to be launched at dawn on Tuesday, October 23. There is no reason to suppose that this would have fared any better than the Jordanians' second attack, which their commander Hajhouj had launched at dawn on October 20. That had been a rerun of the first.

The Jordanian 40th Armored Brigade again struck north, trying to cut through the Israeli advance. But this time it was the Syrians who neglected to provide flank support. And the Syrian Air Force—belatedly appearing after Israeli Phantoms and Mirages began to strafe the Jordanians—contrived to mistake the Jordanians' Centurions for the Israelis' and proceeded to shoot up their allies as well. Once again, a furious Hajhouj had to withdraw. In all, the Jordanian expedition to Syria cost twelve tanks, with another thirty-five hit; plus twenty-three dead and fifty wounded.

Shakkour's next great "combined" assault had been fixed for Sunday, October 21, but the Iraqis asked for a forty-eight-hour postponement. Hussein took advantage of this to send into Syria a second brigade, the 92nd, to reinforce the battered remnants of the 40th.

But late on Monday, October 22, Asad called off the attack. Under Ambassador Mykhitdinov's pressure, he had little choice. Asad's main anger, though, was directed at Sadat, who—he afterward claimed—had not forewarned him of the cease-fire. Sadat's private reply after the war that, in fact, he had warned Asad of the possibility on October 19 raised wry smiles in Amman. On the evening of Sunday, October 21, Sadat sent a message to Hussein assuring him that the battle would continue for weeks yet. Sadat must have drafted that only hours before getting word of the cease-fire deal the Soviets had agreed with Kissinger.

At the very least, therefore, the Soviet Union—having expended such effort and political goodwill to bring about that cease-fire— was unlikely to be impressed by pleas of U.S. helplessness in the face of Israel's encirclement of the Egyptian Third Army. It was more probable, indeed, that Kissinger's instant reaction was correct: Moscow would think he had double-crossed them.

That fear now underlay Kissinger's reactions. By the time he touched down in Washington after his fifteen-hour flight, it was midmorning Tuesday in Israel and the encirclement of the Third Army was well under way. The U.S. ambassador, Kenneth Keating, promptly made what were later described as "serious representations" to Foreign Minister Eban of the dangers were the cease-fire not observed. When that transparently had no effect, Kissinger himself telephoned Mrs. Meir. It was early Tuesday evening in Israel. Kissinger did not hide his fury. Tersely, he told her that Israel's "land grab" had gone far enough, and that she was undermining his position *vis-à-vis* the Soviet Union. According to Dayan, Kissinger even threatened that, should Israel not observe the cease-fire, the United States would not stand in the way of Soviet action to enforce it. It is barely conceivable that Kissinger could have said that—at least, with any hope of credibility. But it may be seen as a parable of the pressure he did put on Mrs. Meir.

Whether Kissinger demanded that Israel withdraw from its new positions is, however, disputed. Washington sources say he did; Israeli sources deny this. In all probability, Kissinger was concerned simply to persuade Israel to go no farther: The question

of withdrawal could come later. Yet this was a crucial issue—
as events in New York now demonstrated.

While pressuring Israel, Kissinger was at the same time trying
to reassure Moscow—through Ambassador Dobrynin—of his good
faith. He found a device to convince them. When, at Sadat's
urgent request, the Security Council convened for another emergency session late on Tuesday, it was once again the two superpowers who came up with a joint resolution.

Although it made no attempt to allocate blame for the breakdown of the cease-fire, Resolution 339 had a stormier passage than
its predecessor. The Chinese deputy foreign minister, Chiao Kuan-
hua, deplored "the malicious practice of using the Security Council
as a tool to be juggled by the two superpowers at will," and the
session had to be suspended for twenty minutes after an angry
shouting match developed among Chiao, the Israeli, and the Soviet
delegates. When passions cooled, the Council endorsed by fourteen votes to none (with China abstaining) the following:

> The Security Council, referring to its Resolution 338 (1973)
> of 22 October 1973,
> 1. Confirms its decision on an immediate cessation of all
> kinds of firing and all military action, and urges that the
> forces be *returned to the positions they occupied at the
> moment the cease-fire became effective* [our italics].
> 2. Requests the Secretary General to take measures for im-
> mediate dispatch of United Nations observers to supervise
> the observance of the cease-fire between the forces of Israel
> and the Arab Republic of Egypt, using for this purpose the
> personnel of the United Nations now in the Middle East
> and first of all the personnel now in Cairo.

The resolution, with its specific mention of UN observers, at
least provided a mechanism for monitoring the truce. But it was
the stipulation in the first clause that Israel withdraw to the
October 22 lines—release the Egyptian Third Army from the
trap—that Kissinger *and* the Soviets saw as the earnestness of U.S.
good faith. In agreeing to that demand, however, Kissinger had
put his own and the United States' credibility still more heavily
in pawn to Israeli moderation—a quality that remained, on the

evidence so far, somewhat hypothetical in nature; for the new resolution's provision for the immediate dispatch of observers did not guarantee their immediate arrival through Israeli lines. Nor was there much chance of their finding agreement between the Israeli and Egyptian forces about their October 22 cease-fire positions when they did arrive. Against this background of ill-substantiated optimism, the new cease-fire was scheduled for 0500 hours GMT (7 A.M. in the battle zone) on Wednesday morning.

Meanwhile, Syria announced acceptance of the October 22 cease-fire, although on terms that seemed likely to create a fresh *casus belli* in the future. The Syrian acceptance was made "on the basis that it means the complete withdrawal of Israeli forces from all Arab territories occupied in June 1967 and after. . . ." (In presenting her acceptance of the cease-fire to the Knesset some hours earlier, Mrs. Meir had given precisely the opposite assurance that it did not imply a return to the pre-1967 borders, which made Israel "a temptation to aggression." Apart from the obvious domestic reasons for that assurance, Mrs. Meir was clearly trying to get on record the promise Kissinger had made privately during his stopover.) If yet another clash was thus brewing over 242, the fact that Syria had even endorsed a UN proposal that referred to 242 and direct negotiations with Israel—neither of which had previously been acceptable in Damascus—was hopeful. Which was more than could now be said for events across the canal.

Shortly after 10 A.M. on Wednesday, October 24, seven UN patrols left Cairo on their way to the forward Egyptian positions. By early evening, two had established themselves on the east bank of the canal—one east of Port Said, the other east of Kantara. Another two took up positions on the west bank at Abu Suweir and south of the Abu Sultan road. The three patrols that headed southwest down the crucial roads to Suez never reached their objective. They made it as far as Jebel Oweida and Bastat El Hemira, only to learn that there was still a war going on.

UN Secretary General Kurt Waldheim later explained to the Security Council that they "had to withdraw westward due to the intense exchange of tank and artillery fire between Egyptian and Israeli forces." Units of the beleaguered Egyptian Third Army were trying to break out. Soon afterward a convoy of Red Cross trucks, laden with medical supplies and blood plasma for the

Third Army, was turned back by the Israelis outside Suez. In Tel Aviv, General Haim Herzog, interviewed for an Israeli overseas broadcast, observed that the only option open to the Egyptian Third Army was "surrender with honor."

Confronted by Israel's evident determination to humiliate the Third Army, Sadat requested yet another Security Council meeting. This time his Foreign Minister, Zayyat, had instructions to urge the Council "to call on the Soviet Union and the United States . . . each to send forces immediately from the forces stationed near the area to supervise the implementation of the cease-fire. . . ." Sadat repeated this plea in personal messages to both Brezhnev and Nixon. The unenforced cease-fire was turning out to be worse than useless. Something a little more potent than a few Jeeploads of UN observers would have to be injected into the truce-keeping operation. The Egyptian view of what was happening was pithily put by Sadat's information advisor, Ashraf Ghorbal: "Israel is cheating on the cease-fire, and the United States is helping it to cheat." The most alarming question now was: Did Moscow agree?

Wednesday evening's Security Council meeting was thus an edgy occasion. Although the Soviet delegate, Yakov Malik, did not comment directly on the readiness of the Soviet Union to commit troops, he indulged in some cudgeling rhetoric about "the war criminals of Tel Aviv." In his view, Israel's "brazen violations" of the cease-fire amounted to a "carefully prepared criminal and hypocritical imperialist provocation." It was not the kind of talk calculated to foster a spirit of cooperation between the two superpowers.

Malik went on to to say: "The only possible way of correcting the situation and directing the course of events is that Israel must immediately be compelled to comply with the decisions of the Security Council, and the United States is obliged and bound to play a decisive role as a permanent member of the Security Council and as a cosponsor of the two resolutions." Egypt's call for the superpowers' troops as guarantors of the peace was, Malik felt, "undoubtedly justified and . . . entirely in accordance with the Charter of the United Nations." The implication seemed to be that, if the Security Council felt troops ought to be committed, the Soviet Union was ready to do its duty—and the

United States should do likewise. The U.S. ambassador to the UN, John Scali, did not much like the implication. "This is not a time," he said, "in which involvement by the great powers, through the dispatch of their armed forces, could be helpful in creating conditions of peace."

While the Security Council talked on until past midnight without reaching any decision, the first steps toward escalation were being taken in Washington. Thursday, October 25, was to be the day when the loose ends of Middle Eastern conflict and superpower diplomacy seemed suddenly woven together into a tripwire for world holocaust.

Washington was already in a nervous condition, for reasons totally unconnected with the Middle East. The Watergate scandal—an amalgam of electoral and national security abuses that had defaced Nixon's re-election in 1972—had already affected the U.S. responses in the Middle East. We have related how the Washington intelligence warnings of possible conflict had fallen through the summer on ears deaf to anything but the reverberations of the scandal. But by Wednesday, October 24, Watergate had gone critical—as a result of the President's decision a few days earlier to fire his special prosecutor, Archibald Cox, who had been investigating the affair. Cox's dismissal caused an uproar; and the idea of impeaching Nixon—or forcing him to resign—was publicly canvassed by erstwhile supporters in his own party. In an attempt to restore his position, Nixon announced that he would, after a short period of retreat in Camp David, address the nation on network television.

While the President was in Camp David, the thankless task of mollifying a by now thoroughly aroused Washington press corps fell to his White House chief of staff, General Alexander Haig. At a briefing in which Haig tried to explain the President's position on the Watergate tapes—the secret White House tape recordings which, it was then thought, could establish Nixon's guilt or innocence—he was given a rough time. As he spoke, cars outside could be heard responding to signs that demonstrators (one of them in a Nixon mask and prison garb) had been holding all weekend: "Honk for Impeachment." Haig accurately described the previous few days as a "firestorm." At one stage, Haig said, "We chose Senator Stennis to listen to the [Watergate] tapes first of all because he's . . ." "Deaf," shouted a reporter. (Which the aged senator indeed was.) After the President's return from Camp David, his press secretary announced that he had decided to cancel the promised broadcast. It was a situation in which even the most sober commentators began to express doubts about the President's grasp on reality.

It was against this atmosphere of official defensiveness and public suspicion that the miscalculations in the Middle East now precipitated the test of nuclear will between the two superpowers. The timetable of the drama went roughly as follows:

8 P.M. Wednesday: The Soviet Ambassador, Anatoly Dobrynin, arrived at the State Department in Foggy Bottom to deliver to Kissinger a note from the Soviet leader, Leonid Brezhnev, endorsing Egypt's call for a Soviet-American military presence in the Middle East. The two men had a brief discussion in which Kissinger made clear U.S. objections. (John Scali was publicly expressing the same views at the UN in response to Malik at about the same time).

Kissinger afterward claimed that this note was the first indication he had received of Soviet willingness to contemplate such a direct involvement. Soviet sources maintain, as we have said, that the idea had been broached by Dobrynin—and, to be sure, turned down by Kissinger—on the evening of October 19, after Kosygin's talks with Sadat. What is certain is that, for U.S. policy makers, the idea of sending in troops was uniquely abhorrent. With an attitude colored by "peace-keeping" in Asia, Washington instantly thought in terms of a commitment powerful enough to intervene in the fighting by main force. One U.S. official later suggested that twenty thousand to thirty thousand men was a minimum for such an operation. Whether the Soviets ever meant any such thing is unclear. Certainly, they later settled for a "police force" of merely deterrent or emollient proportions. The effect of Brezhnev's note, however, was to conjure up in Washington fears of an open-ended Vietnam-style involvement on the ground.

10:45 P.M.: Dobrynin returned to see Kissinger with another message from Brezhnev. It was this note, which has been variously described as brutal, threatening, and rough, that triggered the crisis. According to officials who read it, the content was: "We strongly urge that we both send forces to enforce the cease-fire, and if you do not, we may be obliged to consider acting alone." (Lord Cromer, the British ambassador in Washington, who subsequently had the guts of the note read over to him, remembers the language as being considerably tougher, along the lines of: "I shall state plainly that if the United States rejects the opportunity of joining with us in this matter, the Soviet Union will be obliged to examine as a matter of urgency the question of the unilateral institution of appropriate measures to stop Israeli aggression." Either way, the import was unmistakable.) Dobrynin left this second note with Kissinger without obtaining a reply.

10:50 P.M.: Kissinger telephoned President Nixon, who was then in his upper-floor living quarters at the White House. Kissinger suggested that the U.S. response to the latest Soviet communication should be military as well as political. Nixon agreed, asking Kissinger to work out the details and keep him informed.

11 P.M.: Kissinger convened a meeting in the Situation Room in the lower level of the west wing of the White House. It should be said at this point that Kissinger himself was partly to blame for the deep suspicion with which news of the crisis was later received throughout the United States. He was so consistently less than frank about what had happened. He subsequently claimed, for instance, that this meeting was "a special meeting of the National Security Council" at which "all the members of the NSC were unanimous. . . ."

The truth is that such formal National Security Council meetings have been a fiction for years—"a cosmetic," one former NSC staffer called them, adding: "The NSC hasn't been used in the textbook sense since Eisenhower." The function of the full NSC meeting of twenty-six or so members has tended since to be merely to dramatize decisions quietly made elsewhere. Johnson summoned a full NSC meeting—and called the press to photograph it—after Tet in 1968, for instance; but the main policy responses were in fact only decided weeks later. So it was in this crisis. The group Kissinger actually summoned that Wednesday evening was the Washington Special Action Group, which had been meeting on the war since the evening after the conflict began. Formally a committee of the NSC, WASHAC's actual connection is limited to the fact that it is staffed by the same White House officials.

Through the war, WASHAC had tended to meet as a five-man group—the actual participants fluctuating, but the representation remaining pretty constant: State Department, NSC, Defense Department, and CIA. This meeting, however, was sadly depleted. The chairman, the President himself, stayed upstairs. (Why? We cannot discover. Perhaps because Nixon anticipated the cries that the crisis was a put-up job to distract attention from Watergate? Or was he just too exhausted by Watergate to cope?) Another absentee was former Vice President Spiro Agnew, who had recently resigned from office. Those who did attend were James R. Schlesinger, the Defense Secretary, and Kissinger himself in his dual capacity as Secretary of State and the President's national security affairs advisor. An NSC aide was later quoted as saying: "Officially the meeting consisted of Kissinger, Kissinger, and Schlesinger." Also there, in an advisory capacity, were William E. Colby, the director of the CIA, and Admiral Thomas Moorer, chairman of the Joint Chiefs of Staff.

The elements this small group now had to consider were not simply the two Brezhnev notes. By this time there had been some feedback from John Scali about the "ambiguous" position taken at the UN by his Soviet opposite number, Yakov Malik, Scali found some of Malik's remarks "curious." Yet the sequence so far was not hard to unravel. Malik at the UN and Brezhnev in his first note had proposed a joint force to salvage Sadat—an objective that Kissinger had assured Brezhnev was shared by the United States. Scali publicly and Kissinger privately had rejected the plan. Now, three hours later, Brezhnev was warning that the Soviet Union might intervene alone. Nor was Brezhnev's anger hard to fathom. What good were Kissinger's protestations of good faith after Israel's "improvement" of its cease-fire position, if the United States was simultaneously unable itself to control Israel, yet unwilling to join in action that would succeed? Could it be, after all, an American plot? Even if it were not, there was already enough evidence of dissent within the Kremlin between hawks and doves to suggest that Brezhnev could not relish finding himself thus caught on a limb. The question facing the WASHAC meeting was whether Brezhnev's note was meant merely for Kremlin consumption and to strengthen Kissinger's hand with Mrs. Meir; or whether the Soviet Union, whatever its misgivings, really did contemplate intervention. As one NSC staffer put it coarsely afterward: "Were the bastards bluffing?"

Taken as a whole, there was considerable evidence that the Soviet Union was not bluffing. Preparations for a military movement on any scale are lengthy and complex. For an airlift, they include the physical coordination of aircraft, troops, and equipment—all of which can be monitored by satellite or long-range radar. The radio traffic pattern accompanying such a buildup is equally characteristic and equally detectable. At the WASHAC meeting, CIA director Colby now reported indications of a buildup, derived from every sort of surveillance.

British Royal Air Force reconnaissance aircraft operating out of Malta showed a continuing Soviet naval buildup in the Mediterranean southeast of Cyprus. The Soviet fleet there now totaled around seventy vessels—among them seven amphibious assault craft and at least one helicopter carrier, and possibly two. That was inconclusive. There had been bigger Soviet concentrations before.

Several Soviet mechanized infantry and paratroop divisions stationed in East Germany and Poland had been placed on alert within the previous twenty-four hours. Six divisions were thought to be involved. The reason for the alert was unknown. But there had been previous Soviet alerts during the war. So that too was inconclusive.

A seventh division of Soviet airborne troops had been dispatched the previous week from its base just under one hundred miles south of Moscow to an airfield outside Belgrade in Yugoslavia. It was on a higher, "ready to move" alert. But the staff of this division was already in Syrian military headquarters at Katana outside Damascus. If anything, that demonstrated the probability that the Soviet Union would have intervened to prevent the Israeli capture of Damascus. Since Israel was stalled more than twenty miles from the Syrian capital, the precaution had proved unnecessary. Even without its staff, though, the division could be a formidable intervention force in Egypt.

At dawn on Wednesday, October 17—precisely a week earlier—a crack Soviet air transport unit had also shifted to Belgrade. The unit was equipped with about thirty Antonov freighters. What was worrying was that this unit had been the spearhead of the

Soviet invasion of Prague in 1968—indeed, it had been stationed in Prague ever since. (It was one of this unit's aircraft that landed at Prague Airport, rolled to the end of the main runway, and—jamming Prague civilian air traffic control frequencies—became a mobile control tower to bring in the rest of the Soviet invasion fleet.) Why had this unit moved on October 17? Perhaps because of the same Cosmos satellite pictures of the Egyptian tank disaster in Sinai that, on the same analysis, might have been the cause of Kosygin's hurried departure to Cairo on October 16? Had the Soviets foreseen then that they might have to intervene? (After all, one of Kissinger's long-standing fears—as he had revealed in the conversation with Israeli Brigadier Narkiss in the summer of 1969—had been that an Israeli crossing of the canal would precipitate Soviet intervention.)

With the ambiguous exception of the alert to the Warsaw Pact divisions, the nature and timing of all these preparations indicated a Soviet *ability* to intervene rather than a decision to do so. But there was one further item of intelligence that might suggest some sort of decision. This new element was evidence that the Soviet Air Force had pulled most of the big Antonov transports, which had been used to airlift supplies to Egypt and Syria, back to their home bases in the Soviet Union. The supplies had been flown mainly from the Soviet logistics center of Kiev via bases in Hungary and sometimes Yugoslavia. But for twenty-four hours, all flights had ceased. Just before the WASHAC meeting was convened, however, several Antonov-22s were reported heading for Cairo once more. Some Pentagon officials feared that these might be the vanguard of an airlift of Soviet troops. (An alternative reading of the pullback of Soviet aircraft from Hungary could have been that the main job of resupply had already been accomplished and the Soviet Union—in accordance with the Kissinger-Brezhnev understanding of the previous Sunday—was running down its operation. When the AN-22s did land in Cairo it was discovered that they were not carrying troops but supplies as usual. But by then the United States had taken another step up the ladder.)

11:30 P.M.: Sifting this detailed but inconclusive evidence, Kissinger and Schlesinger decided that a firm response by the United States was required. Their reasoning was more complex than a straightforward decision that the Soviet Union should be deterred from taking precipitate and unilateral action. As Kissinger and Schlesinger saw it, the Kremlin was divided—the hawks wanting intervention, the doves against it, with Brezhnev trying to balance the factions. The prime purpose of any U.S. response, therefore, should be to strengthen the hands of the doves by demonstrating the risks that the hawks' policy would carry.

Watergate *was* a factor in the two men's calculations; for it was reasonable to speculate that one argument of the Kremlin hawks would be that Washington was so paralyzed by Watergate that the U. S. Government would be incapable of making a coherent counter to Soviet intervention. A U.S. response was necessary that would—by its dramatic quality—disabuse that belief.

But there was another reason, too, for a decisive American response. There was at least a chance that the Soviet Union had installed nuclear weapons in Egypt. U.S. reconnaissance surveillance had revealed that on a base a few miles east of Cairo, a battery of Soviet Scud missiles had been deployed. And ranged neatly alongside them were what some analysts held were the characteristic shapes of nuclear warheads. And U.S. intelligence could produce other evidence to suggest that nuclear warheads had been shipped to Egypt—though the reliability of this was also disputed.

If the warheads were there, it did not matter whether they were genuine. It was, in fact, improbable that they were. (Even in Eastern Europe, Russia does not just disperse its nuclear warheads to forward bases in that fashion.) What mattered was the message being signaled to the U.S. reconnaissance media. The Soviets were prepared—presumably as a last resort—to use nuclear weapons.

Duly, with a careful leak by the Pentagon in *Aviation Week* of October 22, this American observation of the Scuds was signaled back—though no public mention of their warheads was made. The Soviets would realize without being told that the United States had seen those too. Besides, Washington could not agree if that was what they were.

At that time, there had been little doubt about the circumstances under which these Scuds—with or, more probably, without nuclear warheads—would be used; for in his speech of October 16, President Sadat had boasted of missiles "on their pads, ready with one signal to be fired to the very depths of Israel." He pointed out that they had not been fired, but reminded Mrs. Meir "of what I said and still say: an eye for an eye, a tooth for a tooth, and depth for depth." To be sure, Sadat had claimed that the rockets in question were the Egyptian-made Zafirs. That was rubbish. German ex-Nazi scientists had begun work on the Zafir for Egypt in 1961. But insuperable problems developing guidance telemetry—not to mention a swift campaign by the Israeli secret service to kill or scare away the German scientists—had led to the abandonment of the program in the mid-1960s, though empty Zafir casings were still wheeled through Cairo in parades.

The rocket Sadat was referring to was clearly the Soviet Scud. And, in the wake of the Israeli raids on Damascus and stategic targets throughout Syria, Sadat's reference to "depth for depth" could only mean that the same Israeli tactics against Egypt would bring retaliation by Scuds. That was understandable enough— "junior league balance of terror," one Washington source, recalling the WASHAC deliberations, called it. Besides, the Scud's range of 160 to 180 miles meant that the rockets could not even reach Israel from the Cairo base.

But, considering those rockets, there was a final "doomsday" possibility that the WASHAC meeting had to bear in mind. Israel, as we have said, possesses a small stockpile of atomic bombs. And one factor in the final U.S. decision to resupply Israel with conventional weaponry had been the fear that Israel, facing defeat, would decide to use those bombs. What if the Soviets had feared the same thing? Suppose those nuclear warheads *were* genuine after all? Perhaps the Soviet Union, forgetting the poverty of the U.S. reconnaissance satellite program, had figured that the warheads would be spotted, there on the sand, more quickly than they were? Had the United States been meant to warn defeated Israel not to press the nuclear trigger?

If that "worst case" hypothesis were correct, might the present humiliation of Sadat and his Third Army persuade the Soviets to fire, say, one nuclear Scud at some Israeli target in Sinai—perhaps the bridgehead, perhaps the forward headquarters, perhaps Bir Gifgafa? Was that the "unilateral action" the Kremlin hawks were contemplating? It was all speculation. But the response from WASHAC would have to be such as to deter that threat as well.

In effect, the U.S. reaction would have to persuade the Soviets at least of the possibility that even a tactical nuclear strike against Israeli troop concentrations might be taken by the United States as an act of global nuclear aggression.

So, chased from one bogey to another until at last they confronted the possibility of nuclear war itself, the WASHAC quartet escalated their ideas of the necessary response to Brezhnev's note. Finally, Kissinger and Schlesinger agreed the answer: a dramatic American combat alert. The one they chose was Defense Condition 3: one above normal, and one below that which obtained during the Cuban missile crisis. (There are five "defense conditions" in the U.S. military lexicon: 5. Forces not in state of readiness, troops lack training. 4. Normal peacetime position as troops undergo training. 3. Troops placed on standby and awaiting orders. All leaves canceled. 2. Troops ready for combat. 1. Troops deployed for combat.) They also decided that it should be a worldwide alert, involving virtually all the 2.2 million U.S. military men dotted around the globe.

11:35 P.M.: Receiving the formal order from Schlesinger, Admiral Moorer transmitted it to the various service chiefs, who then passed it on to commands and subunits throughout the world. The order read: "All Commands: Assume Def Con 3." The only significant exception to the general alert involved the Strategic Air Command (SAC) tanker planes along the United States-to-Israel airlift route. These maintained their mid-Atlantic *rendezvous* patterns instead of being sent north for possible refueling of long-range B-52 bombers.

Midnight: Bellevue, Nebraska, where the worldwide nerve center of SAC is located, was unusually animated. It had been a normal day at the base for most of the 11,653 military personnel and their 25,659 dependents. The base newspaper *Air Pulse* featured plans for Halloween celebrations. Around midnight, as Admiral Moorer's alert order came through, hundreds of Air Force personnel—members of SAC's battle staff—were awakened and summoned to the command center in a 7-story building, 4 of the floors underground. Officers filed into balcony seats as computers began to churn out reams of data on weather at potential targets and information on the readiness of the 162,000 SAC personnel worldwide. Around the world SAC bombers were drawn up on the Tarmac, with crews waiting on board for orders to take off. Sixty B-52s were ordered to return from Guam to the United States.

1 A.M., Thursday, October 25: Lord Cromer, the British ambassador, was informed of the contents of Brezhnev's note and the U.S. alert decision. Cromer passed the information to Sir Alec Douglas-Home in London by breakfasttime. He was the first foreign minister to be informed of the U.S. action.

1:30 A.M.: Schlesinger returned to the Pentagon, where he gave further orders to buttress the alert. The aircraft carrier *John F. Kennedy*, with its Skyhawk A-4 fighter-bombers, was sent from the eastern Atlantic into the Mediterranean. The 15,000-man 82nd Airborne Division at Fort Bragg, North Carolina, known as the "quick reaction force," was told to be ready to move by 6 A.M.

2 A.M.: Other NATO members were informed of the alert through the Brussels office of the North Atlantic Council. Pentagon officials later claimed that the various European capitals were not informed until much later in the morning because of a failure in the Brussels communications machinery. (At the headquarters of NATO's Northern Europe Command in Oslo, senior officers were unaware of the alert as late as Thursday lunchtime—more than seven hours after it had been given.)

2:30 A.M.: Back at the State Department, Kissinger finished the draft of his reply to Brezhnev's note. Kissinger warned that the United States could not tolerate unilateral action by the Soviet Union in the Middle East and that any attempt to introduce troops into the war zone would damage the cause of world peace. He also called for further joint action in the United Nations. Kissinger's reply apparently made no specific mention of the alert. He assumed that the Soviets had already found out about this through their own electronic intelligence. Or perhaps President Nixon—sitting upstairs the while and, he later said, in direct contact with Brezhnev through the night—told Moscow.

3 A.M.: Schlesinger and Moorer completed details on the "final package" of the alert. Kissinger went back to the White House and told Nixon, still sitting upstairs, of the moves that had been made. President Nixon, in his capacity as Commander-in-Chief,

formally ratified the initiatives of his Secretary of State and Defense Secretary.

3:30 A.M.: Kissinger went to bed.

The news leaked. By the time he woke up shortly after 7 A.M. that Thursday morning, the alert was on every news program in the United States, although there had been no official Pentagon or White House announcement. A soldier from a missile base in Montana said, according to NBC, that it was the first time since 1962 that the silos had been put in such readiness. The collective United States spine was chilled. Where was Kissinger's vaunted détente?

Kissinger later said privately that he had expected some of the individual alerts—like that of the 82nd Airborne—to become public, but that he was unprepared for the revelation of the whole bag of tricks. After the traumas of the weekend it all seemed too much. Initial reaction among the skeptical in Washington was either that the President had finally flipped, or that it was all a fraud to distract attention from Watergate. At that stage nobody outside the tiny group of decision makers knew that it was Kissinger who had managed the details of the crisis and that Nixon had simply rubber-stamped his decisions. And nobody knew the network of calculations that had prompted the escalation.

Nor did Kissinger enlighten the world outside his small Washington elite, when he met the press later that Thursday—the President, meanwhile, having postponed another scheduled news conference on Watergate. Shortly after midday, Kissinger came into the big briefing room at the State Department to explain how, literally overnight, the policy of détente had been apparently turned into one of nuclear confrontation. He was at pains to minimize the confrontational aspects of the affair, nor did he level any specific charge at the Soviets: "It is," he said, "the ambiguity of some of the [Soviet] actions and communications, and certain readiness measures that were observed, that caused the President, at a special meeting of the National Security Council last night, at 3 A.M., to order certain precautionary measures to be taken by the United States." (An account that glossed over so many points as to strengthen the hands of those who scented a put-up job.)

Kissinger was bitterly dismissive of these suggestions that the alert might have been prompted by domestic considerations. In answer to one question about whether he suspected the Soviet Union of taking advantage of Nixon's Watergate problem he said simply: "One cannot have crises of authority in a society for a period of months without paying a price somewhere along the line"—a reply that might be seen as aimed as much at home as abroad.

But Kissinger's main audience was Moscow. He reminded his audience that both the Soviet Union and the United States had nuclear arsenals "capable of annihilating humanity" and that they both had "a special duty to see to it that confrontations are kept within bounds." The superpowers, he said, had "a very unique relationship": "We are at one and the same time adversaries and partners in the preservation of peace." And he as good as told Brezhnev that the United States did have the power and the will to do what was necessary to bring Israel into line: "None of the issues that are involved in the observance of the cease-fire would warrant unilateral action," he said.

Kissinger, indeed, so smoothed over the crisis that it would have been hard to guess that he had been primarily responsible for putting the superpower debate onto this nuclear footing. But even as he spoke, the Soviet threat—real or imagined—already seemed a thing of the past. Within the Security Council, meeting that Thursday morning, a compromise had been evolved that would exclude the permanent members of the Council—and therefore the two superpowers—from the immediate peace-keeping operation. As one delegate put it: "No one within the UN had fully digested the problem until it seemed solved." The crucial resolution, sponsored by eight nonpermanent members of the Council—Guinea, India, Indonesia, Kenya, Panama, Peru, Sudan, and Yugoslavia—endorsed the use of a UN emergency force, excluding troops from the Big Five (the United States, the Soviet Union, China, Britain, and France). That was Kissinger's idea, and the resolution had been hammered out in a series of discussions among John Scali, the U.S. representative, and delegates from the nonaligned nations. The final piece slotted into place during the delay caused by Kissinger's press conference—which all the delegates broke off to watch on television—when Malik called Moscow and obtained the Soviet go-ahead. The Secretary General, Dr. Waldheim, received unanimous approval to transfer forces of Austria, Finland, and Sweden, then serving the UN in Cyprus, to the Middle East war zone—in all, seven thousand men.

And just in case the brief confrontation had aroused deeper fantasies inside Israel or the United States, Malik took the opportunity to make Soviet policy explicit: "We are firmly in favor of all—I repeat all—states and peoples in the Near East being ensured peace, security and the inviolability of their borders. The Soviet Union is ready to participate in the corresponding guarantees." The superpowers were back on course.

Had the Soviets really intended to intervene? Or was the alert a panic response to "fantastic speculation," as Brezhnev put it, "in some NATO countries?" There was certainly more to the Soviet buildup than speculation. But after the crisis, both superpowers tried to improve their cases by peddling "off the record" briefing stories about how each had been double-crossed by the other. Neither version seemed entirely credible. The American account had it that Sadat's October 24 call for U.S. and Soviet troops had been a put-up job. Both Sadat and Brezhnev knew that the United States could never accede to such a request: It was simply a device to outmaneuver the West at the UN and provide a cover that would enable the Soviet Union to establish a large presence in the Middle East. But that scenario ignored the sequence of Soviet moves since Kosygin went to Cairo on October 16—a sequence that certainly demonstrated Soviet willingness to go to extreme lengths to bail out Sadat, but equally demonstrated a consistent Soviet desire to achieve this jointly with the United States.

The Soviet version of the double-cross was more lurid. They claimed that they had been betrayed at two levels. First, Kissinger had deceived them by flying from Moscow to Israel and hinting to Golda Meir that no harm would ensue if the Israeli armies pressed their military advantages after agreeing to the crease-fire. Second, they claimed that there had been an agreement to send U.S. and Soviet troops to monitor the cease-fire once formal UN Security Council permission was obtained.

The second allegation is flatly contradicted by the U.S. assertion that the question of sending troops was never raised in Moscow. We have already indicated that it may have been part of the Kosygin-Sadat package put to Kissinger shortly before he flew there. But had enforcement of the cease-fire been a serious topic in Moscow, it is improbable that the draft of Resolution 338 thrashed out then would not have contained some reference to this—if only a form of words to appease the self-esteem of other members of the Security Council. Besides, it seems hardly likely that Kissinger, who had spent over four years disentangling the United States from Vietnam, would have contemplated a similar involvement in the Middle East. Nor is there any evidence to suggest that Kissinger gave the Israelis any encouragement to break the cease-fire. On the contrary, sources close to him maintain that he received news of the postcease-fire encirclement of the Egyptian Third Army with considerable dismay—as the opening anecdote of this chapter exemplified.

There were those, of course, to whom the causes of the crisis were less important than its satisfactory resolution. "He stirred. We growled. He heard it and backed down," said a contented U.S. official after a day on the brink. But that was only a hairy-chested way of avoiding the truth: which was that the superpowers could not arbitrate peace and war among their Middle Eastern client states without running themselves into the same, or even greater, risks of conflict.

Indeed, by far the most plausible explanation of the crisis is that a spectacular misunderstanding arose because the whole question of how the truce might actually be organized was never properly discussed. Carving up the world between them, demonstrating that the United Nations was powerless without their prior agreement, confident that their *protégés* were utterly dependent on them, the two superpowers could not apparently permit themselves to think that Israeli and Arab soldiers and politicians might have wills of their own. The U.S. belief appears to have been that the cease-fire could simply be imposed by the two powers principally responsible for the supply of arms—and Brezhnev agreed. From this simple miscalculation, the steps that led to the global confrontation were terrifying precisely because they were so logical—and derived, not from a mad President, but from the momentum and interplay of actual events.

With the establishment of the UN emergency force, the threat of confrontation between the superpowers ebbed away. Soviet observers did arrive in Egypt before the weekend, but they numbered less than a hundred and were armed only with briefcases. They reported meekly to the UNTSO headquarters in Cairo with offers of assistance. The United States announced its willingness to send similar civilian "representatives," if these were requested by the UN. (Egypt made it clear it did not want the Soviets by confining them to their hotel for a few days. In the end, both the United States and the Soviet Union settled for thirty-six "observers" each.) By Friday, the day after the crisis, the alert was already being phased down.

Only President Nixon tried to make some political mileage out of the affair. In a belated press conference that Friday, he claimed emotionally that the world had passed through its "most difficult" crisis since the Cuban missile confrontation of 1962. This seems to have irritated Brezhnev, who had kept the Soviet Union's public reactions conspicuously low-key.

After Kissinger's postalert press conference, the Soviet news agency Tass omitted all mention of the alert, reporting only Moscow's acceptance of the latest Security Council resolution. That might have been simply to disguise defeat, of course. But Brezhnev, in his first public statement on the crisis, was at pains not even to mention the United States, blaming merely "some NATO countries." In the wake of Nixon's high-pitched account of the affair, however, Moscow now claimed more roughly that Washington's response had been "absurd," and that the crisis had been an attempt to "intimidate" the Soviet Union. And for the first time the Soviet press began to report the possibility of Nixon's impeachment over Watergate.

Which was a bit hard on Nixon, because he had ended his account of the crisis by speaking up for the strength of the Soviet-American relationship. "With all the criticism of détente," he said, "I would suggest that without détente we might have had a major conflict in the Mideast. With détente we avoided it." He seemed less enthusiastic about "our European friends" who, he felt, "hadn't been as cooperative as they might have been in attempting to help us work out the Mideast settlement." With some heat, though little logic, Nixon laid into his Western allies. "Europe gets 80 per cent of its oil from the Mideast," he said. "They would have frozen to death this winter if there hadn't been a settlement." That was not how Europe saw things.

6. Europe Keeps Its Head Down

"After the Six-Day War, we warned America," one British diplomat at the heart of the Middle East crisis recalled. "We said: Unless you get a peace, there will be another war. Well, now there is another war. At least we haven't said, 'We told you so.'" It was the quintessential statement of European policy through the Yom Kippur War. And if it seemed to American eyes quiescent, complaisant, or neutralist—well, that was how it was meant to be.

As the same British diplomat put it: "Producing a peace has always meant persuading Israel by logic or force to accept the rest of the world's interpretation of Resolution 242. And when this war ends, unless Israel is persuaded finally to accept 242, there will be another war again. And we have told the United States that as well. Only they have any power over Israel—which I agree is not much. But we in Europe have even less. What can we do? It's America's problem."

The nuclear alert was the breaking point in relations between the United States and Europe over the war. Most European governments—and particularly those on whose soil the United States had bases that had been put on alert—made it fairly publicly clear that they resented what they saw as lack of consultation, besides finding the switchback of superpower diplomacy a little hair-raising for their liking. At the same time in Washington, officials of the State Department and the Pentagon were putting on record their irritation at Europe's failure to rally 'round the American flag in the Middle East. "We were struck," said the State Department spokesman, Robert McCloskey, "by a number of our allies going to some lengths to separate themselves publicly from us. It raised questions as to how that action on their part can be squared with what the Europeans have often referred to as indivisibility on questions of security."

But perceptions of interest in the Middle East had long since ceased to be indivisible. In part, there were genuine differences of political opinion. Most European powers had become irritated by Israel's seeming recalcitrance in the face of "world opinion" as expressed through the UN, and were inclined to blame Israel for the failure of previous attempts to negotiate a workable peace settlement. Europe was divided in its loyalties, of course. Broadly, Holland was the most pro-Israel; France, the most anti-Israel. (The French insistence upon seeking a pro-Arab formula had been a major factor in sterilizing Secretary of State Rogers' attempts to get a joint "Big Four" approach at the time of his talks with the Soviet Union back in 1969.) But, throughout Europe, there was a fair measure of agreement when the war started that the United States not only shared considerable responsibility for the mess but was—as that British diplomat said—the only Western nation with any hope of influencing events.

And Kissinger, to judge from his approach, seemingly shared this view of Europe's irrelevance. In the first thirty-six hours of war, for example, he had more or less requested the British Government to abandon its initial policy—an immediate Security Council resolution calling for a cease-fire—and to leave matters to him thereafter. Having already ascertained that Sadat would ignore such a resolution anyway, Britain readily agreed. But Kissinger did then conduct Middle East policy with only the barest consultation with the United States' nominal allies. To the more disenchanted recipients of this inattention, it seemed as if the episode of Britain and the abortive cease-fire plan at the end of the first week exemplified Kissinger's attitude: that the United States' allies were to regard themselves as being at his beck and call. A French diplomat in Washington put it elegantly: "I think Dr. Kissinger has absorbed the English belief that children should be seen but not heard. And we are his children."

Reactions such as these expressed no more than predictable pique. The Middle East had for so long been the stamping ground of the European powers that their present impotence inevitably galled at times. Fundamentally, however, Europe was devoutly thankful that Kissinger's approach did demand nothing of it except silence. Europe imported 80 per cent of its oil from Arab countries, whereas the United States was dependent on the Middle East for only 11 per cent of its consumption. An oil ban, of the kind that Arabs were showing themselves capable of imposing, could literally destroy many European economies while being no more than a mild embarrassment to America's. Europe simply could not afford the consequences of overt support for U.S. policy in the Middle East. Europe's policy on the Yom Kippur War was thus, in general terms, to keep its head well down and say as little as possible. It was in pursuit of this low-profile policy, for instance, that Britain, in the first week of the war, had banned arms shipments to both sides—a ban which in fact hurt Israel more than Egypt.

Alone of the European nations, however, France was outspokenly pro-Arab—and in characteristically abrasive fashion. On October 11, the French Foreign Minister, Michel Jobert, met Kissinger for an hour at the State Department. He pledged France's full support for Kissinger's efforts to achieve a cease-fire. He even proffered the "good offices" of French diplomacy. A relieved Kissinger called the meeting "extremely constructive"; and State Department spokesmen claimed it had been "the best meeting with a French Foreign Minister we could recall." A few days later, Jobert stood up in the National Assembly in Paris, demanded with a flourish of rhetoric whether "it is necessarily unforeseen aggression to try to go home"—an unequivocally pro-Arab stance—and poured scorn on Brezhnev and, particularly, Kissinger, "now a Nobel Peace Prize winner, shaking hands while sending thousands of tons of arms by air in to the combatants." Reportedly, when Kissinger read the speech, he "literally couldn't believe it."

But France was, as ever, the exception. For most of NATO, the prospect of a U.S. airlift to Israel thus posed an embarrassing dilemma. Almost certainly, the United States would want overflight rights—perhaps even stopover facilities in the countries in which it had bases. The dilemma was whether to accede to this request and offend the Arabs, or refuse it and alienate the United States. It is, in a sense, a backhanded compliment to the United States that so many chose the latter course: At least, Europe assumed, Washington would be understanding. And relations could always be patched up later.

In practice, most of the countries likely to be asked to help the airlift tried to forestall the request before it could be made. On October 9, Spain—90 per cent dependent on Arab oil, and on the direct U.S.-to-Israel flight path—told the U.S. military mission in Madrid that it hoped overflight rights would not be requested. On October 11, Italy said the same thing. So did Greece and Turkey.

Britain was spared the choice. By the end of the first week—as the U.S. airlift got under way—relations between Britain and America were so bad in the wake of Kissinger's abortive cease-fire bid that the British Government, to its intense relief, was simply never asked to help. One of the main U.S. overseas air bases is in Britain, at Mildenhall in Suffolk. And the British Government was, so far as we can judge, prepared to turn a blind eye to flights in and out of the base—so long as Britain's permission was not asked. Should the Arabs subsequently tax Britain with permitting the airlift, the government could then deny all knowledge with suitable, if transparent, indignation. To the British Government, that did not seem unreasonable—and there is some evidence that a suggestion along these lines was delicately put to Washington.

But, apart from his anger over the cease-fire confusion, Kissinger was by now irate over a similar ploy Britain had already put forward. Midway through the first week of war, the United States was desperate to run high-altitude reconnaissance flights over the battle fronts—partly to take pictures, but mainly to pick up electronic intelligence on the SAM-6s that were crippling the Israeli Air Force.

The United States wanted to base its aircraft for this purpose—the Lockheed SR-71A spy plane, successor to the U-2—at a British base—apparently Mildenhall or one of the other USAF bomber bases. The request went to the British Prime Minister, Edward Heath, who agreed to it—but stipulated that the flights should be not only secret but deniable by the British Government in the event of a leak. If necessary, in other words, the U. S. Government was to "admit" that it had not asked Britain's permission. Kissinger was furious. (The Washington *Post* broke this story; but British sources claim that the *Post* was wrong to attribute

Kissinger's anger to the demand for secrecy. It was the request for deniability that apparently riled him.)

Yet Heath's stipulation was a prudent one, as the embarrassment of West Germany now demonstrated. Willy Brandt, the West German Chancellor, did allow the airlift to operate out of the vast U.S. base at Ramstein in the Rhineland—one of the U.S. military's main logistics centers in Europe. While the bulk of the supplies to Israel came direct from the United States, most of the replacement tanks were flown out of Ramstein, along with numbers of aircraft stripped from U.S. squadrons in Germany.

Within three days of the start of this airlift, West Germany was under pressure from the Arabs. On Tuesday, October 16, West German Foreign Minister Walter Scheel politely but firmly indicated to the U.S. ambassador in Bonn, Martin Hillebrand, that he hoped the airlift would end shortly. Scheel was frank about the pressures. Germany staved off the Arabs, however, until October 23—the day after the supposed cease-fire—when Scheel told Hillebrand that West Germany would now like the arms shipments to cease. Hillebrand reassured him that, so far as he knew, they had already stopped. The German ambassador in Cairo told this to the Arabs.

But Hillebrand was wrong—as the West German Government learned the next day, when a local newspaper telephoned to inquire about the two Israeli freighters loading military cargo at Bremerhaven under the guard of U.S. military police. Scheel complained bitterly to the U. S. Embassy—to be told lamely by Hillebrand's deputy, Frank Cash, that he thought clearance had been given by the West Germans for these all-too-public shipments. The Arabs, of course, thought the West Germans had lied to them.

To Brandt and his colleagues, the nuclear alert the day after that was the last straw. On October 25, the West German Government put out a stiffly worded statement that the United States had been requested to stop all shipments to Israel at once. It was unnecessary: Those two ships were the only ones, and the airlift from Ramstein had ceased. But Brandt needed to salvage some sort of position *vis-à-vis* the Arabs. Kissinger's response was to call in the West German ambassador in Washington, Berndt von

Staden, and lecture him on Europe's duties in the Western alliance.

Kissinger may genuinely have been "disgusted" over Europe's behavior—as he was plausibly reported to have muttered after a Senate hearing. (The aside, having achieved its impact, was then denied.) He certainly admonished a group of European parliamentarians in Washington on their inadequacies. While the United States "had to make significant decisions," he said, "the Europeans acted as though the North Atlantic alliance did not exist." Europe appeared "more interested in gaining marginal individual advantages than in cooperating on united actions."

But what was "marginal" about Europe's need for Arab oil? What did the West German episode demonstrate except, to put it politely, a cavalier U.S. attitude toward the real difficulties of an ally trying to be helpful? What "united actions" had Kissinger requested of Europe? And how could Nixon justify the claim, implicit in his picture of Europe freezing to death, that a united European front against the Arabs would somehow have persuaded the Arabs to supply the West with more and not less oil? Nor did the United States even have the right to excoriate the Arab oil embargo, having itself enforced one against Cuba for years. To many Europeans, Kissinger's strictures sounded merely arrogant. The British ambassador in Washington, Lord Cromer, had a more sophisticated understanding of Kissinger's problems than that, but even he could not resist the last word. When Kissinger lamented to him that during the war "those we consulted most supported us least," Cromer replied deadpan: "You must be referring to the Russians, Henry."

Paradoxically, however much damage the alert did to the United States' relations with Europe, it arguably served to strengthen the accommodation between the superpowers. Both now knew, with no possibility of error, the limits to which each would go. What still remained unresolved, however, were the limits to which either superpower could control its client in the battle zone. On Thursday, October 25—as the world first adjusted to the news of the alert—another attempt by the Egyptian Third Army to break out sparked renewed fighting around the town of Suez. While the Security Council at last debated the sending of a full-scale peace-keeping force, small teams of UN observers once again set out from Cairo to separate the combatants—and once again failed to establish any satisfactory cease-fire line. A UN patrol that had set out from the Israeli side did make it to Port Suez; but they confessed on arrival that they had no very clear idea where they should take up permanent positions.

7. Saving Egypt's Third Army

The plight of the twenty thousand men of the Third Army was desperate. They had been cut off for four days, and on the most generous estimate could not expect to hold out for more than another week. Some military experts thought that another three days would be their limit. That Thursday afternoon, the Israelis again underlined the superiority of their position by announcing that they had agreed, after a request from Cairo relayed through the International Committee of the Red Cross, to permit the shipment of two hundred containers of blood plasma for treatment of the wounded in the Third Army, but on condition that these came from the Red Cross headquarters in Tel Aviv. Earlier, the Israelis had turned back three attempts—two by the Red Crescent (the Egyptian equivalent of the Red Cross) and one by the Red Cross—to send convoys with medical supplies down the Cairo-to-Suez road. No mention of the shipment from Tel Aviv was made on Cairo radio. Sadat's government, under pressure to show that it had not fought the war for nothing—or worse than nothing—was not about to tell its citizens that the succor of its wounded military heroes depended on the enemy's grace and favor.

Cairo, indeed, was still claiming that a remarkable victory had been won. Egyptian spokesmen harked back to the triumph of the fall of the Bar-Lev defenses—"considered stronger than the Maginot and Siegfried lines"—denounced the U.S. supply operation, and remained studiously vague about Israeli "infiltration" into Egyptian territory. This sort of propaganda made the Israelis even more determined to press home their advantage around Suez. The influential commentator, Zeev Schiff, put the official line very precisely in Thursday's Ha'aretz: "The Egyptians are going to try, with the aid of the Russians, to turn the resounding defeat of their Third Army into a victory. This should not fluster us. We must not make a false step and lose this card from our hand. We have no obligation to permit supplies to reach this army. We must remember that it is an enemy army which has shed much of our blood and killed many of our sons, and that any minute may bring a renewal of the fighting.

"This is not the same as the Six-Day War, when Egyptian soldiers retreating in the desert were given drinking water after their defeat. Providing the Third Army with water at this point would mean strengthening it and helping to turn it into a well-consolidated base from which future aggression could threaten us. What we should do is allow the Third Army men to return to Egypt, after leaving their arms in Sinai.

"If they want to drink water, let them go home and drink."

But the Arabs held two cards of their own. Neither was of great military significance but both had a strong emotional content. The first was the maintenance of a naval blockade on the Bab-el-Mandeb straits at the southern entrance to the Red Sea, which the Israelis viewed as an act of war and a violation of the cease-fire. The second, and much more explosive, was the question of prisoners of war.

In accordance with the Geneva Convention of 1949, the Israelis had regularly forwarded to the Red Cross details of Arab prisoners captured. These showed that by the morning of October 24 the Israelis held 1,300 POWs—988 Egyptians, 295 Syrians, 12 Iraqis, and 5 Moroccans. The reporting procedure on the Arab side had been notably more negligent. Egypt had reported only 48 Israelis captured, and Syria, which had exhibited captured Israeli soldiers on television, had reported none. Israel's estimate of its "missing presumed captured" numbered almost 400. But how many were still alive? The first rumors of atrocity stories had already appeared in the Israeli press.

The Israeli military had known for some days, from captured Syrians, of the murders and mutilations on Mount Hermon. On Golan, the graves had now been found in which twenty-eight Israeli soldiers, blindfolded and with their hands manacled, had been buried after being shot. (Soldiers of the Israeli Ordnance Corps, combing Golan for repairable vehicles, had by chance discovered the first bodies at the end of the first week of war, but the

Israeli authorities had kept the finding a close secret.) Israel had the disagreeable impression that the two Arab countries were deliberately avoiding their obligations under the Geneva Convention in order to create uncertainty about the fate of their POWs while Egypt was uncertain about the fate of its Third Army. (Arab diplomats in London said privately that the killings on Mount Hermon, and perhaps others, had been the work of the contingent of Moroccan troops that had fought throughout the war on the northern sector of Golan.)

Friday, October 26, was the first day of the Qorban Bairam holiday, which marks the end of Ramadan. It is a festive occasion, but in Cairo the celebrations were unusually subdued; government offices and factories were told to continue working as normal. The tone of the Egyptian media on the subject of the war was now reassuring rather than euphoric—as if they were slowly preparing their readers for the truth. *Al Gomhouria* warned against the hope of quick solutions, noting that "the popular war of liberation is a continuous one." In *Al Ahram* Heikal urged his readers to "rally 'round the flag and at the side of the decision maker." Sadat, he explained, had to agree to a ceasefire because Egypt found itself "up against direct American intervention. . . . The United States gave Israel weapons which she herself has not used in action." Heikal also sought to allay popular suspicions of superpower collusion at Egypt's expense.

The reality, of course, was that a new phase of superpower collusion was beginning—but at Israel's expense. Implicit in the defusing of confrontation was Kissinger's promise that the United States would now take all necessary steps to preserve the Third Army. In accepting this task, Kissinger could have been under no illusion but that it would entail the most intense pressure upon Israel yet. But it was necessary, as he saw it, to preserve any hope of constructing a long-term settlement. "Let me tell you something about my view of solving disputes," he told Heikal in a later interview. "If we wish to solve a critical dispute the point from which we should start should be one at which each party will feel that it has got something." If the Third Army went under, any chance of negotiation would be dead—the humiliation for Egypt, and the sense of betrayal among the Arabs generally, would be too great. They would have won nothing.

Nor did Kissinger have very long in which to work. While the other fronts stayed quiet on Friday, the encircled Third Army made another, and final, desperate attempt to improve its position. Under cover of tank and artillery fire, the Egyptians attempted to take control of their old pontoon bridges south of the Little Bitter Lake and to lay a new one across the canal south of Port Suez. After a battle lasting three hours, in which the Israeli Air Force played a prominent part, the attempt to establish an east-to-west linkup between the Egyptian forces was foiled and the Arabs' new bridge lay in ruins. The day also brought more positive evidence of the disintegration of Third Army morale as the Israelis rounded up numerous small bands of soldiers—often without a fight—who had detached themselves from the main force and were trying to make their own way back to the Egyptian heartland. Some of the Egyptians carried leaflets advising them to surrender, which had been dropped by Israeli planes over their positions earlier in the week.

Meanwhile, fifty-six Finnish soldiers, members of the UN emergency force hurriedly flown from Cyprus to Cairo, spent illtempered hours at an Israeli roadblock on the Cairo-to-Suez road. They had finally decided that they might as well return to Cairo, when the Israelis announced that Defense Minister Dayan would personally accompany them into position. But Dayan did not arrive—and finally the Finns were told that he had been summoned to a special Cabinet meeting. Kissinger had begun to put on the pressure.

Kissinger tackled the problem that Friday afternoon by talking with Israel, Egypt, and the Soviet Union directly—though UN Secretary General Kurt Waldheim was kept informed. The first surprise was how well Kissinger got on with Egypt's new Foreign Minister, Ismail Fahmy, who had flown to Washington immediately on taking over from Mohammed Zayyat. The first meeting of Kissinger and Fahmy on Friday was "promising and productive," according to State Department officials afterward. And the relationship did seem to move almost at once to a more than formal cordiality: Posing for pictures afterward, Kissinger with his arm around Fahmy's waist, the pair looked the very model of togetherness.

That was the easy part. Having pared Fahmy's demands to

the minimum—by pleading, with considerable frankness, his limited power to work miracles—Kissinger then tackled the Israeli ambassador, Simcha Dinitz. In the early hours of Thursday morning, Kissinger had told Dinitz of the alert and the Soviet moves that had sparked it. The news lost nothing in the telling: Kissinger painted a horrific picture of the Soviet Union teetering on the brink of war. Now, according to Israeli sources, Kissinger played that card to Dinitz once again. He said that the Soviet Union was still fundamentally committed to saving the beleaguered Egyptian force. He implied that Israeli intransigence in the Suez area was a danger to international stability—because, he concluded, the United States could not back down from its publicly expressed opposition to Soviet troop involvement. As a result of the brinkmanship of the preceding days, the Israeli Government found itself unsubtly landed by Kissinger with the custody of world peace.

It was Dinitz's cabled report of this conversation that led Mrs. Meir to summon the hasty Cabinet meeting that prevented Dayan from escorting the Finns of the UN force into position around Suez. It was now late Friday afternoon in Washington, late evening in Israel. And although impressed by the starkness of Soviet determination, as relayed down the Kissinger-to-Dinitz line, Mrs. Meir found it politically impossible to let the Third Army off the hook without something in return. The fate of Israel's missing prisoners was now the main public concern: The Israeli Government would have to make progress on that topic. Besides, Kissinger had told her in Tel Aviv that the Soviets had privately agreed to an exchange of prisoners within seventy-two hours of a cease-fire.

When that was relayed by Dinitz, Kissinger himself telephoned Mrs. Meir. It was now around 6 P.M. in Washington, midnight in Israel. It was impossible for the Egyptians to agree to release prisoners, Kissinger said, unless at the same time Sadat could demonstrate some victory more tangible than an army preserved by Israeli good grace. Sadat, too, had his domestic problems: The more insecure politically he became, the more intransigent Sadat would have to make his demands—and the prospect of peace would recede still farther.

In a conversation of steadily rising heat, Mrs. Meir stuck to her demand. Kissinger threatened that if the Third Army remained unsupplied, the United States would have to demonstrate good faith to the Soviet Union by ceasing supplies to Israel. Mrs. Meir held on. Finally, according to the authors of *Hamechdal*, Kissinger burst out: "Mrs. Meir, you are playing with the future of your people. Would you prefer supplies to the Third Army to be sent in Russian helicopters?" This was no empty threat. The Soviets had already said they would do it if necessary. And it would not have taken any large-scale intervention: merely the publicized insertion of a handful of Soviet pilots to fly Egypt's surviving fleet of Soviet Mi-8 helicopters.

Mrs. Meir gave in. As Dayan said later: "We had no choice." The Israeli Chief of Staff was of the same view: "We were compelled to agree," Elazar said. "It was imposed on us to arrange the convoy." The U. S. State Department was content to soften the affair. As a result of its "good offices," the statement read, agreement had been reached between Egypt and Israel that "would permit a convoy of men and supplies" to go through to the Egyptian Third Army, under the aegis of the UN and the Red Cross.

As the statement implied, a way had been worked out to save Mrs. Meir's face as well as Sadat's. The idea was dreamed up jointly by Ambassador Dinitz and the Israeli military attaché, Mordechai Gur. When they put it to Kissinger early that Friday evening, he was skeptical of its success; but he agreed to try it on Fahmy—who, with a little pressure, agreed. The idea was simple. If Israel could not get its prisoners back in exchange for supplying the Third Army, at least it could gain something else it wanted: face-to-face talks with Egypt. And what better topic to open with than the organization of those supplies?

At Kissinger's behest, Major General Ensio Siilasvuo, the Finnish commander of the UN force wearily trying to establish itself between the armies, arranged the hurried meeting. Barely an hour after Kissinger's talk with Mrs. Meir, at 1:30 A.M. on the morning of Saturday, October 27, an Egyptian officer, Major General Adly el Sherif, strode through the barbed wire of the Israeli lines around Suez and entered a large tent emblazoned with the Star of David. The place was called Wadi el Jandalin, and the tent was pitched not far from a milestone on the Suez-to-

Cairo highway sixty-three miles from the Egyptian capital: Kilometer 101. Waiting under the bright desert starlight to greet Sherif was Major General Aharon Yariv. He was a shrewd choice by Mrs. Meir: After nine years as head of Israeli military intelligence until his retirement in 1972, Yariv understands the Arabs, comprehends their predicament and their pride, more than anyone else in the Israeli establishment.

As recorded by the *Newsweek* reporter on the scene, Yariv's greeting befitted the occasion: "Two valiant armies have fought for three weeks," he said to Sherif. "Now let's try to work out an honorable peace." So, on Saturday, October 27, the guns at last fell silent on both fronts—twenty-four days and thousands of lives after Yom Kippur.

Even now, however, the portents were not wholly encouraging. The Israeli leadership did not feel inclined to disguise its irritation with this anticlimactic end to its Egyptian campaign. Interviewed the next day, Sunday, by the American CBS team, Mrs. Meir ended up by taking charge. "I want to tell you something," she said. "Sadat must, I think, be given time to enjoy his defeat. And not immediately, by political manipulations, turn that into a victory, not because I want him defeated or humiliated, but for God's sake, he started a war, our people are killed, his in the many thousands are killed, and he has been defeated. And then by political arrangements, he is handed a victory and has become or thinks he has become a hero in the eyes of the Egyptian people."

And although Yariv and Sherif had talked for a cordial two hours, immediate problems remained there too. Yariv had agreed to let 125 trucks of supplies through to the Third Army, but after 2 days only 25 had in fact negotiated the Israeli roadblocks. And when Yariv and Sherif began to probe the wider issues, both officers naturally echoed their governments' demands. Yariv wanted an exchange of prisoners and then a pullback to the prewar lines. Sherif demanded that Israel withdraw to the October 22 ceasefire lines. It was deadlock.

When Mrs. Meir flew into Washington on Thursday, November 1, she looked tired; but she stonewalled the press conference questions vigorously enough. She denied United States pressure upon Israel. "There is no pressure," she said. So why had she come? "Just to find out that there is no pressure." It was an expected diplomatic lie. Israel's relationship with the United States was now one of grudging retreat in the face of unrelenting pressure. That was why, in the wake of the Yariv-Sherif talks, the Israeli Cabinet had decided that Mrs. Meir should come to Washington for some straight talking. Mrs. Meir and her ministers seem to have thought that direct liaison with President Nixon might soften Israel's problems. They presumably recalled the similar gap Mrs. Meir had exploited between the President and his Secretary of State over arms supplies in the first week of war. It was not that Kissinger departed from Nixon's policies; on the other hand, he did take up more advanced positions than Nixon himself would hold when personally challenged. So perhaps Mrs. Meir could undercut Kissinger by making Nixon back off.

She was disappointed. By the time Mrs. Meir landed in Washington, Kissinger had already talked at length with Soviet ambassador Dobrynin and met once more with Egyptian Foreign Minister Fahmy. Before the unfortunate spasm of confrontation, Kissinger and Dobrynin had already been discussing "the site, the participation, and the procedures" of proper cease-fire talks. Now, the United States and the Soviet Union had reached agreement: a peace conference just before Christmas at the United Nations or, if Israel really objected, somewhere in Europe—probably Switzerland. The talks to be face-to-face. Arab participation to be agreed among the Arabs. And the aim a settlement along the lines of Rogers' plan turned down by the Soviets at the end of 1969: broadly, a phased Israeli withdrawal from virtually all its 1967 gains, with demilitarized zones, an international peace-keeping force if necessary, and a top dressing of superpower guarantees.

But quite as important as that objective was a further U.S.-Soviet accord on how it should be reached. In effect, Kissinger persuaded the Soviets that no worthwhile settlement could be imposed. To be sure, the superpowers could pressure both sides to keep talking, to make concessions. But any settlement must derive organically from such direct negotiations between the parties. Arabs and Jews alike would by that process of talking have to come to terms with the facts of life—and death. When Kissinger said that both sides now had the opportunity "to determine their own fate in consultation and negotiation—for the first time in twenty-five years," that was not a platitude but the core of the superpowers' strategy.

Mrs. Meir thus faced in Washington an Administration with a Middle East policy for the first time both determined and clear-minded—and united, as she soon learned. Her first appointment, the Thursday afternoon she arrived, was with Kissinger. He handled her characteristically. At that first meeting, he talked solely of immediate problems connected with the cease-fire. And he confined himself to putting up demands he knew she would knock down. In an atmosphere "verging on the abrasive," as the State Department later blandly put it, Mrs. Meir complained of the United States pressure on Israel and rejected any future attempts to limit her freedom of maneuver. When Kissinger broached the maintenance of the cease-fire and the continued supplying of the Third Army, Mrs. Meir countered with demands for the lifting of the Bab-el-Mandeb blockade—and, more emotionally, the listing of Israeli prisoners by Egypt and, if possible, their exchange. "The issue of the Third Army is very much second to the issue of our boys," she said. "One issue is simple decency and international law. The other is an effort to help Sadat out of the military mess he got himself into by starting the war." Kissinger agreed.

So did Nixon. Nixon agreed with almost everything Mrs. Meir said when she met him later that Thursday afternoon. Kissinger and Ambassador Dinitz went to the Oval Office as well. It was a jovial meeting—Mrs. Meir being moved to make her crack about Kissinger's English. And the Israeli Prime Minister later spoke of what she called Nixon's "reassurance" that the United States would continue to support and protect Israel. But beneath the jokes, the reality was bleaker. Nixon made it very clear that he was content to leave U.S. policy in Kissinger's hands. When Mrs. Meir raised the question of arms, Nixon brushed that aside too. Of course, Israel could have arms. How many? "Why don't we arrange for you to meet with Schlesinger on that one," he said. Nixon presented a convincing picture of a President uninterested in detail. Israel had U.S. goodwill: That went without saying. The United States stood for the survival and security of

Israel: That too went without saying. But the price Israel would have to pay? On those details, she should talk to Kissinger.

When Mrs. Meir did see Defense Secretary James Schlesinger the next day, Friday, November 2, he too retreated behind generalities. Of course, Israel could have arms. But there were two problems: their availability and Senate approval. The supplies sent during the war had, for the most part, been stripped from American active service units. The Phantom F-4s, for example, had come mainly from the U. S. Air Force fighter wing at Seymour Johnson Air Force Base near Greensboro in North Carolina. The rest had been lifted from the Sixth Fleet's two attack carriers in the Mediterranean, the U.S.S. *Independence* and the U.S.S. *Roosevelt*. The Skyhawk A-4s had come partly from U.S. bases in Europe; but six had been raided from the U. S. Navy fighter weapons school at Miramar in California: Training was now almost at a standstill. Similarly, the tanks, bombs, and rockets had all come from the United States' own tactical inventories. Schlesinger's first priority, he made clear to Mrs. Meir, was to restock his own forces before he beefed up Israel's. And that could take time. McDonnell Douglas, for example, could at best supply only half a dozen Phantoms a month to the U. S. Air Force. To make up the forty sent to Israel would take over six months.

Senate approval was another problem. Nixon's request for a $2.2 billion appropriation for arms to Israel had been before Congress since October 19. And Congress was showing no inclination to hurry it. Nor was there any secret about the reason. Congressmen reported a flood of mail from constituents concerned that the United States might be sucked into the Middle East after the manner of Vietnam. The key senator in controlling, at this stage, the pace of Senate consideration of Nixon's request was the chairman of the Senate appropriations subcommittee on foreign operations, Daniel Inouye of Hawaii. Inouye was blunt: "All of us in Congress have been receiving letters from anxious constituents who remind us how we became involved in Vietnam, which started with technical assistance, logistical assistance, observers and advisers."

The alert had catalyzed these fears. When war broke out, the first batch of congressional mail had been overwhelmingly pro-Israel. But news of the $2.2 billion appropriation, followed by the scare of the alert, swung the pattern of mail sharply. One midwestern senator told Si Kenen, the main Israeli lobbyist on the Hill, that by the end of the second week of war, though his national mail was running 50–50 on the issue, his home mail was now 99–1 against supplying all that Israel required.

Yet until congressional approval of long-term loans or outright grant aid came through, Schlesinger concluded, Israel would have to pay for what it received within 120 days. And Israel had already gotten $1 billion worth of fresh equipment—which by no stretch of the imagination could it pay for in time. For even before those war resupplies, Israel had already owed the United States $1.7 billion, of which $500 million was due in cash. Schlesinger counseled caution before incurring further debt.

An undaunted Mrs. Meir proceeded to itemize the new equipment Israel required—"the Santa Claus list," Schlesinger's deputy secretary, William Clements, wryly called it. High on her list was the U.S. version of Scud, the Lance battlefield support missile. Schlesinger, like Nixon, shied from such detail. Far better let a joint U.S.-Israel technical team work out precise needs, he told Mrs. Meir. And those needs, of course, would depend upon the shape of the cease-fire and the prospects for peace.

All roads in Washington led back to Kissinger, it seemed. And Washington was fully aware of the leverage that Israel's need for arms now gave him. In musing over Israel's debts, Schlesinger had merely put obliquely what Kissinger's assistant for Near East affairs, Joseph Sisco, had spelled out to the House Foreign Relations Committee on the eve of Mrs. Meir's visit: that Israel had little choice but to listen to what the United States wanted. On Sunday, November 4, a grim-faced Mrs. Meir saw Kissinger once more.

Kissinger made concessions. The United States would free Israel's hand to negotiate with Egypt. The United States would back Israel's decision not to release its stranglehold on the Third Army by withdrawing to the positions of the abortive October 22 cease-fire. Finally, the United States had no map of the Middle East's ultimate boundaries to impose upon Israel. None of these points was a genuine concession, in the sense that—whatever he might have told Mrs. Meir at their first meeting—Kissinger had never intended to insist upon any of those points. On the issue of the Third Army, he realized that even if Mrs. Meir were prepared to release it—which she most certainly was not—she could not do so without encompassing her own political destruction. As for Israel's negotiating freedom, and the absence of an American map, the Kissinger-Dobrynin strategy of avoiding an imposed solution demanded such apparent freedom.

But after the good news, the bad news: Kissinger told Mrs. Meir what he did want. Immediately, he wanted a corridor through the Israeli lines for Egyptian supplies to the Third Army. The corridor route was to be the Cairo-to-Suez road. In the medium term, since the present military positions were absurd—and a danger to peace, which meant to the United States' relationship with the Soviet Union—he wanted an Israeli withdrawal back into Sinai. This would be part of a mutual disengagement. Finally, to set the atmosphere for disengagement, to enable Sadat to make concessions too, Kissinger wanted Israel to prepare positive and constructive proposals for withdrawal from most of its 1967 gains.

In other meetings in Washington, notably with a group of senators, Mrs. Meir portrayed an image of agreeable flexibility—though hedged about with stipulations: agreeing to a withdrawal from Sinai, for instance, provided Israel could have a "long lease" on Sharm el Sheikh; agreeing to withdraw from the West Bank of the Jordan with "only" a token military presence remaining; sadly concluding that Golan would have to be put on a "back burner" until Syria had a "more rational" government. It pleased the senators—though in practical terms it begged just the questions that negotiations would force Israel to face. But negotiating with Kissinger, Mrs. Meir was much tougher.

Thus, Mrs. Meir adamantly rejected all three of Kissinger's requests. A corridor was impossible: It would split Israel's forces. A corridor under Egyptian control was unthinkable: The Third Army would simply rearm. A corridor under Israeli control she felt sure Sadat would not accept. As for Israeli withdrawal to the east bank, that was possible only if Egypt's forces withdrew to the west bank—in effect, returned to the prewar lines. And Israeli proposals for a more extensive pullback from the occupied territories, were also unthinkable until after the Israeli elections—and until Sadat had demonstrated a serious desire for face-to-face negotiations toward an over-all settlement. Sadat's first step must be the provision of the names of Israeli prisoners.

All of which Kissinger had expected. He explored one area of her answer. In the unlikely event that Sadat would accept a corridor to the Third Army under Israeli control, did he understand Mrs. Meir to mean that Israel would then agree to that? Mrs. Meir thought Israel would agree. On that, they parted.

What Kissinger did not tell Mrs. Meir was that before seeing her, he had talked once again with Dobrynin and Fahmy. Fahmy had consulted Sadat; and the Soviet deputy foreign minister, Vasily Kuznetsov, had flown into Cairo too. And although Fahmy reported Sadat's continued determination to achieve an Israeli pullback to the October 22 lines, Kissinger had gathered enough hints from Dobrynin to make him think that Sadat—with a little prodding from the Soviets—would in fact settle for a corridor. When Kissinger put this point to Fahmy, the Egyptian Foreign Minister's reaction had been the mirror image of Mrs. Meir's: Only a corridor under Egyptian control would do, and that Israel would never support.

But who controlled the corridor was a gap that a form of words would bridge—if enough pressure were now applied. Kissinger had whittled the problem of saving the Third Army down to manageable size. The rest could be solved on the spot.

8. The High Price of Victory

On Monday, November 5, Kissinger took off for the Middle East. His departure was accompanied by an orchestrated chorus of woe. Things, it seemed, had never looked worse to Washington. "It is going so badly I think we will have another explosion," one of Kissinger's aides was reported as saying. It was even solemnly suggested that "American intelligence" feared Israel was about to launch a preemptive strike. (At what, Cairo?) True, Sadat had warned foreign newspapermen in Cairo that his more hawkish generals were anxious to renew the war against Israel. And he claimed that the Egyptian Army—thanks to Soviet supplies—was as strong as ever. (In major offensive terms, this was not true: The Soviets had nowhere near made up Egypt's tank losses. But for defense against an Israeli attack, or for a limited assault on the Israeli armor in the Suez salient, it was true that the Egyptian Army was now fully resupplied with Sagger, RPG, and SAM-6 missiles.) But even Sadat's forebodings had their hopeful aspect: A leader under that pressure was badly in need of quick political dividends. As he had said at that October 31 press conference, "I cannot afford to stand with my hands tied." Since Kissinger's aim was to suggest a compromise, the Wagnerian overture of alleged fears in Washington made a useful opening to his tour: It would concentrate Sadat's mind still further.

Kissinger began his Middle East tour in Morocco. It was a tactful gesture: A contingent of King Hassan's troops had fought through the war on Golan, so Morocco qualified as a possible participant in peace talks. And Kissinger knew that one of Sadat's problems would be to sell any compromise solution to his Arab colleagues. So Kissinger helped the process along a bit—and boosted King Hassan's prestige at home—by being photographed in flattering conclave with the Moroccan ruler. Then, on the evening of Tuesday, November 6, Kissinger arrived in Cairo.

The fact of the visit was itself significant. Egypt had severed diplomatic relations with the United States in the wake of the 1967 war, and few people expected a swift reconciliation between Egypt and her enemy's principal armorer. But next morning the surprise happened: Kissinger and Sadat appeared together for an impromptu press conference, looking for all the world like long-lost friends. Egypt and the United States were to resume diplomatic relations. Sadat said he would like Kissinger to remain a mediator in the Middle East conflict. When Kissinger said, "I think we are moving towards peace," Sadat immediately chimed in, "I think I agree with him." In less than twenty-four hours, Sadat and Kissinger had reached a six-point cease-fire agreement. It was an extraordinary achievement; and in retrospect it offers a fascinating insight into Kissinger's working methods.

To some extent, it was done through sheer empathy. Sadat was fascinated by Kissinger—the insecure, mercurial man responding to the confidence and certainty the American radiated. For most of the time, the Egyptian President saw Kissinger without the former's advisors. And he agreed to Kissinger's plan almost without demur. Sadat was later criticized for this by some of his ministers, who held that he had given away too much too soon. But Sadat was shrewder than that. As he later explained privately: "I liked Kissinger very much. I regard him as a friend. And I don't like to haggle with my friends. Besides, I wanted to show him that I am a very very reasonable man—unlike Mrs. Meir. She will haggle over every point. I have given him everything I have. There is no point his coming to ask for more. I have nothing more to give. Now I want something in return."

Kissinger liked Sadat too. (Kissinger in fact has proved to get on well with Egyptians in general. Some part of him seems to respond to their quick intelligence, their almost feminine temperament.) But his approach to Sadat was calculating enough. A blunt description of Kissinger's strategy would be that he promised jam tomorrow in exchange for concessions today. Yet it was more complex than that.

Kissinger deliberately personalized his diplomacy. By talking

with extreme candor, he convinced Sadat that, whatever his misgivings about the United States as a whole, he could trust Kissinger personally—because he also had too much at stake to allow
failure. And the burden of this candor was Kissinger's warning,
reiterated to Sadat, not merely that Egypt's ultimate objectives—
restitution of the Arabs' lost lands, resolution of the Palestinian
tragedy—would take time to achieve, but that the chances of
securing these long-term objectives at all would be diminished
rather than heightened by a concentration upon petty triumphs in
the short term.

Nor, at another level, did Kissinger attempt to conceal that this
was his approach. To be sure, in public the seventeen-man press
corps traveling with him aboard *Air Force One*—"The Yo-Yo
Express," the newsmen called it—were treated largely to jokes.
Sample: Kissinger emerging from the tiny burial chamber at the
heart of the Great Pyramid of the Pharaoh Kufu: "That would
make a nice State Department press room." But his background-
ers seem to have been fairly frank. And to the journalist who
mattered most—Mohammed Heikal, then editor of *Al Ahram* and
by far the most influential newspaperman in the Arab world—
Kissinger devoted 2½ hours on Wednesday evening, after his
talks with Sadat, to what must surely have been one of the most
cunningly revealing self-portraits ever given by a statesman at
work.

"I will tell you two things about my method of tackling disputes," Kissinger said. "The first is that I do not like to approach
any dispute unless I feel that its basic elements—or at least the
great part of its basic elements—are within the grip of my hand.
That was the case in the Vietnam war. American public opinion
was by then anxious to see an end to that war. That was also the
case in Peking and Moscow. The facts of the new age were moving
in the same direction I was moving in. But in the Middle East
crisis I cannot assess precisely what basic elements of the crisis I
have in my grip. . . . I know I am tackling a difficult and complicated dispute. I find it more difficult than Vietnam. I also find
it more difficult than détente with the Soviet Union. But the
second thing is that I hate failure. I have a fund of success which
I do not want to dissipate. I am not speaking of the Nobel Peace
Prize. Let me tell you, some of my son's schoolmates went up to

him and said: 'Do you know that some of our friends say that your father doesn't deserve the Nobel Prize? We are angry with them and said they shouldn't say that.' But my son told his chums: 'What does it matter? My mother told me the same thing.'

"The result of those two factors is that I find myself in the middle of a dispute in which I represent American concern, while all I can do is to rely on my own personal reputation and my own fund of personal success. I believe, nevertheless, that in spite of difficult circumstances there is still a chance of success. But I need time. I want the two sides to give me their patience. That is what I need now: patience. I confess that I fear Arab romanticism. I fear that you may imagine that the solution lies around the first bend in the road. I believe, in fact, that we need an interval of between six months to a year even to reach the beginning of something reasonable.

"When I met the four Arab foreign ministers at the beginning of war, some of them said to me: 'The man who has been able to resolve the Vietnam war, to open the gates of China and to build a détente with the Soviet Union, can surely resolve the Middle East dispute.' But I said to them: 'Please don't look just at the last two weeks in Paris, or at the last few days in Peking or Moscow. Those days were preceded by preparation and work for many long years before we could get to those decisive weeks or days.' I told them: 'Neither I nor anyone else can work miracles. International politics is not a job for a magician.' . . ."

Why should Egypt trust the United States? "I do not represent a direct party in the dispute. This much I can say. Nor do I represent the role of a mediator in the dispute. This much you can say. [Heikal had pointed out that since the United States was not neutral as between Israel and Egypt, Kissinger could not properly be accepted as a mediator.] Well, let us then say, let us agree, that I represent the United States' 'concern' in a grave dispute which takes place in an area which, to us, is a delicate area, an area in which we have strategic interests which we are anxious to maintain and to protect—apart, of course, from our interest in world peace and apart also from our eagerness to keep up our friendship with the peoples of this area.

"Let us therefore say this much. One, we have strategic interests in the area. Two, the other superpower, the Soviet Union, also has interests in this area. Three, we are trying to set up a new world order which rests upon a détente following the disappearance of the era of the Cold War. Yet that détente will not lead us to leave the area to the influence of the other superpower. Four, we do not want any dispute to be escalated to the point of affecting that détente. The dangers of this would be far graver than humanity could stand. Five, we have a special relationship with Israel. We are committed to the protection of its security. But we consider that that security can only be achieved through respect of your sovereignty. Six, in having that special relationship with Israel, we do not find this at all inconsistent with our desire to develop and strengthen our friendship with you. Seven, neither alone, nor in collaboration with others, do we wish to have tutelage over this area. We want the peoples of this area to build up their own system of life and security as they see fit—in consonance with the major factors of the world. These are the elements of our position as President Nixon conceives them and as I conceive them also.

"The Soviet Union can give you weapons. But the United States can give you a fair and just solution whereby your lands can come back to you—especially now that you have actually changed the situation on the ground. Don't imagine that Israel is happy with all that we do. At the same time we cannot possibly imagine that you will be happy with all we do. But politics in our age, today, are not a matter of sentiment but of the facts of power."

It was a brilliant performance. And while Heikal was clever enough to spot the questions Kissinger so adeptly begged, he still found him "a personality that really calls for admiration." His main reservation, however, was particularly relevant. "There is a problem about Henry Kissinger's practical approach to things," Heikal wrote afterward. "He belongs to the school which believes that a fact is what we see at this very moment and not what we think or believe in the light of what has gone before. This, in fact, is a diminution of the importance of history in major conflicts."

In a moving anecdote, Heikal had tried to impress upon Kissinger the importance that their history had for the Arabs. "How long has Sinai been Egyptian?" Kissinger asked him. And Heikal replied: "I will send you a collection of love letters written on papyri some five thousand years ago. They were written by the Egyptian commander of the Egyptian garrison in El Arish [in what is now the Gaza Strip on the northeast coastal corner of Sinai]. They were written to his wife, a Pharaonic princess. And he says: 'I remember you in this remote place, where I wait to repel the enemies from the borders of the sacred fatherland.'" Heikal ended simply: "You are now in the midst of the oldest people in history." But the Jews too, are an ancient people. Had Kissinger the emigré really come to terms with the complexities such heritages bring? Heikal doubted it:

"In his estimation, facts of power come before any other factor in the calculation of disputes. This point calls for special vigilance. Because the facts of power do not freeze at a given moment but are a continuous and ceaseless debate between events. In practical application, this means that, if Israel can change the conditions of power through the battlefield, we may find ourselves called upon to accept those new conditions as a fresh basis. But this was precisely the problem which we had to face after the Security Council resolution of October 22." In the weeks ahead, as Kissinger called upon the Arabs in vain to relax their oil embargo, he might have reflected upon the irony that he had by his very candor persuaded at least one influential Arab of the importance of maintaining it—as a continuous "fact of power."

But as Kissinger prepared to leave Cairo on Thursday, November 8, it was not the Arabs but Israel that seemed likely to give trouble over the "facts of power." While Joseph Sisco flew from Cairo to Israel with the still-secret agreement in his pocket, Kissinger told his press corps that further news would have to await Sisco's return—adding thoughtfully: "That is, if Joe returns." Indeed, Mrs. Meir and her ministers were once again outraged at the demands Sisco summarily presented to them.

In the deal Kissinger had struck, Sadat basically swapped Israeli prisoners and Egypt's attendance at face-to-face peace talks without prior Israeli territorial concessions, for a corridor through Israeli lines to the Third Army. This of course involved Sadat giving up his demand that Israel withdraw to the first cease-fire lines. To sweeten the bargain, Kissinger gave his personal assurances to Sadat that he would ensure a swift start to serious peace talks, and that the aim in view was a virtually total Israeli withdrawal from its 1967 gains—and from all of Sinai—within a year of the opening of those talks.

After listening to this deal—or as much of it as Sisco spelled out—Mrs. Meir angrily replied that she thought she had obtained President Nixon's assurance that the fate of Israeli prisoners would not be traded against the fate of the Third Army. Sisco replied that this was the deal Kissinger had made.

For hours at home that Thursday evening, Mrs. Meir talked over the deal with Allon, Dayan, and the ex-intelligence chief, Yariv. For another four hours the next morning, the full Israeli Cabinet continued the argument. Predictably, Mrs. Meir then returned to Sisco with a long list of Israeli modifications to the deal. She was stunned to be told by Sisco that, like the super-powers' draft of Resolution 338, this cease-fire agreement could not be altered. Mrs. Meir flatly refused to sign. In the end, they compromised. Mrs. Meir reduced Israel's demands to two: that Israeli troops should control the corridor and that Egypt should lift the Bab-el-Mandeb blockade. And Sisco transmitted these demands to Kissinger—who was by now in the Saudi capital, Riyadh.

The Bab-el-Mandeb blockade was easy enough to resolve. Kissinger replied the next day, Saturday, that it was not necessary to write the lifting of the blockade into the agreement because, being an act of war, it would terminate automatically when the cease-fire was signed. That was a semantic maneuver: In fact, Kissinger had meanwhile contacted Sadat and persuaded him to lift the blockade; but for reasons of face, Sadat wanted nothing on paper. Sadat also argued, disingenuously, that it was solely an affair for the Yemeni Government, whose waters the straits were.

The control point was potentially trickier. Kissinger had persuaded Sadat to drop his demand for an Israeli withdrawal to the first cease-fire positions only on condition that the corridor through their present lines was controlled by the UN forces. But Sadat had seen the reasonableness of Israel's fear that supplies sent over the canal to the Third Army might be military. So he had agreed to an Israeli canalbank inspection. Now

Mrs. Meir wanted to control the whole road. While in theory that was not incompatible with UN checkpoints, would the Israelis try to check all supplies down it? Kissinger took a chance. Israel, he cabled back to Mrs. Meir, would retain control of the Cairo-to-Suez road so long as a UN presence was also allowed. To save Sadat's face, however, could the public fiction be maintained that the corridor was under UN control? On that basis, Mrs. Meir took it on herself that Saturday afternoon, November 10, to agree to the six-point cease-fire.

It was a strange document, part nitty-gritty, part face-saving fiction:

Clause 1 merely bound both sides to observe the cease-fire.

Clause 2 promised discussions toward a return to the October 22 lines—but within the framework of UN-supervised disengagement. Since there was not a chance of Israel withdrawing to the October 22 lines without some equally substantial Egyptian territorial withdrawal, the clause was merely a face-saver for Sadat.

Clause 3 pledged the Israelis to allow supplies into the town of Suez and to allow wounded civilians out. There was no mention of Israeli checks.

Clause 4 pledged no Israeli impediment to nonmilitary supplies to the Third Army.

Clause 5 specified a UN takeover of the Cairo-to-Suez road and agreed that Israel might check material over the canal.

Clause 6 concluded that with all UN points established on the road, both sides would exchange prisoners.

In the early afternoon of Sunday, November 11, Egypt and Israel—Major General Aharon Yariv for Israel and the Egyptian director of operations, Lieutenant General Abdel Ghani el Gamasy—met once more at Kilometer 101 on the Cairo-to-Suez road, this time in a UN tent newly erected midway between the rival lines. Kissinger's risk promptly backfired. Briskly, as if it were hardly up for discussion, Yariv told Gamasy that while there was no problem with supplies to the Third Army or to the town of Suez, the question of Israeli supervision of these supplies had still to be thrashed out. Gamasy said there was nothing to discuss. Israel's rights were in the agreement.

The deadlock lasted for two days—while fistfights broke out on the road outside, as Finnish troops of the UN force tried to put up checkpoints and Israeli soldiers tore them down. As a negotiating stance, Yariv—at Dayan's insistence—was now demanding Israeli control of supplies even into Suez. Gamasy replied that the agreement Mrs. Meir, Sadat, and Kissinger had all signed specified only Israeli checks on supplies over the canal. It took two more visits to Mrs. Meir by the U.S. ambassador, Kenneth Keating—relaying further pressure from Kissinger and Sisco—before, on Wednesday, November 14, the Israeli Prime Minister told Yariv to sign. By this time, Yariv had won the concession he wanted anyway: The Israelis did not get a checkpoint at the entrance to the town of Suez, but they could inspect the supplies at a nearby UN-controlled parking lot. The whole process, in fact, had closely followed a British diplomat's weary description of negotiating with the Israelis: "They don't have a maximum and a minimum position. They just have a maximum one, and they go on increasing it."

At 8 A.M. the next day, Thursday, November 15, the exchange of prisoners began, as the UN at last set up its checkpoints on the Cairo-to-Suez road. By November 22, the last of the 8,301 Egyptian and 241 Israeli prisoners were home. The Israelis made heroes of theirs—weeping crowds greeting them at Lod Airport or around the gates of the hospital to which the wounded were taken. Egypt smuggled hers back to a Cairo military airfield closed to public view. The Red Cross flights that ferried the prisoners to and fro were the first direct flights between Cairo and Tel Aviv for a generation. (Even Sisco had detoured via Cyprus.) "At last," said Dayan, "we have arranged this by talking like human beings."

It was a valiant attempt to extract consolation from a gloomy and equivocal peace. Even the fate of the Israeli prisoners held by Syria was still unknown. Fearful of reprisals on those that survived, Israel had said nothing about its gruesome discoveries on Golan; until, on November 10—despairing of its own powerlessness and hoping that the international community might be shocked into action—Israel officially complained to the International Red Cross. The photographs and circumstantial evidence Israel produced clearly indicated that, at 4 places on Golan, 28 Israeli soldiers had been murdered. The news led to riots in Israel by the families of the 113 still listed as missing on that front. The Syrians were unmoved: President Asad saw the surviving prisoners as Syria's sole bargaining counter against a thoroughly victorious Israel.

At any rate, the brute statistics of war indicated an Israeli victory. The combined Arab forces were estimated to have lost about 2,000 tanks and some 450 planes, compared with Israel's loss of 800 tanks and 115 aircraft. In terms of territory controlled, Israel also had an advantage: In Syria it occupied positions well in advance of the 1967 line, and its west bank salient in Egypt more than made up for the Egyptian gains on the east. Yet it was a victory that had little savor for a nation grown accustomed to clear-cut military achievement.

Both Egypt and Syria had lost perhaps 8,000 men each. The cost to Israel in lives had been barely a third of either. Yet still, the toll for Israel was greater than in any conflict since 1948. The figures subsequently released revealed that 2,523 Israelis had been killed in the fighting, more than twice the number killed in the Six-Day War. But the Six-Day War had been one of rapid and triumphant advance, at the end of which Israel had made huge territorial gains—including all of Jerusalem, which has an emotional value greater than any territory.

The real comparison is with the War of Independence, in which about 6,200 Israelis were killed. On the face of it, those losses were much higher. But they were spread over a much longer period. Allowing for the cease-fires that interrupted hostilities, there were roughly 240 days of fighting in the War of Independence. In crude terms, then, Israel lost an average 25 killed for each day of fighting. In 1973, losses ran at the rate of 115 killed per day up to October 27, when fighting stopped on both fronts. (The early days' losses, as we have said, were in fact much higher.) Allowing for the fact that the Jewish population is now five times larger, this suggests that the cost in lives was roughly comparable. Certainly, in terms of Israeli deaths, the Yom Kippur War was more like the War of Independence than the campaigns of the fifties and sixties.

Relative to its population, Israel's losses were light, of course —about 0.01 per cent of the population, roughly equivalent to the error in a census. And Israel, a young country, could readily replace all but the most skilled of them. In October, with the war actually in progress, the Soviet Union gave exit visas to

4,980 Soviet Jews, a record total. "Look at it like this," one Israeli military expert said, "in manpower terms, and allowing for the dependents these immigrants bring with them, we have lost less than two months' supply of Russian Jews." There were few Israelis who could view the deaths in such Olympian fashion. The cost of being Sharon's "military superpower" seemed suddenly much greater than most people—though not Dayan—had envisaged.

Moreover, Israel's economy seemed to have little chance of a rapid recovery. Certainly, there was little hope of early demobilization for Israel's citizen soldiers, as their leaders debated disengagement with the Egyptians at Kilometer 101. Yariv, leader of Israel's negotiating team, was greeted by his soldiers each time he emerged from the UN tent with shouts of "Can we go home?" He could only shake his head. Egypt might have failed to impose a war of attrition on Israel, but the attrition on nerves ground down by this half-peace was only faintly more bearable. To assist young mothers, the Israeli education service set up seminars in the elementary schools to help explain to their children why their fathers were so long at the war. A child psychologist advising one such group in Jerusalem said: "Make it simple. Even if it isn't." But Israel was not the only people in the Middle East to find the aftermath of war suddenly bewildering.

SIX

"A QUESTION THAT HAS NOTHING TO DO WITH YOU"

1. The Forgotten Palestinians

October 25, 1973, was the day of the United States' nuclear alert; and the day when the United Nations agreed to send a peace-keeping force to the Middle East to supervise the cease-fire. It was also the day when a disturbing UN report on the refugee camps that house and care for more than six hundred thousand Palestinians was published. The report made little impact; by now, the war had pushed the problems of the Palestinians right off-stage.

The Palestinian guerrillas understood this perfectly. One day during the war, in the southern Lebanese town of Tyre, the funeral of a dead commando was taking place. A cheap American car carried the body. Armed men in camouflage outfits somewhat unsteadily rode shotgun on the back of the makeshift hearse; files of commandos marched behind, their automatic rifles reversed at odd angles. An incessant chant against Israel crackled from a loudspeaker van through a converted Japanese stereo set. Suddenly, the double sonic boom of two Israeli fighters was heard. The cortege stopped. The commandos looked up to see, far off over the Golan Heights, the smoke trails of two SAMs fired at the aircraft. The rockets exploded, missing the fighters. Three minutes later, the aircraft turned and, passing over Tyre once more, flew out to sea beyond the harbor wall. The funeral moved on. "We're irrelevant in all this," said one commando. "But it's supposed to be for us."

The feeling was shared by many of the Palestinians living in the sixty-three refugee camps run by the UN Relief and Works Agency (UNRWA). But even though the Palestinians were left out of the 1973 war, they could not be left out of the subsequent peace. Any settlement that did not involve them would result in a continuance of the guerrilla war. And the UNRWA report, published on October 25, described a situation where Palestinian support for guerrilla warfare was certain to increase.

UNRWA, it said, faced "a cash crisis" at the beginning of 1974. The projected deficit for 1974—ten million dollars—was roughly what the war had been consuming every half hour. But the deficit was enough for a cutback in UNRWA's work which, the report concluded, "would cause more hardship, frustration, and bitterness among the Palestinian refugees . . . and would heighten tension and encourage further violence in the region."

There are about 2½ million Palestinian Arabs living outside Israel. A million live under Israeli occupation in the Gaza Strip or the West Bank of the Jordan; 900,000 live on the East Bank of the Jordan, and another 500,000 live in Syria and Lebanon. The rest are scattered around the world: Fifteen thousand are estimated to live in West Germany, and 7,000 in the United States. Altogether, 3 out of 5 Palestinian Arabs (that is, 1½ million) have been given refugee status by the UN, though only 600,000 of the refugees live in UN camps. Most refugees left their homes during the 1948–49 war; the rest left in 1967.

In one sense, even before the Yom Kippur War, the Palestinians did have a choice: The Jordan Government had offered full citizenship to Palestinians who wished to settle in Jordan. But more than one third of the refugees in UNRWA's care live in camps in Jordan, and very few ever decide to give up their refugee status. Partly, this is because the camps offer at least shelter and a subsistence diet. More significantly, though, it is the experience of the camps that has created and sustained the refugees' growing sense of a Palestinian national identity. This in turn is partly a product of bitterness—the children in the camps being brought up to share their parents' feelings. UNRWA's largest refugee camp is Baka'a, twelve miles north of Amman. It cares for fifty thousand Palestinians. Eight-year-old Rashid is typical of the children growing up in the camp. "I am from Haifa," he said. "My home is in Haifa. I live in a white house by the sea. We have orange groves behind my home." Rashid has never seen Haifa: His family left in 1948.

Yet there is now more to the "Palestinian entity" than this simple—and itself in no way ignoble—longing for home. The image of the Palestinian is commonly that of a family huddled with blank faces before a dreary camp hut. But a growing minority have achieved success in their new countries. The Palestinians have come to provide a disproportionate share of the skilled workers, the technical and bureaucratic elites in those countries. In some of the Gulf oil sheikdoms, Palestinians probably comprise the biggest single cadre of the administration. Statistics are hard to unravel, but plausible studies suggest that among the Arab peoples the Palestinians have one of the highest levels of education. Again, much of the credit for this is due to the UNRWA education programs—another reason why so many Palestinians retain refugee status. But the result has been the dawning of a new class of Palestinian whose articulate and self-conscious claim to nationality is now independent of the old roots back in the mandate territory.

The Israelis had been able to ignore this development by concentrating upon the territorial aspect of the Palestinians' problem. Even in the wake of the Yom Kippur War, this attitude survived. Dayan, for example, dismissed the problem entirely: "There used to be a Palestine, and there is no more. Had the Palestinians wanted to keep their political entity, they could have done so in 1948. They preferred to join Jordan, and with that an end was put to political Palestine. The ambition of the refugees' leaders is to establish Palestine in the place of Israel, not by the side of Israel." But Israel's own experience in occupying the West Bank of the Jordan since 1967 had undermined such simplicity, as Dayan himself was aware. It was Dayan, after all, who had justified Israeli suppression of political activity among the West Bank Arabs with the comment that there was no point in allowing such activity since the demands it would throw up were certain to be unacceptable to the Israeli occupiers.

And, while it was true that, until the Yom Kippur War, the demand of all Palestinian leaders—whatever their tactical differences—was the establishment of a Palestinian state with the same borders as the old mandate territory, the war forced a Palestinian reappraisal too. This was sufficiently surprising to warrant optimism; for it was readily apparent that for a permanent peace settlement to be successful, it must embody two symmetrical conclusions: Israeli acceptance of a Palestinian Arab state somewhere, and Palestinian acceptance of a Jewish state. In practice, this demanded of the Palestinians the greater concession, because the only parts of Palestine over which Israel was conceivably likely to relinquish control were the occupied Gaza strip and the West Bank. Compared with the dream of returning to orange groves in Haifa, that was bound to seem to Palestinians a meager substitute.

Yet the war, although not directly involving the Palestinians, led to the first signs that some of their exiled leaders would accept just that. An article appeared in *The Times* of London on November 16 by Said Hammami, the London representative of the Palestine Liberation Organization (PLO), the umbrella organization for all the Palestinian groups—including those concentrating upon terrorism. Hammami accepted the possibility of a negotiated settlement with Israel, with a Palestinian state consisting of Gaza and the Jordan West Bank. Such a state, he wrote, "would lead to the emptying and closing down of the refugee camps, thereby drawing out the poison at the heart of the Arab-Israeli enmity."

The article, though carefully presented as a personal view, was in fact written after close consultation with other PLO leaders. It represented the views of many PLO officials who wanted to exploit the new opportunities that the war opened up. Before 1973, there was no immediate prospect of Palestinian Arab control over any part of Palestine—so there was no incentive to offer territorial compromises. When King Hussein had first proposed his plan for a Palestinian state on the West Bank, other Arab leaders—including Sadat—had broken relations with him. Now, in the wake of the cease-fire, Egypt and the Soviet Union both made it clear that they envisaged a Gaza-West Bank Palestinian state following Israeli withdrawal. And they made their support even for this compromise conditional on Palestinian acceptance of it.

In Cairo, the leader of the PLO, Yasir Arafat, said privately that he would accept the plan—as a first step. His second step was now not the overrunning of Israel, however, but the remaking of Jordan. "There is nothing sacred about Jordan," Arafat said. "Its boundaries were drawn, and the Hashemite dynasty established, by Winston Churchill. What he made, others can unmake." (Though oversimplified, that is broadly correct: Transjordan was established, and Hussein's grandfather installed as its ruler, in the hectic British maneuvers that attended the creation of Palestine during and after World War I—maneuvers in which Churchill had a big hand.) Other PLO leaders agreed with Arafat: If Sadat had failed in his last military attempt to force Israel to make concessions, then the last chance to establish a coastal Palestinian state in place of Israel had effectively failed with it. Far better look eastward now, to the sole surviving kingdom on Israel's borders, Jordan.

The immediate imperative for the PLO leaders was thus to exclude Jordan from the opening moves toward the creation of an independent Palestinian state on the West Bank of the Jordan. King Hussein had traditionally been as reluctant as Israeli leaders to accept the idea. Although he had been the only Arab leader to come up with any concrete proposals on the Palestinian issue, his prewar plan had envisaged a Palestine-Jordan *federation*, with the federal capital in Amman. For Hussein there would be immense practical advantages in such a solution: It would once again link the East Bank of the Jordan to the more prosperous West Bank; it would also re-establish Hussein's leadership over the Palestinians.

But few West Bank Palestinians seemed to like Hussein's idea. The West Bank folk have always been different from the East Bank Bedouin among whom Hussein's power lies. A survey of West Bank attitudes conducted shortly before the Yom Kippur War by the Israel Institute of Applied Social Research (with field work done by West Bank Arabs) found that only 8 per cent supported Hussein's idea. A larger minority—19 per cent—preferred a return to direct rule by Jordan; 44 per cent wanted an independent Palestinian state; most of the others thought the West Bank should be placed under international control. These figures must be treated with great caution; but the survey remains the best guide we have to West Bank opinion (and it suggests what an opportunity Israel missed after 1967 in not encouraging an independent Palestinian West Bank—a move that in time might have defused a significant proportion of the Palestinian unrest).

In the aftermath of the war, Jordanian officials were naturally anxious to defer as long as possible the embarrassing problem of facing the demands of the Palestinians. "We must first secure the end to the occupation by the Israelis," one of Hussein's ministers said. If Jordan succeeded in recovering the West Bank without first reaching an agreement with the Palestinians, Hussein would obviously be in a strong position: The future of the West Bank would then have to be negotiated directly with him, rather than in the wider context of an international peace conference. The point was not lost on the Palestinians.

It was partly for this reason that after the war many Palestinians suddenly espoused the idea of an international peace conference: If they could participate at some stage as an independent delegation, they would have their best chance in years of outflanking Hussein. And in Algeria in late November, a meeting of Arab leaders (with the notable absence of King Hussein, President Qaddafi, and the Iraqis) recognized the PLO as the sole voice of the Palestinians. Amman was virtually removed from the Palestinian equation.

Behind the scenes, too, there were strong pressures—particularly from Moscow—for the PLO to become a more broadly based movement. The carrot Moscow held out was that the PLO transform itself into a self-styled government-in-exile. But since a government without a territory might be held to be a contradiction in terms, the real purpose was to wean the Palestinians away from their diet of rhetoric and killing toward a more sober political approach to the now possibly soluble problem of their own future.

So much depended upon Israeli attitudes, however. Would Israel—already worried over the dilution of its Jewish population by the Arabs whose homes it had overrun in 1967—be willing to accept back any of the exiled Palestinians? Or would the international community simply have to find the cash to buy off the Palestinians' outstanding claims to the houses and land they had left behind a generation ago? (The claims were all logged and proved by a land valuation expert in the mid-1950s.) That was certainly the conclusion of one noted expert on the problem, John Reddaway, who was for some years in charge of UNRWA's work among the refugees. And it appeared to be the implication behind the superpowers' drafting of the cease-fire Resolution 338. But what did Israel want?

2. Israel's Search for Security

Israelis emerged from the sixteen-day war shocked by its cost in dead, wounded, and missing; disillusioned and frightened by the early military setbacks; and with their suspicions of Arab intentions confirmed. The realization that the war had brought about a complete change in Israel's way of life came only slowly, and was shot through with paradox.

At the onset of the Arab assault, there had been anger and a determination to "get it over in a few days." When this did not happen, there was bewildered acceptance of the Arab success but stubborn confidence that Israel's total victory was merely deferred. The Golan advance, followed by Sharon's crossing of the canal, precipitated a mood of euphoria; but it too was short-lived. Israelis' fury, when the superpowers stepped in to prevent their Army from routing the Egyptian forces, was the greater for their dawning awareness that their six years of apparently total supremacy on the battlefield were over. There would, from now on, be no clean victories.

Israel's doves derived hope from this. Arie Eliav, a former secretary general of the ruling Labor party, said: "We are coming out of the fool's paradise of the last six and a half years. Now everybody must see that safety does not lie only in military strength." But few were as sanguine as that. The gloomy consensus in Israel was rather that, for all the pieties uttered by Henry Kissinger and the UN, the Arab states did not want to make a permanent peace —above all, now that they had discovered the oil weapon. There were reports, widely credited (though untrue), that Sadat still maintained that Security Council Resolution 242 did not call upon Egypt to recognize Israel, but only its borders. On November 12–13, a poll by the Israel Institute of Social Research of Israel's urban Jews (about 70 per cent of the population) found that over four-fifths believed that the Arab goal had been the destruction of Israel, and that the Arabs would return to the attack in a year or two with the same purpose.

During the war, Israeli opinion had inevitably hardened against compromise. The Arab attack had strengthened the argument that Israel's security was dependent on the retention of some occupied territory—the expanse of Sinai had enabled the Army to buy time with space. But with the publication of the casualty figures, anger focused with unprecedented sharpness on the military leadership, which itself was indulging in mutual recrimination in the Western press.

Sharon started it, with detailed—and, it should be said, much cleaned-up—accounts of his canal triumph to several American reporters, in which he criticized virtually the entire military leadership except Dayan. (After all, though Sharon did not say so, Dayan had recommended that he take over the Sinai command.) Bar-Lev joined in, ostensibly to defend the leadership—but himself proceeded to talk of "grave errors." Gonen, finally incensed by Sharon's rewriting of history, on November 13 formally—though privately—requested Chief of Staff Elazar to begin inquiries into Sharon's conduct with a view to a court-martial. On November 20, Gonen submitted his detailed charges. On November 22, he was removed from his command—and posted to Sharm-el-Sheikh. Having done that, Elazar was not in the best position to make an appeal for an end to such infighting. Mrs. Meir had already ordered a military inquiry into the conduct of the war. Now, in the face of mounting public criticism, she appointed a five-man committee, under the president of Israel's Supreme Court, to inquire into the runup to war—in effect, into her own government's handling of events.

For the military debate was inseparable from politics—inevitably, since the Israeli elections, postponed because of the war, were now rescheduled for December 31. At a more fundamental level, as Eliav's comment implied, the debate about whether Israel had been adequately "prepared" depended in part upon a view of what constituted "security." But this reopened in bitter form the long argument over borders that Israel had been quite unable to resolve since 1967. On two counts, therefore, the main target for popular criticism became Defense Minister Moshe Dayan—before the war, the Labor party's greatest electoral asset. He was blamed for complacency about Arab intentions. And his "maximalist" approach to the territorial issue also came in for reproach from those Israelis who argued that it was Israel's obduracy in the face of Arab demands for the return of their land that had made war inevitable.

Even before the war, the question of Israel's borders had been central to the impending general election. Then, the Labor coalition's compromise platform had favored Moshe Dayan's policies over those of the deputy premier, Yigal Allon. The document enshrining the compromise, drawn up by the influential Minister without Portfolio, Israel Galili, envisaged a limited expansion of Israeli settlements in the occupied territories. (Allon had held that this policy of "creeping annexation" would fatally injure Israel's chances of ever reaching a settlement with the Arabs.) On September 10, Dayan had set out his "five noes" for *Ha'aretz*: Gaza must not be Egyptian; Golan must not be Syrian; there must be no Palestinian state; no Arab Jerusalem; and Israel would not desert the settlements it had founded in the occupied territories.

Yet the territorial issue had perennially been linked to two arguments—often voiced by the same persons, but essentially separate. "Greater Israel" implied both the size and nature of the country. Even if Israel could afford, military and diplomatically, to retain control of all the territories captured in the 1967 war, that would mean creating a predominantly Arab Israel. Acceptance of this demographic fact was implied in the "not one inch" platform of Sharon's right-wing Likud coalition. But most Israelis, and their leaders, wished to maintain a Jewish state—and this very concept excluded the acceptance of borders at their expanded post-June 1967 cease-fire limits (short of forced expulsion of the Arabs, of course).

In some respects, the interim arrangements after 1967 had worked: The Arabs in Israel and the occupied territories were considerably better off in economic terms—jobs were available, and they were relatively well paid. And the labor pool provided in particular by the refugees in the Gaza Strip had proved invaluable to the Israeli economy. For all the fury that Israel's policy of creating Jewish settlements in the administered territories had aroused in the Arab world, some kind of working arrangement had been achieved by 1973. This partly derived from the special nature of the conquered people, however. The Gaza Strip was until 1967 administered, indifferently, by the Egyptian military. And the people of the West Bank, as we have said, had little in common with those in the rest of Jordan.

Still, the facts were hopeful: During the fighting, two things had emerged from regular opinion surveys. One was that quite consistently through the war, more than half the Israeli Jews who were polled said that they did not hate the Arabs at all (only 11 per cent hated "all of them"). The other was that Arabs on the West Bank responded to the war in a pacific way. The bridges across the river Jordan remained open and commerce continued; and guerrilla appeals for industrial sabotage by Arab workers in Israeli-held territory were notably ineffective—though most of the West Bank Arabs working in Israel chose to remain home with their families for much of the war. The Institute of Applied Social Research survey of November 13 recorded that 40 per cent of Israeli Jews believed that the loyalty of Arabs in Israel, and their "identification with the state," had increased during the war. To some extent, this degree of Arab acquiescence was due to the fact that Israel is not an apartheid state; and Arabs had benefited from Israeli government in ways which, politics aside, they had clearly come to recognize. It was tangible progress, however.

But the realities after the 1973 war—the oil embargo, Soviet-U.S. détente, and Kissinger's determination to achieve a lasting solution—ruled out any possibility of reasserting Israel's hold over its 1967 gains. Israel was thus thrown back to the task of defining "secure and recognized boundaries"—and to the even harder question of what it would consider "security" at all. Mrs. Meir's speech to the Knesset on November 13—her first since October 23—reflected this. Predicting a "struggle over future frontiers and over the conditions of peace," she served warning that Israel could respond to U.S. pressure only up to a point: "Anybody who thinks this war taught us that deep and defensible borders have no value in conditions of modern warfare is in error. We did not learn that we must return to the borders of June 4, 1967, which tempt our neighbors to aggression."

Map 13 The shape of Israel as the fighting ceased
At a cost of more than twenty-five hundred dead, Israel had broken the Arab assault and even gained territory—though with vulnerable defense lines.

On the same day, however, the Social Research Institute's poll found that three quarters of urban Jews were prepared to give up all or nearly all of the land occupied in both wars in exchange for peace—a return, after the wartime drop to 50 per cent, to the pre-October response to the same question. And despite their doubts about Arab sincerity, 73 per cent supported the government's decision to sign the cease-fire pact; over half those polled also believed that the Arabs might now be willing at least to enter negotiations. There was a strong feeling that peace talks, however impermanent the results, were the only option.

External factors, apart from superpower politics, reinforced this conviction. Diplomatic pressure upon Israel was becoming more and more intense. During November, eleven African states broke off diplomatic relations, bringing the total number of hostile African states to twenty-eight. (The Africans got no reward: To their chagrin, the Arab oil price rises—and the embargo, as evened out by the international oil companies—hit Africa the same as everywhere else. Various African politicians later reflected publicly that perhaps they had been a touch naïve.) Immediately after the war, as Sharon began giving politically slanted interviews from his active service headquarters on the western side of the canal, a joke began to circulate in Tel Aviv—Question: "Who is the only political leader in Africa friendly to the Israeli Government?" Answer; "Arik Sharon—and he's not all that friendly."

But the reactions of Europe mattered to Israel rather more than those of Africa. And by now the oil embargo was hurting. To the chagrin of the radicals at the Kuwait meeting of Arab oil producers, the subsequent declaration had singled out no specific European targets, but had concentrated instead upon pressuring the United States through a global cutback in production—though leaving the way open for later action against specific pro-Israel nations. But on October 21, the day after the outraged King Faisal had cut all Saudi shipments to the United States, the Algerian oil minister Abdel Abdessalam—one of those disappointed at Kuwait —had finally aimed the oil weapon directly at Europe. Denouncing the Dutch for what he called their position "in hostility to the Arab countries," Abdessalam prohibited Algerian oil shipments to Rotterdam. Within ten days, the other Arab producers had followed suit.

To an extent, the Dutch had brought this upon themselves by imprudence or courage, or both. The Dutch Defense Minister had been a conspicuous participant at an Amsterdam rally in support of Israel. And the Dutch Foreign Minister, Max van der Stoel, had summoned the Arab ambassadors to his office in

The Hague and treated them to a lecture on the justice of Israel's cause—"as if the Dutch were Afrikaaners dealing with helpless kaffirs," one of the Arab delegates later recalled with distaste.

The cutting of shipments to Rotterdam hit far more than Holland, however. For the Europort at Rotterdam—the mouth of the Rhine—is one of Europe's main oil terminals. Suddenly, Europe faced the prospect of severe disruption of its most vital single energy resource. (Just over 40 per cent of Europe's energy needs are supplied by Arab oil.) And when, on November 4, the Arab oil ministers—again meeting in Kuwait—tightened the tap still further by consolidating the somewhat rambling pattern of sanctions to date into an over-all 25 per cent cut in production, with a promise of another 5 per cent cut in December, the foreseeable disruption of world oil supplies was such that even supposedly "friendly" nations such as those of Europe faced crisis.

Israel's relations with Western European states had inevitably cooled as their oil reserves thus diminished, despite strong public support for Israel at nongovernmental levels. And first Japan and then Holland were forced by their need for oil into public assertions of the justice of the Arabs' claims to their lost lands. This process of accommodating European policy to the new realities of Arab oil power was not unaccompanied by moral debate. But, despite the predictable slogans, the analogy with the capitulation to Hitler's demands upon Czechoslovakia at Munich in 1938 was wide of the mark. No European country—with the possible exception of Holland—thought the Arab demands were unreasonable. And few uncommitted observers feared that the Arabs were bent upon genocide.

Israel's outrage at Europe's arabesques was readily understandable. Even so, many Israelis missed the point. When Israeli novelist Amos Oz told Joseph Kraft: "We have come to understand that sympathy for the Jews is a very brief episode in world history. It lasted for about twenty-five years after Buchenwald and Auschwitz," he touched one of the cores of Israel's policy: the assumption that the world, for reasons of recent and unspeakable history, would acknowledge a special Israeli right to understanding. Mrs. Meir had even assumed that in her early meetings with Kissinger. He had tellingly disabused her, as the authors of *Hame-*

chdal recount. On Thursday, November 1, Mrs. Meir's first evening in Washington, Kissinger attended a small dinner for her at
the Israeli Embassy. Mrs. Meir appealed to him for sympathy:
"You, Mr. Kissinger," she reportedly said, "who were born in the
city of Fürth, not far from the gas chambers of Dachau where
millions of our people were liquidated, ought to understand well
the problem of the existence of the people of Israel and their preoccupation with the problems of security." "Madame Prime Minister," Kissinger apparently replied, "we are not discussing faith
here. We are looking for practical alternatives for the solution of
problems." It was a response most European governments would
have silently applauded, though few would have had the courage
to make themselves.

On the home front, Israel's economy—already beset by inflation
before the war—was placed under acute strain by manpower
shortages, although the effects were not immediately assessable.
Mobilization, which cut the Israeli labor force by almost half, was
hitting building programs and industrial output severely. Casualties
had disproportionately drained the skilled sector; and side effects
of the war included shortages of civilian transport, sharp reduc-
tions in tourism (a major foreign-exchange earner), and shortages
in the shops allied to rocketing prices. The war—and now the
dragging out of cease-fire talks—would cost Israel about one
billion dollars, or around 15 per cent of its Gross National Product.
And although Jewish organizations around the world had already
raised stupendous sums—perhaps one billion dollars in the United
States alone—and looked likely to continue this rate of contribution at least through 1974, the Israelis, already the most heavily
taxed people in the world, faced even harsher burdens in the reconstruction of their postwar economy.

Such an inconclusive ending to the most painful war for a
generation necessarily sharpened debate in Israel on the questions
of the likelihood of peace, and the sacrifices its leaders should
be prepared to make to obtain it. A captain interviewed on the
Syrian cease-fire line shrugged off the impact of the war on his
men: "I believe that everyone is more convinced now of what
he thought before." But confidence in the political leadership—
in Golda Meir as well as Moshe Dayan—was seriously eroded.
And an increasing number of people argued that the costs of

Israel's present relations with the Arab world were exorbitant. The difficulty was to translate these feelings into political reality. In a poll conducted for *Ha'aretz* at the end of November, more than half the respondents thought that Mrs. Meir should resign—except that 39 per cent could not think of anyone to replace her.

Israel is an open democracy, whose citizens express their opinions with striking articulacy and volatility. But its electoral system—a complex mixture of corporate institutions and proportional representation—is stable to the point of stagnation. Everything militates against change and, as in France, favors the political median. This makes it very hard to articulate new or radical thought in the international field, as the account of Israel's prewar diplomacy that opened this book indicated. But any deal with the Arabs would demand a radically new line of approach; and even the task of drawing up a political list of candidates ready to endorse a peace package might prove almost impossible. There was much flexibility among the electorate at the end of the war. But this would not necessarily find embodiment in a working formula for flexible policies.

There were still those who echoed the Likud in its call for "no concessions." For all the beating Dayan's reputation had taken, uncertainty about the future merely heightened many Israelis' desire for territorial security at almost any diplomatic price. "Securitism," as this doctrine of the prime importance of expanded borders was called in Israel (*bitkhonism* in colloquial Hebrew), was assailed by the doves in the Knesset. A retired brigadier general, Matatyahu Peled, encapsulated the argument: "When reality refutes their doctrines [the belief of "Securitists" that the 1967 borders were necessary to deter an Arab attack—as opposed to smaller "nonsecure" borders that would, in Mrs. Meir's words, "invite the enemy to attack"], one may guess that not the faintest doubt will be cast on the sanctity of 'the security borders.' What is sure to happen is that this principle will be sanctified more vigorously than ever. Except that for its realization, we shall all be called upon to make further sacrifices."

There were harder-line "solutions" than securitism advocated. One plan considered during the war had been to administer such a blow to the Arabs that their "entire military and economic infrastructure," as one contributor to *Davar* put it on October 16,

would be permanently crushed. This had, indeed, been a strand
in Israel's bombing campaign against Syria. And if Syria had not
been permanently crushed, it had been savagely bruised. Its economic minister later put the damage at $1.8 billion—equivalent to
Syria's GNP for an entire year. And that was merely the damage
to plant—80 to 90 per cent of Syria's electricity generation capacity was destroyed, for example. It did not take account of the
military losses—or, more significantly, the economic damage of
Syria's horrendous casualty figures. But if there was one thing the
October war had made clear, it was that the United States was
not prepared to tolerate the possibility of any action of that kind
against the Arab economy that mattered, Egypt's.

Which brought the argument full circle; for the assumption
behind such proposals had always been that "the real issue today,
as it was in 1967, is the determination by Egypt and Syria to
destroy Israel." It was so expressed, in the context of a plea for
an "end to the language of hate and vilification," in a letter
published by the New York *Review of Books* on November 15.
Signed by the distinguished historian Jacob Talmon and twenty of
his colleagues at the Hebrew University, the letter recalled the
Arab refusal to negotiate in 1967 and their continuing demand
that Israel should make a prior commitment to withdraw from all
the occupied territories—a "gesture" that they did not see as
"morally acceptable or practically feasible." They appealed for
"a peace process" and "free negotiation"; but their tone scarcely
suggested optimism that these would materialize. The letter probably reflected majority opinion in Israel.

If this argument presupposed perpetual Arab enmity, the other
side's was based on something equally difficult to prove. Another
of Israel's leading academics, Professor Daniel Amit, published his
response a week later. Acknowledging that there had, in the early
years of Israel, been an Arab "desire for the annihilation of the
Jewish state," he asked: "Is it possible to force such a straitjacket
on the interpretation of events for all time to come?" Amit argued
that for some years, Arab foreign policy (apart from that of Syria)
had "related to Israel as Israel" and that "almost without exception all the aggressive declarations of the Arab states in the
past few years have concerned their occupied territories." Would
the war have broken out, "had the government of Israel declared,

before fighting began, that she accepted as a basic element in any agreement the right of the Egyptians and the Syrians to all the territories captured in 1967, and that she recognized the existence of the Palestinians as a party in the Israeli-Arab conflict?" Israel might have "many reasons for distrusting the Arabs," but what were they in turn to make of Dayan's "five noes?" Amit closed with a warning. "There are now clear signs of possible escalation in which the local balance of power will become irrelevant . . . with all the attendant dangers this poses to the very existence of Israel."

If the Arabs were genuinely willing to coexist with Israel, that knocked away the foundation of securitism. But for an outsider to ask Israel to accept that was an impossibly arrogant demand. The Israelis themselves would have to learn it. A reserve officer back from the front line wrote an open letter to Mrs. Meir published by *Ha'aretz* on November 12. Israel had been wrong, he said, to trust to its strength, within borders "whose physical solidity is shattered by their doubtful legitimacy." Dayan's confidence that the status quo might last for ten or twenty years had proved unfounded, he argued; and now that "the Arabs have overcome the barrier of fear, the Jews must overcome the barrier of trust." Israel, in other words, did not really have a choice.

3. "A Right to Feel a Sense of Bitterness"

There was, of course, a much simpler reason why that was true. Kissinger was determined to force continued progress toward a settlement on both sides—as his activities after the cease-fire demonstrated. At Kilometer 101, Yariv and Gamasy had continued to talk about disengagement, as specified in Clause 2 of the cease-fire agreement. Through November, they had seven main sessions; but although they got on personally—and made progress—the talks broke down on November 29. It was inevitable that they should.

A withdrawal to the lines of the abortive October 22 cease-fire—Gamasy's original demand, and specified in the cease-fire agreement—was military nonsense for both sides, and would do nothing to lower tension between the rival lines. By mid-November both negotiators were exploring more sweeping schemes. Gamasy's position was that any Israeli withdrawal actually into Sinai would have virtually to be back to Israel's old borders. Yariv —under instructions from Dayan—explored what Egypt might give for Israeli withdrawal to, say, the passes. Would Egypt, in return, withdraw from the east bank? The strip between could be patrolled by the UN.

There was logic behind Yariv's proposal: To hold the passes would require far fewer Israeli troops than the present lines, particularly with Egypt back across the canal. Israel could partially demobilize and begin to get its economy going again. Gamasy rejected the idea. Egypt's presence in Sinai was "irrevocable and not negotiable," he said. It was, after all, Sadat's only gain. But Gamasy did seem to be willing to contemplate another way of giving Israel a measure of security: At least, he did not flinch at a suggestion by Yariv that Egypt might so reduce its heavy weaponry in Sinai that the potential for a renewed Egyptian advance was

undermined. Gamasy at once placed an impossibly high figure on
the number of tanks Egypt would require in Sinai: He specified
four hundred. But to whittle that down was a task of relatively
straightforward bargaining.

Both sides ran out of time. Sadat faced the summit meeting
of Arab leaders in Algeria on November 26. The Israeli Government had to prepare for the December 31 elections. And, in the
meantime, there was the opening of the Geneva peace talks,
scheduled by Kissinger to start on December 17 or 18. Yariv
told Gamasy frankly that he could get no further negotiating
instructions until at least after Geneva and probably not until
after the election. For form's sake, Gamasy protested; in fact, he
understood.

What those instructions would be, however, remained quite
unclear; for the battle within the Israeli party to thrash out a
postwar election policy produced, at best, an equivocal compromise—and, at worst, a platform that confirmed the doves' deepest
forebodings. Basically concerted around Deputy Premier Allon,
Finance Minister Pinhas Sapir, and former Secretary General
Eliav, the Labor party doves wanted, first, a new slate of Labor
candidates chosen to reflect changing attitudes in the wake of
war; and second, a postponement of the elections to allow time
for a full post-mortem of the war's conduct and lessons. At an
all-day meeting of the party's central committee on November 28,
both requests were rejected by more than two to one, respectively.
And on December 5, after a fifteen-hour debate, Mrs. Meir won
another sweeping victory, when Labor's fourteen-point program
was adopted with overwhelming majorities by the central committee.

It was, on some readings, a bleak document. To be sure, the
third of the fourteen points affirmed: "The central objective of
Israel is the achievement of peace with the neighboring countries
and the weaving of cooperative ties with the region's peoples . . . ," though proceeding, predictably, to lay the failure to
achieve this solely at the Arabs' feet. But Clause 10 decreed that
"Israel rejects the setting up of an additional separate Arab Palestinian state west of the Jordan," and laid down that the Palestinians would simply have to integrate with the Jordanians.
Worst of all, Clause 12 said: ". . . measures will be taken to

continue with and consolidate settlement and colonization (*hity-ashvut vehitnalchalut*) . . ." of the occupied territories—in other words, "creeping annexation," as defined by the prewar Galili document.

For international consumption, it was explained afterward that Clause 12 carefully muted the issue; that, effectively, the Galili document had been repudiated. In the decisive central committee debate, Mrs. Meir certainly did not think so: "There is nothing wrong with the Galili document," she said. "A vote should be taken so there will be no uncertainty." Dayan even wanted a vote on a resolution explicitly reiterating the validity of the Galili document. The only concession that Sapir could win for the doves was to stave off those votes. And while Sapir, as Finance Minister, might claim that the Galili document was "in shreds" basically because Israel had no money to finance its proposed settlements, that was irrelevant. It was the attitude revealed that mattered—as Mrs. Meir's former Justice Minister, Yacov Shapira, pointed out.

Shapira had been forced by Mrs. Meir to resign from the Cabinet in the wake of the war after calling for Dayan's resignation. Shapira had been one of those ministers who had learned of the crisis only at the Cabinet meeting at midday on October 6, and he bitterly resented this. Now he attacked what he saw as the blindness of Labor's platform: "The new document, by completely overlooking UN Resolution 242, does nothing more than postpone—who knows for how long?—the major basis upon which any peace negotiations may be conducted." And he despaired of the platform's arrogance: "A simple Jordanian-Palestinian state east of Israel is no doubt convenient for us; but the decision is that of the Jordanians and the Palestinians and not ours. Can we dictate on the matter? Who can accept the view that we have the right to tell the Palestinians that they *have* to be joined to Jordan?"

But Shapira exaggerated in saying that the platform "completely" overlooked Resolution 242. One clause did pledge Labor to seek at Geneva "defensible borders that will ensure Israel's ability to protect herself effectively . . . and which will be based on territorial compromise." That, of course, moved nowhere far enough to satisfy the Arabs—or Henry Kissinger. The crucial point, however, was that in emphasizing its readiness for territorial concessions in such vague terms, Labor was allowing as much leeway as possible for untrammeled negotiations—and at a moment when opinion in Israel was again beginning to harden. That took political nerve on Mrs. Meir's part; for the risk was that if the concessions required of Israel appeared likely before the elections to be too stiff for Israelis to accept, the Labor party's platform would be extremely vulnerable to a Likud attack that played on popular anxieties.

Nor did the Arabs seem at first glance inclined to compromise on those demands—at least, to judge from the communiqué of the Algerian summit, published on November 28. The summit had given Sadat a mandate to embark on negotiations at Geneva, and even agreed that he might sign a satisfactory agreement. But it did not give him a free hand in deciding what would be satisfactory. The communiqué announced two "paramount and unchangeable" conditions for any peace agreement. First: "Evacuation by Israel of the occupied Arab territories and first of all Jerusalem." Second: "Re-establishment of full national rights for the Palestinian people."

The communiqué promptly strengthened the influence of those in Israel who argued that any agreement was likely to carry almost unacceptable risks—that it would only be a first, sly step toward annihilating the Jewish state. The specific reference to Jerusalem was calculated to evoke a xenophobic response from the Israelis; and the term "re-establishment of full national rights" could be taken as implying full backing for the maximum demands by the Palestinians—particularly as the summit had also backed Arafat rather than Hussein as the "sole representative" of the Palestinians, and endorsed in extravagant terms the creation of a Palestinian government-in-exile.

On closer inspection, however, the communiqué—like Labor's manifesto—offered grounds for hope. True, the demand for Jerusalem was unequivocal. That reflected the influence of King Faisal. But the remarkable point was that Jerusalem was the *only* piece of territory so specifically claimed. The communiqué did not even refer to "*all* the occupied territories"; instead, it echoed the ambiguity of Resolution 242. And the reasoning behind the creation of a Palestinian government-in-exile was, as we have already explained, more pacific than it might seem. Besides, the communiqué did not specify *where* the Palestinians were to re-establish their nationhood. But the most significant development of all was the simplest: On whatever terms their first negotiating stance might demand, the assembled Arab leaders (with the exception of Libya, Syria, Iraq, and Jordan) had finally and formally agreed to a peace treaty with Israel.

In one sense, the Arabs could afford to be conciliatory. They were convinced that their oil embargo would produce such Western pressure on Israel that whatever terms they set would have to be met. And there appeared to be nothing that Kissinger or Europe could do about it.

The key country in setting up—or removing—the oil embargo was Saudi Arabia, producer of almost half the Arab oil in question. Kissinger had seen King Faisal on November 9, during Kissinger's first tour of the Middle East. He was not unsympathetic to Faisal's disillusion with United States policy in the Middle East. In Cairo, Heikal told Kissinger: "You will find King Faisal harder than many thought—including, I confess, myself." And Heikal warned: "The Arabhood of Jerusalem is to him, moreover, an issue which permits of no discussion at all. And on that point the whole Arab *ummah* [world] is with him." "Before I left Washington," Kissinger replied, "I read three letters which he had written to three different American Presidents—Kennedy, Johnson, and Nixon—and I think that Faisal has a right to feel a sense of bitterness."

In Riyadh, Kissinger had evidently been successful in conveying that opinion. The Saudi Foreign Minister, Omar Saqqaf, said afterward that Faisal had been impressed by Kissinger as a "sincere man" genuinely seeking a just peace. But Heikal had been right in predicting that Kissinger would have a tough time in Riyadh. According to Faisal's later account of the meeting, the crucial interchange went like this:

KISSINGER: "We have proved our good intentions by the positive steps we have taken and are taking."

FAISAL: "So far we have observed nothing but words, and so far these have not been turned into steps and actions with tangible consequences."

KISSINGER: "American public opinion expects a development in the Arab attitude that will help us to continue our efforts."

FAISAL: "Any development in our attitude to you must be preceded by serious actions with definite results on your part. You must believe that we shall not easily change our attitude to you, and that we shall not allow our emotions to master our reason . . ."

KISSINGER: "The operation of withdrawal from the occupied territories, and other points that have been raised, will take a considerable time."

FAISAL: "If intentions are good, you can oblige Israel to withdraw at once. . . . The withdrawal need not take more than three weeks."

KISSINGER: "It certainly needs months."

FAISAL: "No, it could be done in three weeks."

After that unpromising start, however, Kissinger obtained the compromise he sought from Faisal. The King backed off from the Arabs' previous position that only after total Israeli withdrawal would the oil flow once more. Now, Faisal agreed that he, at least, would end the embargo as soon as Israel agreed to such withdrawal—so long as the United States would guarantee the agreement. That would still not restore full oil supplies, because on top of the total embargo to "unfriendly" countries—notably the United States, Canada, and Holland—the Arabs had only a week before imposed the over-all 25 per cent cut in production. This, Faisal said, would be restored only in phase with actual Israeli withdrawal—thus preserving a measure of Arab leverage.

The compromise was a personal tribute to Kissinger, though it had to be kept secret for some time. What Faisal would not compromise, however, was his definition of an acceptable settlement. He made it clear that he would prefer to stop production altogether than see *any* of the occupied lands ceded to Israel. In particular, he said, Israel must give East Jerusalem back: He was, as defender of the holy places of Mecca, Medina, and Jerusalem, determined to pray in Jerusalem's Al Aqsar Mosque before he died. In purely temporal terms, Faisal could afford to take this strong line: Saudi Arabia could live off its accumulated oil revenues for more than three years without receiving another cent in royalties.

Through November, the embargo plus the over-all production cuts achieved steadily greater economic and political impact. The

European Economic Community faced the most divisive crisis in its history as its nine member nations failed, acrimoniously, to agree on an oil pooling policy to help out Holland. Even convinced "Europeans" wondered gloomily whether the painfully constructed community could long survive disunity on so crucial an issue. The United States' relations with Japan hit trouble. In Tokyo in mid-November, Kissinger urged the Japanese not to break relations with Israel—as the Saudis had suggested they should if they wanted to achieve "friendly" status and obtain almost all their oil once more. But when the Japanese Prime Minister asked whether in that case the United States was prepared to supply Japan itself, Kissinger was irked by the request. What else could the Japanese hope for, though? They had to import virtually all their oil—45 per cent or more from Arab producers.

Even the United States itself was hit harder than most people had expected. In the first eight months of 1973, the United States had imported 3.46 million barrels of crude oil per day (bbd). That was under a quarter of total U.S. domestic consumption of about 17 million bbd. And of those imports, a quarter came from the Arab producers. In all, therefore, only one twentieth or so of U.S. oil needs would in theory be affected by the embargo. One of Nixon's White House energy aides was quoted as saying that the cuts did not appear to be "harmful" to the United States in the short term. (When later U.S. oil import figures were released in November, they showed that in September, the last month before the war, U.S. imports had risen to 3.9 million bbd, which 28.8 per cent had been Arab oil. The dependence was creeping up.)

What the initially blithe White House reaction overlooked, however, was two additional factors. On top of these shipments of Arab crude, the United States was also importing around another million barrels a day of petroleum products from overseas refineries dependent, in turn, upon Arab crude. And, on top of that again, the United States had also been planning to import through the winter of 1973 at least another 550,000 bbd of refined heating oil—principally for home central heating. The U. S. Department of the Interior, in fact, put the need at 650,000 bbd; some oil industry estimates went as high as 1 million bbd. Most of this would have come from the main European oil entrepot, Rotterdam. But the Arab embargo on supplies to Holland wrecked that scheme. In all, therefore, something like 12 per cent of America's total oil supplies were jeopardized by the Arab embargo.

In the early stages of the embargo—say, to the last week of October—the international oil companies were able to do a great deal to even out supply patterns so as to spread the shortages worldwide. (This was not sentiment: The companies' lawyers figured that, on balance, that was the policy likely to provide the best defense against staggering international suits for breach of contract.) But by the end of October, it was clear that the companies' ability to do this would steadily diminish. In the first place, consumer nations on the Arabs' "friendly" list refused to accept any cuts in supply at all—and several, notably in Western Europe, had sufficient clout to enforce fairly complete acquiescence on the part of the companies. More significantly, the Arabs learned to manipulate the embargo with greater precision by means of more complex destination controls on oil shipments from the Gulf.

To survey this prospect, the U. S. Foreign Petroleum Supply Committee—a joint government-industry committee whose members included representatives from twenty-one U.S. oil companies —met in Washington in the first days of November to discuss the scale of the U.S. crisis. The conclusion the committee reached was in sharp contrast to early optimism. The industry executives convinced skeptical Administration officials that the shortfall in U.S. imports could be 2 million bbd by the end of November and as much as 3 million bbd by January (1.8 million bbd of crude oil, 1.2 million bbd of refined products). On November 7 President Nixon went on nationwide television to break this news: "We must therefore face up to a very stark fact. We are heading toward the most acute shortages of energy since World War II. Our supply of petroleum this winter will be at least 10 per cent short of our anticipated demands and it could fall short by as much as 17 per cent. . . ." (It did not, in fact, turn out quite that bad: By January the shortfall was a little over 1 million bbd below the prewar figure, which meant around 1 million bbd below U.S. needs.)

The impact of this shortfall upon the United States was nothing like as severe as it would have been upon economies more dependent upon Arab oil. But it came as a considerable shock to a people accustomed to think of themselves as independent of the rest of the world's problems. (The worst problem the world now faced, of course, was not the oil embargo but the staggering price rises that the producers were simultaneously imposing. But these had little or nothing to do with the war. Indeed, the most aggressive advocate of these rises was the "friendly, pro-Western" Shah of Iran—and it was the Saudis who *restrained* his more vaulting ambitions.)

Nor did there seem any way of alleviating the situation. By the latter half of November—as the talks ground on inconclusively at Kilometer 101; as the Arabs prepared for the Algerian summit; and as the Israelis turned to political battles among themselves— the prospect even of an outline Middle East settlement looked dauntingly remote.

On November 21, Kissinger—alarmed over this slow pace toward peace, and the political damage the oil crisis was doing meanwhile to U.S. relations with Europe and Japan—warned that if the embargo continued "unreasonably and indefinitely," the West would have to consider countermeasures. It was a paper tiger. As one British diplomat said privately: "The instant Arab reaction to any such move would be a total oil embargo. They could easily do it. And they know it. There is no conceivable action that the West could take—even if it could unite sufficiently to agree on action—that would hurt the Arabs one tenth as fast as an oil shutdown would cripple us. It's just not on."

The most feasible possibility, in fact, seemed to be military retaliation: A Western takeover of the Gulf oil fields. This was considered. In the first days of the war, the U. S. Joint Chiefs of Staff convened a top-level study group to examine the feasibility of military intervention. The conclusion was that any such action would be "out of order." But the reason for this decision was not essentially military. The Arabs—anticipating that the more hawkish of their Western customers might toy with such plans—warned that they had made preparations to demolish utterly their oil fields' wellhead installations, pumping gear, pipelines, and tank farms in the event of an attack. The damage, they said confidently, would take years to repair. But, according to a source with access to the work of the Washington study group, the Pentagon assessment dismissed this as bombast and was optimistic about the speed with which full production might be restored. In the "worst case"—apparently assumed to be severe damage to almost all Gulf installations—the Pentagon thought something approaching full production might be resumed in three months. And the "most likely" case apparently predicted damage to a third or less of the installations, in which event production could be resumed in little more than a month. In either case, the military subjugation of the oil states themselves was apparently thought to require no more than a week. (Exercises to this end had already been carried out by the U.S. troops in California and Texas.) The flaw in this planning was that nobody knew what the Soviets would do. That was the reason the Pentagon ruled intervention "out of order." (It should be said that we know of no evidence to suggest that the Nixon administration did consider military action. These calculations seem to have remained at the level of contingency planning by military men paid precisely to make such plans.)

Yet something had to be done—and done rapidly. The relative economic importance to the West of the war itself, and of the oil embargo, which only started to have a serious effect after the fighting stopped, can be gauged by those sensitive barometers of capitalism, stock exchange prices. The main indices in London, New York, and Tokyo were all marginally higher at the end of the war than at the beginning. But in the following month, all three dropped sharply—New York and London by over 15 per cent, Tokyo by 10 per cent—and dropped again in December. On December 6, when rumors circulated that the Arabs might manipulate their Western currency reserves as an additional weapon, the London stock exchange promptly suffered one of its sharpest falls on record. (The Arabs are thought to hold up to $15 billion in Western currency.) The markets had taken little notice of the fluctuating fortunes on the battlefield; but now they winced at each change, or hint of change, in Arab oil or monetary policy. So long as the new-found unity between President Sadat and King Faisal could be made to last, the Arabs had a potent weapon for aiming at the West.

4. Prospects for Peace

On Thursday, December 13, Kissinger set off once more for the Middle East. He had two objectives: to persuade Faisal to relax the oil embargo; and to ensure that both sides would turn up in Geneva for the peace talks now scheduled to start on December 18. He failed in his first aim and had only limited success in his second.

In Riyadh on December 14, Faisal listened patiently as Kissinger explained all the steps he and the United States had taken publicly and privately to advance a Middle East settlement since he had last come to Saudi Arabia. He contested that the effects of the embargo upon the U.S. domestic political climate were such that his freedom of maneuver was being diminished. He argued that the Arabs were in danger of forfeiting by their disruption of oil supplies the undoubted gains they had made in Western sympathy during and after the war. Faisal listened politely and then—according to Arab diplomatic sources—asked Kissinger simply: "What progress on Jerusalem?" Kissinger apparently had to reply: "Well, er, none yet." "In that case," Faisal is said to have replied, "no oil."

Nor did anyone have the power to sway him. When a Western friend pointed out to Sadat late in November how damaging the oil weapon could be to the world economy, Sadat replied: "I realize that. But what can I do? It's Faisal. He is determined to pray at Al Aqsar Mosque in Jerusalem before he dies. And he's getting on. He's sixty-eight, an old man in a hurry. None of us has any power over him." As the Algerian summit communiqué had implicitly revealed, Sadat had been able to wean Faisal from his initial "not one inch" position. Sadat had persuaded Faisal that if Egypt or Syria or Jordan negotiated away any of their territory, that was their affair. But Faisal saw himself as guardian of the holy places of Jerusalem: On those he would not budge. Presumably, Kissinger got much the same explanation when he saw Sadat on December 14.

But Kissinger did get the main adversaries to Geneva. Neither Egypt nor Israel was particularly enamored of the process by which he did so. His diplomacy followed its by now familiar pattern: promises to both sides that, to put it politely, verged on mutual inconsistency; the concentration upon an appearance of progress as the most important ingredient in problem-solving; the willingness to store up troubles for the future so long as a way is found to solve a problem today; the belief that, in the last analysis, it does not matter if two protagonists arrive at a meeting with widely differing views of the ground rules, just so long as they turn up. It was, once again, a brilliant technical feat. But how rapidly Kissinger was expending his store of goodwill, only Sadat, Mrs. Meir, and presumably time could tell.

Sadat had wanted some Israeli agreement on disengagement as a token of good faith before Geneva. Kissinger talked him out of it. The Israelis were tougher. Mrs. Meir considered that Kissinger had welched on three more promises. The first was that, in the wake of the Algerian summit, it now looked as if the Palestinians were going to attend Geneva at the Arabs' behest. But Mrs. Meir had understood from Kissinger that Israel would be able to veto Palestinian participation. (Why Mrs. Meir thought Israel should be able to tell the Arabs who they could summon might be seen as another example of what her former Justice Minister, Shapira, had criticized so harshly in the party platform. Besides, some of Israel's most prominent politicians had themselves begun their careers as terrorists against both the British mandate forces and the Arabs. All of which does not alter the possibility, of course, that Kissinger had indeed conveyed some oblique promise of an Israeli veto.) Kissinger solved that problem by persuading the Arabs not to insist upon Palestinian attendance at this opening session in Geneva—a move that brought the bonus of Jordanian attendance at Geneva instead. (Hussein had said he would not go to Geneva if Arafat went.)

The second Israeli complaint—that the United Nations had now passed a resolution calling upon Secretary General Waldheim to play a full part at Geneva—was harder for Kissinger to fix. The opening of Geneva was delayed for three days while he argued Mrs. Meir around. In the end, Kissinger simply persuaded her of the truth: which was that the UN had been reduced to total and visible impotence over the Middle East, so why could she not shut her eyes to the polite fiction of Waldheim's role? Kissinger and the Soviet Foreign Minister, Andrei Gromyko, would in reality be running the show.

The final Israeli demand solved itself. Mrs. Meir had all along warned that Israel would refuse to sit down at Geneva with the Syrian representative unless Syria had first supplied a list of its Israeli prisoners and allowed Red Cross access to them. Kissinger arrived in Damascus on December 15 to fix up some compromise with President Asad. (It was the first visit to Syria by a U. S. Secretary of State in twenty years. The last intrepid traveler had been John Foster Dulles—a piquant contrast to the incumbent who now confronted Asad.) According to the version of the meeting later relayed by Kissinger's staff, the two men had a seemingly constructive and forward-looking discussion. At the end, Kissinger apparently asked Asad: "Is there anything else on your mind?" Asad replied: "The invitation is fine except for this one line where it says the parties are agreeing to come to the conference at Geneva. We are agreeing to no such thing." A stunned Kissinger could not talk the Syrian President around. Still, that did sidestep the problem: In the absence of Syria, Israel could attend Geneva without the issue of its Golan prisoners having been advanced one inch.

So, on Friday, December 21, Israel, Egypt, and Jordan met at Geneva. The talks were three days behind schedule, but in the context of a generation that was trivial. There at last—in the Council chamber of the Palais des Nations, home of the pre-World War II League of Nations—was a ring of seven tables, ends carefully not touching: one each for Israel, Egypt, Syria, Jordan, the UN, the Soviet Union, and the United States. Waldheim's table tactfully separated those of Israel and Egypt; Israel and Syria were divided by the superpowers; the Syrian table was unoccupied. On the wall above was a sepia fresco depicting, so guides would explain to visitors, "man's advance from barbarism."

It was an objective the old League had notably failed to achieve —but then, they had precisely *not* managed to impose an oil embargo. The omens appeared more hopeful this time. To be sure, the rhetoric at that opening session was fundamentalist. The Egyptian Foreign Minister, Ismail Fahmy, accused Israel of aggression, mass murder, and terror. The Israeli Foreign Minister, Abba Eban, accused the Arabs of "the mentality and ideology that produced the gas chambers and gallows of Auschwitz." But, as Kissinger remarked afterward, that was to be expected.

If the process by which the parties had been dragooned to Geneva had displayed some of the more dubious aspects of Kissinger's technique, the conference itself revealed his greatest single strength: an unremitting awareness of the long-term end. "We can exhaust ourselves in maneuvers," he bluntly told the delegates, "or we can remember that this is the first real chance for peace that the Middle East has had in three decades." And after the first rhetorical outbursts, it did seem that the delegates, even in public, were committed to peace. The Arabs carefully, albeit implicitly, did not rule out some boundary adjustments. And Eban talked of Israeli withdrawal, albeit hedged with demands for "secure boundaries."

It was unfortunate that the parties had come to Geneva with opposing views of the acceptable agenda. Egypt wanted first to discuss Israeli withdrawal. Israel wanted first to explore what sort of peace the Arabs would offer. But in private discussions, the discrepancy could be conjured away. Kissinger and his Soviet counterpart, Gromyko, both held intensive talks behind the scenes, working together as much as separately. (Gromyko's private meeting with Eban was the first acknowledged contact at top level between Israel and the Soviet Union since 1967, although there are strong indications of covert contacts since 1970 over Soviet Jewish emigration.) The Soviets' noses had been put somewhat out of joint by Kissinger's personal success in the Middle East; at Geneva, Gromyko really bustled around.

Swiftly, it became clear that the way to reconcile the opposing views of the right approach to peace was through the first phase: disengagement. The package explored at the stalled Kilometer 101 talks was clarified considerably at those private evening sessions at Geneva. Israel would withdraw to the passes. Egypt would thin its armor in Sinai.

To Egypt this gave the bonus of considerable Israeli withdrawal. To Israel it offered as great an advantage, because Sadat would then have no excuse not to dredge and reopen the Suez Canal and to reconstruct and repopulate the ghost towns along it. (Before 1967, for instance, 400,000 people had lived in Port Said; by 1973, its population was down to 25,000; and the 10,000 women and children among these had been evacuated in the latest fighting.) Sadat's agreement to take such steps—in effect, his willingness to provide a new canal and new towns as guarantees of his peaceful intentions—would surely meet Israel's requirement that the Arabs demonstrate a commitment to peace before Israel in turn committed itself to any major territorial withdrawal.

Only the imminence of the Israeli elections prevented such a deal being clarified at Geneva, though it is also true that both sides still made impossible demands on points of detail. Kissinger was so eager to push it through that he even fell in with Gromyko's plan that a joint Soviet-American force of token size might be stationed in the Sinai passes to block incursions by either side. Kissinger said he "would not rule out totally" such an idea—a departure that made the nuclear alert of less than two months before over precisely that Soviet suggestion appear more aberrant than ever.

(Disengagement was not finally to be agreed until mid-January—and then not until another flurry of peripatetic wheeling-dealing by Kissinger had reconciled the points of detail. The Israelis then once more contrived to bargain themselves an improved position. They withdrew not even to the passes, but to positions sixteen to rather over twenty miles back from the canal. Ironically, this new line followed for much of its length the natural defensive row of sand ridges that had been Ismail's first objective in Operation BADR. In return for this withdrawal, Egypt thinned its heavy armaments in Sinai to nominal proportions. The no-man's-land between the lines was to be patrolled by UN troops rather than the superpowers'. The deal was signed on January 18, but the principles had all been thrashed out at Geneva.)

So what would happen now? Israel's elections on December 31 bore witness to the deep confusion and unhappiness that any sympathetic observer would have predicted. Mrs. Meir's Labor Alignment coalition dropped from fifty-six seats in the Knesset to fifty-one—one crucial seat below the effective minimum necessary to form a stable coalition. But Labor's main challenger, the Likud, advanced only from thirty-two seats to thirty-nine—nowhere near strong enough to take over. And the peripheral parties holding between half a dozen and ten seats each all had such disparate ideas on, among other topics, precisely what they would or would not accept in the way of Israeli concessions at peace talks—the obduracy of each party's views being, as ever, in inverse relation to its size—that Mrs. Meir's ability to form any sort of government with real freedom to enter meaningful negotiations seemed in doubt.

Yet the surprise was that the Labor alignment had suffered as little as it had, for there was no doubt that the electorate had a strong desire to punish what was nationally seen as inept handling of the war. But the campaign had polarized not around this, but around the issue of "security." And it is worth quoting at length one of the Labor alignment newspaper advertisements to illustrate what the biggest single segment of Israeli opinion finally chose:

"ON DECEMBER 31 YOU WILL DECIDE THE FUTURE OF THE STATE—YOUR FUTURE. YOU WILL DECIDE:
BETWEEN a prospect of peace with our neighbors
AND the road leading to unceasing war
BETWEEN a policy of close friendship with the U.S.A.
AND adventurism endangering this friendship
BETWEEN a policy of striving for peace and the strengthening of our security
AND the "not one inch" mentality
BETWEEN a checking and adaptation of policy to changing circumstances
AND the inability to learn and change
BETWEEN the declaration of peace and security as central aims
AND the preferring of the Areas [occupied territories] to peace
BETWEEN the wish to maintain the Jewish character of Israel
AND willingness to add a large Arab population
BETWEEN readiness to maintain friendly relations with a Jordanian-Palestinian state

AND the ignoring of the existence and aspirations of the
Palestinians

BETWEEN preparedness to go to a peace conference at any
time, without prior conditions

AND the creation of difficulties, likely to doom the conference to failure before it starts.

ON DECEMBER 31 YOU WILL HAVE TO DECIDE
BETWEEN POLITICAL REALISM AND A REALISTIC
APPROACH TO SECURITY AND EMPTY SLOGANS AND
POLITICAL RIGIDITY."

The voters chose "realism"—but with sufficient misgivings to
deny Mrs. Meir a decisive mandate. The election result, however
inconvenient, was a remarkably accurate reflection of the mood
of Israel.

What then did the Yom Kippur War achieve? The man who
launched it, Egypt's General Ahmed Ismail, had few doubts. "We
have changed our whole image before the entire world," he told
Al Ahram. "Once it thought we were a motionless dead body.
Now the world has awoken to the fact that we can move, can
fight, and can achieve victory." Ismail went on to argue that Israel's theory of secure borders was "false and untenable: The Suez
Canal was not a forbidding barrier; nor was the Bar-Lev Line an
adequate obstacle in the face of readiness to sacrifice." The Arab
blockade of the Bab-el-Mandeb straits at the southern entrance
to the Red Sea had "categorically proved that Sharm-el-Sheikh
does not have the great importance Israel had thought, and on
the basis of which it had built its ambitions in Sinai."

Such words seemed almost perversely optimistic to the Israelis,
who pointed out that Egypt and Syria, setting out to recover
occupied territory by military means, had actually suffered a net
loss by the time of the October cease-fire. Ismail, however, was
talking about the recovery of credibility as much as of territory.
There was no doubt that, by comparison with the debacle of 1967,
the Arab armies—more particularly Egypt's—had made a radically
better showing. Sharon acknowledged it as succinctly as anyone:
"I have been fighting for twenty-five years," he said, "and all the
rest were just battles. This was a real war."

In Ismail's view, "the important thing in the administration of restricted wars is that any fighting army should be able to fulfill its calculated political objective while maintaining the largest bulk of its forces." The Egyptian objective had been to create a new political situation by means of a limited military campaign, and that had certainly been achieved. Explaining in March 1973 why war was inevitable, Sadat had said the world had "fallen asleep over the Mideast crisis." In October, without doubt, there was an awakening. Henry Kissinger told Heikal in Cairo that he had not opened the Middle East file before October 6. "I had imagined it could wait its turn." That was flattering hyperbole. But by breaking through the Bar-Lev Line, Ismail's army had overthrown the order of precedence in international affairs.

Of course, if Sharon had managed to get the Israeli bridge across the canal on schedule, Egypt would have had difficulty in "maintaining the largest bulk of its forces," as Ismail obliquely acknowledged. Given another thirty-six hours Bren Adan's tanks would have consummated the destruction of the Third Army. Had the Israelis been willing to take more casualties, they could possibly have cut off the Second Army to the north as well. One strictly military lesson of the war was that the cumbrous Egyptian military machine was still inadequate in a fluid situation. But Ismail believed he saw more general conclusions.

"I can almost state that the tanks have lost their mastery—not their value, but as I said their mastery—as a result of the development of antitank missiles." The same, he thought, applied to manned aircraft, as a result of the development of antiaircraft missiles. A good many military commentators extended Ismail's cautious assessment into declarations about the "death of the tank" and the "end of the manned aircraft."

On this basis, the end of Israel's military advantage was foretold. But although the war did suggest that reassessment and re-equipment by both sides would be needed on a huge and costly scale, the balance sheet at the end was in reality a complex one.

Given time to deploy, infantry armed with large numbers of personal wire-guided missiles showed that they could effectively deny territory to a tank force. Equally, the battle on October 14 suggested that the Egyptian infantry had to have time to get themselves established before they could hope to stand up to tanks in a fast-moving daylight action. Speed of tactical response re-

mained so much the key to battle situations as to suggest that
the death of the tank has been prematurely announced.

Missiles powerful enough to inflict serious damage against
the present generation of tanks have been pushed a long way in
the direction of lightness and simplicity of handling (while going
up, naturally, in cost). But the mathematics that govern the
penetrating power of the HEAT charge used in slow-moving
antitank missiles mean that a small increase in the tank's armor
thickness could be countered only by a disproportionate increase
in the weight of the missile, its launcher, and its warhead. A
heavier missile would mean a vehicle launcher. And the battle
of vehicle against vehicle inevitably becomes the battle of tank
against tank. And shells are much cheaper than missiles.

The Israeli Army will therefore need to strengthen its existing
armored force with a substantial number of new tanks, proof
against the new missiles. There is clearly no possibility of buying
the new Anglo-German main battle tank that is under development, and there could be problems even with the American MX-1.
Israel may in that case be forced to design and build her next
generation of tanks at home. The technical expertise is available,
and there are some indications that the Israelis have been discreetly discussing new tank designs with European experts.

At the same time, the Arab armies have to face the fact that the
war demonstrated the almost total obsolescence of the T-54/55,
which still makes up the largest part of their armored detachments.
Even the relatively few T-62s they were able to deploy suffered
severely through the lack of any effective fire-control system. And
neither the T-55 nor the T-62 could stand against the American
TOW missile, which the Israeli infantry received partway through
the war. (The Israelis claimed virtually 100 per cent success with
it.) And, of course, Israel itself, once its mechanics have finished,
will be deploying substantial numbers of T-62s improved beyond
the Arab models—mainly by the fitting of the Centurion's 105mm
gun and the M-60's computer gunsight.

Failing a peace agreement that really does establish something
like normal relationships between Israel and Egypt, both sides
will thus have to rebuild their armored forces. Whichever is
damaged the more, both the Egyptian economy and the Israeli
economy will suffer enormous distortions in the process. And the

cost of the air war, too, will increase yet again. Manned aircraft were not rendered useless by antiaircraft missiles—on the contrary, their infinitely flexible destructive capacity was demonstrated yet again. What did emerge was that manned aircraft needed the protection of complex electronic equipment in order to survive. And the rate of obsolescence of each generation of equipment seems to be accelerating.

The choice for both sides in the wake of the Yom Kippur War were thus unenviable—and particularly for the smallest power, Israel. Peace negotiations would be slow and complicated. And if the Arabs had felt, in 1967, that they could not negotiate because any agreement would be made under duress, it was now Israel's turn to fear coercion. But the alternative was to continue living in a state of semimobilization, awaiting the next round of fighting. And even then, as the war had amply demonstrated, the conduct and outcome of any further fighting would be influenced by factors outside Israeli control—the arms and connivance of the superpowers.

The first war between Israel and the Arab nations, in 1948, was an almost entirely local conflict. The concept of superpower diplomacy had not yet arisen. The Soviet Union had not yet emerged from the pro-Zionist phase of its Middle Eastern policy —it was one of the first to accord diplomatic recognition to Israel—and in any case, Soviet influence in the area was almost nonexistent. In 1956, after many border skirmishes, the Israelis and the Arabs played out a subplot in the grotesque drama of Suez: the last attempt by Britain and France to assert the validity of an imperial role that nobody believed in any more.

In 1967, largely by virtue of a preemptive strike, Israel maintained the illusion of independence. And indeed in those days, when the technological and economic burdens of war were just that little bit lighter—and when Israel still had other friends and suppliers in the world—the Israeli Government could afford to treat its own superpower backer with considerable brashness from time to time. (When a U.S. intelligence ship sailed slightly too near the fighting and got shot up by the Israeli Air Force, apologies from Tel Aviv were quite without humility.) But a preemptive strike, as Israel discovered, is a difficult weapon to use more than once.

In the Yom Kippur War, the Arabs gave themselves the illusion of independence by striking first. Whether they obtained Soviet approval for the assault is an oversimple question. The available evidence suggests strongly that the Soviets knew of Sadat's long-term plans, disapproved of them, were unable to stop them, learned at the last minute of Y-Day—and then tried to make what mileage they prudently could. What is certain is that, fairly swiftly, the Soviet Union found itself embarrassed. And the super-powers do not care for this: The Soviet Union found that other aspects of its foreign policy, notably the détente with the United States, were seriously inconvenienced by the intransigence of Arab leaders who refused to accept an early cease-fire. And, as the ability of Egypt and Syria to rearm for a further conflict is almost totally dependent upon the acquiescence of the Soviet Union, it can be expected that the strings attached to any future arms deliveries will be still shorter and more tightly drawn.

Of course, certain and permanent control still eludes the superpowers. Nonetheless, they are the ones who make the conflict possible, who draw up the rules of the game—and whose interests, at the end of the day, are the decisive interests. Logically, of course, this is clear to most of the people in the Middle East. Emotionally, it is perhaps the hardest point of all to accept and act upon. It is not easy to think of one's own compatriots—one's own friends and children—as pawns in a game played by people whose ultimate interest is not even the advancement of the immediate enemy's cause. The point was put by Henry Kissinger shortly after the cease-fire, deliberately with a more brutal clarity than a professional diplomat would normally allow himself.

"There is another consideration which I would wish you to take into account," he said, after his long discussion with Heikal of *Al Ahram* about his approach to the problems of the Middle East. "The consideration is simply this: The United States cannot, either today or tomorrow, allow Soviet arms to achieve a great victory—though it may not be a decisive victory—over American arms. This is a question that has nothing to do with you, nor with Israel either. This is a question which is directly related to the balance of power between the two superpowers."

Thus we arrive at the ultimate paradox. The enforcing of a settlement in the Middle East seems, as we write, to depend upon the wills and efforts of the superpowers, particularly the United States. In the short term, perhaps that is the only way. But for the future, so long as Arabs and Jews are prepared to accept their role as proxies in a struggle that, at bottom, has "nothing to do" with them, then it is difficult to believe that there can be an enduring peace in the Middle East.

INDEX

Zafir (nuclear rocket), 283, 412
Zamir, Major General Zvi, 101,
   108, 109
Zayyat, Mohammed, 61, 105, 404,
   431
Zeira, Major General Eliahu,
   93–94, 95, 97, 101, 108, 114–
   16, 120, 236

Ziegler, Ronald, 24
Zionism, 20, 33, 262, 303, 304,
   355, 381, 389
ZSU-23 anti-aircraft batteries,
   161, 167, 184, 185